RACE IN SOCIETY

THE ENDURING AMERICAN DILEMMA

Margaret L. Andersen

University of Delaware

ROWMAN & LITTLEFIELD

Lanham • Boulder • New York • London

Executive Editor: Nancy Roberts
Associate Editor: Molly White
Editorial Assistant: Megan Manzano
Senior Marketing Manager: Deborah Hudson
Interior Designer: Ilze Lemesis
Cover Designer: Sally Rinehart
Cover Art: Amanda Rose Timoney

Credits and acknowledgments for material borrowed from other sources and reproduced, with permission, in this textbook appear on appropriate page within the text, or in the credits on page 347.

Published by Rowman & Littlefield
A wholly owned subsidiary of The Rowman & Littlefield Publishing Group, Inc.
4501 Forbes Boulevard, Suite 200, Lanham, Maryland 20706
www.rowman.com

Unit A, Whitacre Mews, 26-34 Stannary Street, London SE11 4AB, United Kingdom

British Library Cataloguing in Publication Information Available

Library of Congress Cataloging-in-Publication Data

Names: Andersen, Margaret L., author.

Title: Race in society : the enduring American dilemma / Margaret L.
    Andersen, University of Delaware.

Other titles: Enduring American dilemma

Description: Lanham, MD: Rowman & Littlefield, [2017] | Includes
    bibliographical references and index.

Identifiers: LCCN 2016047560 (print) | LCCN 2016057588 (ebook) | ISBN
    9781442258020 (cloth : alk. paper) | ISBN 9781442258037 (pbk. : alk.
    paper) | ISBN 9781442258044 (electronic)

Subjects: LCSH: United States—Race relations. | Racism—United States. |
    Minorities—United States—Social conditions. | Race.

Classification: LCC E184.A1 A6195 2017 (print) | LCC E184.A1 (ebook) | DDC
    305.800973—dc23

LC record available at https://lccn.loc.gov/2016047560

♾™ The paper used in this publication meets the minimum requirements of American National Standard for Information

Sciences—Permanence of Paper for Printed Library Materials, ANSI/NISO Z39.48-1992.

Printed in the United States of America

Brief Contents

Detailed Contents

Dilemma or Dream? The Quagmire of Race in America

In 1944, Swedish economist and Nobel Prize winner Karl Gunnar Myrdal published one of the most highly influential books on U.S. race relations, titled *An American Dilemma*. Myrdal had been commissioned by the Carnegie Corporation to comprehensively study the status of Black Americans in the United States (referred to at the time and in his book as "Negroes"). The research took four years to complete. The book (almost 1,500 pages long) took another two years to write. *An American Dilemma* has had an enormous impact, including influencing the momentous 1954 Supreme Court decision *Brown v. Board of Education*.

The major conclusion of Myrdal's book—the one for which it continues to be known—was that the problem of race in the United States lay in the "hearts" of Americans. Myrdal professed that there was a fundamental moral contradiction between the American values of "liberty, equality, justice, and fair opportunity" (1944:xlvii) and the persistence of racial discrimination. The dilemma lay in reconciling these two conflicting realities.

More than seventy years since Myrdal's book was published, racial inequality in the United States is still with us. It is certainly nothing like it was in the 1930s and 1940s, but it is entrenched in the structure of this society. Many still imagine race as primarily residing in the hearts and minds of White Americans, as if race were primarily a problem of people's attitudes and beliefs. As people talk about race today, Myrdal's words still resonate, such as in former president Barack Obama's speech commemorating Martin Luther King Day at Ebenezer Baptist Church in Atlanta in 2008 when he said, "Each of us carries with us the task of changing our hearts and minds." The phrase also appears in various appeals to reducing terrorism. In Obama's words, "Our campaign to prevent people around the world from being radicalized to violence is ultimately a battle for hearts and minds" (*Los Angeles Times*, February 17, 2015).

Today's dilemma is far more complex than Myrdal could have imagined. It would be great if changing race relations in the United States were just a matter of changing hearts and minds. As difficult as it is to change attitudes and feelings, changing society itself is even harder. Racial attitudes are a manifestation of the racism that is built into the very fabric of society. Myrdal did understand this, even with his focus on moral conscience. He wrote that America's race problem was an "integral part of the whole complex of problems in [the United States]" and could not be treated in isolation from those problems. He wrote further that the problem of race "exists and changes because of conditions and forces operating in the larger American society" (1944:liii). Race in U.S. society may live in people's hearts and minds, but it is also entrenched in the structure of society.

We no longer think of race as rooted in the moral dilemma that Myrdal described, but we still live with a contradiction between the professed values of equality in the American dream and seemingly intransigent racial inequality. The American dream holds that there is an open door for all who want to better themselves, their families, and their communities. But haunting the dream is the persistence of racial segregation in neighborhoods and schools, high rates of poverty among people of color, and strong racial resentment by many who think people of color now get an unfair advantage. People of color also frequently get accused of having only themselves to blame if they cannot make it in America.

At times the American dream seems even more like a nightmare, especially as we have recently witnessed so many acts of overt racism and hatred in the aftermath of electing Donald

Trump president of the United States. Trump's professed determination to shut U.S. borders to Mexicans and people of Muslim faith and his labeling Mexican immigrants "criminals and rapists"; the shooting and murder of innocent church-goers in Charleston, South Carolina; the mass shooting of predominantly Latinos/as in a gay nightclub in Orlando, Florida: These and possibly other horrific acts of violence that are likely to occur before this book is published reveal a deep vein of bigotry and hatred in the United States. These acts of hatred targeted at different groups reveal a link between racism, homophobia, xenophobia, and gender-based violence. Following the Orlando mass shooting, the editors of the *New York Times* wrote, "Hate crimes don't happen in a vacuum. They occur where bigotry is allowed to fester, where minorities are vilified and where people are scapegoated for political gain" (Editorial Board, *New York Times*, June 15, 2016).

Many people think that the racism of the past is long gone. After all, the nation elected its first African American president in 2008. The U.S. Supreme Court includes a Latina (Puerto Rican woman) and an African American man. Racial diversity is more common in the media, and public opinion polls show a significant decline in overt expressions of prejudice. Yet, during the 2016 presidential election, the nation witnessed almost entirely White audiences at the rallies of candidate Donald Trump, now our nation's forty-fifth president. When during the campaign Trump said that the judge presiding over a lawsuit against Trump was not qualified because of his "Mexican heritage," Republican congressman Paul Ryan accused Trump of "textbook" racism. (The judge was a native of Indiana, born of Mexican immigrant parents.) In the aftermath of Trump's election to the presidency, many of his supporters in the political arena denied that they were racist but did not decry the fact that Trump was enthusiastically endorsed by various proponents of white supremacy. How could this be? The nation seems to be very confused about what racism is and how it is manifested in our daily lives.

Myrdal could not have foreseen the greater complexity of race that we see today. More people than ever (although still a relatively small number) self-identify as "multiracial." Large numbers of diverse immigrant groups populate the United States. The black-white model of understanding race in America is being eroded as Latinos have surpassed African Americans as a proportion of the population. Moreover, this model of understanding race relations never acknowledged the long-standing presence of Asians and Native Americans in this country. Understanding race in this more multiracial, multicultural society is thus more challenging than ever before. Racism in the United States is sometimes quite overt and obvious, but it also takes more covert forms—forms that may not be so publicly witnessed but are daily felt by those who bear the brunt of racism's pain.

The Merriam-Webster dictionary defines *quagmire* as "soft . . . land that shakes or yields under the foot." The quagmire of race in America is just that—a muddy mess that shifts and changes with each historic event that reshapes its meaning and nature. Race is a quagmire indeed, made murky by the many strong feelings and oft-held misconceptions about what race is and how people experience it. The good news is that more people seem to want to understand race, at least as indicated by the frequency with which race now comes up in public and private conversation.

Race in Society introduces readers to the rich scholarship that now anchors sociological thinking about race. It is presented in the hope that it can help better inform public understanding of the changing nature of racial inequality. The book is anchored in contemporary sociological scholarship (and some classic works) and is written in a narrative style to engage reader interest and make it accessible to a wide audience.

Several assumptions underlie this book. They are:

- Most of us want to live in a society where everyone has a fair chance to be safe and secure and has opportunities for well-being.
- Many, if not most, people are misinformed about race, which leads not just to misunderstanding but also to mistrust, fear, anger, and hurt—emotions that stifle positive cross-group relationships.
- It is difficult, if not impossible, to avoid racial stereotyping because of the pervasiveness of pejorative images in popular culture.
- Racism exists despite the fact that so many people deny that it is still with us.
- Racism is not always overt. It may be invisible to those who do not experience its force, yet it can be made visible through education and careful study.
- People may benefit from racism even when they do not think of themselves as racists.
- Changing racial inequality necessitates change in our social institutions and social policies.

You may not agree with these underlying assumptions, but I hope they will guide your reading of this book. I ask you to consider how we might understand race differently from a perspective anchored in the rich scholarship of social science rather than in the popular perspective that generally blames people for their own shortcomings.

Organization of the Book

Thinking in the sociology of race has changed dramatically in recent years, moving from a "racial and ethnic minorities" perspective to one that is more concept-centered. It is no longer adequate to teach about race as a laundry list of different racial-ethnic "minority" group experiences. Rather, new scholarship examines how various group experiences are linked in a racialized social structure, not just how they are said to reflect different "minorities." The smorgasbord approach of comparing the experiences of different racial-ethnic groups no longer reflects the state of research on race and ethnicity; such comparisons have been displaced by scholarship on the social construction of race and its different manifestations within the increasingly diverse racial-ethnic population of the United States.

This book is organized around several major conceptual themes. In part I ("The Social Construction of Race"), chapter 1 examines the social construction of race and ethnicity as they evolve within systems of power and privilege. Chapter 2 looks at the social dynamics of prejudice, bias, and racism, including colorblind racism. Chapter 3 reviews the enormous influence of the media on how people imagine race. And, chapter 4 presents racial identities in their many evolving forms.

Part II ("Understanding Racial Stratification") includes two important chapters. First, chapter 5 briefly details the diverse histories of U.S. racial-ethnic groups.

Although a single chapter cannot possibly do justice to the rich past of so many groups, it is important to have some background in the history of race and ethnicity to understand the present. Chapter 6 details a theoretical framework for the empirical evidence that the book examines.

Part III ("Race and Social Institutions") focuses on institutional racism. Racial inequality continues to be a part of society's major institutions, shaping the opportunities (or lack thereof) available to various groups. Chapter 7 looks at work and the economy, including the connection between race and poverty. Chapter 8 discusses families and communities. Chapters 9, 10, and 11 focus on housing and educational segregation, health and environmental racism, and the criminal justice system, respectively.

Part IV ("Race and Social Change"), consisting only of chapter 12, provides an overview of the roots of racial protest. It concludes with sections that consider different frameworks for social change and how change is likely to be affected by the increasing diversity of the U.S. population.

A Note on Language

Language is fraught with racial connotation, and words can hurt. Any book on race in the United States must be attentive to the words it uses. What we call people, how we express ideas, whose voice is active, whose passive: All of these practices can suggest racial meaning. While writing this book, I became keenly aware of how word choice conveys particular meanings about race—some intended, others not. In a society where race carries such weight, I want to make my choices involving words and labels clear and provide my reasons for using the words I do.

First, race itself is a social construct, as the early chapters of this book will show. Therefore, the language we use to describe and define different racial-ethnic groups is loaded with social meaning. Simply naming major racial-ethnic groups in the United States inevitably reifies the groups, as if our so-called racial population is easily divided five ways: White, Black (or African American), Latino/a (or Hispanic), Asian American, and Native American. We know that each of these groups is highly diverse, complex in its identities, and not fixed or immutable over the course of time and history. I also realize that some groups object to the labels in which they are generally included. The label *Latino*, for example, is an aggregated term that is meant to convey common experiences and linked interests, but it also hides people's specific identities as Chicano/a, Mexican, Puerto Rican, Guatemalan, and so forth. General labels cloak specific identities, but there is no other way to generalize about group experiences than to use aggregated terms. In the end, I just had to live with this contradiction in a desire to be respectful of individual identities, but sociological in analyzing group experiences.

In reporting data from federal agencies or others' research, I have used the terms found in the original source. In the census, for example, those terms are typically non-Hispanic White, Black (or African American), Hispanic, Asian American, and, sometimes, "multiracial." There is maddeningly little data on Native Americans collected as part of routine surveys in many of these sources, so Native Americans are often omitted in some of the empirical data here, especially as presented in charts, figures, and tables.

I have capitalized *White* and *Black* throughout the book primarily when they are used as proper nouns or to modify people. For some this may appear jarring; for others, it is now common practice. The term *White* itself is fraught with political meaning, as new studies of whiteness are also finding. Certainly, not all Whites share the same advantages as the White population writ large. You will note, for reasons elaborated in chapter 1, that I never use the term *Caucasian* because of its racist origins—even though it is widespread as a label in American culture.

I have found it impossible to avoid the term *minority* when referring to racial and ethnic groups who experience discrimination in U.S. society. Many now object to this term because people of color are becoming a numerical majority in the United States. In many places, they already are in the majority. When used here, however, *minority* is used in the sociological sense of the term, that is, to refer to groups that share common historical and cultural experiences of prejudice and discrimination. In other words, *minority* refers to an experience, not numerical representation.

In sum, language often reflects the political and social status of groups, and I have tried to avoid using any language that unintentionally insults or belittles people. We also know that language shapes people's perceptions of reality. Being attentive to the language of race can help reduce racism. The language here may not always be perfect and, as has happened before, language regarding race is likely to change in the future. I only ask that readers be attentive to the language they use, understanding that this is an important part of the path to greater racial equality.

Pedagogical Features of *Race in Society*

This volume includes several features that will help readers think further about the issues raised within. Throughout the book, *textboxes* enhance core material. The box series titled LIVING WITH RACISM provides first-person narratives about the experience of racism. A second box series, LEARNING OUR PAST, provides glimpses into parts of U.S. history that are often unknown or forgotten. Recognizing and understanding some of the harms of the past put the present into perspective and can help debunk some of the myths about racism that abound in the absence of a longer view.

Student exercises are included at the end of each chapter. These are intended to encourage readers to engage actively with the book's content and see for themselves some of the patterns and processes that mark racial and ethnic inequality. For instructors, these exercises can be the basis for class discussions and/or assignments. Each chapter also includes *critical thinking questions* that enable readers to explore the subject matter more deeply.

Another feature is titled *Challenging Questions: Open to Debate,* appearing at the end of each chapter. It poses scenarios or questions on hotly debated current issues, such as the tension brought on by hate speech in the context of the right to free speech, immigration policy, the influence of race versus class, school choice, affirmative action, and other controversial subjects. The purpose is to explore diverse viewpoints on these hot-button issues.

Key terms are listed at the end of each chapter and are included in a *glossary* at the end of the book.

Instructor and Student Resources

Instructor's Manual and *Test Bank*. For each chapter in the text, the Instructor's Manual provides student learning objectives, key terms with definitions, discussion questions, and web resources. The Test Bank includes a variety of multiple choice, true/false, and short answer questions and is available in either Word or Respondus format. In either format, the Test Bank can be fully edited and customized to best meet your needs. The Instructor's Manual and Test Bank are available to adopters for download on the text's catalog page at https://rowman.com/ISBN/9781442258020.

PowerPoint Slides. These provide the tables and figures from the text. The presentation is available for adopters to download on the text's catalog page at https://rowman.com/ISBN/9781442258020.

Companion Website. Accompanying the text is an open-access website designed to reinforce the main topics and help students to master key vocabulary and concepts through flashcards and self-graded quizzes. Students can access the companion website from their computers or mobile devices at http://textbooks.rowman.com/andersen.

Acknowledgments

Writing a book is never a solo project, despite the long hours of sitting alone at one's desk. There are many people to thank for the many ways they have supported me as the book developed.

I am privileged to work amid a network of brilliant colleagues and friends with whom I have had many conversations about race over the years. Those conversations have shaped my thinking and are, no doubt, embedded in this book. As a White woman I have had to learn to listen, respect, question, and always empathize with those whose experiences are so very different from my own. Although I cannot claim to have lived racism in the ways many of my friends have, I have learned tremendously from each of them. These close friendships are at the heart of this book. I especially thank Maxine Baca Zinn, Elizabeth Higginbotham, Howard Taylor, Valerie Hans, and Patricia Hill Collins for the many years of friendship, collaboration, and discussions of new research. I especially thank Maxine, Elizabeth, and Howard for closely reading chapters and providing invaluable encouragement, corrections, and suggestions. Some special thanks also go to James Jones, my colleague at the University of Delaware and founder of the Center for the Study of Diversity. Our work together over the years has been sustaining even when it seemed impossible to transform our institution. I thank you and Olaive for these years of friendship and support.

I also thank all those scholars, many of them cited here, who are doing such profoundly excellent work on the subjects covered in this book. One book could not possibly do justice to all the nuances in your work, but I am profoundly grateful for what I have learned from you and how your work has guided my writing. A special appreciation to the Center for Comparative Studies in Race and Ethnicity at Stanford University for proving such a rich community of scholars doing exciting new research. I give special thanks to David Embrick, Mark Kerr, Amanda Lewis, and Mary Romero: Your various Facebook posts often pointed me to new research and commentaries that guided the development of this book. Thank you! I thank Sally Hillsman for suggesting early on that I "tell stories" to keep readers' attention. Although this book is not fiction, I hope the narrative flow reflects your always sound advice and guidance. Thank you as well to John Ernest, whose commitment to racial justice has, as he has said, put us on a similar path.

I give deep thanks to the many dear friends who have kept me on an even keel through the daily challenges of writing this book: Jack and Carolyn Batty; Claudia and Richard Fischer; Sarah Hedrick; Barb Hicks; Amber, Mark, Clara, and Luke Petry; Amy, Maxx, and Tony Stein-Miksitz; Joan Stock; Randall and JoAnn Stokes; Scott and Suzanne Supplee; Nancy and Tim Targett; and Debbie Watkins. I hope you all know how much your friendship and support mean to me. You helped keep me going even when the writing seemed impossible to complete. I must also give a special recognition to the "BI Institute"—the support team that helped me stay sane while working on this book and holding a senior leadership position. Thank you, Nancy, Lynn, and Kathy for the support and, especially, the laughter. I am also deeply grateful to be part of the Boston Area Feminist Gender Scholars Group: Our deep conversations and examination of feminist scholarship have enriched my thinking and this work. Thank you, Catherine Connell, Karen Hansen, Rosanna Hertz, Debra Kaufman, Nazli Kibria, Peggy Nelson, Debra Osnowitz, Smitha Radhakrishnan, Kelly Rutherford, Cinzia Solari, Maxine Baca Zinn, and Kathrin Zippel—all of you serious scholars whose insights and support continue to shape my thinking and warm my heart! And to Kerry Ann Rockquemore and the National Center for Faculty Development and Diversity: That 14-Day Writing Challenge and the Faculty Success Program got me through a slump and to the finish line!

I must also thank the students who took my Racial Inequality course in the fall of 2015. They read several chapters and provided detailed commentary at a critical stage. Most especially, I thank them for their willingness to explore openly the subject of race in a very diverse, open, and trusting environment. These students provided an extraordinary teaching and learning experience that I will long remember. A very special thank you, then, goes to: John Affriol, Kristen Brokaw, Cameron Brown, Sarah Clark, Edwin Francois, Daniel Hyde, Kevin James, Gabrielle Lanzetta, Carissa Lupton, Yarissa Luna, Hannah Mosios, Allie Norris, Tyler Paul, Taylor Quick, Kathryn Super, Larissa Thermidor, and Zilong Zhou. You give me hope for a transformed world!

I could not be luckier to have Nancy Roberts as my publisher. From the start, she has been enthusiastic about this project. As the work unfolded, she was always supportive and encouraging. I greatly appreciate her commitment to publishing a full body of sociological scholarship even amid the challenges of the electronic revolution. I also thank Molly White for her attention and thoroughness throughout the production of this book. I also sincerely thank Jehanne Schweitzer and Helen Subbio for shepherding this book through the production phase.

Thanks also go to the reviewers who read all or part of the initial manuscript: Shelly Brown-Jeffy, University of North Carolina–Greensboro; Erica Chito Childs, Hunter College/CUNY Graduate Center; Amanda Lewis, University of Illinois–Chicago; Enid Logan, University of Minnesota; ConSandra McNeil, Jackson State University; Mary Romero, Arizona State University; and Amanda Roth, State University of New York–Geneseo.

I am very fortunate to have had strong institutional support. Thank you to the staff at the University of Delaware's Morris Library for making it easy to find resources and for providing a quiet space to work. I also thank Domenico Grasso and Peggy Bottorff in the Provost's Office at the University of Delaware for the support that helped get this done.

Critically important is the support and love I receive from my family. Our family proves that love is stronger than any differences we have based on race, gender, sexual orientation, age, faith, and religion. Thank you to my mom, Emma Johnson; my deceased stepfather, Luther Johnson; Arlene Hanerfeld; Norman Andersen; Jessica Hanerfeld; Sarah Hanerfeld; Kimball Johnson; Mary Brittain; Debbie Lanier; David Carcapo; the adorable Aubrey Hanerfeld; and now-baby Aden Jonathan Carcapo. I love you all!

To my husband/soul mate/captain, Richard Rosenfeld: I can't find new words to thank you again for supporting my writing, but each time I recognize you in a preface like this, it is just as heartfelt as the first time. You patiently listened as I read passages out loud even when I know you would have rather been doing something else. You somehow manage to keep me steady no matter the headwinds or the clutter in our lives. Your advice when I was having my doubts was invaluable—you told me that I might not know all I needed to know but I knew whose work to trust. That was great advice and it helped me pull this together. Despite all the clutter of our life together, you manage to get us through the mess. Now on to our next journey together!

Finally, *I dedicate this book to William Julius Wilson and Lewis M. Killian.* I started my sociological career as clueless as any White person living in the time and space I came from. Bill Wilson's early and ongoing guidance and the depth of his ideas opened a new way of thinking for me. Bill also helped me to get my first book contract; his steadfast support over the years reverberates in how I now think about race. I cannot thank Lewis in person because he is deceased, but as I wrote this book, I kept hearing his many extraordinary lessons. My path has gone in different directions from what I imagined early on, but I still feel the strong influence of these two men. I am solely responsible for any errors, omissions, and oversimplification.

About the Book Cover

The image on the cover of this book is adapted from a mural by Amanda Timoney, a student at the University of California–Santa Cruz where she created it. Students developed the mural project on the UCSC campus to celebrate social justice and community development. Thirty-five murals were created from this community project; you can see all of them at: http://collegenine.ucsc.edu/getinvolved/murals/index.html.

Amanda Timoney's full mural includes four faces of people from indiscernible races. She designed the mural following her experience of living abroad in Ghana, and she says that the mural symbolizes the values of social justice and community. Within the mural, specific symbols from Ghana's culture are depicted. As the artist writes, "The heart (Sankofa) represents the saying that, 'an individual must reflect on the past before performing actions that will define the future.' The square rectangle with notches is a symbol of versatility and change, specifically the skill of being able to take in negative objects/beliefs and change them into something positive for the community. The two lizards that are attached to one another represent unity in diversity. Finally, the circle and triangle represent freedom and the fact that communities attain freedom through violence (the triangle) and peace (the circle)."

The artist left space on the mural so that others could add symbols of their own. As you read this book, you might think about what symbol you would add if you had that opportunity.

About the Author

Margaret L. Andersen (PhD, MA, University of Massachusetts–Amherst; BA, Georgia State University) is the Edward F. and Elizabeth Goodman Rosenberg Professor of Sociology at the University of Delaware, where she also holds joint appointments in Black American Studies and Women's Studies. She is the author of several books, including *Thinking about Women,* published in its tenth edition; the best-selling anthology *Race, Class and Gender* (coedited with Patricia Hill Collins; 9th ed.); *Race and Ethnicity in Society: The Changing Landscape* (coedited with Elizabeth Higginbotham; 4th ed.); *Sociology: The Essentials* (coauthored with Howard F. Taylor, 9th ed.); *Living Art: The Life of African American Art Collector Paul Jones*; and *On Land and On Sea: A Century of Women in the Rosenfeld Collection.*

She is a member and former chair of the National Advisory Board for Stanford University's Center for Comparative Studies in Race and Ethnicity, the past vice president of the American Sociological Association, and the past president of the Eastern Sociological Society. She has received two teaching awards from the University of Delaware and two prestigious awards from her professional organizations: the Eastern Sociological Society Merit Award for career contributions, and the American Sociological Association's Jessie Bernard Award, an award given for expanding the boundaries of sociology to include women. At the University of Delaware, she has served in several senior administrative positions, including vice provost for Faculty Affairs and Diversity, executive director of the President's Diversity Initiative, interim deputy provost, and dean of the College of Arts and Sciences.

CHAPTER 1

Race

A Thoroughly Social Idea

Race is a pigment of the imagination.
—Rubén Rumbaut (2009a)

OBJECTIVES

- Understand the historical origins of the "one drop rule"

- Connect the emergence of racial thinking to its historical origins

- Be able to criticize the idea of race as biologically or genetically based

- Situate racial classification systems in their historical and social context

- Understand race as a social construction

- Explain the concept of racial formation

Suppose that one day a stranger comes to your door and tells you that she discovered that a huge bureaucratic mistake was made when you were born. She says that your birth certificate was bungled at birth, and it records you as a different race from what you have thought all of your life. You are being given the opportunity to change your race, but you must decide by the end of the day.

You are not the only person in this scenario. A very wealthy gentleman is willing to give a very generous sum of money to anyone who agrees to change his or her race to match the state records. Nothing else about you would change. Your ideas, thoughts, level of education, job: Everything else would remain the same, but you would from then on be known and recognized as a member of your "new" race. You would live the rest of your life as a person of a different race.

This hypothetical situation assumes, of course, that a person's race can be changed. As you will learn here, race is a complex social reality and is not solely about appearance. Whether race can be "changed" is also a more complicated matter than you might think. But what if you *could* change your race? *How much money would you want to change your race?*

A scenario like this has actually been studied by researchers who were interested in White people's perceptions of the "cost of being Black" (Mazzocco et al. 2006). The researchers were interested in White people's perceptions, so they only included White people in their research sample. They presented a hypothetical situation similar to the one above to research subjects. In the study, the authors found that White Americans did not want too much money to become Black; on average, Whites wanted about $1,500 a year to change their race—far less than the $1 million subjects wanted to never watch television again. The researchers concluded that White Americans vastly underestimate the cost of being Black in the United States.

If you could change someone's race, how much do you think a White person should want to become Black? A Latino to become Asian? A Black person to become White? In a class taught by this book's author, some Black students said they would not take any amount of money to be White. White students wanted large sums of money to become Black. All students agreed that you couldn't pay them enough to give up television!

Aside from the monetary award, what would it mean to change your race? Would you only change your appearance? Would your attitudes change? Your neighbors? Your friends? Your job? In other words, how would your life be lived differently if you were of a race other than what you have assumed all your life? Such questions help you start to think about the significance and consequences of race. This chapter examines the meaning of race and how it is connected to society.

The One Drop Rule

In some ways, changing race is not as farfetched as this opening scenario suggests. Consider the actual case of Susie Guillory Phipps. Susie Guillory was born in Louisiana in 1934. She grew up White, never thinking of herself in any other way. She married a White man, Andy Phipps. In 1977 she applied for a passport so that she and her husband could travel to South America. When she went to the Division of Vital Records in New Orleans to do so, she was told that her birth certificate recorded both her parents as "col," that is, "colored"—or black (Trillin 1986; Wright 1994). Oddly enough, her children's birth certificates listed her and her two children as "white." Imagine her surprise on learning that the state considered her to be "black."

Susie Phipps tried to get her birth certificate changed to reflect what she believed to be her true identity—"white"—but the state clerks would not budge. As it turns out, Susie Guillory Phipps's great-great-great-grandmother (named Marguerite) was a Black slave—five generations back.[1] A 1970 state law in Louisiana defined anyone with a trace of black ancestry as "black." At the time, it was believed that each race had its own blood type. Blood type was also thought to be correlated with other physical and social features—an idea that we now know to be ludicrous but that nonetheless governed the laws of southern states for years.

Susie Phipps sued the state of Louisiana to have her birth certificate changed. She lost her case in 1983. The law was not overturned until years later.

Louisiana was not unique among southern states in defining a person's race by the **one drop rule** (more formally known as **hypodescent**). The one drop rule refers to the notion that a certain amount of so-called black blood legally defined someone as "black." States varied in the particulars. Mississippi classified individuals as "black" if they had "any appreciable amount of Negro blood." North Carolina, Florida, and Texas defined "black" as anyone having one-eighth Black ancestry.

Oddly enough, you might be considered a given race in one state and not in another. In Virginia, even as late as 1963, you were considered Indian if you lived on a reservation and had at least one Indian grandparent. Off the reservation, you would be considered Black (Cumminos 1963). Your official identity could even change over time within a given state. In 1785 Virginia, any person with "one-fourth part or more Negro blood" was deemed a "colored" person, but in 1910, the proportion was changed to one-sixteenth. In 1924 the Virginia Racial Purity Act decreed that having *any trace* of African ancestry meant you were Black (California Newsreel 2003).

You might be surprised to learn that many of the state laws defining people in one race or another were not enacted until the early twentieth century—1911 in Texas and Arkansas, 1923 in North Carolina, 1924 in Virginia, 1927 in Georgia and Alabama (Murray 1997). Why then?

Known sardonically as the "Golden Age of Racism," the early twentieth century was a period of dramatic change in the racial social order of the United States. Slavery had ended with the close of the Civil War and the passage of the Thirteenth Amendment to the U.S. Constitution in 1865. The period of Reconstruction in the South (1865–1877) had given newly emancipated Black Americans hope for full rights of citizenship but, following Reconstruction, the nation remodeled a system

---

[1] Marguerite was the slave of the wife (Marie Jeanne LaCasse) of a French planter (Joseph Gregory Guillory). After LaCasse's death, Joseph Guillory fathered four children with Marguerite, but she was still listed as Marie Jeanne LaCasse's property. LaCasse's White sons sued Joseph Gregory Guillory for all of LaCasse's property, including Marguerite, and Marguerite was turned over to the eldest son (Jean Baptiste Guillory). Joseph went to his son's home and kidnapped Marguerite at knifepoint. Joseph then freed Marguerite (through what is known as *manumission*), on the condition that she stay with him until his death, which she did. When the sons attempted to have Marguerite returned to them, Marguerite sued in court and won, ensuring both her freedom and that of her four children.

of racial inequality that disenfranchised Black Americans in every aspect of life (Foner 1988).

Retrenchment to a revised system of racial subordination was cemented with the 1898 Supreme Court decision in *Plessy v. Ferguson* that legally sanctioned strict racial segregation. Jim Crow segregation,[2] that is, the separate and fully unequal treatment of Black and White Americans, would govern the American South for years to come. That enactment of racial classification laws is an example of how extreme forms of racism tend to emerge during periods of rapid social change in the preexisting racial order, such as in the one that characterized the late nineteenth and early twentieth centuries in the United States. *Racial backlash* occurs when there is a movement to reestablish a social order defined along lines of race even when social trends have begun to dismantle the prior racial system (Roberts 2012).

Looking at Jim Crow segregation from today's vantage point, the laws and practices seem capricious, but they were taken for granted at least by dominant groups. They constituted one of the mechanisms that maintained and protected a racial order that assured white supremacy in all aspects of life. We are familiar with separate schools, separate restrooms, and separate seating on public buses, but the extremes that the laws went to are sometimes stunning. For example, a 1935 North Carolina law decreed, "Books shall not be interchangeable between the white and colored schools, but shall continued [*sic*] by the race first using them" (1935, c. 422, s.2; cited in Murray 1997:331). Another example can be found in the state of Delaware, where law mandated not only separate schools for Whites and Blacks but also for those identified as Moors or Indians (Murray 1997). The degree to which these Jim Crow laws governed daily life is hard to overemphasize.

Why were laws defining race so important? They were important for several reasons. They defined citizenship and, for African Americans, they had defined ownership under slavery. Such laws were also designed to prevent intermarriage. Racial intermarriage was illegal in all southern states until 1967, when the Supreme Court ruled in a case poignantly named *Loving v. Virginia* that laws prohibiting racial intermarriage were unconstitutional. We will examine interracial marriage later in this book, but the point now is to see how the definition of race emerges for very specific *societal* reasons.

The meaning of race is deeply tied to systems of racial inequality—that is, social systems where dominant groups control, exploit, and *define* subordinate groups (Higginbotham and Andersen 2016). Putting briefly one of the most important lessons of this book, *race is a social construction*. The remainder of this chapter explores in more detail what race as a social construction means.

The Myth of Biological Race

When you encounter a person, most likely one of the first things you notice about the person is race; at least this is so in the United States. On what do you base this? Is it physical appearance? Skin tone? Facial features? Hair? Most people think they can

---

[2] The term *Jim Crow* is said to originate from a White minstrel-show performer who appeared in black-face and danced a ridiculously stereotypical jig, an insulting performance that became a standard part of minstrel shows in the mid-nineteenth century in the United States.

"see" race because physical features are what make race "visible" to others. Scratch the surface, though, and you will discover that race is not as simple as it may seem.

Even now, with years of research to tell us the contrary, many think that race is somehow rooted in biological or genetic differences. Is this true? Using the technique of DNA sequencing, scientists working on the human genome project have mapped the over twenty thousand extant human genes and have soundly concluded that *there is no such thing as a race gene.* Of course, there are identifiable physical differences among human populations, and some of those physical characteristics are produced through genetic expression. A brief lesson in genetics, though, helps you understand that even genetic traits are not as simply determined as you might think (Bonham 2015; Feldman 2010).

The **genotype** of any organism, including humans, is the full set of genes found in a given organism, including the human body. An organism's **phenotype** refers to its *observable* characteristics. The genotype influences the phenotype, but the phenotype is also influenced by an organism's environment or *culture* (see chapter 3). Some genotypic traits are discrete and fixed, that is, they are directly expressed, producing a particular outcome. Blood type is an example: A person is either A, B, AB, or O. Most observable characteristics in people, that is, their phenotype, fall along a continuum, influenced by inherited characteristics *and* the environment. Height is a good example. You might inherit the tendency to be tall or short, but your environment will significantly affect your actual height.

Skin color is a phenotypic trait. That is, although it is partially based on inherited genes, in any human grouping it is also influenced by environmental factors. Scientists now understand that skin color is likely determined by as many as six different genes. Genes also interact with each other. Even if skin color alone defined race, it would not result in discrete categories as does blood type.

Most people do not understand the complexity that geneticists are now discovering. The mass media generally oversimplify research studies about genetics, leading the public to think that there is a direct causal relationship between particular genes and a given condition. This simple causal relationship is generally not true. For example, there can be correlations between genes and particular diseases, but this does not necessarily mean that genes are causal determinants of disease (Brooks and King 2008). Health and disease are influenced by all kinds of social factors, including lifestyle, access to quality health care, and diet—all social and environmental factors, not genetically determined ones.

What about so-called race-based diseases, such as sickle cell anemia? Sickle cell occurs in offspring where both parents carry the sickle cell genetic trait. In the United States, sickle cell anemia is a disease that is most common among African and African American populations. But the genetic trait that produces sickle cell anemia has developed over time as a resistance to malaria. Thus, sickle cell anemia was first found in populations where malaria was most common, in such places as the Middle East, India, Greece, southern Italy, southern Turkey, and West Africa. Certain African populations actually have a very low rate of sickle cell disease. Again, even when a condition like sickle cell anemia is more common in a given population, the trait for it developed earlier in response to environmental conditions. Note that we do not call sickle cell an Italian or Turkish disease. Sickle cell, then, should not now be considered an African American disease either.

Likewise, Tay-Sachs is a disease that is associated with Ashkenazic Jewish people. It is a recessive genetic disorder, but it is not exclusive to Jewish populations. Tay-Sachs is also found among French Canadians, Louisiana Cajuns, and the Pennsylvania Dutch. As in the case of sickle cell anemia, a combination of a population's ancestry and geographic location will condition the likelihood of manifesting this trait (Brooks and King 2008; Villarosa 2002).

Simply put, although there may be some genetic influence on what we call race traits, none of the characteristics we have used to define race (such as skin color, hair texture, or body form) corresponds to any true genetic difference between human populations. You simply cannot look at genes and then separate people into discrete, supposedly "racial" categories based on their genetic makeup. Biologists define a race as "a population that has significant genetic differences from other populations such that it can be considered a subspecies" (Graves, cited in Villarosa 2002). Unlike in the animal kingdom, where you can separate animals into distinct species, there are no separate species of human beings.

At the level of genetic composition, scientists now know that there are far more similarities among people than there are differences. If you take any two people (including two people from supposedly different races) and analyze their genetic composition, you will find that they are far more alike than different. This is a very important point for anyone who thinks of race as a biological given. So-called racial traits do not exist in discrete categories—a condition that would be needed to take any species and divide it into so-called race groups. The fact is that genetic variation among human beings is indeed very small. *There is only one human race.*

This truth has not stopped people over the years from trying to categorize people into so-called race groups. Over time people have created many different schemes for dividing human beings into races. At one time, some even thought that earwax could be used as a "marker" of race (Snipp 2010)! The schemes that have been developed throughout history reflect the racial politics and social systems of the time far more than any true scientific facts.

Notions about how many races there are and what race means have also changed dramatically over time. This is because the meanings that humans have given to race reflect social, not biological, conditions. Contemporary scientists conclude that the "lay concept of race does not correspond to the variation that exists in nature" (Graves 2001:5).

The idea that human beings can be separated into races corresponds closely with the development of social institutions that have exploited people for the profit of others, such as slavery (Graves 2004; Jones 2013). The idea that humans can be divided into so-called races only makes sense within the context of a system of racial inequality. Such exploitation could only be justified (at least by the dominant group) if the group being oppressed is defined as something less than fully human (Fredrickson 2002). To understand the meaning of race, then, you must understand the social context from which the idea stems.

If race is false as a biological notion, then is there no such thing as race? Yes and no. There is no biological reality that divides people into separate races, but race is very real in its vast and significant human impact. As summed up by sociologist Ann Morning, who has extensively studied scientific constructions of race, there is a "longstanding belief that race is etched on the human body" and, as she continues to say, this "has far-reaching physical, social, economic and political consequences" (Morning 2011:7). You will see the consequences of the social construction of race throughout this book but, for now, understand that the consequences of race reach into every dimension of our society. In other words, *race is real, but it is real in its social origins and consequences.*

Race: A Modern Idea

It might surprise you to learn that race is a relatively modern idea. Over the ages, people in society have held negative ideas about those perceived as "other." The term **xenophobia** ("fear of foreigners"), for example, stems from ancient Greece where Greeks thought that all non-Greeks were barbarians (Graves 2004). In the Western world, there is ample evidence that some of the earliest cultures had definitions of groups that ranked them by descent and seeming physical differences (Bethencourt 2014). There is a big difference, though, between seeing strangers as outsiders or "others" and establishing a social system in which people perceived as different are defined as less than human and believed to be innately inferior. Although the ancient Greeks did have slaves and disliked outsiders, whom they defined as somehow different, possibly even innately different, slaves were not treated like property in a formal, state-sanctioned system of slavery (Fredrickson 2002).

It seems that the term *race* was first used in the Middle Ages, but it only referred to animal breeds. With the advent of the scientific revolution, though, early scientists became obsessed with observing and classifying what they saw in nature. It did not take long before they tried to differentiate human groups based on presumed differences in their physical characteristics (Ferber 1998). An uneasy alliance was then forged between budding scientific thinking and the emergence of modern racism.

Historian Winthrop Jordan locates the origins of the idea of race in the early European conquest of African people. Jordan meticulously shows that when European explorers encountered Africans, the Europeans thought of Africans as primitive and savage. This belief was then used to rationalize what became the development of slavery in the New World (Jordan 1968).

Swedish botanist and physician Carolus Linnaeus (1707–1778) was the first to develop elaborate taxonomies of plants and other parts of nature. He organized the plant and animal kingdoms into different species, according to the shared characteristics of these living organisms. Linnaeus identified human beings (*Homo sapiens*) and primates as part of the genus *Homo*. He further differentiated *Homo sapiens* into four groups: Europeans, American Indians, Asians, and Africans. Although he did not explicitly rank them, he did color-code them white, red, yellow, and black. Further, he described each group in what we would now see as a highly value-laden, Eurocentric perspective (Fredrickson 2002; Roberts 2012), describing Europeans as "gentle, acute, inventive . . . governed by customs" and Africans as "crafty, indolent, negligent . . . governed by caprice" (West 1982:56, cited in Ferber 1998:28–29).

Incredibly, the color scheme that Linnaeus invented persists to this day as people continue to describe human groups in terms of presumed color. Following Linnaeus, various other Europeans developed different schemes for classifying human beings as if they were of different biological types. While the Atlantic slave trade was flourishing, pseudoscientific thinkers developed various racial schemes to give supposed legitimacy to a highly unequal and oppressive system of human life.

In the early eighteenth century, French naturalist Georges-Louis Leclerc, Comte de Buffon (1707–1788), introduced the term *race* into the scientific lexicon to categorize human beings. Buffon thought that human variation was the result of differences in the climate where groups lived. He elevated people with white skin to the top of the hierarchy he created, writing that they were the essence of humanity. Absurdly enough, he thought that white was the "natural" color of human beings and that African people were dark because of their greater exposure to the sun. He even thought that if Africans would only move to Europe, their skin would lighten over time (Ferber 1998).

The idea that human beings could be divided into races culminated with the work of Johann Friedrich Blumenbach (1752–1841), a German physician and naturalist. Like other naturalists of the time, Blumenbach believed you could classify humans into a taxonomy of types. He thought there were five separate "varieties" of human beings: Caucasian, Mongolian, Ethiopian, American, and Malay. Blumenbach was particularly smitten with the people of the Russian Caucasus, who were mostly blond and light-skinned. He believed them to be the most beautiful people in the world. He placed them at the "top" of his alleged racial hierarchy of human beings.

Most people now have never heard of Johann Blumenbach, but his racist ideas persist. Have you ever referred to White people as "Caucasian" or checked a box marked "Caucasian" to indicate your race? Now that you know the origin of this label, perhaps you will cringe the next time you hear it. Would you ever have imagined that this term came from one man over two hundred years ago, whose ideas about people from the Russian Caucasus seem so outlandish to us now? This shows how intractable some of the racist thinking of the past is in influencing our lives today.

Where would such menacing ideas come from? Remember that at the time, the Atlantic slave trade was flourishing. Dutch, Spanish, and British empires had colonized much of the world—primarily for purposes of trade and the acquisition of wealth and profit. Human trafficking was pivotal to this system. Within such an economic system, the world was ripe for the scourge of racism. It is no coincidence that ideas about innate human differences were developed as part of the Atlantic slave trade and the development of an institutionalized system of slavery in North and South America. Slavery was a system that *depended on* classifying some groups as innately inferior to White European Americans. Only if some people could be considered something less than fully human could a system of racial subordination emerge.

The racism that was developing in the eighteenth century emerged alongside Western movements for democracy, namely, the French and American revolutions. It may seem inconceivable now that proclamations of equality, at least for men, could exist side by side with a flourishing system of racism. As historian George Fredrickson (2002) argues, aspirations for equality went hand in hand with racism. How? As people were rejecting old notions of traditional order, they had to have some rationalization, if only for themselves, for the exploitation and mistreatment

The social construction of race is reproduced through various forms of everyday behavior. Race becomes defined by color in the various emojis people use on social media platforms.

of others. The idea of race filled that need. If differences between two groups who are unequal were defined as "natural," then there was no need to question the social order.

Antiquated as early thinking about race seems now, its legacy lives on. Many people continue to think of race as somehow reflecting meaningful differences between people, differences that get socially coded by "color." Even very modern technology reflects this thinking: Think of the emojis that people use on the Internet and their smartphones. Developed in Japan, the icon was originally a nonhuman-looking character depicted only in yellow, but it was soon developed to show people in five different colors, ranging from a pink tone to very dark brown (see photo). Not until very recently did developers change the technology so users could shade the human icon, choosing from 151 different options. What is interesting, however, is how color has become the standard for defining human diversity (Phillip 2014).

Who Counts? Racial Classification Systems

Even without there being separate human races, over time, people have put a lot of effort into classifying people into racial categories. The many different ways they have done so are intricately connected to the racial politics and interests of powerful groups in society at given points in the nation's history. This fact reveals how deeply social the concept of race is.

The first attempt to count different populations in the United States came in 1787 with the writing of the U.S. Constitution. Article I, Section 2 of the Constitution mandates that the population be counted every ten years in order to determine taxation and representation in the government. Which people were counted and how they were counted were critical in establishing the political structure of the nation. To this day, the decennial census determines state representation in the U.S. Congress.

As written in 1787, Article I of the U.S. Constitution decreed that apportionment of the states in the national government would be "determined by adding to the whole Number of free Persons, including those bound to Service for a Term of Years, and excluding Indians not taxed, three-fifths of all other Persons" (Anderson 1988:9, cited in Rodríguez 2000:66). With this mandate, Black slaves were constitutionally defined as three fifths of a person. Indentured servants, who were White, were to be counted as free persons. Most Indians were not counted. So-called taxed Indians, those living in European settlements and likely including Indian women married to White men, were few (Rodríguez 2000:66). From the start, race was inscribed into the U.S. Constitution as a category of citizenship (Snipp 2010)—or, in the case of African Americans and Indians, non-citizenship.

Although the first census in the United States in 1790 did not mention "race" per se, it classified people into four groups: free White males, free White females, slaves, and all other free persons, including indentured White servants, free Blacks, and taxed Indians. As the nation developed, census categories evolved to reflect changes in the population and White people's reactions to the growing immigrant population. The 1820 census was thus the first to categorize the "foreign born" population, reflecting concerns about the so-called stock of new immigrant groups (Snipp 2010). This designation still appears in the census today. The 1820 census was also the first to categorize people by color; you were either White, Black, or American Indian. Which category you fell into was the work of census enumerators who were instructed to note a person's "color"—presumably based solely on appearance.

In 1850 the national census added the category "mulatto," the first official acknowledgment of racial intermarriage between Blacks and Whites and between Blacks and American Indians. Thus, the child of a Black-Indian relationship would be counted in a different "race" box than either parent.

"Chinese" and "Asian Indian" were added to the census of 1860, the result of the large-scale immigration of Chinese and other Asian workers who provided so much of the labor for an expanding nation. In 1870, "Japanese" was added as a racial-ethnic category, following the group's widespread immigration, often as contract labor.

Near the turn of the twentieth century, White anxieties about racial purity fueled many of the changes made in census classifications. Even though "race-mixing" has been common throughout U.S. history—through both involuntary and voluntary relationships—dominant ideologies have extolled "racial purity." Concerns about racial purity peaked by the 1890 census, when yet other categories denoting race were added. If you were counted in the 1890 census, you would have been either White, Black, Chinese, Japanese, American Indian (taxed or nontaxed). If you were mixed race, you would have been tallied as mulatto, "quadroon," or "octoroon."

Reflecting the one drop rule, these categories used "blood" as the marker of race. A mixed person was one-half Black; a quadroon, one-quarter; an octoroon, one-eighth.

Racial categories in the census changed again in 1900. Then you would be classified in one of five race groups (White, Black, Indian, Japanese, or Chinese). Mulatto and "other" reappeared in 1910. How was your race determined? You didn't check a box, as you would now. Instead, census counters simply looked at you and were told that "a person of mixed White and Negro blood was to be returned as Negro, no matter how small the percentage of Negro blood; someone part Indian and part Negro was also to be listed as Negro unless the Indian blood predominated" (Bennett 2000:169–70, cited in Snipp 2003).

Change came again in 1930 with new categories labeled Mexican, Hindu, Korean, and Filipino. Such fluctuating categories seem odd to us now, but they followed a racial logic that made sense at the time because of the social definitions imposed on various groups (Lee 1993). These shifting census categories show that one way race has been constructed is through the apparatus of the government— what sociologist C. Matthew Snipp calls "administrative definitions of race" (2010:110).

From 1940 to 1960, the census took little note of race. After the 1960 census the federal government started collecting more information about race, largely the result of the Civil Rights movement and subsequent efforts to monitor racial discrimination. The proliferation of federal agencies that collected data on race fostered great inconsistency in how race was counted. Because of this confusion, in 1977 the federal Office of Management and Budget adopted a policy of requiring agencies to tabulate race using five groups: (1) American Indians and Alaska Natives, (2) Asians and Pacific Islanders, (3) non-Hispanic Blacks, (4) non-Hispanic Whites, and (5) Hispanics of any race.

Consistent with this directive, in 1980, the census included a designation for Hispanic origin for the first time. Advocacy groups, however, argued that some groups were being omitted from the census categories. Arab Americans, for example, fell into none of the census categories. Others, such as native Hawaiians, argued that they should not be lumped together with Asians and Pacific Islanders. How the census classified people into groups was a quite political matter.

As a result of political pressure, in 2000 the federal government once again modified its racial designations, developing designations that are still in place. There are five basic groupings in the census now: White, Black, American Indian and Alaska Native, Asian, and Native Hawaiian and other Pacific Islander. Because Hispanics can be found in any racial group, for the first time in 2000, the census added a separate check box for Hispanic origin, identified as an ethnic group and separate from so-called racial groups (Snipp 2010).

Doesn't it seem a little odd to you that Native Hawaiians would be considered a "race" but Hispanics would not? For that matter, why is it so important to designate races? Perhaps you will quickly conclude that we just shouldn't count people by race and ethnicity at all. But what would this do to our ability to monitor discrimination or to study such things as patterns of disease, school enrollment, voting rights, and the countless other matters that depend on some racial and ethnic designation?

→ **NOTE: Please answer BOTH Question 5 about Hispanic origin and Question 6 about race. For this census, Hispanic origins are not races.**

5. Is this person of Hispanic, Latino, or Spanish origin?

☐ **No,** not of Hispanic, Latino, or Spanish origin
☐ Yes, Mexican, Mexican Am., Chicano
☐ Yes, Puerto Rican
☐ Yes, Cuban
☐ Yes, another Hispanic, Latino, or Spanish origin — *Print origin, for example, Argentinean, Colombian, Dominican, Nicaraguan, Salvadoran, Spaniard, and so on.* ↙

6. What is this person's race? *Mark* ☒ *one or more boxes.*

☐ White
☐ Black, African Am., or Negro
☐ American Indian or Alaska Native — *Print name of enrolled or principal tribe.* ↙

☐ Asian Indian   ☐ Japanese   ☐ Native Hawaiian
☐ Chinese   ☐ Korean   ☐ Guamanian or Chamorro
☐ Filipino   ☐ Vietnamese   ☐ Samoan
☐ Other Asian — *Print race, for example, Hmong, Laotian, Thai, Pakistani, Cambodian, and so on.* ↙   ☐ Other Pacific Islander — *Print race, for example, Fijian, Tongan, and so on.* ↙

☐ Some other race — *Print race.* ↙

FIG. 1.1 The 2010 Census Hispanic Origin and Race Questions

Source: U.S. Bureau of the Census. 2010 Census Questionnaire.

Starting with the 2000 census, a person could also check more than one box to indicate racial heritage. Even though the census now allows people to identify as multiracial, the census still counts Hispanics as a separate ethnic identification (figure 1.1). Within the Hispanic category are various ethnic groups (Mexican Americans, Puerto Ricans, Colombians, and so forth), just as the Black category includes a wide range of ethnic identities (Haitians, African Americans, Nigerians, to name a few). Diversity in human identities often gets disguised by the generation of single labels, such as those created by the census.

Defining Race and Ethnicity: Intersecting Ideas

The distinction between race and ethnicity is complex and blurry—and is also quite specific to a given culture. What race means in the United States, for example, would not hold up in other parts of the world. In fact, people from outside the United States typically find the U.S. conception of race to be quite strange.

Sociologists have long defined race and ethnicity as different concepts. The usual definition of an **ethnic group** is an identifiable group of people who share a common culture, language, regional origin, and/or religion. Ethnic groups also have a definition of themselves as a collective or "we." Jewish Americans constitute an ethnic group, as do Irish Americans, Italian Americans, and Arab Americans. You can see right away, though, that groups considered to be racial groups in the United States also share a common culture, African Americans being a good example. African Americans are certainly considered a racial group in the United States, but they can also be thought of as an ethnic group—sharing a common history, common cultural characteristics, and sometimes a unique dialect. Hispanics are typically defined as an ethnic group, although some may not even speak Spanish. These examples point to the fact that although race and ethnicity are treated as separate concepts, the line between the two is not always firm.

Race is also constructed in relationship to ethnicity, meaning that race and ethnicity can reinforce each other. To explain, immigrants to America have historically faced a Black versus White type of divide. Outsiders themselves, immigrants navigate this terrain in complex ways. Some may have their ethnic identity imposed on them by others, such as Vietnamese immigrants coming to the United States following the Vietnam War. They become "Asian," even though they may never have defined themselves in this way (Kibria, Bowman, and O'Leary 2014).

The meaning of whiteness has also emerged in the context of the nation's history of immigration and race. Some immigrant groups eventually come to be defined as White even though they may have been defined in other terms before (Roediger 2002). Both race and ethnicity have been created in the United States in the context of each group's placement within the nation's system of inequality. People have been sorted into categories that correspond with their placement in the labor market. For example, some Latinos may now be perceived as White if they hold high-status professional jobs, while those in the most menial occupations are perceived as "colored," that is, brown.

Even with a soft distinction between race and ethnicity, ethnicity can be just as damaging as is race. It can turn into **ethnocentrism**, the belief that one's group is superior to all other groups (also see chapter 2). When taken to extremes, ethnocentrism can have murderous consequences. Tragically, there are countless examples of such ethnic hatred: the Jewish Holocaust, the Turkish massacre of Armenians in World War I, the genocide of American Indians, the mass execution of Sunni Muslims in Syria under the rule of President Bashar al-Assad, the suggestion that Muslims should be banned from entry to the United States, and many more.

Ethnicity can, however, also be somewhat mild compared to race, for example, when it is **symbolic ethnicity**, allegiance to an ethnic group that is felt without incorporating ethnicity into one's daily behavior (Gans 1979). Everyone can feel Irish on St. Patrick's Day or Creole during Mardi Gras, but this identification with ethnic celebration or pride comes without cost or consequence.

Both ethnicity and race must be understood in the context of how groups are treated in society. The distinction between them underscores yet again that both are social constructions (Kibria, Bowman, and O'Leary 2014). That is, groups may share a common culture, history, and heritage, *but how they come to be defined in society is a social process*. Moreover, as we will see, there are times when an ethnic group may become defined as a racial group, depending on the circumstances in society at the time.

In this book, **race** is defined as a group treated as distinct in society based on presumed group characteristics that have been interpreted as signifying inferiority and superiority. The designation of a group as a race is then used to produce a social order of domination, power, and exploitation (Higginbotham and Andersen 2016, adapted from Wilson 1973).

Several ideas are included in this definition:

- It is the treatment of groups, not their individual attributes, that defines race and makes it meaningful in society.
- Race in the United States has been constructed through a history of conquest and exploitation.
- Understandings and definitions of race, both formal and informal, are fluid and change over time.
- Race is contextual; that is, you must understand the circumstances in which definitions of race arise to fully understand the idea of race.
- Race is both an individual identity and a collective process (Omi and Winant 1986; Omi and Winant 2015).
- The meaning of race is unstable and can be transformed through political struggle (Omi and Winant 1986).

To further understand the complexity of race and ethnicity, let's go back to the opening scenario of this chapter. How would you describe your race and your ethnicity? People regularly note their race on various official forms—not just in the census but also on credit applications, college admissions forms, driver's licenses, opinion polls and surveys, and any number of other places. Each may reflect a different scheme for counting and defining race and ethnicity.

If you were checking your racial identity on the census form shown in figure 1.1, what would you mark? For some, this may be a simple exercise. For others, not. What if you have a White parent and a Black parent? Would you check Black or White? What if one parent is Asian and the other Hispanic? What race and ethnicity are you?

As you answer these questions, you may see that the one drop rule is still flourishing, even many years after its elimination from the law. Is your understanding of your race based on your appearance? Socialization in your family? Your ancestral past? Your attitudes and behaviors? If you are White, do you regularly think of yourself as even having a racial identity? Certainly, African American and Latino people think of you that way, but White Americans generally do not have to think about their race, as whiteness is a taken-for-granted racial identity. Are there places, other than standard forms, where a White person's race becomes more apparent? What does this suggest to you about race as a *contextual identity*?

In fact, it is difficult to establish a single definition of race that reflects its multi-dimensional and social meaning (Taylor 2008). What are the various ways that one can define race?

- There can be *biological definitions of race*, no matter how problematic they are. Most people think of race as a fixed attribute of a person—something that cannot be changed.
- There are also *administrative or state-based definitions of race* (Snipp 2010; Rodríguez 2000). A good example is the federal acknowledgment process that determines whether a person formally "counts" as an American Indian. Managed through the U.S. Department of the Interior Office of Indian Affairs, this elaborate process requires that you extensively document your membership in one of 554 recognized Indian tribes. Whether you ultimately count administratively as "Indian" may be inconsistent with how you actually define yourself.
- Race can be defined by *how you define yourself*. Racial identity, examined in more detail in chapter 4, is a powerful part of people's self-concept. People can take great pride in their racial identity, placing a high value on being Chicana or part of a long legacy of African American heritage. In fact, people actually "perform race" as part of their daily expression of self, such as by displaying certain symbols or behaviors that signify race to others. "Doing race" (Markus and Moya 2010) can signify your membership as part of a racial group, and you may even be judged by others as "not being black enough" or as not "authentically black" if you do not exhibit certain attitudes and behaviors. In the past, an African American who was very light-skinned might decide to "pass" for White to escape the oppression of slavery of Jim Crow segregation. Interestingly, passing also required some effort by those around you who were willing to keep your secret (Hobbs 2014). This shows again that the definition of race, including how one presents oneself, is a highly social process. Simply put, "how individuals publicly identify is powerfully shaped by the norms of the time and place in which they live" (Saperstein and Penner 2014:188).
- Your race may also be defined by *how others define you*. An interesting experiment reveals how others' stereotypes about race may actually influence how they see and define race. This has been shown in a clever set of research studies by sociologists Aliya Saperstein and Andrew Penner (Saperstein and Penner 2014; Penner and Saperstein 2008, 2013). Saperstein and Penner have studied how interviewers classify a person's race based on certain social statuses. They have conclusively found that a person is much more likely to be classified as Black if he or she is unemployed, on welfare, poor, or incarcerated—all stereotypes associated with being Black. People who are married or living in the suburbs are more likely to be classified as White. This research shows that one's social status can actually define race, at least in the eyes of others.
- Race may be *influenced by social class*. There is a high correlation between skin tone and social class status, most notably in Brazil and Mexico, where, as the saying goes, "Money whitens" (Schwartzman 2007). Lighter-skinned people in these complex systems of racial definition may be more likely to be perceived as White or possibly to perceive themselves as White. At the same time, shifts in racial politics, such as movements that emphasize racial pride, may lessen this tendency.

- Finally, *racial politics* shape the definition of race. The Black Power and Chicano movements, as examples, encouraged people to embrace pride in their racial group membership. Even the language used to describe race changed as a result. Terms such as *people of color* and even the change from *Negro* to (eventually) *African American* reflect the collective political identity that social movements for racial justice can inspire.

As you think about these multiple ways of defining race, you will see that race is not as simple as one might think. One thing becomes especially clear as we have worked through a definition of race: "The actual meaning of race lies not in people's physical characteristics, but in the historical treatment of different groups and the significance that society gives to what is believed to differentiate so-called racial groups" (Higginbotham and Andersen 2016:1). In other words, what is important about race is not biological difference, but how groups are treated.

A multidimensional definition of race emphasizes **racialization**, the social process by which a group comes to be defined as a race (Omi and Winant 1986). Some groups become "racialized"; others do not.

The classic example of racialization is Nazi Germany. During his dictatorship, Adolf Hitler racialized Jewish people. He simply made up the idea that so-called Aryan (white, blue-eyed, and blond) people constituted a superior race; he defined Jewish people as inherently inferior. The extreme **anti-Semitism** of Nazi Germany, that is, the hatred of Jewish people, was based on racializing both groups. Racialization was an explicit racial policy of the Nazi state and had murderous consequences. Over six million Jewish people were exterminated, as were millions of gays, lesbians, disabled people, gypsies, and others who were perceived as unfit or inferior. If you ever doubted that race is a social construction, the Nazi Holocaust is strong evidence of the horrid human acts that can stem from racialization.

Race Is a Process, Not a Thing: Racial Formation

By now you should see that race is not a "thing" or some fixed attribute of individual people. Again, race is a social construction, created through the actions and beliefs of people, most often those with a vested interest in devising and maintaining a system of racial inequality. This idea has been well formulated in the concept of **racial formation** developed by sociologists Michael Omi and Howard Winant (1986, 2015).

Omi and Winant define racial formation as the "process by which racial categories are created, inhabited, transformed, and/or destroyed" (Omi and Winant 1986:64). What they mean is that race is created through the actions of people, especially those with the power to shape race within social institutions. In this sense, race is not an objective thing, but a subjective construction. As Omi and Winant put it, "racial categories and the meaning of race are given concrete expression by the specific social relations and historical context in which they are embedded" (1986:60). We have seen that the meaning of race changes at different points in time although, for most of U.S. history, race has been defined in fairly rigid black/white terms.

The framework of racial formation emphasizes several important sociological points:

- Racial formation is a *process*. That is, race is not a fixed attribute of particular people or groups but, rather, develops in the context of how groups are treated and perceived by others.
- Race is an *emergent* concept—an idea that develops through the course of history.
- The formation of "race" happens at the *macro* level of society through powerful social institutions. Although race is reinforced at the *micro* level of society, that is, in everyday interactions, it is structured into social institutions.
- Race is *contested*. That is, groups can challenge dominant definitions of race such that race can change, for example, through the political efforts of social movements and social protest.

The process of racial formation helps you also understand how a given group comes to be defined as a race. Asian Americans, for example, have been racialized at various points throughout American history. *Asian American* is a term, like *Hispanic*, that lumps together people who come from very different societies and cultures—indeed, societies that have at times even been at war with each other. Moreover, each group's history in the United States differs. Asian Americans are not a monolithic group. Chinese Americans, Japanese Americans, Filipinos, Korean Americans, and more recently, Asian immigrants from Southeast Asia (Vietnam, Laos, and Cambodia, among other places) are much more ethnic groups than they are racial groups, but how they are regarded in American society shows the power of racial formation.

Omi and Winant's concept of racial formation shows that race is not fixed, but rather it changes over time. Think about how different racial-ethnic groups are defined. Would you say that Hispanics are a race? Hispanics have been typically identified as an ethnic group, based on shared cultural characteristics of language and national origin. Included in the category of Hispanics, however, are very different groups who may not share the same histories or current experiences. Some groups even disagree about what they want their group to be called. Hispanic or Latino groups are as diverse as the peoples who figure in these designations—Chicanos/as, Mexican Americans, Puerto Ricans, Cubans, and a variety of Central and South Americans.

With such different origins and histories, should Hispanics even be considered a single group? Hispanics have some but not all cultural characteristics in common. Chicanos, for example, are native to U.S. soil and are only defined as Chicano because of their lands having been confiscated by the U.S. government following the Mexican-American War (1846–1848). Puerto Ricans both on the U.S. mainland and on the island of Puerto Rico hold U.S. citizenship as the result of the 1917 Jones Act. Movement back and forth between the U.S. mainland and the island of Puerto Rico has marked Puerto Ricans' history in the United States.

In short, groups become racialized not because of some inherent characteristics, but because of their position in the U.S. racial hierarchy. Groups can become racialized because of their low status in the social and economic structure of U.S. society, as some would say is happening to many Hispanics (Bonilla-Silva 2004).

Furthermore, race can be deconstructed as well as constructed. That is, some groups previously designated as people of color may be perceived as "whitened" by gains in social and economic status. European immigrant groups in the nineteenth and early twentieth centuries were sometimes initially defined as something other than White, but their ultimate success in America led to a perception of them as White. Asian Americans may also come to be considered White by their social and economic success. Sociologist Min Zhou cautions, however, that perceiving Asian Americans as White—the "model minority" stereotype—overlooks the persistent discrimination and racism that Asian Americans experience. As Zhou says, "Speaking perfect English, adopting mainstream cultural values, and even intermarrying members of the dominant group may help reduce this 'otherness' for particular individuals, but it has little effect on the group as a whole" (2004:35).

When you understand race as a process, not an individual attribute, you can see that races are created, changed, and potentially destroyed through the actions of human beings. This framework also helps you understand that the construction of race is now changing, especially as different groups shape the American racial landscape. No longer is race just about a black-white divide. Even though the black-white divide is still significant, race in the United States—along with ethnicity—is becoming increasingly complicated, as we will see throughout this book.

Conclusion

When you understand that race is a social construction, how does your thinking about race change? This is a question that you can answer as this volume unfolds. Race and the racism that accompanies it are embedded in social practices that are a part of society.

To some people, race appears to have lost its significance in society. The election of the nation's first African American president led some to proclaim that we are now a post-racial society. Additionally, the increasingly complex and diverse character of U.S. society leads many to think that race will become less important over time. Images around you suggest that racial integration is here, but reality is different.

Race and ethnicity continue to shape all matters of human life, including opportunities, income, health, housing, education, criminal justice—as well as interpersonal relationships and group identity.

We have seen in this chapter that race is manufactured by human beings as they construct powerful institutions. Race is a social construction and thus is in some ways a false construct. Still, its effects remain very real, as we will see in the chapters to come. The culprit in the problems of race and racism is a combination of human beliefs, attitudes, and actions, not something inherent in different groups or individuals. What is so dangerous about the formation of race and ethnicity is that they are so deeply enmeshed in the formation of prejudice and racism—subjects to which we turn in the next chapter.

Key Terms

anti-Semitism, 16

ethnic group, 13

ethnocentrism, 13

genotype, 5

hypodescent, 3

one drop rule, 3

phenotype, 5

race, 14

racial formation, 16

racialization, 16

symbolic ethnicity, 13

xenophobia, 7

Critical Thinking Questions

1. Having read this chapter, what would you say to someone who declared, "We are all just human beings. Race doesn't matter anymore."
2. How does the one drop rule continue to influence people's understanding of race?
3. What are the key points in understanding that race is a social construction?

Student Exercises

1.1: As described in the opening scenario in this chapter, ask yourself how much money you would want to change your race. How much would you want to give up your smartphone or to quit watching television? If you can, ask students or friends of different races how they would answer these questions. What do their responses and your own tell you about the value people place on their racial (or ethnic) identity?

1.2: Go to the Public Broadcasting Service (PBS) website for the film *Race: The Power of Illusion*, and do the "Sorting People" exercise. The link is http://www.pbs.org/race/002_SortingPeople/002_00-home.htm.

Answer the following questions:

1. How many did you get right?
2. What did you look for to identify people?
3. When you first meet someone, do you immediately note the person's race? If so, what do you look for to do so?
4. What do you learn about the definition of race from this exercise?

Challenging Questions/Open to Debate

Should we "count" race?

Some think that people should not be asked to indicate their race on the many and various forms where this question is asked. Do you agree or disagree? Explain your answer in detail.

CHAPTER 2

What Do You Think?

Prejudice, Racism, and Colorblindness

Build bridges, instead of walls.
—Associate Supreme Court Justice Sonia Sotomayor (2013)

OBJECTIVES

- Analyze the attitudinal dimensions of prejudice
- Distinguish prejudice as an attitude from discrimination as behavior
- Interpret changes in public attitudes about race
- Compare and contrast the different forms of racism
- Understand the concept of colorblind racism

In the spring of 2015, a video of a busload of University of Oklahoma fraternity members chanting an extremely racist song went viral on the Internet. The chant, by brothers in the Sigma Alpha Epsilon (SAE) fraternity, referred to lynching Black people and used the derogatory *n* word, a word that is highly offensive to Black people particularly when used by Whites. The national SAE organization and the university immediately closed the campus's fraternity chapter, and two of the students were expelled.

In the days following the media storm about this incident, the young men's behavior was described by some as a "horrible cancer." Others defended the young men, describing this deplorable behavior as an aberration and saying that the young men were "good boys" and certainly "not racist."[1]

This wasn't the first time that college students got into trouble for such racist behavior, nor would it be the last. There have been investigations into ghetto theme parties, which are common on many campuses as are party themes that insult Mexican Americans, Arab Americans, Native Americans, and just about any other racial or ethnic group you can imagine. Examples are plentiful, such as a "South of the Border" party on a New Jersey campus attended by female White students dressed as pregnant Latina maids (Georgevich 2007) and parties on other campuses where watermelon is often served to White students in blackface wearing gangsta clothes. How you would feel if you were a Mexican American or African American student on a campus where people ridiculed you by performing such stereotypes? What some White students think is "just for fun" has deeply harmful consequences for others.

Racist theme parties happen even at some of the nation's most prestigious schools in and outside of the Deep South (Wise 2007; Chesler, Lewis, and Crowfoot 2005; Van Dyke and Tester 2014). Studies find that fraternities and sororities can be especially vicious because they are racially homogenous, that is, almost entirely White.[2] The parties also tend to happen behind closed doors.

In these exclusionary environments, researchers have found that White male college students rather than people of color tend to perceive themselves as the victims of racism. Interviews with White male students have uncovered that these students tend to see racism in individualistic terms; they minimize the experience of race and say that people of color are overly sensitive to it. White male students also believe that people of color exploit race to make excuses for their behavior. Moreover, what they learn in college does not change these views (Cabrera 2014).

Incidents like the racist chant and racial theme parties reveal a lot about contemporary prejudice and racism, the subjects of this chapter. Many people seem to be confused about what racism is, thinking of it mostly as bigotry, that is, overt expressions of group hatred. You will learn otherwise in this chapter. You will see,

---

[1] In the aftermath of this event, Brody and Susan Pettit said of their son, Levi, a participant in the chant, "He is a good boy, but what we saw in those videos is disgusting. While it may be difficult for those who only know Levi from the video to understand, we know his heart, and he is not a racist." CNN reported that on March 25, 2015, Levi described himself by saying, "I never thought of myself as a racist. I never considered it a possibility." Also see Stephen Crockett (2015).

[2] Black Greek fraternities, though generally all Black, do not engage in this kind of racist behavior. For analysis of the history and sociology of Black Greek organizations, see Matthew Hughey and Gregory Parks (2011).

first, that although racism can be (and often is) manifested in expressed group hatred, this is not its only form. The description of the fraternity event in Oklahoma as a "horrible cancer" makes it seem that prejudice and racism are found mostly in the minds of a few "sick" individuals. Many people think of prejudice as held primarily by a few easily identified bigots, not the majority of the public. Bigotry is also primarily associated with certain groups, namely the white working class and White southerners.

Second, overt bigotry and individual prejudice are forms of racism, but racism is more complex than individual attitudes. Prejudice is also not the same thing as racism. Even when prejudice is not expressed, racism is pervasive in the very structure of society. Consequently, understanding racism requires more than looking at individual attitudes and behaviors. Both prejudice and racism are important concepts, but understanding the difference between them requires careful analysis of each. We start with a discussion of prejudice.

A Few Bad Apples or Is Everyone a Racist? The Social Dynamics of Prejudice

The social scientific study of prejudice originated with the social psychologist Theodor Adorno. Fleeing persecution, Adorno left Nazi Germany in the 1930s, going first to Britain and then, in 1937, to the United States. He questioned how the human mind could work to lead people to commit such atrocities as the mass execution of Jewish people during the Holocaust. He found his answer in the study of prejudice.

Adorno thought prejudice originated in feelings of insecurity and threat. He identified what he called the **authoritarian personality** (Adorno et al. 1950). He analyzed people with such personalities as having little tolerance for difference, rigid in their judgments about others, and strict and highly obedient to authority. Adorno reached these conclusions by witnessing how many German people succumbed to the influence of Hitler. He concluded that people with authoritarian personalities are particularly prone to prejudice.

Social psychologist Gordon Allport took the study of prejudice in a slightly different direction. Unlike Adorno, who rooted prejudice in the workings of individual personalities, Allport emphasized the social context in which prejudice emerges. Allport's book, *The Nature of Prejudice* (1954), remains a classic analysis of the social dynamics of prejudice.

Allport developed the "lens model" to explain how prejudice targets particular individuals but does so within a broad social and historical context (see figure 2.1). Prejudice originates, according to this model, from a historical background of group conflict, but progresses through various "lenses," starting from the sociocultural context and then proceeding through particular situations, the personality of the observer, and the immediate context (that is, the "phenomenological").

The lens model shows that prejudice is anchored in a context that includes not only immediate situations, but also broad historical forces that shape how groups and people see each other. Without understanding that broader context, you cannot understand the full social psychology of prejudice.

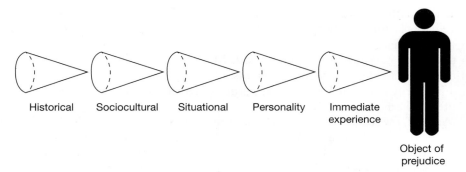

FIG. 2.1 Allport's Lens Model of Prejudice

Source: Adapted from Jones, James M., John F. Dovidio, and Deborah L. Vietze. 2014. *The Psychology of Diversity: Beyond Prejudice and Racism.* Malden, MA: Wiley Blackwell.

Defining Prejudice

The term *prejudice* stems from the ancient term *praejudicium*, meaning "prejudgment." Allport defined **prejudice** as "an avertive or hostile attitude toward a person who belongs to a group, simply because he belongs to that group, and is therefore presumed to have objectionable qualities ascribed to the group" (1954:7).

Prejudgment is central to the concept of prejudice. *Prejudice is an attitude* and people who display this attitude prejudge others based on their presumed characteristics. Prejudice is also presumably linked to discriminatory behavior, to be examined later. For now, keep in mind that prejudice is an attitude or way of thinking. **Discrimination** is behavior or a way of acting, displayed when someone treats a person or group differently because of a presumed characteristic.

There are several ideas about the nature of prejudice embedded in its definition:

- Prejudice is generally a *negative* or hostile attitude. People can express prejudice in a positive way, as in "Women are more nurturing than men," but most of the time and in its most harmful form, prejudice disparages people based on their presumed group membership, as in "All jocks are stupid."
- Prejudice rests on *generalizations*. That is, prejudice is directed at all members of a group just because they are perceived as belonging to that group.
- Prejudice is about *perception*, that is, how people see other people. Perception, not reality, forms prejudiced attitudes.
- Prejudice rests on group *stereotypes*, which flourish especially when people have little information about the targets of prejudice. As we will see, stereotypes are especially pernicious when there is little or minimal contact between different groups.
- Prejudice is *false* and *ill informed*. The perceptions that prejudice fosters are generally based on incorrect ideas or, at the very least, limited true information about people and groups. As Allport himself wrote, prejudice is "thinking ill of others without sufficient warrant" (1954:6).
- Prejudice is *learned*. Prejudice is not something that just "comes naturally." It is commonly learned in the family but can also be learned within peer groups or because of cultural stereotypes in society. Because prejudice is learned, social justice advocates also argue that it can be "unlearned," primarily through education.

- Prejudice is both *affective* (i.e., about emotion) and *cognitive* (about thinking). This means that prejudice is not only about misperception, but it also reflects intense feelings (Forman 2004).

Each of these characteristics of prejudice shows the social basis of prejudiced[3] thinking. Prejudice emerges in the context of group positions relative to one another, not just in some vague sense of feelings (Blumer 1958:3). For example, some White people do not understand why racial theme parties are so offensive. Why does it not seem as wrong if campus parties stereotype Italian mobsters or White businessmen? The answer lies in the power that some groups have over others. There is simply not an equal playing field when it comes to racial inequality. Ridiculing a racial group packs extra insults that would not be a problem were there equivalencies in how different racial and ethnic groups are perceived and treated in society. Prejudice can appear in many forms and against various groups, but it is particularly harmful when it is directed against those who are in positions of less power relative to a dominant group.

Forms of Prejudice

You can probably think of dozens, if not hundreds, of examples of prejudice and the various groups that experience the pain of prejudice. Gay men, lesbians, racial and ethnic minority groups, women, religious minorities, disabled people, and others are all subjected to the harms of prejudice. Anti-Semitism is one form of prejudice that defines Jewish people as inferior and has been used to discriminate against them.

Is prejudice an inevitable feature of social life? Perhaps *ethnocentrism*, that is, the belief that one's group is superior to all others, is unavoidable because people typically see others through the eyes of their own group experience. Ethnocentrism does not necessarily produce prejudice, such as in favoring one's family traditions over those of one's in-laws. But when it results in negative judgments about others, particularly when based on sex, religion, or any other aspect of identity in which group status is a factor, prejudice occurs.

No one is free of prejudice, but certain social facts predict the likelihood of someone being prejudiced. People with more education are far less likely than those with less education to express prejudiced attitudes, at least openly (Kuppens and Spears 2014). Those with fundamentalist religious beliefs are also more likely to be racially prejudiced (Brandt and Reyna 2014). Older people are more likely than younger people to express prejudice (Franssen, Dhont, and Van Hiel 2013). Prejudice emerges in a social context, so it is not surprising that it is more common in some groups than in others.

In his original formulation of prejudice, Allport identified different ways that prejudice is expressed, ranging on a continuum from its most mild forms to its most extreme. At the mild extreme of this continuum is *speaking poorly* of others, what Allport called "anti-locution." Speech can, of course, be harmful, but Allport identified anti-locution as a relatively mild form of expressed prejudice, such as telling

---

[3] Note that *prejudice* is a noun and should be used accordingly. People often misstate the word, using its adjectival form (*prejudiced*) when the noun is appropriate. To illustrate: A person may have a *prejudiced* attitude, but is exhibiting *prejudice*.

racist jokes or saying that all people of a particular group are stupid. As relatively mild as such speech is, however, it is insulting and harmful to members of the targeted group.

At the next point on Allport's continuum is the *avoidance of others*. Holding prejudice may lead people to be fearful of difference and thus avoid social contact with people identified as different. There are countless examples of this, such as when a White person subtly—but surely—steps back when interacting with an Arab American. On campus, not selecting the one Latino student in a class to join a study group is another example. The tendency to avoid interracial contact is exacerbated by the segregation that is present in society.

Acting on one's prejudices also leads to *discrimination*, the next place along Allport's continuum. Being slow to serve someone in a restaurant or excluding an Asian American neighbor from a neighborhood party are examples. As we will see below, prejudice does not always result in taking discriminatory action but, as this book will document, discrimination against racial-ethnic groups is pervasive in society.

At the extreme end of Allport's continuum of prejudice are *physical attack* and *extermination*. Physical attack can mean the destruction of property, such as cross burning or the desecration of Jewish cemeteries, or actual bodily harm. Both forms of physical attack constitute **hate crime**, defined in law as criminal action taken against a person or property with the added element of bias (also see chapter 11). Under laws about hate crime, bias can be based on race, religion, disability, ethnic origin, or sexual orientation. Sadly, there are many examples of physical attack against racial-ethnic minorities. In 2015, Dylann Roof, a twenty-two-year-old White

Many people associate segregation only with Black and White Americans, but the ugliness of racial segregation affects other groups, too, as in this sign from the 1940s.

LIVING WITH RACISM

From the moment my comrades in the military discovered I was an Indian, I was treated differently. My name disappeared. I was no longer Suina, Joseph, or Joe. Suddenly, I was Chief, Indian, or Tonto. Occasionally, I was referred to as Geronimo, Crazy Horse, or some other well-known warrior from the past. It was almost always with an affection that develops in a family, but clearly, I was seen in the light of stereotypes that my fellow Marines from around the country had about Native Americans.

Source: Suina, Joseph. 1994. "Personal Narrative." Pp. 16–17 in *Facing History and Facing Ourselves: Holocaust and Human Behavior*, by Margot Stern Strom. Brookline, MA: Facing History and Facing Ourselves National Foundation.

male was tried and convicted of hate crimes resulting in death, along with other federal charges, after he slaughtered nine Black parishioners at the Emanuel African Methodist Episcopal Church in Charleston, South Carolina, in 2015.

Extermination, which in modern times has come to be thought of as **genocide**, is the most extreme form of prejudice in Allport's formulation. Again, it can be exemplified by what happened to Jewish people and other minority groups during the Holocaust. More recently, the mass killing of Yazidis, a religious minority in Syria and Iraq, by ISIS extremists has been called genocide by the United Nations. The mass slaughter of civilians in Aleppo, Syria, by Syrian troops loyal to President Assad is another atrocious example (Schick 2016). Genocide is an international crime, defined by the United Nations in the aftermath of World War II as the "intent to destroy, in whole or part, a national, ethnical [*sic*], racial, or religious group" (United Nations 1948). Tragically, around the world and throughout history, there is no shortage of examples of extermination based on racial or ethnic prejudice. The killing of racial-ethnic minorities is a tragic fact of U.S. history, such as in the extermination of so many Native Americans by early European conquerors and their descendants.

The various forms of prejudice show the extent of this vicious problem (see, for example, LIVING WITH RACISM). Yet there are ways that prejudice can be reduced. Years of research have shown that contact between groups can reduce prejudice (Pettigrew et al. 2011). This is particularly the case when young children interact in noncompetitive environments (Irizarry 2013). Even something as pleasurable as having a romantic relationship with someone outside your own group tends to reduce prejudice (Orta 2013). One of the strongest preventive strategies for reducing prejudice is education. When people know more about each other, they are less likely to be afflicted with the misinformation about others on which prejudice relies.

Stereotypes and Stereotype Threat

Prejudice relies on stereotypes for its power in society. It seems that people almost inevitably categorize others. You meet someone for the first time and almost instantaneously you categorize the person, probably based at first on race and gender and possibly also by age and social class. These are some of the first salient features that people notice (Andersen and Taylor 2017).

A **stereotype** is an oversimplified set of beliefs about the members of a social group. Stereotypes assign characteristics to people who are presumed to be a part of a group. An example of a stereotype came to the nation's attention during billionaire Donald Trump's 2016 presidential campaign. Trump referred to Mexican immigrants as criminals and rapists, gross stereotypes that completely contradict the well-documented fact that Mexican immigrants are actually *less likely* to commit crimes (including rape) than are native-born citizens (see chapter 11). Even after having made this and numerous other bigoted comments, Trump still claimed, "I'm not a racist. I don't have a racist bone in my body" (*Washington Post*, July 8, 2015). Clearly, Trump *had* invoked a stereotype of Mexican immigrants. Evidence to the contrary was not powerful enough to debunk the stereotype.

Stereotypes are not always so blatant, harmful, or accusatory. Stereotypes can be positive or possibly even neutral, such as the stereotype that all Norwegians are blond. Negative stereotypes are the ones that are quite harmful, regardless of the group they target. In the United States, virtually every racial and ethnic minority group throughout history has been subject to demeaning and insulting stereotypes. The Irish have been stereotyped as hotheaded drunks, Italians as Mafia members, Mexican American women as hypersexual. African Americans are stereotyped as lazy, aggressive, and welfare-dependent. Name a group and you can probably immediately imagine some of the stereotypes that have been negatively associated with it. As we will examine in more detail in the next chapter, stereotypes permeate everyday life, especially in popular culture and the media. Although some people believe that stereotypes are harmless, they actually have consequences that are not always well understood. An Asian student who is only average in math skills may feel extra pressure to do well; the blonde who is very smart may be sensitive to how others view her, regardless of her academic ability; African Americans may take extra effort to be neat in public spaces. Each of these examples shows how even relatively mild stereotypes have consequences for people's self-confidence, academic performance, and general state of stress (Woodcock et al. 2012).

Recent studies show some of the invisible yet consequential results of group stereotyping. Research by psychologist Claude Steele shows that people are very attuned to stereotypes about their own group. Their sensitivity manifests itself in *identity contingencies*, what people have to deal with when they are aware of the social identities that others have bestowed upon them.

One of the identity contingencies Steele and his colleagues identified is **stereotype threat**. Stereotype threat happens when people feel the risk of confirming, through their own behavior, stereotypes that others have about them. Steele's research on stereotype threat, done in laboratory settings, shows that invoking a racial stereotype can actually cause a test taker to perform more poorly than if no stereotype is present (Steele 2010; Steele and Aronson 1995).

Here is how Steele discovered this. Research subjects were told in series of laboratory experiments that they were about to take a test that was "a genuine test of their verbal abilities and limitations," thus invoking for African American research subjects a stereotype that they are innately less intelligent. In another set of tests, research subjects were told they should try hard but that the test would not evaluate their ability. Members of a third group were told they should "take the challenge seriously even though the examiners were not going to evaluate their ability." Only in the first case was a stereotype present, that is, a stereotype threat.

Steele and his colleagues consistently found that only when the threat of the stereotype—that Black students are less intelligent—was present did Black and White test scores differ—and significantly so. In other words, Black test takers, aware that they as a group were perceived as less smart than White students, did actually perform less well when the stereotype was invoked. Without the presence of stereotype threat, as in the second two conditions, Black and White test takers performed equally well.

This result has been tested in other experiments, strongly supporting Steele's original results: Feeling stereotype threat actually *lessens* African American student performance. Furthermore, this finding has been shown to occur for other groups, such as when women are aware of the stereotype that they are supposedly not as good at math as men (Picho, Rodriquez, and Finnie 2013). Likewise, Mexican American students, whether immigrant or not, do less well when faced with the stereotype that Mexican immigrants have little command of English (Guyll et al. 2010).

Most research on stereotype threat has been done in controlled experiments in a laboratory setting. You can probably imagine other real-life scenarios where stereotype threat produces apprehension and thus inhibits a person's behavior. Imagine a Latina student whose professor makes a comment in class that stereotypes Latinos. Might a student's test performance then actually be affected? Flipping this example, if students communicate that Asian faculty members do not speak English clearly or that African American faculty members are not as authoritative as White male faculty (Gutiérrez y Muhs et al. 2012), might the mere presence of this stereotype shape how well a faculty member performs in class? Even seemingly innocuous comments and subtle expressions of stereotypes, made through no particular ill will, can affect the behavior of people who are keenly aware of stereotypes about their group.

Implicit Bias

Research shows that social behavior is affected by prejudice and stereotyping, even when they are not consciously intended. Such a subtle form of prejudice is known as **implicit bias**, which refers to the preference people may have for particular groups and the negative associations they hold, *even when they may not be aware of them*, against other particular groups (Jones, Dovidio, and Vietze 2014:40). It can be guided by unconscious erroneous beliefs about, for example, the inferiority of particular racial-ethnic groups (Jones, Dovidio, and Vietze 2014; Dovidio 2001). Implicit bias can take the form of **aversive racism**, manifested by a person avoiding contact with members of other racial-ethnic groups without specifically intending to do so. There is now a large body of research that documents the implicit biases that people hold against various groups: Blacks, Latinos, gay men, lesbians, disabled people, even older people (Lemm 2006; Greenwald, McGhee, and Schwartz 1998; Wilson and Scior 2014; Archambault et al. 2008).

Implicit bias equates to our culture leaving an invisible imprint on our minds. Most research on prejudice focuses on people's conscious beliefs, often measured in attitudinal surveys. Just beneath the surface, though, lie judgments and associations that are now being discovered by new techniques in neuroscience. Thoughts and feelings are triggered even when we do not realize it.

Implicit bias has been linked to critical behaviors. It may cause physicians to refrain from referring critically ill Black patients to specialists. It may even cause physicians to minimize the seriousness of disease found in people of color (Stepanikova 2012). Implicit bias has also been linked to use of force by police officers as they interact with Black male suspects (Eberhardt 2010).

Implicit bias has been demonstrated through the *Implicit Association Test* (Greenwald, McGhee, and Schwartz 1998). The test, to be taken by individuals on a computer, has people quickly associate positive and negative qualities with rapidly shown images of different people who are presumably identifiable by their race. Bias is shown by the frequency with which people associate negative characteristics with people of color. This cleverly designed experimental test can reveal the implicit (or unconscious) biases that people may hold. The purpose of the test is not only to discover the underlying bias, but also to make people more aware of their biases so they can work harder to overcome them—or at least make them less salient in interactions with others. Implicit bias, for example, has been used to train the police so that they will not so quickly associate Black men with criminality (Eberhardt 2010).

Does Prejudice Cause Racism? The Prejudice-Discrimination Link

Most people assume that prejudice causes discrimination. Does it? Obviously, the two are interconnected, but early work by sociologist Robert Merton (1949) shows that there is not necessarily a causal relationship between prejudice and discrimination. Important as prejudice is in shaping our behavior, it is not the only way to explain racial discrimination.

To show this, Merton developed a typology, a simple of way of showing different possible combinations of the presence or absence of prejudice and discrimination (see table 2.1). He showed four possible outcomes:

1. Both prejudice and discrimination are present (case 1 in table 2.1).
2. Prejudice is present, but discrimination is not (case 2).
3. Prejudice is not present, but discrimination occurs (case 3).
4. Neither prejudice nor discrimination occurs (case 4).

What situations result for each of these scenarios? In case 1, someone is both prejudiced and discriminatory. This is the classic bigot, someone whose views are overtly expressed and whose actions reflect prejudiced attitudes. This is the case that people most associate with prejudice; prejudice and discrimination are overt, intentional, and hostile.

TABLE 2.1 **Prejudice and Discrimination: How Are They Related?**

	Prejudice	
	+	−
Discrimination +	Case 1. + + bigot	Case 3. − + nonprejudiced, discriminator
−	Case 2. + − prejudiced, nondiscriminator	Case 4. − − "all-weather liberal"

It is in cases 2 and 3 that we see that prejudice and discrimination are not necessarily directly linked. In case 2, someone who is prejudiced does not discriminate—perhaps because laws prohibit discrimination. Imagine a bigoted employer whose company rewards bosses who employ a diverse workforce. The boss may dislike Asian and Latino workers but will hire them anyway—and may even reap a reward in pay for himself. Prejudice is present, but discrimination does not occur.

In case 3, one may not be prejudiced but will still discriminate. Think of parents who hold no racial prejudice in their everyday lives but send their children to all-White private schools to "get the best education." Such parents (understandably) want the best education for their children but, in making such a choice, they reproduce the discrimination that is at the core of educational segregation (see chapter 9).

Within case 4 resides the person Merton called the "all-weather liberal." The all-weather liberal may not hold overtly prejudiced views and may not overtly discriminate. This is someone we would now call a *colorblind racist*, explored further in the last section of this chapter. The colorblind racist may benefit from the racial inequality of others but be largely unaware of this advantage. He or she might also think there is little he or she can do to change race relations. The person holds no overt prejudices, does not consciously discriminate against others, yet does little to challenge the racism that is endemic in society.

Merton was ahead of his time when he wrote about this in the 1950s, even though he may not have fully understood or articulated how deeply structural racial inequality was in the United States. Merton shows that there is not an inevitably causal relationship between prejudice and discrimination. Other ways of thinking about racial inequality, beyond prejudice, are needed. The remainder of this chapter addresses that subject.

Polling for Prejudice: The Decline in Jim Crow Racism

Despite its strong and lingering presence in the United States, racial prejudice, at least as overtly expressed, has declined since the period of Jim Crow segregation. Most people consider it inappropriate to express prejudice openly (Picca and Feagin 2007). It is still quite present, but so few people now express overt prejudice that survey researchers no longer ask the same questions that they used earlier to measure racial prejudice. For example, in 1942, a full 68 percent of White Americans said they favored racially segregated schools, compared with only 7 percent who said so in 1985. Researchers no longer ask about school segregation. Similarly, so many Americans now endorse equal treatment at least in principle that surveys no longer ask if people support, in general, equal opportunity values. Instead, pollsters ask such things as people's perceptions of discrimination, whether race relations have improved, and how satisfied people are with the treatment of different groups.

To illustrate, most people, both Black and White, now think that civil rights have improved within their lifetime.[4] However, there are significant and large differences in Black and White opinions about this change. Whites are more likely to say race relations have greatly improved. Black Americans think race relations have improved somewhat but they are far more likely than Whites to think that new civil rights laws are needed to reduce discrimination (53 percent of Blacks versus only 17 percent of Whites; Gallup Editors 2014). Black and White Americans also disagree on how satisfied they are with how Blacks are treated in society; Hispanic opinion about the treatment of Black Americans is mixed, as you can see (figure 2.2).

Change in public opinion is also apparent in other ways. In 1944, a majority of White Americans (55 percent) said that they thought White people should get preferential access to jobs (Bobo 1999). So few would say this now that the question is

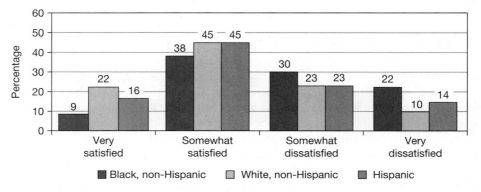

FIG. 2.2 How Satisfied Are You with How Blacks Are Treated in Society?

Source: Saad, Lydia. 2013. "In U.S., 52% of Blacks Unhappy with Societal Treatment." Gallup. Retrieved August 31, 2013 (http://www.gallup.com/poll/163553/blacks-unhappy-societal-treatment.aspx).

[4] Much of the survey research now carried out only reports Black-White differences, leaving us with less information about the perceptions of other racial and ethnic groups.

TABLE 2.2 Public Opinion on Preferential Treatment

Do you agree or disagree? "We should make every effort to improve the position of blacks and minorities, even if it means giving them preferential treatment."

Respondents	Agree (%)	Disagree (%)
White	22	76
Black	58	36
Hispanic	53	35

Source: Pew Research Center. 2009. "Public Backs Affirmative Action, but Not Minority Preferences." Washington, DC: Pew Research Organization. Retrieved January 20, 2017 (http://www.pewresearch.org/2009/06/02/public-backs-affirmative-action-but-not-minority-preferences/).

no longer asked, but the tables have turned: White Americans now overwhelmingly reject preferential treatment for minorities. Seventy-six percent of White Americans disagree that "we should make every effort to improve the position of blacks and minorities, even if it means giving them preferential treatment" (Pew Research Center 2009). On the other hand, 58 percent of Blacks and 53 percent of Hispanics agree with this statement (see table 2.2).

Changes in public opinion have thus evolved over time. Do not conclude from these changes, however, that racist attitudes are disappearing. Prejudice and stereotypes also still abound. When asked about social traits of Black Americans, 25 percent of White Americans (and 10 percent of Blacks) also describe Blacks as "lazy" and "preferring to live on welfare." Fully one-third of White Americans see Blacks as "complaining" and "aggressive or violent" (Bobo 2004:19). So pervasive are these views that political campaigns use subtle reference to these stereotypes to "prime" voters to vote in particular ways (Bobo 2006). You saw evidence to this effect during the 2016 presidential campaign. Largely White audiences at Trump rallies yelling, "Build that wall!" and Trump's repeated references to Black Americans "living in hell" evoked prejudicial images of Latinos as illegal immigrants and Black Americans as mostly violent and poor.

While people seem to have accepted the idea of racial equality, the character of racism has changed. There are huge gaps in the extent to which White and Black people perceive the persistence of racial discrimination. Whites are far less likely to think that Black Americans are treated less fairly by the police, in the workplace, and in other ways (see figure 2.3).

The lessening of old-style prejudice has given way to new beliefs that race no longer matters—or matters less. Recent times have seen an increase in overt racism, but generally racism is less often overtly expressed and, when it is, people deny that they are actually racist. Racism can be present, however, even when not overt or intentional. It may not even be recognizable to those who benefit from it.

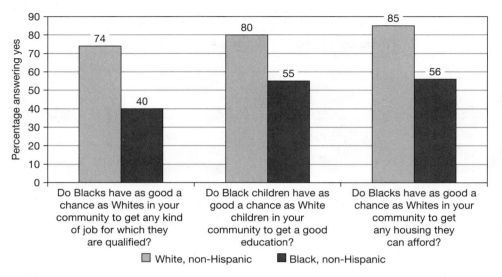

FIG. 2.3 Perceptions of Racial Discrimination

Source: Gallup Editors. 2014. "Gallup Review: Black and White Differences in Views on Race." Princeton, NJ: The Gallup Organization. Retrieved December 30, 2016 (http://www.gallup.com/poll/180107/gallup-review-black-white-differences-views-race.aspx).

"I'm Not a Racist, but . . . ": The New Forms of Racism

Recall the fraternity men in this chapter's opening who, even though described as not racist, chanted a highly racist song about lynching Black people. Most saw this behavior as morally reprehensible. White people are simply not supposed to say deplorable words. The reference to Black lynching on the fraternity's bus seemed to many like a throwback to a racist past. Some people also said that the young men were otherwise "good boys" who were not racist at all, even though they had participated in this extremely racist behavior.

Even when supporters of then candidate Donald Trump yelled, "Build that wall; build that wall!"—a reference to the wall Trump proposed building along the U.S.-Mexican border to keep immigrants from crossing illegally—most of these people would likely say they are not racist. How can this be?

The answer is that racism is more than individual attitudes. The public, especially the White public, tends to think that racism is solely a matter of individually expressed prejudice, when it actually is a more subtle and complex phenomenon. It is deeply rooted in society, not just in people's minds. Racism has structured the very institutions that constitute U.S. society. Racism is not always overt, nor is it always intentional or obvious. Racism is fundamentally different from prejudice.

Racism is a more collective or institutional phenomenon than prejudice, although it can be manifested in some people's thoughts and actions. Racism need not be motivated by irrational thoughts and it may not even be apparent to those who benefit from it. As we will see throughout this book, racism is deeply embedded in the institutions of society (Feagin 2010a; Forman 2004; Bobo 2004; Bonilla-Silva 2003; also see LEARNING OUR PAST).

LEARNING OUR PAST

You can learn a lot about how ideas about race shaped the nation's past by looking at what some of our revered national leaders have said.

I am not nor ever have been, in favor of bringing about in any way the social or political equality of the white and black races. . . . I will say in addition that there is a physical difference between the white and black race which, I suppose, will forever forbid the two races living together upon terms of social and political equality; and in as much as they cannot so live, that while they do remain together there must be a position of the superiors and the inferiors; and that I, as much as any other man, am in favor of the superior being assigned to the white man.

—Abraham Lincoln (1858)

The Number of purely white People in the World is proportionately very small. All Africa is black or tawny. Asia chiefly tawny. America (exclusive of the new Comers) wholly so. And, in Europe, the Spaniards, Italians, French, Russians, and Swedes, are generally of what we call a swarthy Complexion; as are the Germans also the Saxons only excepted, who with the English make the principle Body of White People in the Face of the Earth. I could wish their Numbers were increased. Perhaps I am partial to the Complexion of my Country, for such Kind of Partiality is natural to Mankind. . . . Why increase the Sons of Africa, by planting them in America, where we have so fair an opportunity, by excluding all Blacks and Tawneys, of increasing the lovely White and Red?

—Benjamin Franklin (1751)

Sources: Franklin, Benjamin. [1751] 1961. "Observations Concerning the Increase of Mankind, Peopling of Countries, etc." In *Papers of Benjamin*, Vol. 4, July 1, 1750 –June 30, 1753, edited by Leonard W. Labaree. New Haven, CT: Yale University Press; Lincoln, Abraham. [1858] 1907. "Joint Debate with Stephen A. Douglas." Reprint, *The Outlook* 85:262.

Defining Racism

When you stop thinking about racism solely in terms of prejudice and start thinking about it as an institutional phenomenon, your view of racism changes. Racism emerges not out of people's attitudes, but from what noted historian George Fredrickson calls "overtly racist regimes" (Fredrickson 2002:100).

Fredrickson's observation points to an important element of racism, namely, that it emerges only in societies where there is a racialized system of power. As Fredrickson points out, racism is thought of as if it were some constellation of hostile attitudes and biased treatment toward particular groups. But, racism, as we will learn, is more than just attitudes. When racism exists, it is structured into society's institutions, making it both more difficult to identify and more difficult to change. How is racism defined?

Racism is both a belief system and a social structure. As an ideology, it rests on the idea that a group is inferior because of some presumed cultural, biological, or other differences. As a social structure, **racism** means that groups defined as races are oppressed, controlled, and exploited socially, economically, politically, culturally, and psychologically by a dominant group (adapted from Wilson 1973:32). Racism is not merely an attitude or set of beliefs. Racism is expressed in the "practices, institutions, and structures that a sense of deep difference justifies or validates" (Fredrickson 2002:4). In other words, the ideology of racism attempts to justify, even if wrongly, structured inequality that is based on presumed racial difference.

Important elements of this definition of racism are the following:

- Racism is an ideology, not just an attitude. It is *located in social institutions*, not just individual minds or attitudes.
- Racism emerges because of relationships of *domination and subordination*. This means that racism is about exploitation, not just people's beliefs, although surely those beliefs buttress any system of racial inequality.
- Racism is a belief system and principle of oppression that "defends the advantages whites have because of the subordinated position of racial minorities" (Wellman 1977:xviii). In the United States, this makes *white privilege* central to any discussion of racism.
- Racism is *dynamic, and it changes with changes in society*. Racism may not look the same in the contemporary period as it has in the past. Understanding racism, therefore, has to change with the times.
- Racism is *not just fixed in people's minds*, although it may be manifested there (Wellman 1977). Restricting awareness of racism to individual bigotry misses many of the ways that racism occurs.
- Racism is not a holdover from the past. It continues to be *sanctioned through dominant cultural beliefs*. David Wellman puts it this way: Racism "defends the advantages that whites gain from the presence of Blacks in America" (1977:4).
- Racism develops in a *global context* (Chang 2010). The hierarchy of power from which racism has developed is a worldwide system of economic exploitation. The United States has a unique system of racism, but it is part of a system of global inequality.

Some say that racism is prejudice plus power, but that is too simple a formation. Racism is not just the summation of many attitudes with power thrown in. It is a principle of social domination that has been the very foundation for social institutions in the United States—ever since slavery (see chapter 5). Although first established to justify the exploitation of Black labor and then used to justify formalized racial segregation, racism persists in the form of patterns of racial inequality that remain with us today.

To understand racism thus means understanding it not only as an individual attitude but also as an **ideology** that supports a particular set of social, economic, political, and cultural relationships. Ideology refers to a constellation of beliefs (beliefs that can change over time) that purport to justify and defend the status quo. Racism is an ideology. Its form and shape change as racial domination changes, but this means that it is deeply linked to social institutions and institutional power.

Many sociologists use the term **institutional racism** to refer to patterns of racial advantage and disadvantage. Eliminating racism is not a matter of finding those individuals who harbor racist views and changing their minds, but a matter of transforming social practices and policies in such a way that the institutional basis of racial inequality is addressed. The difference in thinking about racial inequality from a prejudice versus a racism framework is summarized in table 2.3.

TABLE 2.3 **Prejudice versus Racism Framework**

	Prejudice Framework	**Racism Framework**
Level of manifestation:	Individual	Institutional
How it is manifested:	Overtly, explicitly	Sometimes overtly, but also covertly
Where it is located:	Within people's minds (conscious and unconscious)	Endemic in society, culturally sanctioned, embedded in social practices and policies
Cause of the problem:	Misinformation, individual attitudes	Legitimacy in social institutions, defense of white privilege and advantage
Solution to the problem:	Change attitudes, isolate bad people, eliminate bias, build tolerance	Transform social policies and social institutions

The Emergence of Laissez-Faire Racism

New forms of racism that have emerged in the aftermath of Jim Crow segregation are multifaceted and not as obvious as old styles of prejudice. One of the major changes has been that most White people in the United States simply no longer believe that race matters that much, even though race shapes just about every aspect of people's lives in the United States.

One of the most significant new forms of racism is what sociologist Lawrence Bobo has termed **laissez-faire racism.** *Laissez faire*, loosely translated from French, means quite simply "hands off." Laissez-faire racism thus refers to the tendency for White people to "downplay, ignore, and minimize" the effects of racism (Bobo 2004:17). Laissez-faire racism is minimally overt, but it is based on the idea that antiracist policies are no longer needed (thus, "hands off"). Further, there is a strong tendency under laissez-faire racism to blame whatever racial inequalities exist on the cultural values of minorities (Bobo 2004).

Laissez-faire racism has three key components, as identified by Bobo:

1. persistent negative stereotyping of people of color
2. blaming people of color, especially African Americans, for the racial gap in socioeconomic status
3. resisting race-specific policies to ameliorate racial differences in status

Laissez-faire racism is apparent when you hear someone say, "I don't dislike Black people" (or read Latinos, immigrants, or any number of other groups). Or, "I just think people should work hard if they want to make it in this society." Such commonly heard statements presume that anyone who works hard enough in America can succeed; those who do not, fail. This attitude, indeed, lies at the core of the American Dream: that with hard work and the right values, anyone can move "from rags to riches." We examine the reality, not the dream, of this core cultural belief later in this book, but, for now, understand that it is a foundation of laissez-faire racial beliefs.

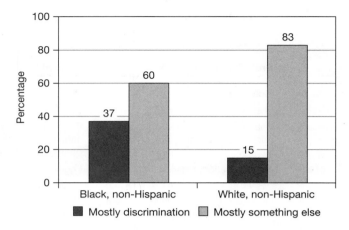

FIG. 2.4 What Is to Blame for Blacks' Inferior Jobs, Income, and Housing Situation?

Source: Gallup Editors. 2014. "Gallup Review: Black and White Differences in Views on Race." Princeton, NJ: The Gallup Organization. Retrieved December 30, 2016 (http://www.gallup.com/poll/180107/gallup-review-black-white-differences-views-race.aspx).

You can also see evidence of laissez-faire racism in figure 2.4. A national sample of adults was asked who is to blame for Blacks' inferior jobs, income, and housing situation. As you can see, a huge majority of Whites say that not discrimination but "something else" is to blame.

Laissez-faire racism is anchored in several beliefs, including:

- The United States is a **meritocracy** where people rise according to their efforts
- People should not notice race
- Any patterns of racial inequality that persist are the result of cultural deficiencies or poor values held by the disadvantaged
- Nothing systemic needs to be done to ameliorate the problem; this is also referred to as "racial apathy" (Forman 2004:45)

Throughout this book, we will be evaluating the evidence for these claims, but there is little doubt that laissez-faire racism has become a dominant viewpoint for how many people, especially White people, interpret the state of race relations today. With the more obvious forms of racial exclusion and discrimination fading, it is more difficult for those who are *not disadvantaged* by race to see its continuing significance. Further, in a society that values the idea of a colorblind society, it is easy for people to not want race to matter even when it does. The value placed on colorblindness has then produced yet another new form of racial thinking.

"Gee, I Never Think of You as . . . ": Colorblind Racism in "Post-Racial" America

The waning of Jim Crow segregation and the increased visibility of prominent people of color in positions of power and influence have led some to conclude that the United States is now a "postracial" society (Pettigrew 2009). A greater acceptance of mixed-race couples, dramatic changes in the racial and ethnic populations of the nation, the removal of overt barriers to the advancement of people of color, and other significant social changes have led many to think that we are now "beyond race" and that whatever racial inequities still exist must be the result of something else.

Such a belief is what is now referred to as **colorblind racism**, the idea that it is best to just ignore race and to look at people as if they are all alike. According to this view, if people would only overlook race and not see "difference," then the effects of racism would just vanish (Andersen and Taylor 2017). It can be manifested by someone saying, for example, with all good intent, "Well, I don't think it's about race anymore. It's all about class."

This belief, even when anchored in a desire for a more racially just society, is problematic for many reasons. To start with, if you are a woman, how would you feel if someone said to you, "Gee, I never think of you as a woman"? If you are a man, would you be insulted if someone said, "Gee, I never think of you as a man"? This is precisely what happens to people of color on a routine basis.

Denying that race matters—or saying that it is about something else—eliminates the significance of race for people's identities and experiences. Moreover, despite the importance of class and its entanglement with race, race still matters and it matters a lot in shaping people's life chances (West 1994). When White people speak from a position of racial privilege and deny what people of color know, they are rebuffing the very real, lived experience of those who do not experience racial privilege, thus making the experiences of people of color seem irrelevant or not significant.

Put in general terms, colorblind racism refers to the denial, usually by people in the dominant group, that racism exists, which minimizes its significance in the lives of people of color *and* in how society continues to be organized around racial inequality. Through the lens of colorblind racism, someone might say, "People are all alike," leading to another conclusion—sometimes implicit, sometimes explicit— that if racial inequality is still present, it must be the result of some character flaw that makes people fail.

Unlike the old style of prejudice, colorblind racism is seldom overt. In fact, people who express colorblind racism likely congratulate themselves on being liberal, well-meaning people, and they likely are. Colorblind racism appears not to be about race, but, in fact, it is actually all about race. Eduardo Bonilla-Silva calls it "racism without racists," because no one appears to be outwardly racist. Colorblind racism instead is "subtle, institutional, and apparently non-racial" (Bonilla-Silva 2003:3). Colorblind racism is also manifested in behavior, not just attitudes. Covert behaviors, such as ignoring when a person of color speaks in a meeting or classroom, reflect colorblind racism. Uprooting racism is then less about "hunting for racists" (Bonilla-Silva 2003) than about transforming commonplace behaviors as well as social policies.

Colorblind racism is also particularly slippery because White people can think they are being nonracist by participating in Black culture. Charles Gallagher (2003) has argued that White people seem to accept the culture of people of color when they engage in hip-hop, wear fashion that emerges from the culture of people of color, or speak the lingo of various minority cultures. But, he continues, doing so does not challenge racism. This commodification of culture disregards the racial hierarchies from which the cultures emerged and bestows further privilege on the

"We're a colourblind company here, Johnson.
To us you are black and invisible."

CartoonStock Ltd./Joseph Rank

White people who consume them. Thus, one can appear "cool" by consuming Black culture even while never challenging the racial status quo.

The problem with colorblind racism is that it also very easily slips into blaming people of color for their own predicament. If racial inequality is not about race, what do people think it is about? By ignoring race, colorblind racism shifts responsibility for racial inequality onto those most likely to suffer from it: those who have the least power and privilege in society.

Colorblind racism is powerful, in part, because it rests on an important value in U.S. society: that all people are created equal. Of course, as prophetically spoken by the Reverend Martin Luther King Jr., we want to live in a society where people are not judged by the color of their skin, but instead by the content of their character. That value, however, does not have to mean disregarding race. The United States is most decidedly not a colorblind society. Even a glance at contemporary events—racism on college campuses, disproportionate numbers of police shootings of Black men, persistent poverty among Latinos and African Americans, joblessness, the racial achievement gap in education, and more—indicates that race still matters. As long as people blame people of color for their own predicament, they will be unable to understand the complex reasons why racial inequality persists. Of course, there are highly visible and successful people of color and their achievements are noteworthy, but are they the products of a truly colorblind society? The evidence screams no, even while the majority of Whites believe that racial discrimination is no longer the cause for ongoing racial disparities.

Conclusion

The new forms of racism the United States is experiencing show how much there is for the public to learn about how and why race matters. The good news is that, as this chapter shows, racism is not a fixed thing. As it has evolved with changes in the racial social structure, people's minds have changed. One can hope that this means even more change can come through information and education that is not rooted in the old ways of racial prejudice and that can also untangle the new ways that racism is appearing. In the following chapter, we turn to some of the common and daily ways in which thinking about race is shaped—by popular culture and the media.

Key Terms

authoritarian personality, 23

aversive racism, 29

colorblind racism, 39

discrimination, 24

genocide, 27

hate crime, 26

ideology, 36

implicit bias, 29

institutional racism, 36

laissez-faire racism, 37

meritocracy, 38

prejudice, 24

racism, 35

stereotype, 28

stereotype threat, 28

Critical Thinking Questions

1. Based on your reading of this chapter, explain this statement: "Prejudiced people are not the only racists in America" (Wellman 1977:1).

2. Look at the detail in the graph below (figure 2.5) and think about the historic events at these different points in time. What might have influenced the attitudes of African American and White people over time? What explains the differences you see between the two groups?

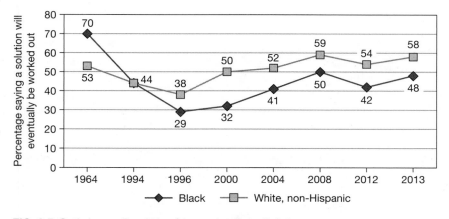

FIG. 2.5 Optimism or Pessimism? Improving Race Relations

Source: Gallup Editors. 2014. "Gallup Review: Black and White Differences in Views on Race." Gallup. Princeton, NJ: The Gallup Organization. Retrieved December 30, 2016 (http://www.gallup.com/poll/180107/gallup-review-black-white-differences-views-race.aspx).

Student Exercises

2.1: Do a small research study where you ask different people the same question that was asked in the national poll shown in the graph above. The question was: "Do you think that relations between blacks and whites will always be a problem for the United States, or that a solution will eventually be worked out?" Be sure to ask the question in these exact words in order to compare to the results above. Try to vary your sample of people to whom you ask the question by at least one characteristic: race, gender, age, or education, among others. What results do you get and how do you explain any differences you find . . . or do not find?

2.2: Go to the website for the Implicit Association Test (https://implicit.harvard. edu/implicit/takeatest.html), and take the demonstration. What results did you get, and what does this teach you about any implicit biases toward a particular group that you might have? Do you think this test is an accurate assessment of your attitudes? If so, why? If not, why not?

Challenging Questions/Open to Debate: Hate Speech

Hate speech is "speech that offends, threatens, or insults groups, based on race, color, religion, national origin, sexual orientation, disability, or other traits" (http://www.americanbar.org). Imagine a scenario where an overtly racist speaker is scheduled to speak on a college campus.

What would you do if you were the college president?
Should the speaker be allowed to speak, given the constitutional right to free speech, or should the speech not be allowed, given penalties under law for hate crimes?

CHAPTER 3

Representing Race

Popular Culture and the Media

The esteem with which we regard the multiple cultures offered in our country enhances our possibilities for healthy survival and continued social development.
—Maya Angelou

OBJECTIVES

- Describe the roles of popular culture and the media in shaping beliefs about race and ethnicity
- Relate the history and origin of racial representations
- Analyze the demographics of media audiences and the racial-ethnic content of media images
- Explain the impact of racial representations on different groups
- Compare and contrast theoretical explanations of media representations of race
- Identify ways that people resist and change representations of race and ethnicity

You might not expect that when you run your errands and go to the grocery store, you would be confronted with an array of racial and ethnic stereotypes. Try this, though: The next time you go to a market to shop, walk through every aisle and take note of the images of people that you see on various products. Here is a sample of what you might see.

Pancake mix has a smiling image of a modern Aunt Jemima, lighter skinned than in the past but an image that still is based on a racial stereotype. Are you looking for drink mix? Margarita mix has a stereotyped Latina on its label—long, flowing hair, big red lips, and an alluring smile. A beguiling Native American woman is there to provide your butter. Native American Indian chiefs in full headdress and feathers are on cornmeal labels. If you want some salsa, there is Paul Newman dressed as a stereotyped Mexican bandit, adorned with a mustache and a sombrero. If food labels are any indication, Asian Americans don't even exist. White men don't get off easily either: Check out the paper towels with big, brawny, muscular men looking like they have spent their lives working out in the gym.

A few products present different racial-ethnic group images for different versions of the same product: Black women's faces appear on some packaging; White women's faces appear on the very same product but with different packaging. Deodorants depict a variety of faces on the same product. Does this mean that your hair and underarms are the only places where a token acknowledgment of diversity is allowed?

If you are looking for racial integration, the only place you will likely find it is in the cereal and diaper aisles. Is the message that it is safe for children of different racial-ethnic groups to be together, but not for adults?

You may never have paid particular attention to these everyday images, but they are pervasive in society. Racial and ethnic images are packaged and sold through a variety of products, media forms, and other avenues where social stereotypes are produced and consumed (see LIVING WITH RACISM). You might think they have no impact on you or anyone else, but research shows otherwise, as we will see in this chapter.

The images that represent race and ethnicity in popular culture and the media are massively important in shaping our views of each other and ourselves. What are these images? How did they originate, and how have they changed? Are they harmless? What purpose do they serve, and how do people understand and, at times, challenge them? These are the questions that guide this chapter.

LIVING WITH RACISM

Even in my local supermarket, I'm reminded that "post-racial" America isn't past its attachment to stereotypes: I went to the customer service desk at King Soopers (a Kroger chain in Colorado, store #36) and asked if they still carry the Cento brand of white clam sauce.

The clerk looked at me and immediately said, "Well, if we do it should be in the Oriental aisle." I glared at her and said, "Uh, well, I'm making linguini with clam sauce."

Source: Asakawa, Gil. 2011. "Being stereotyped out of ignorance isn't as bad as flat-out racism, but . . ." *Nikkei View: The Asian American Blog.* Retrieved May 1, 2015 (http://nikkeiview.com/blog//?s=ignorance).

The Power of Culture: Cultural Racism, Stereotypes, and Controlling Images

The **culture** of any society provides a meaning system that enables its members to understand their world. As cultural analyst Stuart Hall (1997) puts it, culture provides shared meanings that orient people to their environment. Cultural representations are thus crucial in shaping people's understanding of themselves and others, including how race and ethnicity are constructed through culture.

As we have already seen, race is not a fixed thing. It is constantly being changed, transformed, and even contested—a process that plays out through social institutions, but is heavily shaped by cultural representations (Grzanka 2014; hooks 1992). Representations of race and ethnicity provide the meanings that people associate with different groups, even when people may be completely unaware of how such images affect them. Sociologists Danielle Dirks and Jennifer Mueller put it this way: "The power of popular culture lies in its ability to distort, shape, and produce reality, distorting the ways in which we think, feel, and operate in the social world" (2010:116).

In today's world, culture is largely shaped through the enormous power of the mass media and popular culture. The **mass media** refers to all those channels of communication that transmit information to a wide segment of the population (Andersen and Taylor 2017). The mass media now take many forms, including print media (books, newspapers, magazines), television, video, film, and, to name just one component of the vast scope of the Internet, social media (Facebook, Twitter, Snapchat, and perhaps new forms that were not yet invented as this book was being written). One important part of contemporary mass media is **popular culture**—the beliefs, ideas, images, and objects that are part of everyday life. Popular culture may differ within different segments of the population, but it is widely influential in shaping our national values and beliefs. Furthermore, because of their immersion in popular culture, young people, especially children, are particularly susceptible to its influence.

Popular culture is by its very nature ephemeral, that is, it is ever-changing, making it difficult to describe in a lasting way. Especially if you have no other way to "know" them, images in popular culture can have a profound and lasting impact on how you think about racial-ethnic groups other than your own. The cartoon, television, and film characters you love, the music you listen to, the video games you play, the books you read, even the news you watch: All of these forms of culture shape your perception of others and yourself. You cannot help but be influenced by these appearances. Whole generations of White people grew up with images of "little Black Sambo." How could those images not have influenced their perceptions of Black people? What images are shaping people's thinking now?

It is difficult to underestimate the power that the media have to shape ideas and beliefs. Can you imagine life without the media? Probably not. Try ignoring them in all their forms (print and electronic) for just one day and you will see how pervasive the media are in your life. How could such an enormous group not affect our collective consciousness? How could the media not be influencing people's understanding of race and ethnicity?

Culture is, of course, not monolithic. Diversity within culture means that groups do not necessarily share the exact same values or beliefs. The **dominant culture** is the culture associated with the most powerful group in society. It is the culture that is most pervasive throughout society and that tends to bind people together as "one." The dominant culture has the greatest hold on cultural values and ideas and is transmitted through images, texts, and other media throughout society. The dominant culture is what analysts call *hegemonic*. **Cultural hegemony** (pronounced "heh-JEM-o-nee"), then, refers to the pervasive and excessive influence of one culture throughout society (Andersen and Taylor 2017).

As we will see, despite positive changes in how media represent race and ethnicity, the dominant culture still views people of color through a narrow lens that diminishes, distorts, and misrepresents reality. People of color are, of course, not the only groups so distorted. Media images misrepresent many groups, including women, people with disabilities, lesbian, gay, bisexual, and transgender people, and old people. Although all groups can be distorted through the media, people of color get distorted in particular ways, ways that make them seem inferior or "other."

Here are just a few examples: Latinos, if visible at all, are typically cast in stereotypical roles as cheap labor, criminals, hypersexual characters, or law enforcers (Negrón-Muntaner 2015). Native Americans appear as sports mascots—caricatures that make American Indians seem warlike while also cartoonish and childlike, such as the image of the Cleveland Indians mascot. In other venues, such as television, American Indians are rarely even present—a negligible percent of television characters (Bunche Center 2015). African American women athletes, such as the fabulously successful Williams sisters in tennis, are routinely described in terms that emphasize their sexuality, such as the sportswriter who described Venus Williams as "a swirling, whirling street babe" (Philip 2007). Asian Americans are constructed in a variety of ways—sometimes in disparaging ways—and at other times are just ignored. When depicted, they are quite typically stereotyped as the "model minority," as if all Asian Americans are hardworking, compliant, and self-sufficient, values that also become defined as "Asian," not just American. Moreover, the image of the Asian model minority juxtaposes Asian Americans with all others, as if they are expected to discipline other racial-ethnic groups (Wang 2010).

In these and countless other examples, not only studied through research but also visible to a watchful eye, popular culture and the media create **racial frames**—that is, scripts that are fictitious but that frame how we see ourselves and others through a particular lens of race. As explained by sociologists Adia Harvey Wingfield and Joe Feagin, racial framing refers to "the racial perceptions, stereotypes, images, ideologies, narratives, and emotive reactions used to make sense of a given situation, experience, or issue involving racial matters" (Wingfield and Feagin 2012:144; Feagin 2010b). For the most part, the dominant racial frame, whether inadvertent or not, projects the idea of **white supremacy**—that is, that White people are superior; everyone else, inferior.

The Fog of Cultural Racism

Cultural racism refers to the images and other messages that "affirm the assumed superiority of Whites and the assumed inferiority of people of color" (Tatum 1997:6). These images and messages are so pervasive in society that, as college president and educational expert Beverly Tatum says, they are like "smog in the air" (1997:6). You may not even be aware of them—unless of course you are highly offended by them. Even when they are not obvious, they construct an understanding of race and ethnicity that lingers in the imagination.

Here is an example: First introduced in the 1940s, Chiquita Banana was an advertising symbol that promoted the nutritious value of bananas. Chiquita Banana, represented as a stereotypical Central American woman, originally appeared as just coming off a boat from "near the equator." The actual figure was a banana, but designed as a hip-swirling woman who appealed to men with her flirtatious winking and suggestive dancing. At the time the image was introduced, the men, women, and children who worked on U.S.-owned banana plantations in Central America were being subjected to grueling work conditions and serious illness from pesticide poisoning (Gallagher and McWhirter 1998). Wildly popular, the mocking image of Chiquita Banana became the basis for numerous live performances, including by the celebrity Carmen Miranda. To this day, Chiquita Banana advertises bananas. The contemporary image is a Latina dressed in stereotypical Latin clothing and carrying fruit on her head. You can also see and purchase this stereotyped outfit in such places as Pinterest and Halloween costume outlets.

The example of Chiquita Banana shows that images and ideas in the media are manufactured. By their very nature media are illusions that serve particular purposes, whether they are selling products, marketing entertainment, or informing the public about national and world affairs. In a racially stratified society like the United States, cultural representations buttress a system of white supremacy—that is, trivializing, ignoring, and/or disparaging people of color. By stereotyping people of color, popular culture and the media make the dominance of White people seem "natural." As we will see, even when you think "it is just for fun," media images have a tremendous influence on our self-concepts, our understandings of each other, and our knowledge and information about race in society.

Surrounded by Stereotypes

In the previous chapter, a *stereotype* was defined as an oversimplified set of beliefs used to categorize members of a social group. Stereotypes are simplistic constructions, have little nuance, and overlook the complexity of real people, reducing them instead to one-dimensional characters.

The media are a particularly effective vehicle for communicating stereotypes because of this oversimplification. The mass media gain their success by appealing to the largest possible audience, taking little risk, and relying on stock characterizations and commonly held values. The mass media also build their power through repetition, recurring themes, and familiar images (Alsultany 2012), thus facilitating the presentation and perpetuation of stereotypes.

When people have little actual contact with each other, such as in a racially segregated society, stereotypes wield even greater power. With no other basis for knowing each other, stereotypes fill the open space created by segregation. Thus, media images have even greater power to define groups to each other.

Stereotypes are common throughout the media. Select any group and you can probably quickly imagine media stereotypes about that group. Arab Americans, for example, are commonly presented as either terrorists, belly dancers, oppressed women, or sheiks (Shaheen 2014; Alsultany 2012). This leaves little room for non-Arabs to imagine Arab Americans as accomplished scholars, loving family members, working professionals, or in other positive roles. Some groups are stereotyped in the media by not being visible at all, such as Asian Americans and American Indians who are rarely seen in television dramas or, when present, appear as "sidekicks" or shadowy figures in the background.

Racial-ethnic stereotypes also overlap with gender stereotypes. Women of color are routinely stereotyped in suggestive and sexualized ways, often found in a jungle-like setting. If you doubt this, notice how common it is in women's magazines or fashion layouts to see women of color in animal prints, posed in a background dense with foliage. In fact, people of color are often portrayed as somehow closer to nature, a stereotype suggesting that people of color are somehow less than human, more like animals. At certain times in history, such stereotypes have been horribly overt. Now they are more covert but present nonetheless. As you look at the media and popular culture more critically, you may be surprised at how pervasive such stereotyped images are.

Objectifying "Others": The Power of Controlling Images

The concept of a stereotype is important, but even more powerful is the idea of controlling images. A **controlling image** is a reference to stereotypes but with the added recognition that such images actually restrict and manipulate people (Collins 1990). Different from stereotypes, the concept of controlling images emphasizes that these are not free-floating ideas. As the founder of this concept, Patricia Hill Collins has stated that controlling images are "major instruments of power" (1990:68). Controlling images are part of a system of domination—that is, part of the ideological justification for race, class, and gender oppression (Collins 1990).

Examining controlling images further, Collins teaches us that there have been four major controlling images specifically associated with African American women: (1) the mammy, (2) the matriarch, (3) the welfare mother, and (4) Jezebel or the whore (Collins 1990). The "mammy" controlling image depicts Black women as servile and happy to be so. This controlling image sees Black women as content to care for others' children, even if they have to leave their own to do so. Black women are also depicted through this controlling image as "loving the oppressor."

Handed down from slavery, this controlling image is based on the historic oppression of Black women (White 1999). Essential to the containment of women of color in domestic labor, the controlling image of "mammy" is now also found in images of Latinas as domestic workers (Hondagneu-Sotelo 2007). The employer who says that she "loves her Latina domestic worker like a family member" is articulating this controlling image.

The second controlling image of Black women is that of Black women being matriarchs, at least in their own homes. This image depicts Black women as bossy, overly aggressive, and quick to emasculate Black men, thus twisting the historic strength of Black women who have supported their families under the most adverse conditions (Collins 1990). The result is a pejorative and unidimensional caricature that demeans Black women's struggles. The next time you watch a movie that includes a Black woman (that being rare in itself!), note how frequent is the image of the "angry Black woman."

The controlling image of Black women as matriarchs is connected to a third: the image of Black women as welfare mothers. This image asserts that Black women (and by implication other women of color) keep having children to increase the size of their welfare check. This is a tenacious, though false, idea held by many. There are several reasons why this image is false. To begin with, only 2.5 percent of Black Americans and under two percent of Hispanic women receive support from TANF[1]—the federal "welfare" program for needy families (Irving and Loveless 2015). Furthermore, *family-cap policies* deny additional assistance after a child is born if the mother was already receiving assistance before the pregnancy. Family-cap policies, enacted in nineteen states, are an example of what has been called "putting prejudice into practice" in that they punish, not assist, poor women who have children, based on this controlling image of poor women of color as welfare cheats (Bouie 2014). Finally, the median TANF payment of $426 per month is too low to reasonably support families. In no state do such payments raise a family above the poverty line. The value of TANF payments has also actually declined by more than 20 percent since the mid-1990s (Stanley, Floyd, and Hill 2016).

Finally, the fourth controlling image of Black women that Collins describes is that of "Jezebel" or the whore. This controlling image depicts Black women as sexually loose, aggressive, and available. It obscures the painful history of the sexual abuse of Black women by White slave owners. For the Latina experience, this controlling image translates into that of "the Madonna," on the one hand, or the whore, on the other (Vargas 2010). Likewise, Asian American women become constructed as either sexually exotic (the "lotus blossom") or aggressive and domineering (the "dragon lady" or, more recently, "tiger mom"). Muslim women also become objectified as exotically sexual.

Controlling images of all women of color typically engage both race and gender imagery. Each of these controlling images denies women of color full *human agency*—that is, the right to define their own human identity (Vargas 2010). Controlling images rest on a process of **objectification**—the process of making a human being an object or a "thing." Objectification dehumanizes people. When

---

[1] In 1996, the original federal welfare program, Aid to Families with Dependent Children, was replaced with a new program, Temporary Assistance to Needy Families (TANF), discussed further in chapter 7.

you objectify someone as somehow less than human you create a rationale for controlling and manipulating people—a distressingly frequent phenomenon in U.S. and world history. Making someone an "other," as has been the common history of people of color, seems to be a prerequisite for exploiting other human beings.

The Echo of the Past

Many of the images you see today have their origins in an earlier history. Not that long ago, you might have seen statues of black jockeys as lawn ornaments on the properties of wealthy White people. During the late nineteenth century when Chinese people were immigrating to the United States as laborers, the term "yellow peril" was used to define the Chinese as a threat to Whites. The term was later extended to Japanese immigrants as well. Up until 1971, when protests by the National Mexican-American Anti-Defamation Committee forced its elimination, the Frito Bandito was a racist image on packages of corn chips. Frito Bandito spoke in an exaggerated quasi-Spanish accent, wore a huge sombrero, had a gold tooth and bulging stomach, and robbed people of their chips. The character was depicted as a devious villain. Imagine the young person who, knowing no other Hispanic people, might grow up thinking of Latinos through this iconic and insulting invention.

These and many other examples show that racist images in popular culture have a dirty history in the presentation of Black, Latino, Asian, and Native American people. They also continue to appear, such as in the false belief that immigrants are somehow taking over our country. You may recall the oft-repeated phrase in Donald Trump's presidential campaign that "we need to take our country back"—a phrase that reflects this latent anti-immigrant controlling image.

Many of these images and icons of the past continue to influence dominant understandings of race and ethnicity. Historically, racist images have been gross and explicitly demeaning. Black Sambo, Aunt Jemima, Uncle Ben, Speedy Gonzales: These and other racial-ethnic stereotypes have been widely distributed and consumed through popular culture (see LEARNING OUR PAST). Anti-Black images in history have also been used as a "yardstick" against which other groups have been either devalued or elevated (Dirks and Mueller 2010:116).

Over the years, for example, Disney films have been full of negative and stereotyped images of marginalized racial groups, affecting whole generations of children who grow up enamored of these films and other Disney products. The 1941 classic Disney film *Dumbo* shows a group of black crows whose dialect reflects stereotyped American Black speech patterns. The crows are shown happily singing, "Can't wait to spend our pay away" (Markus and Conner 2013). The same film shows a group of Black workers, supervised by a White man, where the workers sing: "We work all day, we work all night, we have no life to read and write, we're happy . . . we don't know when we get our pay, and when we do, we throw our money away" (Towbin et al. 2004). In the film *The Jungle Book*, at the head of a society of apes obviously meant to demean Black people is King Louie, an orangutan, who pleads for help to "be more human."

Disney is not the only company that reproduced such racist images. Looney Tunes cartoon mouse Speedy Gonzales was shelved in the late 1990s after protests

LEARNING OUR PAST

The Real Aunt Jemima

Racial stereotypes, though changeable over time, reemerge on a regular basis in everyday life.

Who was Aunt Jemima? Is she only a stereotyped icon on boxes of pancakes? Yes and no. Certainly the stereotype of Aunt Jemima has persisted over the years. The image, in fact, has changed since its original inception, moving from a more dark-skinned, mammy-like image to a light-skinned Black woman with pearls and curls. There is a history about a real Black woman that is embedded in this iconic image, even though that history is largely unknown.

The real "Aunt Jemima" was a Black woman named Nancy Green, born in 1834 as a slave in Montgomery County, Kentucky. Nancy Green was a gifted storyteller and skilled cook who became one of America's first Black corporate models. In the late nineteenth century, the owners of the Pearl Milling Company wanted to sell a ready-mix, self-rising pancake flour, but needed an image for their product. Inspired by a blackface performer in a vaudeville show who had performed a tune called "Aunt Jemima," company owner R. T. Davis employed Nancy Green in 1890 to be a living trademark. Nancy Green was fifty-six years old.

Davis's company, the Davis Milling Company, promoted the product at the World's Columbian Exposition in Chicago in 1893 with Green serving thousands of pancakes and demonstrating the product. Because of her storytelling and cooking skills, Green was a tremendous hit. The exhibition booth was so popular that special police were hired to keep the crowds moving. Nancy Green signed a lifetime contract and traveled extensively around the country promoting the pancake mix, no doubt earning huge profits for the company. She was killed in a tragic car accident in 1923.

In 2014 two of Nancy Green's descendants (her great-grandsons) filed suit in Chicago for $2 billion claiming that Green was a key formulator of the recipe for pancake mix. That suit is still pending.

What other legacies do you imagine might lie behind some of the common icons that you still see today?

Sources: Hine, Darlene Clark, ed. 1993. *Black Women in America: An Historical Encyclopedia,* Volumes 1 and 2. Brooklyn, NY: Carlson Publishing Inc.; Roberts, Diana. 1994. *The Myth of Aunt Jemima: White Women Representing Black Women.* New York: Routledge; Manning, Maurice M. 1998. *Slave in a Box: The Strange Career of Aunt Jemima.* Charlottesville: University of Virginia Press.

about how racially stereotyped the character was. Speedy Gonzales spoke in an exaggerated Mexican accent and, just as in other Hispanic stereotypes, wore an oversized sombrero and guarded the border against other "mice" coming into the country and getting all the cheese (Basset 2013; Markus and Conner 2013).

You don't have to watch movies and cartoons, though, to see such images. Everyday objects from the post–Civil War period through the 1950s used stereotypical images of Black Americans to do everything from holding seasonings to covering your toaster. Now called "Black collectibles," these were objects used in daily life that exaggerated the presumed features of African Americans, making Black Americans appear to be stupid, lovable, servile, and nonthreatening—and certainly inferior.

Black collectibles such as salt-and-pepper shakers, dolls, lawn jockeys, postcards, and other everyday items were popular from the 1880s through the 1950s. These everyday goods depicted Black people as dark-skinned, servile, and childlike. The "mammy" was typically overweight and smiling, appearing as if she aimed to please (Turner 1994). Now prized among some collectors, these goods presented images of Black people that, in many ways, remain with us today. These everyday objects, however, were part of the racial ideology that cemented the inferiority of Black people in the White imagination. Such seemingly trivial, everyday objects were part of the ruling apparatus of society (Goings 1994).

The iconography of the past provides a window through which we can now understand contemporary representations. Even the exaggerated way that some people now mock Spanish may have its origins in old presentations in which characters speak Spanish in an exaggerated and comical way. They clearly supported notions of white supremacy and the inferiority of everyone else. Viewed from today's perspective, past stereotypes seem exaggerated and offensive but, at the time, they were taken for granted, at least by dominant groups. As you look at current racial and ethnic stereotypes, you can see how some of the old ones have been recycled for a new day (Dirks and Mueller 2010). This is all the more reason to become more critically attuned to current representations.

Who Sees What?

With the growth of social media and an increasing array of media forms and networks, the U.S. public is now exposed to a huge array of images and ideas that communicate notions of race and ethnicity. Television, film, video, social media: These are only a few of the places where the public views racial and ethnic representations. Through advertisements alone, the typical person is exposed to hundreds, perhaps thousands, of images every day. You probably think you do not notice, but ads have an impact—otherwise corporations would not spend the huge sums of money that they do to produce them. Ads are only one way that images are dispersed. Our exposure to manufactured images is so vast that it is almost impossible to measure.

Together, images in the media act as *agents of socialization*. That is, they convey norms, values, and ideas to a public whose thinking and identities are then shaped by the images presented. This is true for all people, but it is especially true for children. Stereotypes learned at an early age, unless challenged, become a strong part of children's identity development (Martin 2008). Children now watch more TV than they did even a few years ago. Black and Latino youth also consume more media than do White children (Greenberg, Mastro, and Brand 2002; Martin 2008). Surveys find that children aged two to five now spend about thirty-two hours per week in front of a TV screen (McDonough 2009). Even young infants are now increasingly exposed to images on the screen. One report finds that 70 percent of infants spend about two hours per day in front of a screen (Rideout, Vandewater, and Wartell 2003). Little wonder that television is sometimes called the nation's babysitter!

When children watch, what do they see? Children of color are now 44 percent of the population, but images of them do not account for anywhere near that proportion in the media forms that they watch, read, and hear. This can lead to feelings of being less important and less valued than others. Research finds that for children of color, not seeing themselves portrayed in a positive light is associated with reduced self-esteem (Martin 2008; Ward 2004). Other than on Spanish-language television, Latino youth will find very few portrayals of themselves in the media. Studies find that frequent exposure of children of color to mainstream programming is associated with lower self-esteem. Among Latino high school and college students, greater exposure to mainstream media is particularly associated with a more negative body image (Rivadeneyra, Ward, and Gordon 2005).

Children's media is also a place where White children learn racial stereotypes. Even as early as age three, the racial and ethnic images that White children see in the media teach them to exclude other children from play (Van Ausdale and Feagin 2000). Children's books and films now also reflect the racism of colorblindness. They largely ignore African American history, the realities of racism, and the struggles of people of color (Winograd 2011). There are exceptions, of course, but you have to look to alternative networks long and hard to find them—an ongoing challenge for parents who want to raise their children with a vision of a more racially inclusive society.

Analyzing Sites of Cultural Production

Social scientists use content analysis to document the images seen in the media. **Content analysis** is a method of research that systematically documents the images that appear in various cultural artifacts. It is a way of recording the images that appear in the media and assessing the changes that may or may not occur over time. Because content analysis only details what appears in the media, it cannot tell you how people react to these images. For that, other methods of research are needed. Still, content analysis reveals the systematic content of media images, even when those images may be taken for granted and barely noticed in any critical way by casual observers.

What does content analysis tell us about the representations found in some of the common sites of **cultural production**, meaning those places where cultural images and ideas are actually made? There is no doubt that images of people of color have improved in recent years, especially as advertisers have tuned in to the increased diversity of the U.S. population. The expansion of civil rights and resulting job opportunities for people of color in the media make for a more diverse workforce and then fewer stereotyped images. What do we see in some of the most common sites of production?

The Race-Ethnicity Gap in the Media

* 87 percent of video game heroes are White.
* No Latino men played leading roles in films in the period 2010–2013.
* 94 percent of film executives are White; all of them are men.
* In the 2013 TV season, minorities played only 6.5 percent of lead roles on scripted broadcast TV programs.
* In 2013, Native Americans constituted a mere 0.4 percent of television characters.
* Stories about Latinos are less than 1 percent of news media coverage.

Sources: Bunche Center for African American Studies at UCLA. 2015. "2015 Hollywood Diversity Report: Flipping the Script" (http://www.bunchecenter.ucla.edu/wp-content/uploads/2015/02/2015-Hollywood-Diversity-Report-2-25-15.pdf); Frances Negrón-Muntaner. 2015. *The Latino Media Gap*. New York: Columbia University, Center for the Study of Ethnicity and Race.

Television

Even with the rise of social media and the ability to stream film and video, television remains the most popular medium for viewers, even though it is giving way to streaming video. Ninety-seven percent of homes in the United States have at least one TV; most have more. In any given week, 83 percent of the population watches prime-time television. The average person watches five or more hours of television per day, even more as he or she grows older (U.S. Bureau of the Census 2012b). African Americans watch more television than any other group—200 hours of television per month compared to 155 hours for Whites, 117 hours for Hispanics, and 82 hours per month for Asians, who watch the least television. Americans also watch more television by far than people in other nations (Nielsen Company 2014).

As producers have become more aware of population diversity, they have seized the market by projecting more images that reflect this diversity. Yet, for example, on television American Indians are almost invisible, comprising a tiny percentage of those shown on TV. Indeed, Native Americans are even more rare now than they were in the 1950s and 1960s, when Westerns were very popular. Then, however, American Indians were crudely stereotyped and typically shown as sidekicks or background figures. Current portrayals of American Indians, rare as they are, either place them in earlier centuries or portray them as spiritual figures or as beleaguered by social problems (Leavitt et al. 2015).

Because the vast majority of TV shows are now set in urban locations, you might expect to see more diverse people on television and in a variety of roles, but television presents a narrow range of characters, especially for people of color. African Americans are most commonly seen as entertainers, athletes, criminals, or sidekicks, and they are disproportionately shown in sitcoms and crime dramas. African American representation on television increased significantly in the 1980s, when they were about 22 percent of prime-time characters, but their representation has dropped since to about 14 percent of characters now (Mastro 2015).

Latinos are vastly underrepresented on television, except on Spanish-language television, which is rarely watched by White audiences. When Latinos appear on mainstream television, they are most often portrayed as hypersexual, subservient, or just plain stupid (Mastro 2015). South Asian Americans, when seen at all, are often stereotyped as cab drivers and convenience store clerks. Other Asian Americans are typically depicted as linked to technology (Thakore 2014).

The invisibility and stereotyping of people of color on television results in what cultural critics call **symbolic annihilation** (Gerbner 1972). Symbolic annihilation refers to the under- and misrepresentation of certain groups of people in the media. When people of color are "symbolically annihilated," stereotypes fill the void.

If America actually looked like the limited representation of people of color on television, what would the nation look like? Figure 3.1 shows you. This figure is based on a study of 325 prime-time television programs conducted over a twenty-two-year time span. As you can see, prime-time television suggests that White people are as much as 80 percent of the U.S. population. In reality, Whites are 62 percent of the U.S. population (Mastro 2015; U.S. Bureau of the Census 2015c). Images in the media simply do not reflect reality.

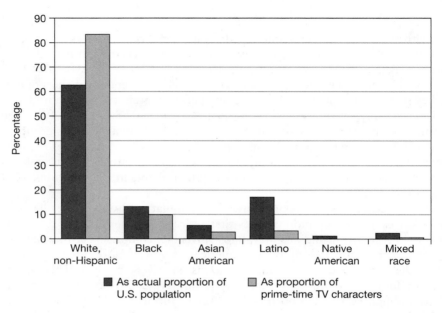

FIG. 3.1　What Does America Look Like? Reality vs. TV

Sources: Tukachinsky, Riva, Dana Mastro, and Moran Yarchi. 2015. "Documenting Portrayals of Race/Ethnicity on Primetime Television over a 20-Year Span and Their Association with National-Level Racial/Ethnic Attitudes." *Journal of Social Issues* 71(1):17–38; U.S. Bureau of the Census. 2015c. *State and County Quick Facts.* Washington, DC: U.S. Department of Commerce.

Film

Film audiences are, in fact, a highly diverse population. Twelve percent of moviegoers are Black Americans, 17 percent are Hispanics, 64 percent are White—a fairly close approximation of the actual population. In fact, half of all frequent moviegoers are now people of color (Bunche Center 2015).

There is a greater presence now of people of color in film than in past years. Racial-ethnic groups have a higher percentage of leading roles. Cast diversity in films has also increased, yet stereotypes remain. Asian Americans in the movies are stereotyped in particular ways. Asian women are heavily sexualized as "exotic" but submissive beauties. Asian men are routinely shown in the context of martial arts where they are usually beaten by White guys. Rarely are Asian men seen with White women, whereas Asian women are usually paired with non-Asian men (Bunche Center 2015).

In film, African Americans are all too frequently portrayed as victims saved by White people (Hughey 2014; Vera and Gordon 2003). Even in 2014, a so-called breakout year for African Americans in film, minority leads were more likely to appear in comedies, while White leads were more prominent in dramas. Even with the increased presence of people of color in film, the top credits are still more likely to go to White actors, especially to White men.

Latinos actually see more movies and listen to more radio than any other demographic group (Koyen 2012). Yet in the movies, there are fewer lead Latino actors than there were seventy years ago. Looking at a recent time period (2010–2013), scholars have found that Latino men played *no* leading roles in either the top ten films and/or in the most popular TV shows (measured by size of the viewing audience). Moreover, Latinos were less than three percent of those in supporting roles.

Progress is being made, especially as more people of color enter employment in the filmmaking industry. Even here, however, people of color are underrepresented as directors, writers, and producers (Bunche Center 2015; Erigha 2015).

Video Games

Video gaming is another site of cultural production, although few people probably think of it as a place where racial-ethnic images are produced. For many, playing video games now surpasses time spent watching television. As with other media, these games can have a significant impact on the formation of identity and beliefs about race and ethnicity.

Asian Americans are the group most likely to be video gamers. Eighty-one percent of Asian Americans play video games, followed by African Americans (71 percent), then non-Hispanic Whites (61 percent), and, finally, Hispanics (55 percent). Asian Americans and Whites are overrepresented as characters in video games, at least relative to their proportion in the U.S. population. White characters are a full 85 percent of primary characters in video games; Blacks, 9.6 percent; Asians, 1.7 percent. Hispanics and Native Americans only appear as secondary characters (Williams et al. 2009; Nielsen Company 2015).

In video games with characters, nearly all the heroes are White (87 percent). African Americans and Latinos are most often portrayed as athletes; Asians and Pacific Islanders, as wrestlers or fighters. Especially interesting is that when African American characters in video games are the victims of violence, they are likely to be shown as unharmed. African American women are the group most likely to be portrayed as victims of violence (Glaubke et al. 2001). Research shows that video game play has a significant effect on White players' views of Black and Asian Americans: The more time Whites spend playing video games, the less likely they are to have egalitarian views of Black and Asian people (Behm-Morawitz and Ta 2014).

News

The one place where you might expect greater accuracy in the representation and portrayal of race and ethnicity is in the news. Given its mission to report national and world events, we count on news for facts and accuracy. Yet even in the news, people of color are under- and misrepresented. Turn on any Sunday morning news program and see who appear as experts. White men dominate, even when talking about racial issues.

Careful analyses of news coverage have found that major newspapers feature seven times more quotes from men than from women. Even with somewhat greater inclusion of people of color as reporters and commentators now, there are few people of color as the primary anchors on the national evening news. As of 2015, all of the hosts of Sunday morning political talk shows were White men (Boguhn 2015; also see figure 3.2).

How people appear in the news also matters. As we will see next, people of color are overreported as criminals relative to the amount of crime they commit.

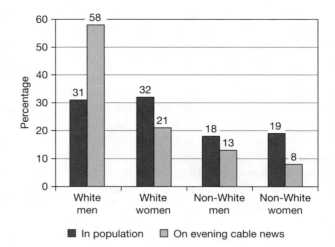

FIG. 3.2   Who Narrates the News? Representation in the Population vs. Evening Cable News

Source: Savillo, Rob, and Oliver Willis. 2013. "Diversity on Evening Cable News in 13 Charts." Media Matters. Retrieved January 21, 2017 (https://mediamatters.org/research/2013/05/13/report-diversity-on-evening-cable-news-in-13-ch/194012).

Of the Latinos who appear in the news, two-thirds are shown as either criminals or illegal immigrants. A slim 2.7 percent of guests on talk shows are Latino (Negrón-Muntaner 2015; Savillo and Willis 2013). With such limited and misrepresentative imagery on the news, is it any wonder that viewers end up with such a limited understanding of the issues facing people of color in today's world?

Internet

Finally, cyberspace is an increasingly important site for the production of culture. Facebook, Twitter, Snapchat, Instagram, and other social media play an increasingly important role in the cultural life of all Americans. A digital divide remains in who uses the Internet, although this gap is closing. African Americans trail White Americans by seven percentage points in how many use the Internet (87 percent of Whites, 80 percent of African Americans). Among young people, the gap however has disappeared, although fewer African Americans have Internet access in the home. On social media, Whites are 78 percent of those using social media; Blacks, 10 percent; Asians, 3 percent; and Hispanics, 12 percent (Nielsen Company 2011; Smith 2014).[2]

The development and use of social media give people the opportunity to share information and entertainment in a highly democratic way, in that people can be less dependent on mainstream media for sharing information. African Americans,

---

[2] The figures do not total 100 percent because Hispanics can fall into multiple groups.

for example, are more likely to use Twitter than other groups. Analyses of social media indicate the presence of rampant racism (Daniels 2013), raising new ethical issues about how much free speech should be tolerated in these new forms of communication.

Social media are an increasingly important source of how people get the news. Many of us are now in information networks that are less dependent on the dominant media outlets. But people tend to be in social media feeds that provide information that they already agree with, making it less likely that the media are a source for alternative and possibly opposing views. Moreover, the ease of posting on social media means that people are easily susceptible to so-called fake news, meaning news that is completely untrue and yet easily shared and widely dispersed through social media. At the same time, however, social media can be used to construct alternative narratives that are important in political activism, as has been shown in how organizers in movements such as Black Lives Matter use social media for mobilizing support (Rose 2013).

Crime, Sex, and Aliens: The Media Constructs Race

Taken together, stereotypes in television, film, the news, the Internet, and other cultural sites distort the reality of life for people of color. Even with some minor variation, certain themes recur in the presentation of racial-ethnic groups, especially:

- associating race and criminality
- representing people of color as hypersexual
- constructing people of color as alien or "other"

In the absence of other images, these recurring themes leave a stamp on people's consciousness. Representations of groups that are pervasive in society orient people in their social environment and provide a way for people to communicate with and understand each other.

Race and Criminalization

All media vastly overrepresent African Americans as criminals. At the same time, White people are underrepresented as criminals relative to the proportion of crimes they actually commit. This has happened largely because of the expansion of local news coverage. Local news now takes up more time in television than it did in the not-too-distant past; therefore, local news affiliates need to fill the time allotted and do it inexpensively. Images of violent crime are more dramatic than images that would be associated with nonviolent crimes such as tax evasion, embezzlement, or government kickbacks (Iyengar 2010). The result is a dramatic increase in televised images of urban African American crime. This leaves the public with a very distorted image of the incidence and causes of crime by Black Americans (Gilliam et al. 1996).

White people's increased exposure to crime shows inflates their perception of the actual crime rate, especially that by people of color. With more exposure to crime shows, White people are also then more likely to support punitive criminal justice policies (Gilliam and Iyengar 2000; Hurley et al. 2015). Repeated images of Black

Americans reproduce common stereotypes of race and increase fear of crime. Even as the actual crime rate has declined, an increasing percentage of Americans cite crime as one of the most important problems in the United States (Iyengar 2010). As we have tragically seen, police who associate African Americans with danger and crime are more likely to shoot African Americans compared to police who do not have this association (Eberhardt 2010).

Sexualizing the Body

A second recurring theme in the portrayal of people of color is hypersexuality. The body is one of the places where "the prevailing rules of a culture are written" (Gimlin 2002:3). For people of color, the body becomes a site for scripting racism. In countless examples, Black American women and Latinas are depicted as oversexed and sexually loose, feeding some of the controlling images that we have already discussed. The sexualization of women of color is especially played out in music videos that routinely portray Black women with large breasts and big hips, and Latinas as "hot," seductive, overly emotional, and dressed in loud colors (Vargas 2010).

Sports are also a place where Black American bodies are on display. As with crime, relative to their proportion in the population, Blacks are overrepresented in sports; Whites, underrepresented. Narrations by sports announcers also tend to stereotype Black male athletes as naturally athletic, quick, and powerful. On the other hand, White male athletes are touted for their hard work, effort, and mental skill (Eastman and Billings 2001; McKay and Johnson 2008).

Making People Other: The Alien Narrative

The third theme recurring in the media is the presentation of people of color as "alien" or "other." This is especially true for how Mexican immigrants are presented. Even the language used to describe immigrants communicates "otherness," thus influencing how immigrants are understood. As an example, think of how the image conjured up by the term "illegal alien" differs from that of the "undocumented worker."

Over the years, various immigrant groups, including Latinos and Asians, have been described as a "contagion," "pollutants," "perils," and other terms that clearly imply that immigrants are invaders who threaten the fabric of American life—much the way that Chinese and Japanese immigrants were constructed in the earlier part of the twentieth century. Mexican immigrants especially have been stereotyped as a threat, different from earlier European immigrants who instead are seen as becoming part of the nation (Chavez 2008; Cisneros 2008).

Images of immigrants as "invaders" generate support for punitive immigration policies, such as Donald Trump's calls to "build a wall" and create a massive deportation force. Such policies rest on a stereotype of Mexican immigrants as dangerous criminals. Donald Trump's call to close the borders to Syrian refugees also rests on a narrow stereotype of refugees as terrorists and killers. Such inflammatory language of "othering" thwarts any chance for empathy or understanding about the actual lived conditions and hard work of either Mexican workers or Syrians fleeing violence and war in their home county.

Isn't It Just for Fun?

By now you might be thinking that all these images do not really affect you. After all, most of them come from the world of entertainment, so surely it is just for fun and does not really shape how you think about yourself or others, right? Research shows otherwise.

Take the case of Native American sports mascots. You go to the stadium, root for your team, perhaps even chant the "tomahawk chop" as you sit on the edge of your seat, maybe wearing a T-shirt with an image of an Indian as your team's logo. What possible harm could come from this?

When you picture the typical representation of a Native American mascot, you probably see a male wearing feathers, with big teeth and a grin on his face, and also appearing comical or fearsome. Think of the symbol of the Cleveland Indians for a clear example! This image seriously distorts who Native people are. For one thing, why are the mascots always men? Where are Native American women in this representation? The suggestion that Native people are fierce and warlike also miscasts the actual history of aggression against American Indians. Mainly, this iconic image of American Indians offends people who see it as degrading and insulting to the complexity and richness of Native American nations.

Social psychologist Stephanie Fryberg asked whether Native American mascots are just for fun or whether they cause harm (Fryberg and Watts 2010). She devised a series of carefully designed experiments to test the effect of Native American mascots on young Native American children, asking how exposure to these mascots affects their self-image and academic achievement. She conducted her experiments at three Native American schools and one Native American college.

After being exposed to the typical mascot image, the students wrote down the first five thoughts that came to mind. Using social psychological instruments to measure various outcomes, Fryberg found that students who were exposed to the mascot image reported lower self-esteem and a lower sense of community worth than did students who were not exposed to the mascot. This consequence emerged regardless of whether the mascot image was more positive or more negative. In a second experiment, Fryberg also found that students reported lower goals for their future after exposure to the mascot image. She then tested a sample of European American students, using the exact same research protocol. She found that, following exposure to the mascots, European American students actually reported that their self-esteem *went up!*

Fryberg's research shows us that mascot images not only have a deleterious effect on young Native Americans but they also elevate how White people think of themselves. These mascots have become so commonplace that few White people ever think about the harm they do to others, but imagine how you might feel if your town had a team named the Pittsburgh Polacks or the Kansas City Kikes or the Detroit Dykes or the Wisconsin Wetbacks (Churchill 1993). Are those of us who are not Native American so accustomed to ridiculing them that we no longer empathize or even understand why these images are so hurtful? What does it tell you about our culture that people can so blithely participate in stereotypes that mock Native American people? Are there any other racial-ethnic stereotypes that are so commonplace that you hardly even see them anymore—unless, of course, they are applied to you?

Consider how some people celebrate Halloween. Holidays are occasions that confirm group identities, that is, they involve rituals that socialize people into a sense of community and help shape the collective consciousness (Durkheim 1964 [1895]). In the case of Halloween, costumes that portray racial and ethnic stereotypes can reinforce identity for White people. This has been illustrated by a study of college students who wrote diaries about their Halloween experiences. Students recorded how racial images were portrayed in Halloween costumes. The researchers concluded from the students' observations that Halloween costumes became "vehicles for transmitting racial judgments about people of color" (Mueller, Dirks, and Picca 2007:324), therefore, at the same time confirming whiteness as a "normal" identity.

Research finds other consequences of exposure to racial stereotypes. Seeing African Americans in stereotypical roles on television, for example, influences how audiences understand the occupational roles of Black people (Punyanunt-Carter 2008). Frequent television viewing is also associated with greater endorsement of negative stereotypes by White people. On a more positive note, even brief exposure to positive and likable images in the media leads to better racial attitudes among White people (Schmader, Block, and Lickel 2015; Oliver et al. 2015). All told, despite the cavalier attitude by some that stereotypes do not matter that much, the fact is that they do.

Markets, Makers, and Money: The Media Makes Race

Popular culture and the media provide a basis for a shared experience in society, even though different groups use and experience the media in diverse ways. What we see in popular culture and the media is, of course, "fake," that is, consisting of images produced by people with very specific purposes, most often commercial ones. Why are the images what they are?

There are three ways we can explain racial and ethnic representations in popular culture and the media:

1. demographic changes in the population
2. the status of people of color in media organization
3. critical race theory

First, *demographic changes in the population* mean that media audiences are more diverse than ever before. In a related sidenote, because the majority of media outlets are commercially owned, the advertiser—not the customer—is king. For continued success, the broadcaster knows that it is crucial to appeal to the widest possible audience, delivering "superficial content with wide appeal" (Iyengar 2010:254). Advertisers and producers have recognized the importance of appealing to a diverse population, so they have increased the representation of diverse groups in their advertising and programming, compared to the past. Particularly given the growth of the Latino and Asian populations, you can expect that advertisers will want to promote content that capitalizes on these growing markets. Changes in media images can be heavily attributed to these market forces.

Second, change in racial representations has also come with *greater inclusion of people of color in the media workforce*. The images we see in popular culture and the media are manufactured. Like other products, media images are produced and distributed by those employed in media organizations. Without diversity in the workforce, workers might project only a limited view, one filled with group stereotypes. People of color have made many inroads into the media as employees; African American, Latino, Native American, and Asian American people figure among film directors, reporters, and other media employees. There is still room for improvement (see figure3.3). With greater inclusion, especially in the top positions, it seems likely that the representation and depiction of people of color in the media will change.

A third perspective, **critical race theory**, takes the viewpoint that the media and popular culture reflect and re-create hierarchical systems of race, class, and gender in society (Brooks and Hébert 2006; Dines and Humez 2014; Dirks and Mueller 2010). This interdisciplinary perspective emphasizes the role of power in constructing the meaning of race and its intersection with other social factors, such as gender and social class. Critical race theory situates the representations of race and ethnicity in the fact that the United States is a capitalist society. **Capitalism** is an economic system based on the pursuit of profit and private ownership. The mass media in 2017 include a vast number of media forms and outlets but, in truth, the majority of news and media outlets are owned by only a few. As just one example, a company called National Amusements has controlling interests in both CBS and Viacom. CBS owns the CBS Television Network, Showtime, countless television and radio stations, and various online properties. Viacom owns several cable networks, including BET, MTV, Nickelodeon, Comedy Central, and others, plus Paramount Pictures and more ("Who Owns What" 2015). With so much of the media in the hands of so few,

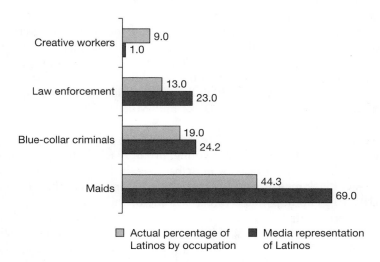

FIG. 3.3 Latino Roles in the Media and in the Actual Labor Force

Source: Negrón-Muntaner, Frances. 2015. *The Latino Media Gap.*
New York: Columbia University, Center for the Study of Ethnicity and Race.

you cannot help but ask whose interests are served by the racial representations that appear in the media. From the perspective of critical race theory, representations produced in the media and popular culture are essential for maintaining particular systems of control and power.

Race, Resistance, and Alternative Visions

We have seen how images of race and ethnicity in society are fundamental to how we think about race. At the same time, culture can be a vehicle for change and alternative images and visions for racial justice. Although dominant representations reflect and reproduce racial inequality, it is also possible for culture to liberate us from the negativity and misrepresentation that is all too common in popular culture and the media. In other words, although the media and popular culture produce and reflect racial perceptions, they can also subvert them (Grzanka 2014).

Throughout history, including recently, people have organized to resist racist images and to insist that there be better representation of people of color in the media. Many of the changes that we now see are the result of mobilization by people of color insisting that more affirming and positive images be reflected in the dominant culture.

A **culture of resistance** refers to the cultural forms that people create explicitly to challenge the stereotypes and controlling images that appear in the dominant culture. There are numerous examples of cultures of resistance throughout American history and now.

Sometimes cultures of resistance appear as protests against corporations that produce racist images in their products. One such example occurred when Abercrombie and Fitch marketed a T-shirt in 2003 featuring this slogan: "Wong Brothers Laundry: Two Wongs Make It White." A massive national outcry was raised as students and others led a petition campaign to have the shirt removed because it was so offensive to Asian Americans and their allies. Abercrombie and Fitch responded by saying that their company did not single Asian Americans out—that, in fact, they ran campaigns that offended everybody! In the end, given the public outcry, Abercrombie and Fitch pulled the shirt from its shelves. Two years later, Abercrombie and Fitch had to pay $40 million in a settlement for widespread ethnic and gender discrimination in hiring (Dirks and Mueller 2010; *New York Times*, November 17, 2004).

Another example of a culture of resistance is hip-hop. Hip-hop as a musical style has now become mainstream, but young, urban Black men (and some women) first created hip-hop in the 1970s to fight back against mainstream cultural messages that depict Black men, especially, as "dangerous and disposable" (Morgan and Fischer 2010:510). Hip-hop was a direct critique of the U.S. system of justice. By deploying the vernacular language of the streets, young Black teens reclaimed the cultural space to define themselves. Hip-hop thus became a tool to defy racism.

This cultural invention also showcases the talents of many young Black men who were otherwise dispossessed by the dominant culture. Composed of rhyming and acrobatic dancing in the streets, hip-hop was made by artists who may have had no formal art education and none of the race or class privileges that some other artists enjoy. Hip-hop has now become a global movement. Indeed, some would argue that White consumers have appropriated hip-hop style, thus softening its original political message. Other contemporary art forms, such as slam poetry, stem from the hip-hop movement and show how culture can be a source of affirmation, not just degradation, for those excluded from dominant cultural institutions.

The hip-hop phenomenon also shows that a culture of resistance can also be a **culture of affirmation,** that is, culture can be the medium by which groups develop and assert a strongly positive identity for themselves. As with cultures of resistance, a culture of affirmation shows the creativity of people who produce new cultural forms with the specific purpose of showcasing the talents and strong identities of people of color (or other minorities). Again, there are numerous examples throughout American history; among the best is the Harlem Renaissance (Marks 1999; Huggins 2007; Lewis 1981). The Harlem Renaissance spanned the period from the end of World War I until about the beginning of the Great Depression in the early 1930s. It was a period a tremendous cultural expression by Black artists focused in Harlem in the areas of music, literature, dance, intellectual works, and the arts. Many of those artists are recognized today as among the greats of American culture: Romare Bearden, Langston Hughes, "Dizzy" Gillespie, Nella Larsen, Ella Fitzgerald, Bessie Smith, Billie Holiday, Louis Armstrong, and many others too numerous to mention.

Cultures of resistance and cultures of affirmation teach us that, as people construct and see positive images of themselves and others, they can transform our understanding of race and ethnicity, and such cultures can be the basis for movements for social justice. This takes looking at the dominant culture with a critical eye, but doing so without appropriating the culture of others (Gallagher 2003).

In today's world, Black culture has become especially popular among White youth. People can now "consume" Black culture through participation in a mainstream popular culture that has been very much influenced by African American culture—especially African American urban culture (Pitcher 2014). How that culture was made to flow into the mainstream has to do with the phenomenon of **cultural appropriation,** which occurs when privileged groups consume and "claim" the culture of an oppressed or colonized group. White people can now participate in "blackness" without incurring any of the costs of being Black. Movie star Amandla Stenberg puts it well: "What would America be like if it loved Black people as much as it loves Black culture?" (Stenberg 2015)?

Any person can work to produce more affirming and positive views of race and ethnicity. One example is found in the cartoon character Dora the Explorer. When Dora was developed in 2000, the creators hired sociologist Clara Rodriguez, an expert in media representations of Latinos/as, as a consultant to be sure that Dora would be a positive influence for young children. As Dora was developed, everything was "carefully crafted to make sure that Dora accurately portrayed Latinos" (Havrilla 2010). Dora, a seven-year-old Latina, is goal-oriented and adventurous—a very different image from the typical Latina image in the media. By introducing Dora and, later, her companion Diego as positive Latina/o role models, Rodriguez and the cartoon's producers have influenced how White children see Latinas/os and boosted the self-respect of Latino/a children.

A. DOTING MUM
B. LOVES A GIRLS' NIGHT OUT
C. PROFESSIONAL ACCOUNTANT
D. ALL OF THE ABOVE

SEE BEYOND RACE.

Challenging racial stereotypes is an important step in reducing prejudice in its various forms.

Racial boundaries, hierarchies, and definitions are challenged by those who produce new visions for what is possible. The fact that race is fluid makes change possible. Culture is a major medium through which this can happen. As one small example, research finds that those who view inspiring videos about people of color develop stronger feelings of connectedness with diverse racial-ethnic groups (Oliver et al. 2015). Seeing more positive images also reduces stereotypes (Ramasubramanian 2015). Especially if you are a member of the dominant group, this requires looking with a critical eye and changing your way of thinking.

Conclusion

The mass media and popular culture have increasing influence on how people see each other and how they understand the society in which they live. Put simply, the media constructs reality but does not reflect it (Brooks and Hébert 2006; Gamson et al. 1992). Sometimes the images in the media support the belief in colorblind racism, that is, the idea that race no longer matters and that everyone has the same chance to succeed, which we examined in the previous chapter.

Racial images in the media also have become something that White Americans can consume and enjoy but without any consequence for their status in society (Gallagher 2003). Race, then, becomes a style, not a matter of social inequality. As we have seen throughout this chapter, though, popular culture and the media continue to reproduce images that distort and undermine people of color through the vehicle of culture. Although improvements have been made in the representation of people of color, much needs to be done if we are to project a more inclusive and realistic portrait of race and ethnicity in the United States. Because race and ethnicity are social constructions, transforming these images in the media is an important part of the process of change.

Key Terms

capitalism, 63

content analysis, 54

controlling image, 48

critical race theory, 63

cultural appropriation, 65

cultural hegemony, 46

cultural production, 54

cultural racism, 47

culture, 45

culture of affirmation, 65

culture of resistance, 64

dominant culture, 46

mass media, 45

objectification, 49

popular culture, 45

racial frames, 46

symbolic annihilation, 55

white supremacy, 47

Critical Thinking Questions

1. Go back to the quote by Maya Angelou that opened this chapter. How can popular culture and the media help build the esteem for multiple cultures in the United States that Angelou writes about?

2. How have you been influenced by some of the controlling images that are found in the media that you are most likely to use on a regular basis? How does the answer to this question likely differ if you are a person of color or a White person?

Student Exercises

3.1: Take a visit to your local grocery store. Walk through every aisle, making note of any stereotypes that you see. What does this exercise tell you about the presence of stereotypes in everyday life?

3.2: Your goal here is to do a content analysis of some form of media or popular culture. First identify a very specific genre (sitcoms, police "reality" shows, advertisements in a particular theme magazine, or something quite focused so you can be systematic in your research). Then, develop a careful plan by which you can do a content analysis of the images in this particular form of media. Describe your results in terms of the images that you find and what they portray. What do you conclude from this exercise? Does it change how you see the media and popular culture?

Challenging Questions/Open to Debate

Suppose that a student government has arranged to bring a comedian to campus for an evening of student entertainment. The contracts are signed, publicity is out, and the student organization has committed a lot of its budget to this event. As it turns out, the performer uses a lot of racial stereotypes in the stand-up comedy act and some student groups on campus are protesting the event.

Should the event be canceled, given the student demonstrations against it?

Would your answer change depending on which groups were being offended by the comedian?

If the performance is not canceled, are there other courses of action?

CHAPTER 4

Who Do You Think You Are?

Racial Identities and Relationships

It is a peculiar sensation, this double-consciousness, this sense of always looking at one's self through the eyes of others, of measuring one's soul by the tape of a world that looks on in amused contempt and pity.
—William Edward Burghardt Du Bois (1903)

OBJECTIVES

- Understand the social structural basis for racial identities
- Identify and explain white privilege
- Detail the significance of racial microaggressions
- Discuss the factors that influence the development of interracial relationships

In the summer of 2015, Rachel Dolezal resigned as president of the Spokane, Washington, chapter of the National Association for the Advancement of Colored People (NAACP).[1] She did so following a national uproar when her parents (from whom she was estranged) announced to the national media that Rachel was White, not Black, as Rachel had claimed. As the news unfolded, we learned that Rachel Dolezal had changed her appearance over the years by darkening her skin, wearing an Afro-like hairstyle, and changing other things about her demeanor. As far as most people could tell, she looked like a light-skinned, African American person. Her ex-husband was African American. Dolezal was a passionate advocate for civil rights, had taught in an Africana Studies program, and served as a campus advisor to Black students. Few had questioned her commitment to racial justice.

As this controversy ensued, people on all sides of the political spectrum weighed in on Rachel's racial identity. She was called an impostor, but she insisted she was "not White." Her estranged parents wanted her to have a DNA test to prove that she was their White offspring. What if she was? Could she reasonably claim to be biracial, transracial, or Black—all terms she used at various times to describe herself? How is one's racial identity determined? Did she have the right to call herself Black? How would we know?

We learned in chapters 1 and 2 that race is a multidimensional social construct. Nowhere has this been clearer than in this fascinating case of someone who seems to be "biologically White" even while claiming to be Black. Is your racial identity simply a matter of your ancestry, or is it something that emerges in the context of your lifetime relationships?

Think about this in another context. Imagine a day when a baby is born. Everyone in the child's large extended family is excited about the new life that has come into the world. Let's suppose the child's mother identifies as Latina and has a Latina mother and a Black father. The baby's father is White, raised Jewish. What is the baby? When the delivery room nurse completes the birth certificate, what would she pick to identify the child's race—Black? Hispanic? White? Other? None of the above?

Taking this one step further, would it matter where the hospital was located? Did you assume this was happening in the United States? What if the birth happened in a Caribbean nation? Canada? Europe? What if you had been born in 1950—in a southern U.S. hospital? What race you would be? And why does it matter? If you were considered White at birth, might you later change your identity to Black or "multiracial"? Once you grew up to be an adult, what would you put on the census form?

All of these questions are pivotal in a discussion of racial identity—the subject of this chapter. The questions iterate a central point made throughout this book: that race is a social construction, as is your racial identity—or, perhaps, identities. This chapter explores the formation and significance of racial identity and the interracial relationships that develop or are impeded in a racially unequal society.

---

[1] The NAACP was founded in 1909 by a coalition of African Americans and White liberals. The long-standing organization advocates for civil rights, focusing largely, though not exclusively, on African Americans. W. E. B. Du Bois, Ida Wells Barnett, and Mary Church Terrell were among its founders.

In doing so, we are looking at what sociologists call the *micro level of society*, that is, the part of society that is up close and quite directly observable. You might think of this as the individual level of society—how we see ourselves, how others see us, and how we relate to each other. It is important to see, however, that the micro level of society is shaped by the *macro level* or large-scale social systems and institutions that together constitute society.

In the case of race and ethnic relations, the macro level of racial-ethnic inequality very much shapes who we are as individuals and how we relate to people in different racial-ethnic groups. Even as we go through our daily lives and form highly personal relationships, the macro level of society is ever present. This chapter begins with a discussion of the "closest in" level of society: our racial and ethnic identities.

Who Am I? Racial Identities in a Racialized Society

Who do you think you are? This simple question packs a lot of meaning and cuts to the heart of the human experience: Humans are not just a bundle of physiological processes. Our capacity for reflection is part of what makes us human. That is, we have a consciousness of ourselves. It is in that consciousness—or self-reflection—that our sense of ourselves as human beings in society is realized. Human consciousness provides the ability to know one's self and the world around you. It also provides a way we can reimagine the possibilities for more equitable intergroup relations.

Individuals in Society: The Formation of Identity

Identity is a person's conception of self. We think of our identity as an individual thing, but identity is very much the result of social relationships and social structures. This does not mean that you are not an individual, but it means that your identity emerges from your relationships with others and from your specific location in society. Identity is not fixed; it is formed over the course of one's lifetime and is constantly emerging. Certain experiences, especially during childhood but also in adolescence and adulthood, can be critical moments for identity formation (Kramer, Burke and Charles 2015). A particular relationship, a traumatic encounter, a new experience, a life of wealth or extreme poverty, living in racially segregated or integrated environments: These and other social factors all have a lasting impact on one's identity.

Several key thinkers are important for understanding the social significance of identity. George Herbert Mead (1863–1931) and Charles Horton Cooley (1864–1921) of the Chicago School of Sociology formulated sociological analyses of identity and the self. Cooley's concept of the *looking glass self* teaches us that we see ourselves as others see us. The self is the cumulated identity we have that results from the iteration between observation and reflection (Cooley 1902; Erikson 1968). We see how others see us and we incorporate that awareness into our notion of who we are. Our concept of "self" emerges from this ongoing process. Mead wrote that it is through internalizing how those in our surrounding circles see us that we formulate a sense of self—a process he referred to as *taking the role of the other* (Mead 1934).

The noteworthy psychologist Erik Erikson (1902–1994) conceptualized identity as a process by which we integrate different experiences and characteristics into a stable definition of oneself. This process begins at birth and continues through adolescence and adulthood. We do this through our membership in different social groups, including, as we will see, our racial-ethnic group (Christian 2000). To Erikson, one's identity is the point of intersection between the individual and community. Although our identity emerges through the specific circumstances of our individual life, we are located in communities that attach us to particular expectations, values, and worldviews.

George Herbert Mead referred to this as the *generalized other*—the collective expectations that others have of us, especially those who are *significant others*. Mead used the term significant others to refer to the most important people in our social circle, a broader usage than how the term is often used today to refer to one's partner. This formulation of identity means that the social environment is critical to the development of identity, regardless of how personal and individual we think we are. How race is understood in that social environment is then a critical part of the identities we form.

Racial Identity: A Sense of Belonging

Racial identity is the sense one has of oneself as belonging to a racial group (Steck, Heckert, and Heckert 2003). In a nation such as the United States where race is so significant in shaping social institutions, race is a key component of people's identity. When you grow up in a society tinged with racism, your racial identity—whatever it is—is bound to be affected. Racial identity is often a *master status*, that is, it trumps other forms of identity while also intersecting with other master statuses, such as gender and age.

Racial identities attach us not only to specific racial groups but also to particular histories. Your racial identity gives you a sense of common belonging, although this varies in the degree to which it is felt. If you are a member of a racial or ethnic **minority group**,[2] your racial-ethnic identity is likely to be far more salient than it is to those in the majority group.

In a racially stratified society like the United States, racial identity is formed as we navigate the various borders that construct race in society and, thus, our own sense of who we are. Sometimes, as is the case for people with a mixed racial heritage, many feel a sense of belonging to more than one racial or ethnic group, something we explore further later in this chapter.

Feeling a common attachment to others in your racial or ethnic group anchors you to a racial past and present, one that you may not always know but that connects you to a social structure that extends beyond your individual life. Such

---

[2] In sociological usage, *minority group* refers to any group with less power than a dominant (or majority) group. A racial minority group need not be numerically smaller than the dominant group. In fact, there are many instances in which a minority group, defined in terms of power and subordination, is actually larger than the most powerful or dominating group. South Africa is a case in point. Under apartheid, Whites were a small numerical portion of the population (about 10 percent); Blacks and other persons of color were about 90 percent, but Whites exercised total power and control over Blacks and colored people, the racial designations used in South African society.

attachments give you a sense of collective belonging, although strong attachments to particular groups or identities can also be the basis for the exclusion of others. In the United States, the attachment that people of color have with each other provides a strong feeling of collective identity. Whites tend to have more individualistic identities (Ai et al. 2011; Bethel 1999; Triandis 1989).

Racial identity comes with particular expectations about how we behave and what we believe (Schwalbe 2014; Schwalbe et al. 2000). Although people respond to these expectations in different ways, the dominant expectations regarding race both constrain and enable us, depending on our place in the racial hierarchy. As one sociologist has put it, we act in "recognizable patterns and in ways that produce . . . allegiance to racial scripts" (Hughey 2015:148). The White teacher who scolds a young Latino student for "speaking with an accent"; the Black teen whose parents instruct him on how to behave if stopped by a police officer; the biracial adolescent who switches between thinking of herself as Latina and as Black: These and other examples are scripts about race and ethnicity that are played out through routine social interactions. Although we may not always recognize that we are playing racial scripts, they permeate interactions both within and across racial-ethnic groups. What else would it mean to say that someone is "acting White" (Carbado and Gulati 2013) or as being not "authentically Black"?

Seeing ourselves as others see us is especially complicated in a racially unequal society. Those in racially subordinated groups will see themselves both through the eyes of those in their racial group *and* through the eyes of the dominant group. W. E. B. Du Bois's well-known quotation that opens this chapter speaks to this reality for African American people. Du Bois wrote that African American people develop a unique racial identity in that they must strive to reconcile two selves—that defined by Whites and that derived from their own community. Within this sense of "twoness," African Americans have to find strength to keep "from being torn asunder" (Du Bois 1996:5). This process is not necessarily unique to African Americans. Immigrants who bridge two cultures, even while identifying as American, may also feel that sense of "twoness."

The dilemma that Du Bois so eloquently expressed is today known as an **identity contingency**. Identity contingencies are "the things you have to deal with because you have a given social identity" (Steele 2010:3). If that contingency is racism or ethnic prejudice, your identity will be shaped by these realities. People of color must learn to deal with identity contingencies. African American parents, for example, must teach their children about racism early in life, as will Asian, Native American, and Latino parents. White children, on the other hand, may grow up rarely thinking about or talking about race—that is, until confronted with a racial conflict or other awakening experience. Racial identities develop in a social system grounded in the idea that Whites are dominant and all others as subordinate. Navigating this environment thus differs for dominant and subordinate groups.

In overtly racist regimes, a Black person who has the physical characteristics of a White person may try to pass as White to escape racism. Historically, many African Americans engaged in passing, often having to leave behind families and communities, lest their "white" identity be betrayed. By presenting themselves as White (perhaps even for a lifetime), these individuals would have better opportunities and would not be subjected to the ravages of racism (see LEARNING OUR PAST).

LEARNING OUR PAST

Can you imagine leaving your family and the community where you grew up to pass as someone from a different racial background than that to which you were born? That is precisely what some African Americans did during slavery and through the mid-twentieth century. Passing was a way to escape the conditions of racism, but it also involved considerable risks of its own. Only some could do it, by virtue of their appearance. They also had to change their clothing, manners of speech, life history, appearance (if possible), and any other markers that would reveal their true identity.

Other people have also used passing as a way of escaping from brutal ethnic, sexual, and gender oppression. Jewish people might try to pass to escape anti-Semitism. There are many instances of women who have passed as men for their entire lives (Middlebrook 1998). LGBT people might even liken passing to being "in the closet" to protect themselves from the threat of homophobia. For any individual, no matter the motivation, passing is very risky, given the constant possibility of having one's true identity revealed.

Historian Allyson Hobbs, who has studied African American passing, argues that "the core issue of passing is not becoming what you pass for, but losing what you pass away from" (2014:18). Although passing by African Americans is now (and always has been) relatively rare, it reveals the lengths to which people will go in pursuit of freedom and fair treatment.

Sources: Hobbs, Allyson. 2014. *A Chosen Exile: A History of Racial Passing in American Life*. Cambridge, MA: Harvard University Press; Middlebrook, Diane Wood. 1998. *Suits Me: The Double Life of Billy Tipton*. New York. Houghton Mifflin.

The passing person, however, would also experience a great sense of loss, having left the African American community. Even now, some biracial people may "pass" by emphasizing their White identity over their Black identity, perhaps even just in some situation, in order to protect themselves from racial threats (Hobbs 2014; Wilton, Sanchez, and Garcia 2013).

Like other identities, *racial identity is emergent.* Your identity is not fixed at birth; rather, it develops over the life course. Your racial identity may even change as you encounter new ideas and new life circumstances, which could lead you to define yourself differently. A White adolescent girl may discover that she has a mixed-race heritage and start hanging out mostly with Black friends, constructing herself as "Black" in the process. Or a second-generation Korean American who was raised to be "American" may leave home for college and begin to explore his Asian heritage. He may take courses in Asian American Studies, surround himself with Asian students from many different backgrounds, and start defining himself as "Asian American." In each of these examples and others, you can see that racial-ethnic identity is emergent and fluid at the same time that it can be quite stable.

The work of developing racial identity addresses a question that White people often ask when they see a group of people of color clustered together in a predominantly White environment, a question exemplified by *Why Are All the Black Kids Sitting Together in the Cafeteria?* This question is the title of psychologist and former college president Beverly Tatum's book (1997). Are Black students sitting together in a predominantly White environment "self-segregating"? Tatum's answer is no. She explains that subordinated groups develop a strong racial identity even when faced with racial and ethnic stereotypes and negative racial encounters.

Tatum's work teaches us that, if you are a minority group member, immersing yourself in the culture of your affinity group is an important part of the process of identity formation. Joining a Latino student organization or participating in the Black student union provides a safe space where people of color can explore and then internalize a positive racial or ethnic identity. This is especially relevant during adolescence and early adulthood when one's identity is being so significantly shaped. If located in a mostly White environment, people of color may surround themselves with symbols and relationships that affirm, not deny, their racial identity. Immersion in one's own group as a minority person is thus a necessary route, according to Tatum, for developing a strong and stable racial identity (Tatum 1997). *Identity safety* is achieved when "people believe their social identity is an asset, rather than a barrier . . . and that they are welcomed, supported and valued whatever their background" (Steele and Cohn-Vargas 2013:5).

Several points summarize this discussion of racial identity:

- *Racial identity emerges in particular social and historical contexts.* C. Wright Mills (1959), in founding one of the central concepts in sociology, identified the central task of sociology as understanding the link between people's lives and the historical and social context in which they lived. The *sociological imagination* reveals this link between biography and history, that is, understanding the patterns and social processes that shape individual lives. In the case of racial identities, dominant groups "set the parameters within which the subordinates operate" (Tatum 1997:23). As a result, people of color have to pay attention to those who control their outcomes. They will be highly attuned to the dynamics of race, while those in the dominant group will take their racial identity for granted—a point we return to below, in a discussion of whiteness.
- *Racial identity is linked to other significant identities.* Gender, age, social class, sexuality, and nationality, among other factors, are also integral parts of our identity. Although one factor may be more salient at a given moment than another, they intersect and overlap, together constituting who we are. A Native American woman does not think of herself as Native at one moment and a woman at another. But if someone makes a disparaging remark about Native people in front of her, her identity as Native may at that moment seem particularly sharp, just as a sexist comment might heighten her gender identity. In a society structured around inequalities of race, class, gender, and sexuality, each of these social facts intersects with the others in forming our identities and our **identity matrix** (Rockquemore 2002; Thomas, Hacker, and Hoxha 2011). Put another way, the matrix is the configuration of social factors that, taken together, constitute one's definition of self.
- *Racial identity is consequential.* Identity is not only who we think we are, but it has outcomes for our well-being—sometimes for the better, sometimes not. People who grow up in a context of being consistently told by powerful people

that they are worthless or incompetent may develop a low sense of self-worth. As a member of a racial-ethnic minority group, this is a risk unless there are countervailing forces within one's family or peer group. Research finds that, although there are psychological risks for people of color growing up in a racist society, developing a strong racial identity is nonetheless beneficial. Numerous studies find that even though society writ large may devalue people of color, having a strong collective attachment as a racial minority can reduce stress, allow a more positive sense of well-being, and help in contending with prevailing racial and ethnic stereotypes (Way et al. 2013).

To sum up, racial identity is multidimensional (Sellers et al. 1998) and linked to the social structure of society. How you see yourself and how others see you happen as people experience how race is constructed in society. Because the social construction of race is such a complex phenomenon, so is the social construction of racial identities. This is particularly revealed when thinking about multiracial identity (see figure 4.1).

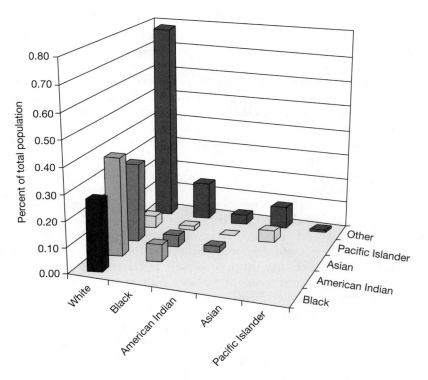

FIG. 4.1 Who's with Who? Multiracial Relationship Combinations

This figure shows you the frequency of different racial-ethnic combinations, as people identified themselves in the U.S. census. Which identities are most common? Least common? Why?

Source: Social Science Data Analysis Network. N.d. "CensusScope—Multiracial Population Statistics." CensusScope. (http://www.censusscope.org/us/chart_multi.html.)

Borders and Binaries: The Complexities of Multiracial Identity

The number of people who define themselves as more than one race is increasing, although the number is still relatively small in official terms. Although official census counts are not a perfect indication of how people define themselves, the number of people who said in the census that they were of more than one race doubled between 2000 and 2010 (from 2.4 to 4.5 percent of the U.S. population). The census of 2000 was the first one in which people could indicate membership in more than one racial and/or ethnic group. It is projected that in a few years a significant number of U.S. citizens will likely have a relative or at least know someone who is of mixed race (Alba 2009). Multiracial people are more likely to live in Hawaii and Alaska; the West and the Southwest, especially California and Oklahoma; and limited pockets on the Atlantic Coast, as you can see in figure 4.2 (also see Brunsma 2006a).

Giving people the option to identify as multiracial in the census resulted from the mobilization of multiracial groups who lobbied hard for greater recognition. Politics around how the Bureau of the Census defines race, debates about race and

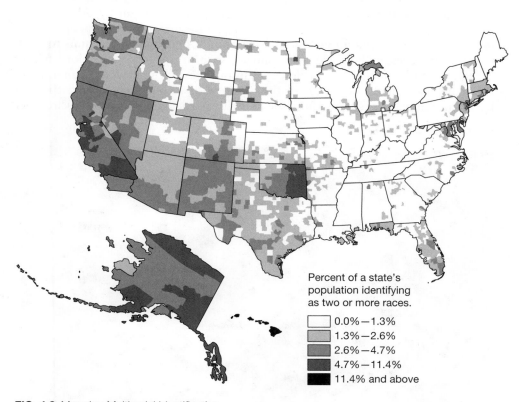

Percent of a state's population identifying as two or more races.

- 0.0%—1.3%
- 1.3%—2.6%
- 2.6%—4.7%
- 4.7%—11.4%
- 11.4% and above

FIG. 4.2 Mapping Multiracial Identification

This map shows the regional distribution of those who define themselves as more than one race. What factors do you think influence this distribution? This map was drawn from 2000 census data; what would you expect to see when the data are available from the 2020 census?

Source: Social Science Data Analysis Network. N.d. "CensusScope—Demographic Maps: Multiracial Population." CensusScope. (http://www.censusscope.org/us/chart_multi.html.)

adoption, the growth of scholarly research on multiracialism, and the popularity of multiracial celebrities such as Tiger Woods fueled this movement and called public attention to multiracial identities (Dalmage 2004; DaCosta 2007; Williams 2006).

People with multiracial identities have had to navigate a black-white binary that has long defined race relations in the United States. Studies of multiracialism actually challenge the binary thinking that earlier defined people as either White or Black. Living on the margins of two or more groups can mean forming a "merged identity" (Root 1992, 1996). For example, how does a woman born to a Black father and a Latina mother define herself? Maybe Latina? Maybe Black? Maybe both? Either way, the person has to establish a racial-ethnic identity in a more complex process than is true for others (Khanna 2011b). One's sense of pride in a particular origin group has a strong influence on whether a person identifies as multiracial or not. For example, children whose parents include an American Indian and someone of another race are more likely to adopt an Indian identity if they live on American Indian homelands (Liebler 2010; Liebler and Zacher 2013).

Identity work is the process by which people construct and maintain positive identities distinct from the negative ones applied to them by others (Snow and Anderson 1987; Goffman 1963). Identity work for multiracial people might involve displaying certain racial or ethnic symbols, making verbal claims to identity, perhaps even making physical changes, such as in one's hair color, style of dress, or even lightening one's skin color. In this way, identity work is an attempt to align oneself with the norms of the group with whom a person most identifies. A multiracial person might associate with particular groups or disclose her

Just as you cannot judge a book by its cover, you should not assess race based on how people look. These two women are non-identical twin sisters.

LIVING WITH RACISM

Racial identity is a complex and shifting way that people see themselves. How do people of mixed backgrounds understand their racial identity? "I just say I'm brown," McKenzi McPherson, 9, says. "And I think, Why do you want to know?" This has been explored in a recent *National Geographic* article:

Maximillian Sugiura, 29, says he responds with whatever ethnicity provides a situational advantage. Loyalties figure in too, especially when one's heritage doesn't show up in phenotypical facial features, hair, or skin. Yudah Holman, 29, self-identifies as half Thai and half black, but marks Asian on forms and always puts Thai first, "because my mother raised me, so I'm really proud of being Thai."

Sandra Williams, 46 [in 2012], grew up at a time when the nation still turned on a black-white axis. The 1960 census depicted a country that was still 99 percent black or white, and when Williams was born six years later to parents of mixed black and white ancestry, 17 states still had laws against interracial marriage. In Williams's western Virginia hometown, there was only one Asian child in her school. To link her own fair skin and hair to her white ancestry, Williams says, would have been seen by blacks as a rejection. And so, though she views race as a social construction, she checks black on the census. "It's what my parents checked," she says.

People with complex cultural and racial origins become more fluid and playful with what they call themselves. On playgrounds and college campuses, you'll find such homespun terms as Blackanese, Filatino, Chicanese, and Korgentinian. When Joshua Ahsoak, 34, attended college, his heritage of Inupiat (Eskimo) and midwestern Jewish earned him the moniker Juskimo, a term he still uses to describe himself (a practicing Jew who breaks kosher dietary laws not for bacon but for walrus and seal meat). Tracey Williams Bautista says her seven-year-old son, Yoel Chac Bautista, identifies himself as black when he's with her, his African-American parent. When he's with his father, he'll say Mexican. "We call him a Blaxican," she jokes, and says she and her husband are raising him in a home where Martin Luther King, Jr., is displayed next to Frida Kahlo. Black relatives warn Williams about the persistence of the one-drop rule, the long-standing practice of seeing anyone with a trace of black "blood" as black. "They say, 'He may be half, but he's still the N word.'"

Source: Funderburg, Lisa. 2013. "The Changing Face of America." *National Geographic* 224(4):80–91.

identity only in certain contexts. Through identity work, biracial people "engage in a range of activities to create, present, or sustain identities that are congruent with or supportive of their self-concept" (see LIVING WITH RACISM; Snow and Anderson 1987:1348; Khanna 2011a).

With more cross-race unions and more people defining themselves in more than one ethnic or racial category, what will this mean for the social construction of race? Only time will tell. Some suggest that America will become a tripartite society composed of Whites, Blacks, and Latinos (Bonilla-Silva 2004; also see chapter 12), but others think the black-white binary will persist, with some groups becoming perceived as "white," while others are "blackened."

Some argue that the focus on generating new categories of racial membership only reinforces the idea of race as an immutable characteristic even while the concept of race is unraveling (Brunsma 2006b). As one critic of the multiracial category has argued, the very nature of African American identity is multiracial, given the millions of African American people who have been conceived through multiracial unions. Some say then that developing a new category of race to acknowledge multiracial identity only reproduces (even if implicitly) the old one drop rule, thereby defining race and "blackness" as somehow fixed or immutable (Spencer 2006). Some also fear that the separation of multiracial people into a distinct category could dilute the civil rights agenda by undercounting those traditionally thought to be African American (Thompson 2007).

Multiracialism underscores the fluidity in the definition of race (Brunsma 2006b; Rockquemore, Brunsma, and Delgado 2009). It reminds us how cultural, social, and political forces shape the very meaning of race in society. Racial boundaries that have been established through law and social practices are actually permeable, even though they are presented to us through the dominant culture as immutable. The complexities of racial identity make this apparent as people try to situate themselves within a racial order that extends far beyond their personal lives. Racial identity, like race, is experienced at the individual (or micro) level, but it is constructed at the macro level.

Out of Many, One: Panethnic Identities

The diversity of racial and ethnic groups in U.S. society has also led to a new form of racial-ethnic identity referred to as panethnicity. **Panethnicity** is the collective identity that is formed when multiple ethnic groups forge a sense of shared belonging, also creating a new name for one's group (Okamoto 2014; Okamoto and Mora 2014:220; Espiritu 1992). As different ethnic, tribal, religious, or national groups come to think of themselves as having a common history or shared political, cultural, or social interests, they may form a panethnic identity. Activists, for example, may use slogans such as "brown power" or "yellow power" to bring together diverse ethnic groups, organized under a single label to wield more collective power (Okamoto and Mora 2014).

There are numerous examples of panethnic identity. Native American is a panethnic identity in that it consolidates the many and very different American Indian nations into a forged sense of being "one." Likewise, Latino, Asian American, "people of color," and, for that matter, African American are also panethnic identities in that they link people together under a single name even when there is great diversity of ethnic, regional, and/or national origin under this umbrella (Ocampo 2014).

Panethnicity is often self-generated, but it can be imposed when a dominant group forces consolidation onto diverse ethnic or tribal groups, usually to delineate group rights. When the British colonized Malaysia, for example, they created the category "Malay" to lump together different ethnic groups and distinguish them from the Chinese. These divisions then determined various group rights—or lack thereof. The former Soviet Union also created "Russian" people even when people from the various nations that made up the former Soviet Union would have defined themselves as Ukrainian, Armenian, or other nationalities from within the federated states of the former Soviet Union. These examples show how panethnicity can be the result of government actions that consolidate the power of a dominant group (Okamoto and Mora 2014).

A panethnic label, especially when self-generated, is strongly associated with a sense of a common history and a linked fate, including the idea that the fate of others in the group affects you (Wong et al. 2011; Okamoto and Mora 2014:223). When panethnicity is imposed, not self-generated, people are more likely to hold on to their original identity. Panethnicity allows groups to present a united front, especially when they see themselves as mistreated by more powerful groups. In other words, they develop an identity as "insiders" even while being perceived as "outsiders" by the dominant culture.

Panethnic identity can also emerge in response to racial discrimination. People who migrate from Latin America, for example, may not initially think of themselves as Hispanic or Latino. If they encounter discrimination once they enter the United States, they are more likely to develop a Hispanic/Latino identity (Golash-Boza and Darity 2008). In her seminal study of panethnicity, Yen Le Espiritu describes Asian American panethnicity as "the development of bridging organizations and solidarities among several ethnic and immigrant groups of Asian ancestry" (1992:14). Her work presents panethnicity as a response to widespread anti-Asian violence and discrimination. Panethnicity among Asian Americans provides a consciousness of collective social standing, even though diverse Asian people may have previously thought of themselves as Korean, Chinese, Japanese, or some other more specific Asian origin. With too many subgroups to be effective, people sometimes organize under a panethnic label to be more able to unite against a common oppressor.

Within the United States, panethnic identity has grown in recent years as diverse groups have mobilized to grow and protect their civil rights. Two-thirds of Asian Americans now use the *panethnic* term as part of their identification (Lien, Conway, and Wong 2003). In the early 1990s, only 40 percent of Mexican Americans, Puerto Ricans, and Cuban Americans identified with panethnic labels, by 2008, the percentage had doubled to over 80 percent (Fraga 2012; Jones-Correa and Leal 1996; Tienda and Ortiz 1986).

The extent to which people embrace panethnic identity differs within particular groups. Among immigrants, younger generations may be more likely to adopt a panethnic identity as parents try to hold on to their national identity. Among Latinos, those in the second generation and those with higher levels of education and income are more likely to identify as Latino or Hispanic (de La Garza 1992; Jones-Correa and Leal 1996; Portes and MacLeod 1996). An increasing number of first-generation Latino immigrants now identify as panethnic. Cuban Americans, though, are less likely than Mexican Americans and Puerto Ricans to identify as Hispanic or Latino (Fraga et al. 2010; Fraga 2012). Among Asian Americans, class and educational differences correlate with panethnic identity (Kibria 2003; Lee 2004; Lien, Conway, and Wong 2003; Masuoka 2006). Among Asian Americans, Koreans are the most likely to identify with panethnicity; Japanese, the least likely (Wong et al. 2011).

Sometimes members of a group will adopt a panethnic identity to assert what they are not. For example, a study of Arab Americans in Detroit found that Arab Americans have adopted a panethnic identity because they do not want to be thought of as "white" (Ajrouch and Jamal 2007). Some African immigrants to the United States also reject an African American identity because they see themselves as having unique values and aspirations. They identify instead as African (Imoagene 2012).

Single-ethnic and panethnic identities can also exist side by side, being separately exercised at different times and in different situations. A specific encounter or context may make one feel more affiliated with his or her subgroup identity, whereas in other contexts, one might embrace a more collective identity. These different identities are then interlocking and simultaneous (Espiritu 1992; Vo 2004; Nakano 2013).

Panethnic labels can be quite controversial. Many Chicanos, for example, vehemently object to being called Latino, wanting instead to hold on to their specific group history and identity. Chicano activist groups in the U.S. Southwest have viewed Hispanic and Latino labels as a threat to their nationalist projects (Oboler 1995). Some Cubans also object to being called Hispanic, as seen in the bumper stickers that have appeared throughout Miami declaring, "Don't call me Hispanic, I'm Cuban" (Okamoto and Mora 2014:223). Studies of American Indians also confirm the importance of one's "home" identity. In other words, the pride that one feels in being a part of a particular ethnic group can override any political interest in becoming part of a panethnic collectivity.

Some groups may also fear that adopting a panethnic label will lead to their group being racialized. Some West Indians, for example, do not want to be considered "Black" because of the racism associated with that group status. Panethnicity is usually self-created, but racialization is something that happens to you through the action of others. Rejecting panethnicity can be a way of protecting oneself and one's group against the ravages of racism (Itzigsohn 2004; Itzigsohn and Dore-Cabral 2000). Indeed, panethnicity and the racialization process go hand in hand because, without the backdrop of a society marked by race and racism, panethnicity would not likely emerge (Brown and Jones 2015).

Research on panethnicity, like that on multiracial identity, underscores how fluid racial identities can be. Because identity emerges through group interaction and one's social, historical, and political context, racial identity for some can change over time. Fundamentally, understanding panethnicity underscores the point that racial identities are constructed via group interrelationships and boundaries (Okamoto and Mora 2014).

Who's White and Why Does It Matter?
Whiteness and White Privilege

Until now, we have largely been looking at racial identity for people of color. If you are White, do you think of yourself as having a race? Perhaps you do, although it is not likely to be something that you think about very often. People of color certainly think of you as White; it is very likely one of the first things they take note of when meeting you, given the decades of distrust that have marked Black-White relations. Unlike racial minority identities, race is typically not a salient identity for White people. That is, White people are usually not very conscious of their racial status because they can take it for granted in a society where whiteness brings certain privileges and advantages, regardless of whether one thinks about it or not (Wise 2008).

You can see this based on a simple test. In this experiment, research subjects are asked to list twenty responses to the simple question, "Who am I?" How would you answer? This is known as the Twenty Statements Test (TST). First developed in the

1950s, the TST has been used to study people's most salient identities. Theoretically, the more important a particular identity is, the more likely someone will list it. How close something is to the top of the list also reveals the salience of a given identity.

The TST can also be used to compare the salience of identities for different groups. Over the years, researchers have found that people in racial or ethnic minority groups almost always mention that aspect of themselves, and mention it near the top of their list. White people rarely do either one (Tatum 1997). More specifically, half of Whites never mention their race, whereas hardly any Black Americans (only 12 percent) say race never crosses their mind (Forman 2004; Forman and Lewis 2006). Simply put, racial identity is far more salient for members of minority groups than for White people, even though the salience of racial identity varies for different groups and at different points in time (Steck, Heckert, and Heckert 2003).

White identity has been called "transparent" (Doane and Bonilla-Silva 2003; Flagg 1997). Whiteness establishes an invisible norm, meaning that it usually goes unexamined.[3] Whiteness bestows specific and unquestioned privileges and expectations, even though people assume whiteness to be "raceless." The reality is, though, that race is operative even when only White people are present (Andersen 2003). Here's a somewhat trivial yet telling example: If you do a generic search on Google for an image such as "hand," "finger," or "woman," the images default to white. To date, the campaign to change this has had no effect.

Although White people do not see their race as salient, it certainly is. Even when White people do not take note of their race, people of color will see it as salient, just as men do not typically see their gender status but women do. As we will see next, White people benefit from their racial status even when they are not conscious of their **white privilege,** the social, cultural, and economic benefits that White people accrue relative to others in a society marked by racial hierarchy. The few White people who understand this are more likely to support policies designed to alleviate racial inequality (Bunyasi 2015).

Peggy McIntosh (1988) has called white privilege the "invisible backpack," something White people carry around with them but do not see. McIntosh has listed the many ways—large and small—that whiteness confers privilege. For example, when a White person does something wrong, it will not be attributed to the person's race. See additional examples in "White Privilege: The Invisible Backpack."

How did the idea of whiteness come to exist? People have long had so-called white skin, but the idea of people being white is relatively recent. It originated in the eighteenth century, when notions of race were first developed (see chapter 1; also, Painter 2010). Like other meanings of race, "white" is an idea and an identity that was invented in the context of racial inequality and perceived difference. Prior to the invention of "white," people in Western Europe were known by their tribe or ethnicity: Celts, Gauls, Phoenicians, Greeks, Romans, and so forth (Painter 2010). With the development of slavery in the New World, "white" developed as a way of distinguishing categories of laborers; White people were free or indentured, but Black slaves were not.

---

[3] By now you will have noticed that White is capitalized when referring to a proper noun. See the preface for a discussion of why.

WHITE PRIVILEGE

The Invisible Backpack

Peggy McIntosh's influential work on white privilege includes a list of some of the ways that white privilege is manifested in everyday life; examples are shown below. If you were making such a list, what would you add?

- I can go shopping pretty sure that I will not be followed or harassed.
- In the media, I can see people like me well represented.
- I can dress in used clothes or sloppy outfits without people attributing my look to my bad morals.
- I can remain oblivious to the heritage of people of color.
- I can be pretty sure that if I speak to "the person in charge," I will be facing a person of my race.
- If I am stopped for speeding, I will not feel like I have been singled out because of my race.
- I can easily buy greeting cards, books, toys, and so forth that represent people like me.
- I can take a job without someone saying I got the position because of my race.
- I can be fairly sure that if I need medical or legal help, my race will not work against me.

Source: Adapted from McIntosh, Peggy. 1988. "White Privilege and Male Privilege: A Personal Account of Coming to See Correspondences through Work in Women's Studies." Working Paper 189. Wellesley, MA: Wellesley Centers for Women.

Who gets defined as White and, thus, benefits from the privilege of being White? As we have seen, the meaning of racial categories shifts over time. Some groups now perceived as White were once considered to be otherwise. Like other racial and ethnic groups, "white" is not a monolithic category and not all White people benefit equally from white privilege. Also, although some groups may not define themselves as White, if successful, they may be treated as such. In this regard, the "borders of whiteness are expanding" (Gallagher 2004:60), meaning that some groups, such as middle-class Asian Americans, become perceived as like Whites because of their economic and social success. In this sense, "white" has more to do with privilege than skin color per se (Zhou 2004). But, just as the borders of whiteness can expand, can they also contract, "blackening" those who are unable to make their way?

In a related vein, some people may define themselves as White but not be seen by others as such. A telling example comes from a study by Nicholas Vargas. Vargas asked a national sample of Latinos how they identified themselves and how they perceived others as defining them. Vargas found that 40 percent of Latinos identified as White, but only 6 percent said that others saw them as White. In other words, although a significant number of Latinos self-identify as White, others usually defined them as Hispanic. There was a much greater likelihood of Latinos being perceived by others as White if they had lighter skin and a higher socioeconomic status (Vargas 2015). Vargas's research findings are similar to those found for other groups. Dominicans in the United States, for example, are likely to define themselves as Hispano/a or Indio/a, but others simply perceive them as Black (Itzigsohn, Gorguli, and Vazquez 2005).

How can White people become allies for building a more racially just society? To develop an antiracist identity White people first have to recognize institutional racism. Once they do so, however, it might be easier to fall back into preconceived ideas than to become allies for racial justice. Becoming an ally does mean taking some risks—including the risk that White people feel just talking about race. More often than not, Whites will remain silent about race, afraid they will say the wrong thing. Ignoring race and racism, however, just reaffirms its presence. For White people to become racial allies means taking several steps: recognizing the invisibility of their own racial identity, acknowledging the privilege that comes with being White, identifying their own learned racism, and taking responsibility for social change (Ford and Orlandella 2015).

The Consequences of Color

The study of whiteness teaches us that having light skin matters. A system of advantage accrues to people identified as White. We see this in how people in various racial and ethnic groups may be judged and treated differently within their own groups based on the *tone* of their skin. The phenomenon is called **colorism,** "the discriminatory treatment of individuals falling within the same 'racial group' on the basis of skin color" (Herring 2004:3).

Colorism is based on the higher value placed on so-called European, or white, features. Although colorism is an issue that people within racial-ethnic communities may not want to acknowledge (at least not outside of their own group), it is a phenomenon with notable consequences, including how people's appearance is judged. Lighter-skinned people tend to reach higher income and educational levels than those with darker skin (Herring, Keith, and Horton 2004; Hochschild and Weaver 2007).

Colorism does not just occur within the United States. In Latin American societies, skin color is a factor of the stratification system, with those of darker color holding lower status. In India, darker-skinned Hindus have experienced particularly strong prejudice and discrimination (Herring, Keith, and Horton 2004; Hall 1995).

The origins of colorism lie in the history of European colonialism throughout the Western world and in the development of slavery in North America. These patterns of conquest and enslavement, as we know, were based on a system of white supremacy. That would make it seem particularly capricious for people of color to judge others in their group by the shade of their skin, but there is little doubt that this happens. To some degree, being light- rather than dark-skinned has historically provided higher status for African Americans *within* the African American community.

In Latin America and Mexico, colorism began with the Spanish conquest of indigenous people. Spanish colonialists justified their domination through an ideology that portrayed native, darker-skinned people as savage and heathen (Chavez-Duenas, Adames, and Organista 2014; Hunter 2007, 2004). In the United States, White slave owners also assigned labor according to relative color. They might also have extended some privileges to mixed-race children whom they had fathered (Hunter 2004; Billingsley 1968).

The complexity of color stratification is especially apparent in Brazil where color and class have become intermixed. As the result of this complex system of stratification, a person considered Black in the United States might not be considered so in Brazil. Being "Black" in Brazil is a much fuzzier category. In Brazil, people are more likely to use the term "color" than to think of color as race. Nonetheless, as with race in the United States, color in Brazil has particular consequences for one's social status and relative privilege or advantage. Color differences in Brazil are also used to refer to the entire population, whereas in the United States, shades of color are only thought of within minority racial or ethnic groups (Telles 2009). In the United States, for example, White people do not differentiate among themselves in terms of skin tone.

Differences in how color is considered in Brazil and the United States are the result of specific histories in both places, emphasizing again how racial identity is dependent on specific social contexts. In the American Southwest, Anglos (White people of non-Hispanic descent) were more willing to grant citizenship to lighter-skinned Mexicans than to darker-skinned Mexican laborers (Hunter 2004). To this day, Mexican Americans and Asians—particularly darker men—report lower earnings and more experiences of discrimination (Ortiz and Telles 2008; Edwards, Carter-Tellison, and Herring 2004).

Now as in the past, skin tone is also connected to standards of beauty (Craig 2002; Thompson and Keith 2001). Successful women of color have to appear "more white." Popular stars Jennifer Lopez, Beyoncé, and Christina Aguilera, for example, have become more blond and thin as they have become more successful (Vargas 2010). The growing use of skin-lightening products is also evidence of the perceived importance of light skin among women of color (Glenn 2008; Hill 2002, 2000).

Colorism and racism are clearly interrelated because colorism stems from a system of racial inequality. They are not, however, the same thing. Racism is an institutionalized system of exploitation. Although colorism differentiates people based on skin tone, colorism has not structured social institutions nor denied people rights based solely on their membership in particular groups. Certainly, colorism involves judgments about people, but it is a manifestation of racism, not an institutionalized system of inequality.

With an increase in the number of multiracial people, will colorism persist? Perhaps not, if there is greater acceptance of multiracial people, but judgments about people based on skin color have been obstinate. If nothing else, this discussion of color emphasizes once again how race is constructed through specific social and historical behaviors.

It's the Little Things That Count: Racial Microaggressions

The patterns of race in society are everywhere around you—in your head, in your self-concept, and in the interactions you have with others. Where there are common and repetitive behaviors that minimize, ignore, or insult people of color, there is *everyday racism* (adapted from Essed 1991:52). Everyday racism happens in encounters between dominant and subordinate groups. These behaviors happen at the individual or micro level, but they take place in the context of a power structure.

It is usually harder for dominant groups to see how racism is played out in everyday life. The invisibility of racism to dominant groups has been compared to the presence of spikes in some parking lots: The spikes are hardly apparent as long as you go in the right direction, but they will shred your tires if you drive over them backward (Wah et al. 1994). Like the tire spikes, everyday racism can go unnoticed by White people who easily "flow" with the system. For people of color they are a constant reminder of one's status to those who are "other."

The behaviors of everyday racism are what are now called **microaggressions**, "brief and commonplace daily verbal, behavioral, or environmental indignities, whether intentional or unintentional, that communicate hostile, derogatory, or negative racial slights and insults toward people of color" (Sue et al. 2007:271; Sue 2010). These can be momentary and subtle exchanges, possibly not even recognized by the offender. Although often unintentional, they reflect how stereotypes are activated in the minds and, thus, in the behavior of dominant groups. Something as seemingly innocuous as a nonverbal exchange, such as the White woman who clutches her bag tightly as a Black man approaches, is an ongoing reminder to him of his presumed status.

There are countless examples of microaggression. Ignoring what a Black woman says in a meeting, assuming a Latina to be the maid or a Black man to be a servant at a party, a store clerk following a Black woman but not a White woman around a shop: All of these and many more that people of color experience on a routine basis are examples of microaggression. They may seem small to some, but they add up and, in the context of racial inequality, the seemingly simplest things take on greater meaning. Also, what may seem perfectly acceptable and normal to people of the same social status may be insulting and offensive when the very same behavior occurs between people of unequal status—such as calling a man a "boy"—highly demeaning when a White person refers to a Black person in this way, but probably only a term of endearment or kidding around between friends of equal status. You saw another example of this when presidential candidate Donald Trump referred to Mexican immigrants as "bad hombres." Almost instantaneously, opponents of Trump who were peers to one another seized this language, using it to reflect "insider status" and as a political statement against Trump's microaggressions.

Microaggressions have to be understood in the context of power relationships. For example, everyone has probably at some point had the experience of getting slow service in a restaurant, but people of color may experience this on a routine basis. Any one instance of such slow service can trigger a reminder of one's status in society (Allen 2013; Gutiérrez y Muhs et al. 2012). If the person of color so offended mentions this to a White person, the White person may say, "It is no big deal" or "You're wearing race on your sleeve," thus diminishing the person of color's experience—which may consist of much more negativity than this one single instance. Further, the result for the person of color is yet another microaggression!

Derand Wing Sue and his colleagues, who have extensively studied microaggressions, describe them as occurring in three ways: micro insults, micro assaults, and micro invalidations. *Micro insults* are interactions that convey stereotypes and biased messages. In a cross-race interaction, this could be a situation in which a dominant group member treats the other as second class, unimportant, stupid, incompetent, or perhaps even criminal. A White student, for example, who disregards the authority of a Black professor or who presumes that the Latina professor is somehow less competent than the White man is engaging in a micro insult. In a work environment, the absence of symbols that depict people like you can also be a micro insult.

The second type of microaggression is a *micro assault*. These are explicit remarks or behaviors that disparage and insult people. Using racial epithets, serving White people before people of color, and name-calling are examples. Asking students in a classroom to "speak for their race" is another example (McCabe 2009). Such micro assaults are very similar to old styles of racism in that they tend to be more deliberate and conscious than other forms of microaggression.

Finally, Sue and his colleagues discuss *micro invalidations*. These are comments and behavior that negate the experience of a person of color. An example might be a comment such as "I never see a person's color" or "Gee, you speak good English." Such comments invalidate the person of color's experience even while heightening his or her identity as someone "different."

Microaggressions can be directed against various groups, including women, gays and lesbians, and disabled people. Although these everyday expressions of racism are more subtly expressed than overt racism, they have serious consequences—in the form of stress, anger, or simply the avoidance of others. Researchers who have studied microaggressions conclude that they are cumulative, weighing on people of color, and becoming a "never-ending burden" (Pierce et al. 1978:66; Solórzano, Ceja, and Yosso 2000).

Microaggression can also affect how people of color act in mixed-race settings. It can also affect people's performance, such as on examinations or in workplaces (Basford, Offermann, and Behrend 2014). One example comes from research on Asian American undergraduates in elite universities. Asian students in "white institutional space" typically encounter racism, but seldom challenge it. Especially for Asian American women, the mix of racism and sexism in such environments is demeaning at the least and can be highly traumatic (Chou, Lee, and Ho 2015).

The stress of dealing with microaggression even has physiological consequences. Studies find that Black people's level of stress increases (measured in biometric ways) when interacting with White people. There are also physiological consequences for White people as the result of interracial tensions: When interacting with Black people, White people's heart rate increases (Blascovich et al. 2001; Markus and Conner 2013). Clearly, we would all be better off if we could understand and stop the everyday actions that produce such results. Some do, as we will now see in a brief discussion of interracial friendships.

Who Do You Know? Interracial Friendships

When you make a friend, you are probably not thinking about the social forces that make that friendship possible or that influence whether it will last. Even though you may be unaware of them, those social forces are present, including the social forces of race and racism. Whether or not you even have friends from a different racial or ethnic background is influenced by race.

Take a wedding party. Your wedding is about as personal as an occasion can get. You are probably going to invite your best friends to be your bridesmaids or groomsmen.

Research finds that integrated wedding parties are quite unusual, an unobtrusive measure of the degree to which close, interracial friendships are formed.

Will they be the same race as you? A clever study of more than one thousand published wedding photographs found in a random search on the web reveals the paucity of inter-racial friendships, at least as indicated by the racial makeup of each bridal party. Only 3.7 percent of White brides, but 22 percent of Black brides, had a friend from another race who was close enough to be in their wedding party. Whites are only half as likely to have Black friends among their guests as Blacks are to include White friends. Blacks are also more likely to invite Asians than Whites into their wedding party, but Asians are only one-fifth as likely to invite Blacks (Berry 2011). While such a study, based as it is on photographs, can only determine race based on appearance, it is an interesting indication of the influence of race on close friendship patterns.

Social science research can teach us about the conditions under which cross-race relationships are most likely to be made. Figure 4.3 shows you that younger generations tend to get along better with others than is true for older generations.

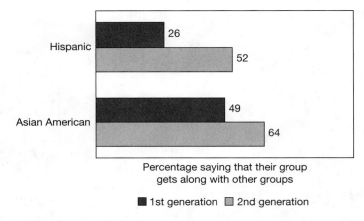

FIG. 4.3 Why Can't We All Get Along? Do Generations Matter?

How well does your group get along with other groups? This graph shows the percentages of first- and second-generation Hispanics and Asian Americans who say their group gets along well with other groups.

Sources: Pew Research Center. 2012b. *2012 National Survey of Latinos.* Washington, DC: Pew Research Center; Pew Research Center. 2012a. *2012 Asian American Survey.* Washington, DC: Pew Research Center.

By far one of the most important factors predicting cross-race friendships is residential and educational segregation (Kim and White 2010). Studies have found that among elementary school children interracial friendships become more common as the student body approaches an equal mix (de Souza 2007; Mouw and Entwisle 2006; Quillian and Campbell 2003). People who have experienced interracial contact in schools and neighborhoods are also more likely as adults to have racially diverse friendship circles, although this pattern does not hold for Asian Americans (Emerson, Kimbro, and Yancey 2002). Within schools, educational tracking also results in a lower probability of students forming interracial friendships because tracking tends to separate racial groups (Stearns, Buchmann, and Bonneau 2009). You can see in Figure 4.4 that the odds of forming an interracial friendship in school are not that good relative to the actual racial mix of people in schools.

Segregated patterns of friendship can, however, be changed by engaging students in programs and activities that bring different groups together. Researchers have found that extracurricular activities that engage people of different backgrounds in common activities build more interracial ties. Socializing with coworkers, engaging in diverse civic activities, and attending multiracial religious services are also linked to more cross-race friendships (Tavares 2011). In college, students who enter college having already had interracial connections through participation in sports, the arts, and political activities are more likely than other students to build cross-race friendships in college (Benediktsson 2012).

Interaction between people of different racial-ethnic backgrounds can be challenging. Anxiety about interacting with people from different backgrounds, as well as the fear of rejection, are obstacles to people establishing cross-race friends. These obstacles to friendship can be overcome, however, as demonstrated by a very interesting study of friendship building. In a clever experiment, social psychologists put

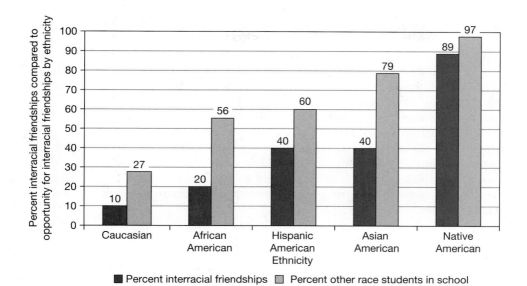

FIG. 4.4 Taking a Chance: What Are the Odds of Having an Interracial Friendship?

This chart shows the percentage of students of other races in schools, compared to the actual percentage of interracial friendships formed. As you can see, the possibility for cross-race friendships is greater than the realization of such friendships. How would you describe the reasons for this gap?

Sources: Page-Gould, Elizabeth. 2004. *Research on Cross-Race Relationships: An Annotated Bibliography.* (http://greatergood.berkeley.edu/article/item/cross-race_relationships_an_annotated_bibliography); Joyner, Kara, and Grace Kao. 2005. "Interracial Relationships and the Transition to Adulthood." *American Sociological Review* 70(4):563–81.

Latino and White college students (otherwise unknown to each other) in a laboratory setting where the students engaged in closeness-building tasks over a period of three weeks. Prior to the shared activity, the investigators measured the students' level of implicit prejudice, background characteristics, and levels of anxiety (measured by physiological indicators). Following the three weeks of friendship-building activities, the students kept a ten-day diary, recording their interactions with people outside of the laboratory. Interestingly, it was students who were the most prejudiced at the beginning of the study who reported seeking out more cross-group interactions in the weeks following the initial experiment. Their anxiety levels were also significantly reduced (Page-Gould, Mendoza-Denton, and Tropp 2008).

Such a study shows that people can learn to cross the boundaries of race. Other studies also find that once students have acquired more cross-group friends in their first two years of college, they experience far less anxiety and are more likely to interact with people from a different race by the end of their four years in college (Levin, Laar, and Sidanius 2003). Studies also find that although attitudes have an impact on the formation of interracial friendships, campus diversity is important in predicting friendship patterns. Having a cross-race roommate, experiencing more interracial contact in residence halls, and participating in various interracial extracurricular activities are strongly related to the formation of interracial friendships

(Stearns, Buchmann, and Bonneau 2009). Students of color on campus have more diversity in their friendships than do White students, but this usual difference nearly disappears when schools are more diverse (Fischer 2008).

For people of color, having friends *within* one's own racial-ethnic group is also important. Researchers found, for example, that Black and Asian American middle schoolers who have *only* cross-race friendships report lower emotional well-being than those whose best friends are of their race (McGill, Way, and Hughes 2012). Friendship patterns also differ for African American, Latino, and Asian American adolescents. Latino and Black adolescents tend to establish and maintain friendships for a longer time than do Asian adolescents. Among people of color, Asian American adolescents are also least likely to form close friendships, especially if they are discouraged by their parents from spending time with friends outside of school (Way et al. 2005).

Multiracial youth have unique challenges in establishing friends. If they are rejected by their single-race peers, they will have smaller friendship networks. But, multiracial adolescents also form more racially diverse friendship networks than single-race adolescents, and they are more likely to bridge or socially connect with diverse friendship networks. Biracial adolescents with Black ancestry also have an especially high rate of friendship, forming bridges between Black persons and people in other racial groups (Quillian and Redd 2009).

There is some evidence to suggest that interracial relationships are difficult to maintain. In general, interracial friends report engaging in fewer shared activities than do intraracial friends (Kao and Joyner 2004). Interracial friendships are less likely to be reciprocal, that is, characterized by both people reporting the other as a friend (Vaquera and Kao 2008; Rude 2010).

Despite the interpersonal challenges that racism presents in the making of cross-race friendships, these connections are good for you. Interracial contact in the form of friendship brings more interracial closeness. For people of color it can diminish the effects of perceived discrimination (Tropp 2007). For Whites, interracial friendship is also related to a whole host of transforming attitudes about racial issues, such as acceptance of interracial marriage, a topic examined in chapter 7 (Jacobson and Johnson 2006). All told, interracial friendship is one path to eliminating the fears, misunderstanding, and mistrust that racism produces.

Conclusion

As you have seen, race and racial identity are changing in U.S. society. A black-white model of race relations no longer makes sense of the complex, shifting, and emergent forms that racial identities and interactions are taking. Throughout this chapter, you have seen that racial identities develop—and potentially shift—in a context where the social meaning of race per se is also evolving. Attention to racial identity thus necessarily hinges on the particular constellation of racial meanings that exist at any given time in society.

Even in this kaleidoscope of racial meanings, the one thing that persists is that, as one sociologist has put it, "race is both deeply personal and strongly political" (Dalmage 2004:5). The meaning of race and, therefore, the meaning of racial identities is complex and sometimes blurry as new groups enter society, intermarry, and change how they think about race. One simply cannot understand racial identity—either one's own or identities writ large—without understanding the structural and material realities of race (Lewis 2004). The next section of this book moves from examining race on micro levels to the structural and institutional systems of race in America.

Key Terms

colorism, 85

identity, 71

identity contingency, 73

identity matrix, 75

identity work, 78

microaggressions, 87

minority group, 72

panethnicity, 80

racial identity, 72

white privilege, 83

Critical Thinking Questions

1. Do you think the increasing numbers of people with multiracial identities will reduce racism in the United States? Why or why not?
2. Does creating new categories to count "race" reify the idea that race is "real" and not a social construction? How can we recognize racial differences without stumbling into racism?
3. Are there some groups in contemporary society who seem to have the privileges of "whiteness" even if they are not White? What does this teach you about the social construction of whiteness?

Student Exercises

4.1: Ask a mixed-race group of individuals to try the Twenty Statements Test. Simply ask them to write down everything they think of to answer the question, "Who am I?" Once they have done so, ask them to note their race and gender at the bottom of the page. Then, compare people in different groups, analyzing whether or not people listed their racial and/or ethnic identities. How near the top of the answers were racial and ethnic identities for those who named them? Do you see any (other) patterns? How do you explain your findings?

4.2: Do you have a friend (or more than one) from a different racial background than your own? If so, how did you meet? What were the social conditions that enabled this friendship to be formed? If you do not have such friends, what conditions have prevented such a friendship?

Challenging Questions/Open to Debate

Census counts are important for purposes of representation and apportionment of seats in Congress. Some argue that creating new census categories to count multiracial people weakens the representation of others, especially African Americans. Others think, to the contrary, that multiracial people need to be recognized on their own terms. If you were the director of the census, what would you do, and why?

CHAPTER 5

Diverse Histories/Common Threads

Race and Ethnicity Build a Nation

As Americans, we originally came from many different shores, and our diversity has been at the center of the making of America.
—Ronald Takaki (1993)

What would it take for you to uproot yourself, perhaps leave your family behind, and travel across an ocean or a desert to settle in a new place? Can you imagine being seized by an agent of a shipping company, forced to walk hundreds of miles, and then put into the cargo hold of a ship, crammed together with hundreds of others, and taken thousands of miles away to work for nothing, that is, if you survived the horrific journey at all? In another scenario, what if your land was seized, your home was declared part of another nation, and you were then stripped all of your rights?

Each scenario describes the experiences by which some groups became a part of the United States. The scenarios describe the cruel realities of parts of our nation's history. The diverse racial and ethnic groups who today make up this nation have origins that are a tale of exploitation, forced labor, seizure of lands, and, in many cases, death and extermination. At the same time, U.S. history is also a tale of opportunity seeking, community building, and achievement against the odds. Our nation's most horrid historic episodes are behind us, but understanding the present realities of race and ethnicity requires knowing something about the origins of our diverse population.

Different racial and ethnic groups have unique histories in the United States. Of course, it would be impossible to provide even a brief historical account of all of them in a single chapter of a single book, but certain aspects are common to all.

One aspect is *labor*. How people worked and what various groups provided to build this nation are a critical part of the history of race and ethnicity—indeed, the nation's history. Slavery, indentured servitude, contract labor, and being niched into particular forms of work are how racial and ethnic groups have become part of this society.

A second aspect in this mosaic of history is *property*. Whether losing property, being treated as property, or trying to hold or gain property, different groups have specific relationships to patterns of ownership. Property might be in the form of land, but it can also be in the form of money and other financial resources. Our racial-ethnic history has created vast property for some, robbed others of what they held, and provided little, if any, to others. As you will see, the accumulation of property by some, even at the expense of others, has been one of the driving forces of U.S. history.

A third aspect in the history of different groups is *social control*. Whether through armed conflict, violence, the use of law, or the propagation of controlling belief systems, powerful groups have used their resources to control the lives of others. Indeed, labor, property, and social control are part of the fabric of U.S. history. One group might work the land for a more powerful group, resulting in the accumulation of property for those who use their power to create laws and social practices that control the labor and lives of others.

You can see the influence of the quest for labor, property, and social control in the concept of **settler colonialism**, which refers to the process by which newcomers try to acquire land and property for the purpose of forming new communities even while overpowering indigenous (native) communities. They do so through the social control of others—often a group whose racial and/or ethnic identity differs from that of the colonist. Frequently in this process, indigenous groups such as American Indians become racialized through an ideological process that is part of the newly imposed social control. Settler colonialism has marked not only U.S. history but also the global processes of the acquisition of labor and property over the long course of world history. As we will see below, in the histories of diverse groups within the United States, settler colonialism typically means containing others, erasing their indigenous culture, terrorizing people, and, in the extreme, removing them or moving them to places where their labor is needed (Glenn 2015).

As you think about the history of the diverse races and ethnicities in the United States, you will see that settler colonialism and the dynamics of property, labor, and social control run throughout the experiences of each racial-ethnic minority group. We turn now to the brief discussion of each group's history that is necessary for understanding the foundation on which the nation was built.

Land of the Free, Home of Native Americans

Of all the racial-ethnic groups in the United States, American Indians and, as you will see, some Mexican Americans are the only people who are indigenous to the United States—that is, native to this land. Estimates of the number of Native Americans in the earliest years are impossible to know but are guessed to be anywhere from one to ten million people. Some Indian societies were nomadic, moving (perhaps seasonally) for food and water and because of climate. Others built great nations with vast amounts of land and natural resources. Given the great diversity of Native societies, how communities were organized and governed varied, depending on the different conditions that groups faced (Takaki 1993).

When Europeans first came to the Americas, Native tribes were widely scattered, especially in what is now the United States. In Latin America, Indians were more numerous and organized in larger communities. With the migration of Europeans to the Americas, conquest and the clash of cultures became the dominant pattern. Over time, the population of Native Americans was decimated by disease, war, and removal from their homelands. In fact, the history of Native American and European relations can be mostly described as one of conquest, famine, and genocide. Native Americans' traditional way of life was brutally crushed.

Sociologist Matt Snipp (1996) outlines five periods that frame and help us understand Native American history: *removal, assimilation, the Indian New Deal, termination/relocation,* and *self-determination.* When the first U.S. colonies settled in what are now Virginia and Massachusetts, there was a period of relative harmony between the new colonists and the Native groups (Philbrick 2006). But any semblance of harmony soon dissipated with the expansion of the European population, the federal government's increased political and military capability, and White desire for more territory.

During the period of *removal*, the U.S. federal government negotiated various treaties that forced Native groups to relinquish their lands, pushing those in the east to the west. As much as Native nations fought for their survival, with the expansion of the United States to the western frontier, removal became an even more explicit policy of the federal government. During the Andrew Jackson presidency, in 1830, Congress passed the **Indian Removal Act**, mandating the removal of all Indian groups to the area identified as Indian Territory (now the state of Oklahoma). In the now infamous "Trail of Tears" (in 1838) over seventeen thousand Cherokees were forced to leave their homes and march to Indian Territory; half died from cold, disease, and starvation. Those who survived this period witnessed the devastation of long-standing community structures by the federal removal policy, which left former societies of Native people profoundly disrupted.

As the result of federal policies, by the nineteenth century Native Americans were near extinction. Those who remained were isolated on Indian reservations where their lives were bleak. White reformers actually argued that the government should "humanely ease American Indians into extinction" (Snipp 1996:392), thus ushering in the period of *assimilation*. The federal government wanted Native Americans to adopt the dominant culture and relinquish their traditions and ways of life. The government created the Bureau of Indian Affairs to "civilize" Indians— forcing them into Christianity, educating them to adopt so-called American values, and trying to inculcate the value of private property (Snipp 1996). Indian boarding schools were created to indoctrinate Indian children who were, as a result, removed from their parents' homes and educated to think that European cultural values were superior to those of tribal nations.

In 1887, the Congress passed the General Allotment Act, otherwise known as the Dawes Act. The stated purpose of this law was to integrate Indians into the mainstream, but it did so by forcing them to relinquish communal property. The government seized over ninety million acres of Indian land (two-thirds of all Indian land at the time), thus further isolating Native American groups who were then scattered across remote reservations (Snipp 1996).

In the 1930s the *Indian New Deal* reversed the allotment process and acknowledged the value of traditional tribal cultures. A component of President Franklin Roosevelt's New Deal, the Indian New Deal briefly brought some relief to Native Americans, including support for various infrastructure improvements. Federal programs such as the Civilian Conservation Corps and the Works Progress Administration that benefitted countless numbers of other Americans also benefitted Indians, but only for a short period of time. In 1934, passage of the *Indian Reorganization Act* allowed tribal governments to be self-governing. The Act was not without controversy, because some Indians thought that the law imposed on reservations an "alien form of government—representative democracy" (Snipp 1996:393).

Following World War II, Congress tried to terminate all special relationships with Indian tribes, including all reservations. Native Americans vigorously opposed such changes; only two reservations were actually abolished. Still, the federal government pursued policies that encouraged Indians to move to urban areas. Those policies, coupled with the dire need to find jobs, meant that many Indians left reservations only to encounter urban poverty. This period of *termination/relocation* can still be seen in the fact that the vast majority of American Indians (80 percent, according to the Bureau of the Census) live in urban areas. Although many have moved to urban areas in search of work, the period of termination and relocation persists in contemporary residential patterns.

The final period Snipp identifies is *self-determination*. American Indians have a long tradition of resisting the policies and incursions of the federal government. Inspired by the Civil Rights movement of the 1960s, American Indian activism became even more pronounced. In 1969 several hundred Native American activists and their supporters occupied Alcatraz Island in San Francisco Bay. They demanded to control the island and set up a cultural center there for Native American studies. The occupation lasted for nineteen months until the U.S. government forcibly removed the protesters, many of whom had remained even after the government had shut down power and telephone service to the island. The Alcatraz occupation, though it failed in its objectives, called public attention to the plight of Native peoples and heralded a new direction in Native American activism. The American Indian Self-Determination and Education Assistance Act, passed in 1975, authorized Native Americans to oversee the affairs of their own communities, giving tribal governments a much greater role in reservation affairs.

Today, there are about 5.2 million American Indians and Alaska Natives (the category now used by the Bureau of the Census to enumerate Alaskan native people). The population of American Indians and Alaska Natives is also growing at a rate faster than the rest of the U.S. population. They are predicted to become a slightly larger share of the U.S. population by 2060 (from 1.7 to 2.5 percent: U.S. Bureau of the Census 2012a). A small proportion (20 percent) live on reservations, although this is more common for those who identify as "American Indian alone," that is, not in combination with other racial or ethnic identities (Norris, Vines, and Hoeffel 2012). Native Americans have a higher poverty rate than the nation as a whole (28.4 percent in 2010, compared to 15 percent of the national population at that time; U.S. Bureau of the Census 2011).

Although the poverty rate among American Indians is high, a new stereotype of Indians has emerged that depicts them as growing fabulously wealthy through casino gambling. Is this true? The *Indian Gaming Regulatory Act* in 1988 allowed tribal nations to conduct gaming activities, including casino gambling. Because tribes are recognized as sovereign entities, states cannot prohibit Indian gaming. Casino gambling has generated revenue for many groups and is a major means of economic development for Indian communities. As a result of this law, more than one hundred tribes now distribute resources from gaming to tribal members. Indian gaming is not, however, as lucrative as many think, nor is its impact uniform across all tribes. The benefit tends to be greater for tribes operating casinos in more populous states where incomes are higher and where Indians are not competing with other casinos (Connor 2013). To summarize, the overall impact of allowing Indian gaming has been generally positive in terms of more employment, better health, and overall economic development, but not in every case (Wolfe et al. 2012; Gonzales, Lyson, and Mauer 2007).

Stereotypes of American Indians as poor, uneducated, and drunk have obscured the reality of their lives; so have other albeit more positive stereotypes of Indians as exotic and romantic figures who live in an idealized state, somehow closer to nature. Native Americans have been highly vulnerable to the social and economic stresses that many other groups have also faced, such as a lack of job opportunities and poor education. A combination of these and other factors such as stolen lands and various federal policies to control and remove their numbers has had a particularly deleterious effect on this group.

The Peculiar Institution: Slavery and Its Aftermath

As you think about the different histories of racial and ethnic groups in American society, you have to imagine simultaneous trails of events. Like railroad tracks crossing the country, these trails are separate lines of history, but they crisscross in the weaving of the nation's development. So as the nation was pushing Indians away, it was also developing an economic system dependent on the slave labor of Black people. While Native Americans were being forcibly removed to the west, Black Americans were laboring in slavery, and the conflicts that ultimately led to the Civil War were simmering.

Other societies have had slaves, but only in the Americas did slavery develop into a full-blown social and economic institution. Precolonial African nations, for example, depended on slave labor (Fredrickson 2002), but in African societies slaves could marry free people and their children would be free as well. What distinguishes slavery here from other forms of slavery is that in the United States, slavery became the "bedrock of the economy and of the social order" (Kolchin 1993:29). Central to slavery in the New World was the principle of slaves as **chattel**, that is, human beings and their offspring were the property of others for a lifetime.

The first Africans landed in what became the United States at Jamestown, Virginia, in 1619. Historical data are sketchy, but it seems the first Black people on U.S. soil were servants, not slaves. Many of the earliest White settlers were themselves indentured servants, bound for a period of time to their employers. In the early days of the Virginia colony, most of the workers were White indentured servants; in fact, 75 percent of those arriving in the seventeenth century were indentured servants. Outcasts from England, Germany, and Ireland, many Whites arrived involuntarily at the hands of unscrupulous recruiters. Neither Whites nor Blacks in the early colonies were truly free, and Black and White workers shared class exploitation. Records show that sometimes they were even partners in running away or were publicly whipped together for having had sex. As the nation developed over the course of the seventeenth century, slavery emerged as an economic institution. By the middle of the seventeenth century, the courts were starting to recognize the status of Black people as distinct from that of White servants. Over time, Black servants saw their condition worsen, culminating in what became the institution of slavery (Takaki 1993).

It is impossible to know how many slaves were transported from western Africa to the New World. The best estimates are between ten and twelve million people,

It is believed that many of the millions of African people who were sold into slavery in the Americas left Africa through the Door of No Return in Senegal, which now stands as a haunting reminder of this horrid period in world history.

the vast majority of whom were imported to Brazil and the Caribbean. The United States received relatively few (600,000–650,000), about six percent of the total (Genovese 1972; Kolchin 1993).

This forced migration of African people was one of the most brutal in world history. During the excruciating Middle Passage (the transatlantic transport), men and women were usually chained and packed tightly together so that slave traders could import as many persons as possible and increase their profits. Thousands of women and men died from disease while in passage, and their bodies were dumped into the sea. Some simply jumped overboard, preferring death to the horror of living. Historians estimate that those who died during the Middle Passage accounted for somewhere between 5 and 20 percent of all transported men and women (Kolchin 1993; Meier and Rudwick 1970).

In the United States, slavery was first developed around Tidewater Virginia and Maryland—the area surrounding the Chesapeake Bay. Slavery provided an ideal labor solution for an expanding capitalist economy. The major crops in the Tidewater area were tobacco and wheat, cultivated for transport to Europe. Although most people associate slavery with the Deep South, up until 1790, two-thirds of the slave population resided in the area surrounding the Chesapeake Bay (Fogel and Engermann 1974).

Slaves provided the free labor that built the profits both for the plantation class and for Northern industrialists who benefitted from sales of tobacco, wheat, rice, indigo, and—later—cotton. Indentured servants had provided sufficient labor through most of the seventeenth century, but as the nation's economy grew, there was a greater need for workers. Unable to enslave Indians because of their familiarity with their "home turf," colonists turned to the slave trade for the nation's labor force (Kolchin 1993). The slave population of 700,000 in 1790 quickly grew to 3.2 million by 1850 and 4 million by 1860.

At the very time that the nation was being founded upon the principles of freedom, independence, and the "natural rights of man," a new institution was developing in which men and women were being forced into a system of slave labor. How could people reconcile this fundamental contradiction in their professed beliefs? The answer was racism, reflected in the emerging belief that Blacks were somehow different, not fully human. Reconciling this inhumane treatment of people with the ideals of the new nation was epitomized in the compromise that defined the original American political system. To settle conflicting state interests between the North and South, for purposes of political representation each Black slave was counted as three-fifths of a person with none of the rights or privileges given to White men (Meier and Rudwick 1970).

Several features differentiate U.S. slavery from slavery in the Caribbean and Latin America. In the United States as opposed to the Caribbean, White people were still a significant proportion of the working population; thus it was necessary to develop an ideology that differentiated slave and free labor. Again, racism filled this void. Also, in the United States as opposed to the Caribbean and Latin America, the slave population soon began to reproduce itself, reducing the need to import slaves via the slave trade. Historians have yet to understand why there were higher birth rates and lower death rates in the United States compared to nations farther south. Perhaps the climate or the harsh conditions in the sugar industry suppressed the rate of population growth in the Caribbean and Latin America, but whatever the explanation, when Britain outlawed the Atlantic slave trade in 1807, the United States had lost its need to continue importing slaves (Kolchin 1993).

The slavery that most people probably imagine now is *antebellum slavery*—the slavery that had developed around the growth of the cotton industry, beginning around 1800 and existing until the end of the Civil War. Antebellum slavery actually filled a relatively short period in American history. Most slaves prior to 1790 had been in the Tidewater region, but by 1820 two-thirds of the slave population had been relocated into the Deep South where cotton predominated (Fogel and Engermann 1974).

Slaves revolted in a number of ways: running away, holding work stoppages, feigning illness, and organizing outright rebellions. Enslaved people did all they could to preserve their sense of dignity and humanity. While slaves might have pretended to be docile as a means of avoiding worse treatment, they did not internalize a low sense of self-worth. There is plenty of evidence that slaves resisted slavery in any way they possibly could (Kolchin 1993).

The Emancipation Proclamation of 1863 notwithstanding, slavery lingered until the end of the Civil War in 1865 and was finally outlawed by the Thirteenth Amendment to the U.S. Constitution that same year. The plantation economy of slavery had concentrated power in the South in the hands of a White aristocracy. Although only a small number (about one-quarter in 1860) of White southern families actually owned slaves, they wielded enormous power. White workers, no longer indentured, also had little power in this system, but racist ideology prevented them from seeing that they had any common interests with Black labor (Wilson 1978).

Following slavery, a period of *Reconstruction* brought new freedoms and new hopes to Black Americans. During Reconstruction, Black Americans had an unprecedented role in public life, yet the period was also marked by racial violence and the attempt to reestablish a Black labor force to redevelop the southern economy. The *Black Codes* were enacted to give newly freed Blacks the right to own property, marry, and make contracts, but the Codes also kept Black labor virtually enslaved, even if under new rules and regulations, as White southerners worked to reestablish the system of labor that had been destroyed by the Civil War.

Reconstruction temporarily transformed the racial order by enfranchising Black men and creating the belief in the possibility for freedom (Hobbs 2014; Foner 1988). But when a negotiated settlement in 1876 between northern and southern states gave Rutherford Hayes the presidency of the United States and ended Reconstruction, Black Americans, now free people, once again became the pawns in a political compromise between conflicting White interests. When Hayes became president, federal troops were withdrawn from the South, and the idea established during Reconstruction that the national government would protect the rights of *all* U.S. citizens (Foner 1988:582) was withdrawn as well. "Home rule" was returned to southern states. Virulent opposition to Black freedom initiated in the South a period of intense repression, violence, and the dismissal of whatever rights Black Americans had achieved during Reconstruction.

The period culminated in 1896 with *Plessy v. Ferguson* and the Supreme Court ruling (in favor of the principle of "separate but equal" that reigned for more than half a century). The grip of Jim Crow segregation strictly controlled Black-White interactions in the South until the principle of "separate but equal" was overturned by *Brown v. Board of Education* in 1954 (see chapter 9).

As Black Americans entered the twentieth century, many remained in the South, laboring in agriculture, manufacturing, and, for women, in domestic work. Thousands, however, left as they could to seek new forms of work in the expanding industrial economy of northern and midwestern cities. During this **Great Migration**, many African Americans made a new way for themselves in cities where Jim Crow was not the prevalent social order, although racism was surely present. As we will see below, urbanization and industrialization transformed race relations in the United States. A population that had been mostly enslaved became ready for the dawn of the Civil Rights movement (see chapter 12).

Today, African Americans constitute 13.3 percent of the U.S. population, slightly higher if you include those who identify themselves in combination with other races. African Americans now include many who do not date their ancestry from slavery. More recent immigrants come from such diverse places as Nigeria, Ethiopia, the Dominican Republic, and Haiti, among many others. Poverty afflicts many Black Americans, but there is also a significant Black middle class. Many African Americans have risen to the top echelons of American power and are now found in positions of economic, military, and political leadership, including the forty-fourth president of the United States, Barack Obama. Still, the inequality between Black and White Americans has proven to be somewhat intractable, that is, characterized by progress for many but stagnation for others, as we will see in later chapters.

Annexing the Southwest: The Mexican American Experience

Latinos are a highly diverse population comprised of many different groups. Like other labels used to describe other racial and ethnic groups, *Latino* is an umbrella term used to convey common interests shared by diverse people of Spanish descent in the United States, even while recognizing their unique pasts and present circumstances. Mexican Americans make up the largest Latino group, representing 66 percent of the current Latino population in the United States. Indigenous Mexican Americans (called Chicanos/as)[1] were the first Latinos to be in what is now the United States. It is that history to which we now turn, with more information on other Latino groups later in this chapter.

Over the course of the sixteenth and seventeenth centuries, Spanish explorers made several expeditions to the California coast as they sought to expand world trade. Organized Spanish colonization of the area now encompassing California began in the mid-eighteenth century when Father Junípero Serra founded the first mission, San Diego de Alcalá. Junípero Serra is infamous for his brutal treatment of native Indians, whom he and other Spanish colonizers sought to colonize and convert to Catholicism. The Spanish established twenty-one missions, stretching over five hundred miles through California from San Diego to Sonoma (Takaki 1993).

Other than native Indians, the original settlers in California were Mexicans whose social order was marked by an elaborate stratification system. At the top of the hierarchy were the landed elite and prosperous officials. Some were Spanish, but most were *mestizo* ("mixed"). In the middle were small-scale ranchers and farmers. At the bottom were laborers, artisans, and other skilled workers; many were Indians, although their numbers were diminishing (Camarillo 1979). In the early nineteenth century, the Mexican government offered land grants to Mexicans in what is now California on the condition that they convert to Catholicism, and some did so. But by the 1840s, attracted to California's natural resources, more and more Anglos moved west. Once the U.S. federal government clearly articulated its objective to annex California (Takaki 1993), a period of conflict over property between the United States and Mexico commenced.

In 1830 the Mexican government outlawed slavery, but cotton planters in the southern United States were anxious to expand into the Mexican territory that would become Texas. In 1836, armed Anglo Americans in Texas began an insurrection against Mexican authority in the now infamous battle at the Alamo. A brutal military campaign followed, eventually leading to the Mexican-American War (1846–1848). Outgunned, the Mexican government lost the war and signed the *Treaty of Guadalupe Hidalgo* (Acuña 2014; Carrasco 2010).

---

[1] *Chicano/a* refers to Mexican people who became incorporated into the United States as the result of a war treaty. Some Mexican Americans born in the United States prefer to be called Chicano/Chicana because of its association with pride. There is debate within the Mexican American community over what people want to be called. Chicano/Chicana emerged in the 1960s as part of a movement for recognition and rights. Some claim that, despite this affirming terminology, the term Chicano had been used earlier as an insult. Activists often reclaim such negative terms, however, during social movements to affirm a positive and collective identity (see chapter 4). For more discussion of the politics of language, see the preface to this book.

With this treaty, Mexico ceded over one million square miles to the United States, extending the southern U.S. border to the Rio Grande. The land that now includes the states of Texas, California, New Mexico, Nevada, and parts of Colorado, Arizona, and Utah became U.S. territory, an area of land that was roughly half of what had been Mexico. Overnight, the fifty thousand or so Mexicans living in these areas were declared to be U.S. citizens and were given full citizenship rights—in principle but not in practice (De Genova and Ramos-Zayas 2001; Takaki 1993). Once a majority in their own lands, Mexican Americans soon became a minority in the sociological sense of that word (Massey 2008; also see the preface of this volume). As some say today, "We didn't cross the border; the border crossed us" (Baca Zinn 2015, personal correspondence).

The quarter century following the Mexican-American War continues to shape the experiences of many Mexican Americans in the United States. As California and the Southwest changed from a primarily pastoral economy to an industrial one, Mexican workers in the United States increasingly were incorporated into the needs of capitalism. Those who had been landed often became landless. Many who had held large tracts of land as ranchers moved from "riches to rags" (Camarillo 1979:67) as Anglos increasingly took control of the new economic system.

Although in 1848, at the conclusion of the Mexican-American War, Mexicans had outnumbered Anglos by ten to one, the discovery of gold that same year changed everything. People throughout the United States headed west, thinking they would become wealthy as prospectors. Soon, the Anglo population overwhelmed the Mexican American population, and Mexican Americans found themselves thoroughly subjected to Anglo domination. Laws and other ordinances were put in place that restricted Mexican American rights. Lands were stolen and Mexican Americans were targeted for all manner of abuses. The growing hatred and stereotyping of Mexicans is well illustrated by an antivagrancy act passed in California in 1865 that was actually called the "Greaser Act" (Takaki 1993; Feagin and Cobas 2014).

With virtually no immigration laws, Mexicans and others found it relatively easy to migrate to the land that had just become the United States. As the economic base of the nation was expanding, there was an increasing need for labor— especially cheap labor that could enrich the profits of business owners. Ranching, agriculture, and mining drew many Mexicans to the Southwest. Growers and industrialists recruited people from far and wide, spending thousands to recruit and transport Mexicans to where they were needed to work, including such places as Colorado, Wyoming, Iowa, Nebraska, and the city of Chicago, Illinois. The rate of immigration of Mexican laborers to the United States became particularly high after the United States restricted Asian immigration in the late nineteenth and early twentieth centuries. As employers actively recruited Mexican workers, the number of Mexican immigrants jumped from about 17,000 per year in 1910 to about 50,000 per year in the 1920s and 740,000 by 1930 (Massey 2008).

As the Mexican population in the United States grew larger, White opposition intensified. By the late 1920s, when the Great Depression unfolded, Mexicans became the scapegoats for the failing U.S. economy, and a period of intense anti-Mexican sentiment ensued. During massive deportation from 1929 to 1934, authorities rounded up Mexicans through raids in neighborhoods, factories, and fields, often without a chance for people to gather their belongings. Steeped in anti-Mexican stereotypes, officials often did not attempt to distinguish Mexican immigrants from Mexican American citizens. Thousands of children, including many born in the United States and thus U.S. citizens, were also deported regardless of their citizenship status. This massive deportation cut the population of Mexicans in the United States in half (Olivas 2010; Romo 1996).

By the time the United States entered World War II, the need for labor returned and the country opened its doors to Mexican immigrants again. In 1942 the United States and Mexico created the *bracero* **program**—a formal agreement that permitted Mexican citizens to work in the United States for temporary, renewable periods. The agreement also prohibited discrimination, which was largely ignored both by U.S. growers and the federal government (Massey 2008; Rodríguez, Sáenz, and Menjívar 2008).

Over a half million braceros worked under this arrangement. Mexicans in the bracero program endured poor food, excessive charges for rent, discrimination, and exposure to pesticides, but the program provided growers with a large source of cheap labor. Even after World War II, when U.S. soldiers returned home wanting jobs, the program was kept alive because of the interests of agribusiness. The bracero program brought nearly five million Mexicans to the United States between 1942 and 1964. It was finally ended over protests about horrific working conditions. Many Mexican Americans today can still trace their roots to this program and can recall vividly horrible memories of it (Olivas 2010; Carrasco 1997).

The Mexican Americans who had fought in World War II were able to take advantage of GI benefits and seek higher education. But others, viewed as disposable labor, worked in low-wage jobs, were segregated in barrios, and attended segregated schools (Perea 2004; Smith 2008). Mexican Americans were subjected to some of the same indignities that afflicted Black Americans under Jim Crow. In the postwar period, Mexican Americans organized extensively for protection of their civil rights, orchestrating the now well-known grape boycott led by Cesar Chavez and others. The grape boycott, a protest against working conditions for many migrant workers, lasted from 1965 to 1970 and resulted in unionization for grape workers for the first time, which set an important precedent for other agricultural laborers (Romo 1996; Ferris and Sandoval 1997).

Mexican American history teaches us a lot about how racial-ethnic groups have been drawn in as cheap sources of labor while being denied basic rights of citizenship. But Mexican Americans today are just one group of various Latino peoples with different histories and traditions.

Latinos are now the most rapidly growing "minority" population in the United States, including Chicanos, newly arrived Mexican Americans, Puerto Ricans, Cubans, and immigrants from South and Central America. By 2010, people self-identifying as Hispanic were 16 percent of the U.S. population, and that percentage is expected to grow to 29 percent by 2060. Latinos now are widely dispersed across the country, although more concentrated in certain areas. Three-quarters of the Hispanic population live in the West or the South, two-thirds in California, Texas, Florida, or New York (Ennis, Rios-Vargas, and Elbert 2011; U.S. Bureau of the Census 2015c).

Poverty among Latinos is high (23.5 percent in 2013), nearly matching that of African Americans. As with African Americans, there is also a significant middle class. Class status also varies among the different groups that make up the Latino population. Like African Americans, Latinos have a visible presence in some of the most powerful positions in the land, and they are a population that is increasingly important in shaping national politics. You will learn more about Latinos in the chapters to follow.

Opening the Nation's Doors—and Slamming Them Closed

Asian Americans also come from very diverse backgrounds, but the early history of Asian migration centers on Chinese and Japanese movement into the United States. Their history, like that of other groups, involves the expansion and contraction of the need for labor. Both groups were also subjected to the vagaries of lawmakers who used their power to restrict Chinese and Japanese rights of citizenship.

Chinese Americans

California's annexation by the United States in the Treaty of Guadalupe Hidalgo opened a new door for the country to expand into Asia and for Asians to enter the United States (Takaki 1993). Many Chinese people came to the United States to escape harsh conditions in China. They saw the United States as a place where they could have plenty to eat, have opportunities to work, and establish homes. Men arrived with the intention of becoming established and then moving their families. Most came through a "credit-ticket" system in which a broker would lend them the money for passage, and they would repay the broker, with interest, from their earnings in the United States (Takaki 1993).

Between 1850 and 1882, over three hundred thousand Chinese people left southern China to work in America. Many were imported to work as strikebreakers, and they were also relegated to the most dangerous and difficult work available. By 1870, there were sixty-three thousand Chinese people in the United States, three-quarters of whom lived in California (Takaki 1993).

Labor recruiters preferred to recruit young, able-bodied men from China; this and other factors allowed for very few Chinese women to come to the United States. Women's traditional roles in China, the cost of travel, and Chinese women's fears of physical/sexual assault in the United States created a huge imbalance in the ratio of men to women among the Chinese in America (Chow 1996). As an example, of the 11,787 Chinese who came to the United States in 1852, only seven were women. Some Chinese women managed to enter as indentured servants. The extreme sex imbalance created bachelor communities and a lucrative market for prostitution, especially since California law prevented Chinese people from marrying Whites. In the census of 1870, 61 percent of Chinese women living in California listed their occupation as "prostitute" (Takaki 1993).

At first, Chinese laborers worked mostly in the mining industry, but the decline of mining, the resistance of White labor, and the building of the transcontinental railroad changed the course of Chinese immigration. Thousands of Chinese workers labored to build the Central Pacific Railroad between 1864 and 1869. White workers considered the work too dangerous and demanded better pay and working conditions. Employing Chinese workers saved railroad owners one-third of their costs, and Chinese workers ultimately made up 90 percent of the railroad labor force. Chinese workers also sought improvements in their situation and organized a strike in 1867, but the railroad owners cut off their food supply and forced them back to work without any change in their status (Takaki 1993).

Once the railroad was completed in 1869, most of the Chinese workers returned to San Francisco, Sacramento, and other places, mostly in California, where new Chinese communities were being formed. San Francisco was also becoming a focal point of industry, and by 1870, half of the city's labor force was Chinese. Chinese people were concentrated in low-wage work and/or were paid less than Whites when they did the same work. Some turned to farming, helping to develop the fruit industry and teaching growers how to construct irrigation systems. Others, shut out of work opportunities, moved into service work, such as laundering (Takaki 1989, 1993).

By the 1880s, the need for Chinese workers dissipated. Throughout the course of their labor history in America, Chinese people had been defined as ideal workers, but they were now perceived as a "yellow peril"—a menace to White society. In 1882, the U.S. Congress passed the **Chinese Exclusion Act** denying the entry of additional Chinese laborers. The door of opportunity that had been briefly opened was now slammed shut. The only Chinese allowed entry to the United States were those who were merchants, teachers, diplomats, students, and tourists (see LEARNING OUR PAST for a brief discussion of Chinese detention on Angel Island in California). Women could only enter if they were married to a merchant. Only because of a natural disaster in 1906 were some Chinese able to re-form families. The San Francisco earthquake of 1906 and a subsequent fire destroyed local official records that provided proof of family relations, prompting many Chinese to then claim they had been born in San Francisco. They would then travel back to China and return with those they claimed as "sons"—so-called **paper sons** (Dill 1988). The Chinese Exclusion Act was not rescinded until 1943 when China and the United States became allies in World War II (Chow 1996).

Japanese Americans

Japanese immigration to the United States primarily occurred between 1890 and 1924. Most of the first Japanese immigrants were men, but unlike among Chinese immigrants, Japanese women were far more likely to emigrate. The strong central Japanese government wanted Japan to appear "noble" to others and thus strictly regulated emigration, requiring those who left to be healthy and literate. The Japanese government thus allowed Japanese women to emigrate as family members (Dill 1988; Takaki 1989). In Japan in the late nineteenth century, poor farming conditions meant that many farmers lost their land and crops. Like the Chinese, many Japanese people thought that coming to the United States would mean high wages and a more successful life.

With some need for labor and the Chinese now excluded, Japanese workers were initially welcomed into the United States and Hawaii. Between 1885 and 1924, 200,000 Japanese people emigrated to Hawaii and another 180,000 to the U.S. mainland, where they were a smaller proportion of the population. In Hawaii, the government also stipulated that a certain percentage of workers had to be women. Once there, women were assigned to work in the fields. On the mainland, women assisted husbands as unpaid workers in shops and as farmers.

LEARNING OUR PAST

Remembering Angel Island

When people think of the historic points of entry for immigrants into the United States, most probably think of Ellis Island, the entry point in New York City for thousands of Europeans. Immigrants arriving in San Francisco from the Pacific between 1910 and 1940 were separated by nationality by customs agents. Coming mostly from Asia, but also from Mexico and Russia, they were ferried to Angel Island, where they were held in quarantine. Chinese people, in particular, were detained on Angel Island, sometimes for weeks, months, and even years, interrogated about their background, and often sent back. A fire badly damaged the poorly kept facility in 1940 and only recently were poems discovered that detainees had carved into the walls expressing their hopes, fears, and yearnings.

If you are ever in San Francisco, a visit to the museum at Angel Island, now a state park, is a very moving and educational experience. The island is now beautiful, with flowers and biking and walking trails, but once you learn about the history of people who were held there, you will feel some of the ghosts of the past.

You can read some of the narratives that detainees at Angel Island wrote, as well as view photographs that have been preserved, at the following sites:

http://www.aiisf.org/immigrant-voices/read-a-story
http://www.angel-island.com/history.html

Whereas many White people associate the entry of immigrants with Ellis Island in New York City, most Chinese and Japanese immigrants entered through the Angel Island Immigration Station in San Francisco Bay. Often forced to stay for there for months, they experienced inhumane conditions and extreme overcrowding.

Organized White U.S. workers scorned and attacked Japanese workers and also denied them access to industrial employment where they might have found better jobs. Instead, the Japanese were relegated to work in farming and, for some, shop-keeping. By 1910, Japanese laborers in California were producing 70 percent of the strawberries, 95 percent of the soybeans, 95 percent of the celery, and huge proportions of the rest of the nation's fruit and vegetable diet (Takaki 1993).

Many Japanese believed that their success in agriculture would be the ticket to acceptance, but sadly they were wrong. Anti-immigrant sentiment in the United States began curtailing Japanese immigration. The **Gentleman's Agreement of 1907**—an agreement between the United States and Japan—barred further entry of Japanese laborers, significantly reducing Japanese immigration. This agreement only allowed women to come as wives of merchants. The result was a system of **picture brides**—marriages arranged by a broker (as was the custom in Japan). A Japanese man in the United States who could not afford to return to Japan selected a wife from picture books provided by brokers. Between 1909 and 1923, 71 percent of the Japanese women arriving in the United States came as picture brides (Glenn 1986; Glenn and Parreñas 1996).

Like the Chinese in America, Japanese people were denied the basic rights of citizenship. This was highlighted in 1922 in a case that ultimately went to the U.S. Supreme Court: *Ozawa v. United States*. Takao Ozawa had emigrated from Japan, graduated from a U.S. high school and attended the University of California–Berkeley. He moved to Hawaii, where he worked for an American family and raised his family. But when he applied for naturalization, he was denied. His case ultimately went to the U.S. Supreme Court, where he was denied the right to file for citizenship based on the argument that he was not "Caucasian" (Takaki 1989). The Ozawa case reflects the development of whiteness as a legal construct.

The first generation of Japanese (*Issei*) in the United States had great hopes that the second generation (*Nisei*) would benefit from their hard work by qualifying for higher education and stronger employment. Issei hopes, however, were dashed in December 1941, when the Japanese bombed Pearl Harbor and set off nationwide outrage against the Japanese, including those who were American citizens either by birth or naturalization. In 1942 President Franklin Roosevelt issued an executive order removing all Japanese people from the American West and ordering them into internment camps throughout the western states. Japanese Americans were first housed in stockyards and on fairgrounds and racetracks; eventually they were relocated to ten different internment camps. All of their financial assets were frozen, and a massive propaganda campaign targeted them as traitors and "enemy aliens." The U.S. government ultimately paid sixteen billion dollars in reparations to detainees and their descendants. For a personal account of the experience of internment, see LIVING WITH RACISM.

Waves of Whiteness: European Immigration

White ethnic groups have not been immune to the forces of prejudice and hatred that have marked the experiences of people of color. The earliest immigrants in the seventeenth century were English. Even as late as 1790, when over 80 percent of the

LIVING WITH RACISM

The Alien Land Law and Japanese Americans

Marvin Uratsu was born in Sacramento in 1925. When the Japanese were forcibly removed from the West Coast, he spent his junior year of high school at the Tule Lake internment camp. He has been interviewed about his life experience for a student oral history project documenting the lived history of older Americans of different racial and ethnic backgrounds. (You can read and listen to these interviews at http://www.tellingstories.org.) Here is an excerpt from Marvin Uratsu's experience.

> There was this Alien Land Law that made it impossible for my father to buy land. There was a period before the Alien Land Law that some Japanese American families were able to buy land before the law came into effect. And that was like my wife's family. They were able to buy land before the law went into effect. But in our case, the Uratsu family's case, the law was passed and they couldn't buy land. That was one of the biggest things. It made it kind of hard for us. We couldn't get citizenship. People from Europe would come over and after so many years they were able to get their U.S. citizenship, but that wasn't the case for the Japanese so there were two or three other things that made it difficult to live here and have to work as a day laborer on the farms.

Source: Uratsu, Marvin. 2007. "Marvin Uratsu." Interview. Telling Their Stories. Retrieved December 30, 2016 (http://www.tellingstories.org/internment/muratsu/index.html).

U.S. population was White, between 60 and 70 percent of the White population was of English ancestry. The rest were mostly Irish, Scots, and German. By 1920, following extensive European immigration, 90 percent of the population was White, but less than half (44 percent) of the White population was descended from England (Schneiderman 1996).

Two great waves mark European immigration to the United States. The first wave, roughly from 1815 to 1865, brought primarily German, Irish, and Scandinavian immigrants—that is, mostly northern and western Europeans. Jewish immigrants also arrived around 1849, largely from Germany. Later Jewish immigrants would come from other parts of eastern Europe, as we will see below.

In the late nineteenth and early twentieth centuries, crop failures and deteriorating economic conditions in Sweden, Norway, and Denmark brought another wave of thousands of people from these countries to U.S. shores. Even while Black Americans were still being held in slavery, the *Homestead Act of 1862* gave free land to those who would farm it for five years. This attracted Scandinavians especially to the upper Midwest (Hansen 2013).

Between 1820 and 1930, about 4.5 million Irish came to the United States; indeed, by 1840 half of all immigrants were Irish. The potato famine in Ireland in the late 1840s caused the population of the island to decrease by four million. Two million died of starvation. The other two million were people who were able to leave Ireland, and many of them came to the United States. The least expensive route to the United States took the Irish to Boston, one of the major ports of settlement. Given the conditions in Ireland, many arrived dependent on charity. There were few jobs, and the Irish had little to invest in their future. The men took the least skilled, lowest paying jobs, digging canals, building bridges, and doing other manual labor, while Irish women worked as domestic servants.

At the time, the Irish were blamed for many of the nation's ills, as are today's immigrants. Stereotyped, ridiculed, and attacked by anti-Irish mobs, Irish immigrants were nonetheless able to gain a foothold in urban politics—for reasons not fully understood. This ultimately led to their upward mobility at least into the working class, if not higher. The anti-Irish anger that they encountered also helped them build a strong Irish identity that only further exacerbated hostility toward them (Diner 1996). Arriving in a nation that largely defined itself as Protestant, the Irish were harshly subjected to **nativism** in the form of anti-Catholic hostility. Nativist organizations promoted the idea of the United States as a Protestant country. Such anti-Catholic sentiments surfaced again in 1960 when John Fitzgerald Kennedy, descended from Irish immigrants, was elected the nation's first Catholic U.S. president.

Jewish immigrants to the United States came in their largest numbers between 1880 and 1924. About one-third of all Jewish people in eastern Europe, numbering about two million, migrated to the United States within that time frame to escape anti-Semitism. By the beginning of World War I alone, one-third of all the Jews in Russia and Eastern Europe—mostly Poland, Austria, Hungary, and Romania—had emigrated. By 1920, 1.6 million Jewish people were in New York City, accounting for 43 percent of the city's population (Foner 2005; Takaki 1993). Their arrival was facilitated by the German Jews who had started arriving in the 1840s and settled in urban areas to work as bankers and merchants. Many had settled in the Lower East Side of Manhattan, where slum conditions in housing tenements were the norm.

Jewish people in the United States have faced exclusion and discrimination, but they have also been more successful than many other White ethnics. Although this has led to numerous false stereotypes of Jewish people, the fact is that they arrived more skilled, better educated, and more accustomed to urban life, which facilitated their social and economic mobility (Gold and Phillips 1996).

The second wave of European immigration came roughly between 1880 and 1920, bringing mostly people from southern Europe, especially Italians. Approximately 2.5 million Italians came to the United States, mostly through Ellis Island. By 1920 there were over eight hundred thousand Italians living in New York City alone, more than the population of most Italian cities at the time (Foner 2005; National Institute of Italian Statistics 2015). Spurred to emigrate because their way of life in southern Italy had been disrupted by negative developments in their agrarian lifestyle, most Italians were dislocated peasants. Arriving in an expanding urban-industrial economy with limited skills, they formed "urban villages" in the major cities of the East Coast and worked mostly in factories and in the construction, sanitation, and food industries.

As opposed to other immigrants, many Italians thought of their move as temporary and held out hope of returning to Italy. They maintained a close connection to their homeland; many did, in fact, repatriate. But they were slow to develop an "Italian" identity; more often than not, "homeland" for an Italian was a region of Italy, such as Sicily or Calabria. Italians became another despised immigrant group in the United States; they were perceived as "swarthy" and associated with criminal tendencies in general and the Mafia in particular. Second- and third-generation Italian Americans, however, became assimilated into the American mainstream (Alba 1996).

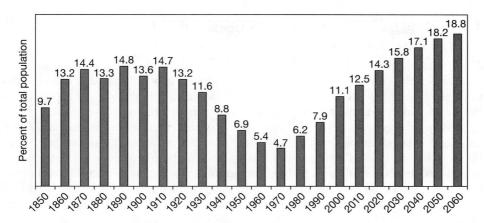

FIG. 5.1 The Foreign-Born Population in the United States, 1850–2010

Note: Percentages for 2020 and beyond are based on U.S. Census Bureau projections.

Sources: Gibson, Campbell, and Kay Jung. 2006. *Historical Census Statistics on the Foreign-Born Population of the United States, 1850–2000.* Washington, DC: U.S. Bureau of the Census; Colby, Sandra L., and Jennifer M. Ortman. 2015. *Projections of the Size and Composition of the U.S. Population, 2014–2060.* Washington, DC: U.S. Bureau of the Census.

As immigrants became an increasingly large share of the U.S. population in the early twentieth century (see figure 5.1), nativist sentiments surged. White workers perceived immigrant workers as a threat. Hostility and claims that America was a "white" nation were rampant. White supremacists claimed that the surge of immigrants would "dilute the moral fiber of the nation" (Portes and Rumbaut 2014:9), a sentiment that has echoed in current times as right-wing movements have declared that immigrants are threatening the moral fabric of American life.

During earlier periods of immigration, once business no longer needed the cheap source of labor that so many immigrants had provided, the nation changed its laws to shut down immigration. The **National Origins Act** (also called the *Johnson-Reed Act*) was passed in 1924, and it put a virtual halt to immigration by establishing a quota system that restricted the entry of new immigrants to 2 percent of the total number of people of each nationality that had been in the United States in 1890. An exception to this quota system, which favored immigrants from Western Europe, was that it explicitly forbade immigrants from Asia. Between the Great Depression and World War II, immigration plummeted, especially for those from southern Europe, Italy in particular. The law favored immigrants from northern Europe, especially Germany, Britain, and Ireland (Pedraza 1996). Opportunities for immigrants, once believed to be the path to success, were no longer available.

The National Origins Act reduced immigration to a trickle until 1965, when legislation eliminating the national origins quota was passed. Knowing the earlier history provides a context for understanding some of the resurgent social forces that are shaping debates about immigration today.

The New Immigration: Changing the Face of the Nation

The twentieth century brought new developments that continue to influence racial and ethnic relations to this day. Ebbs and flows in the demand for labor track alongside the ebbs and flows of different racial-ethnic groups, mirroring the evolution of the racial order into the twenty-first century (Alba and Foner 2015; Alba 2012). Especially at times when native White workers find themselves economically and socially displaced, immigrants then become scapegoats for woes that actually have their origins in the social structures of society. This has been especially evident recently as calls to "build a wall" and to halt immigration altogether from certain countries have become rallying cries for a new nativist and populist movement. White, working-class men especially may feel intense anger about their own loss of status, and they may displace that anger onto immigrants, who become objectified as "other."

In the early twentieth century, urbanization and industrialization rapidly expanded, changing the nature of work and transforming the nation's cities. It bears repeating that, with the possibility of employment in an expanding industrial economy and the desire to be free of the grip of Jim Crow racism in the South, approximately six million African American people participated in the Great Migration between about 1915 and 1970 (Marks 1989; Wilkerson 2010). They headed north in one of the greatest population shifts in U.S. history.

The demand for industrial labor also brought increasing numbers of Puerto Ricans to the U.S. mainland beginning in the early twentieth century and expanding through the post–World War II period. Puerto Rican migration is somewhat different from that of other groups, primarily because Puerto Ricans are U.S. citizens and, thus, not immigrants. Puerto Rico became a colony of the United States in 1898 following the Spanish-American War. Puerto Ricans were then granted citizenship under the *Jones Act of 1917*. Puerto Ricans began to travel back and forth between the island and the U.S. mainland in significant numbers after World War II.

Like immigrants, Puerto Ricans were drawn to the jobs that the postwar economy provided. By 1950 there were three hundred thousand Puerto Ricans on the mainland, most of them in New York City. By 1970, there were 1.5 million Puerto Ricans on the mainland, a number that has grown to more than 4.9 million in the early twenty-first century. Typically employed in low-wage, often seasonal, jobs, Puerto Ricans have provided much of the work that sustains others, even while their back-and-forth migration patterns have disrupted many Puerto Rican families (Brown and Patten 2013; Carrasquillo and Sánchez-Korrol 1996).

The period from the Great Depression until the mid-1960s in the United States was a period of retrenchment in immigration. Mexicans who were working under the bracero program, Black southern migrants, and Puerto Ricans were replacing the need for immigrant labor (Portes and Rumbaut 2014). Through the 1930s, there were few jobs and, therefore, little incentive for people to migrate. The Second World War, though, provided a big boost to the economy and again brought about the need for workers. The stage was set for the pattern of immigration that marks the contemporary period.

With a surging economy and postwar affluence, the United States was poised for a change in its immigration laws. In 1965, the Congress passed the *Immigration and Nationality Act of 1965*, usually referred to as the **Hart-Celler Act**. This law has

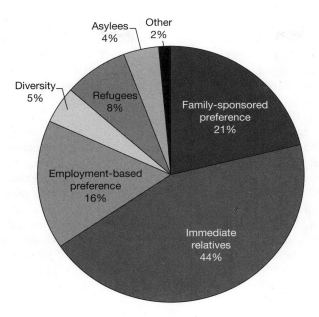

FIG. 5.2 Reasons for Immigrant Admission, 2013

Note: "Other" includes such diverse reasons as cancellation of removal, children born, refugees from Haiti and Nicaragua admitted under unique policies, parolees, and other reasons.

Source: Office of Immigration Statistics. 2013. *2013 Yearbook of Immigration Statistics.* Washington, DC: U.S. Department of Homeland Security.

changed the face of U.S. society. The Hart-Celler Act eliminated the national origins quota created by the National Origins Act of 1924. The new law also gave priority to family reunification, replacing occupational skill as the preferred reason for entry (see figure 5.2). The Hart-Celler Act continues to guide the character of immigration as of 2017.

Hart-Celler has had a number of unintended consequences. Recall that one year before the passage of the 1965 law, the Congress had ended the bracero program. The program itself no longer supplied cheap labor, but employers (mostly ranchers and farmers) continued to turn to the same group of laborers, who would now work under clandestine arrangements. Soon these laborers would be known as "illegal immigrants."

The Hart-Celler law also opened the door to highly skilled immigrants, drawing in well-educated people who were ready to assume professional positions. The result was the bifurcated immigrant labor market that still exists, which consists of highly skilled, often science- and technology-based immigrant workers, at the high end and millions of other, both legal and illegal, immigrants working in low-wage and service work (Portes and Rumbaut 2014; also see chapter 7 of this volume).

As the result of the 1965 law, immigration to the United States dramatically increased, almost reaching the same proportions as during the waves of European immigration from 1880 to 1920. Between 1980 and 2014, the proportion of foreign-born people in the United States rapidly increased from 6.2 percent of the population to 13 percent and from 6.7 percent of the civilian labor force to 16.5 percent (Newburger and Gryn 2009; U.S. Bureau of Labor Statistics 2015d). Half of the foreign born are now between eighteen and forty-four years of age, compared to one-third of native-born people. The foreign born are also more likely to be married and to have children (Grieco et al. 2012).

Among the new immigrants are those who are undocumented, that is, those who have entered the country illegally. Undocumented immigration fuels current debates about immigration policy—debates that are often clouded by myths about who these people are and what they do. There are approximately eleven million undocumented immigrants in the United States, a number that has been declining since 2007 because the labor market is shrinking. While many Americans imagine most undocumented immigrants to be Mexican, Mexicans only make up about one-half of those who are undocumented. Others come from different Central and South American nations. Unauthorized immigrants make up about 5 percent of the U.S. workforce and, despite social myths, two-thirds of these workers pay state and federal taxes and Social Security (Krogstad and Passel 2015; Massey 2005).

Post-1965 immigration differs from earlier European immigration in a number of ways:

1. Current immigrant populations are coming from different parts of the world, including Southeast Asia, Central and South America, Africa, the Middle East, and the Caribbean (see figure 5.3). With the exception of those from China and Japan, earlier immigrants to the United States came largely from the western hemisphere: the westernmost European nations and Mexico. Now, immigrants mostly come from places that differ more in terms of culture, and they are more likely to be perceived as racially different from White Americans (Alba and Nee 2003).
2. New immigrants are more geographically dispersed throughout the nation than was true when earlier immigration waves settled mostly in the nation's cities (Hirschman and Massey 2008).
3. Today's immigrants are more diverse in their educational and occupational backgrounds (Kibria, Bowman, and O'Leary 2014). Although immigrants are stereotyped as poor and uneducated, seldom do the poorest in any nation immigrate. Immigration takes resources in terms of both financial and social networks.
4. Whereas many earlier immigrants, especially those originating from European nations, experienced upward social mobility over time, post-1965 immigrants are more likely to experience downward mobility. Those who were physicians in their country of origin might become medical technicians, professors, or teachers. College-educated women may immigrate into domestic work (Gans 1992, 2009; Hondagneu-Sotelo 2007).

In sum, the experience of coming to the United States varies. For some, entrance means new opportunities and, perhaps, mobility into a new social status. For others, it means menial labor, poverty, and perhaps disappointment by dashed hopes for a new life. The ugly side of the immigrant experience is that those who arrive with darker skin may find themselves racialized, even though they likely came from a culture where race has little or no meaning (see chapter 2). The wish of many

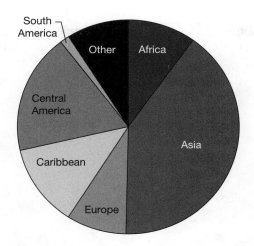

FIG. 5.3 Immigrant Origins, 2013

Note: "Other" includes such diverse places as Oceania, Canada, and Bermuda, and even "unknown." Countries from the Middle East are included in Asia (Afghanistan, Jordan, Kuwait, Syria, Saudi Arabia, Iran, Iraq, and others) or, in some cases, Africa (Libya, Egypt, Sudan, and others).

Source: Migration Policy Institute. 2014. "Inflow of New Legal Residents by Country of Birth, 1990–2013." *MPI Data Hub: Facts, Stats, and Maps*. Washington, DC: Migration Policy Institute.

Americans to see the United States as a white society means that the reception for some is colored by racial ideology (Chavez 2013).

The new character of immigration is shaping national debates about immigration policy. Even though strong anti-immigrant sentiments have been expressed in recent times, most Americans think that immigrants strengthen the nation through their hard work and talents. A large majority (72 percent) think that undocumented immigrants should be allowed to stay if they meet certain requirements. A majority (61 percent) oppose building a wall along the U.S.-Mexico border. Black and Hispanic Americans (76 percent of each) are especially opposed to building such a wall, and there are clear partisan differences, with 84 percent of Democrats and 34 percent of Republicans opposed to building such a wall (Pew Research Center 2015, 2016). The country is clearly divided over exactly how to handle immigration reform (Abrajano and Hajnal 2015). As one commentator has said, "Immigration is the civil rights struggle of our times" (Rodriguez 2014).

Immigration is bringing cultural changes that are welcomed by many who see immigrants as enriching the American mosaic. Others think these changes threaten the national identity (Katznelson 2014). Should the United States focus primarily on securing its borders? Should we deport undocumented immigrants, even if they have children who have been born here? Should people who are undocumented but who have been working, paying taxes, and contributing to the national economy be given a path to citizenship? Are we really a melting pot or simply a simmering stew about to boil over?

As debates about immigration intensify, we are reminded that immigration policies have long disrupted families whose members are otherwise only trying to improve their lives.

These questions are not easily answered, and they spark intense debate. As we will see in the chapters to follow, immigrants are a part of every major social institution in the United States. As this chapter has briefly detailed, all of the groups that now make up American society have followed their respective unique routes to their current status. Linking these group experiences together has been the chain of history.

Conclusion

This chapter opened by identifying three elements central to the history of racial-ethnic groups in the United States: *property*, *labor*, and *social control*. You now see how each played out in the development of the nation's resources. Property was taken from some and acquired by others, even as some people were defined as the property of others. Patterns of immigration or exclusion have tracked alongside the need for cheap sources of labor during periods of economic growth or contraction. In each of the histories told here, social control has been exercised—sometimes through the rule of law but other times through violence or the imposition of belief systems.

Why have some made it and others not? This chapter has provided some of the background needed to begin answering that question. The following chapter details an analytical framework that can further help you to understand the status of different racial-ethnic groups in society.

Key Terms

bracero program, 106

chattel, 100

Chinese Exclusion Act (1882), 108

Gentleman's Agreement (1907), 110

Great Migration, 103

Hart-Celler Act (1965), 115

Indian Removal Act, 98

National Origins Act (1924), 113

nativism, 112

paper sons, 108

picture brides, 110

settler colonialism, 97

Critical Thinking Questions

1. Based on what you have learned in this chapter, what common experiences would you say diverse racial-ethnic groups have had during their incorporation into the United States? Do you see similar patterns as you examine contemporary immigration and race relations?
2. This chapter opened by identifying three themes that organize the racial-ethnic history of the United States: property, labor, and social control. Using your own racial-ethnic group as an example, how do you see these factors reflected in your group's history?

Student Exercises

5.1: Interview someone in your family (immediate or extended) who knows something about your family history. How is your family history similar to or different from any one of the group experiences examined here?

5.2: Analyze the content of one major national news outlet over the course of one week. Identify every mention of contemporary immigration. Then write a brief analysis of how immigration is understood—at least through the perspective of this news outlet. Ask yourself, is it accurate? If so, how? If not, why not?

Challenging Question/Open to Debate

Few doubt that U.S. immigration policy is in need of reform. The collision of different interests, however, fractures the many constituencies with an interest in immigration policy, including immigrant families and their allies, business interests, state and federal government officials (including police and border patrol agents), and the general public, to name a few. Acknowledging this complexity, how would you prioritize the following concerns in framing a new immigration policy: family unification, economic opportunity, labor needs, national and regional security? You might want to inform your answer by examining public opinion on this issue (see, e.g., current polling from the Pew Research Center on immigration policy: http://www.pewresearch.org/topics/immigration/).

CHAPTER 6

Roots of Racial Inequality

Framing the Discussion

*If you are neutral in situations of injustice, you have chosen the side
of the oppressor. If an elephant has its foot on the tail of a mouse,
and you say that you are neutral, the mouse will not appreciate
your neutrality.*

—Archbishop Desmond Tutu (cited in Brown 1984)

OBJECTIVES

- Understand the social processes that facilitate ethnic assimilation
- Identify key elements in a structural explanation of racial inequality
- Explain how race and class are interrelated
- Be able to debate the relative influence of culture and structure in shaping racial inequality

Ask someone why racial inequality exists and you will likely hear at least one of these statements:

> "We need to get over the past and let old prejudices fade away."
> "As society becomes more multiracial, racism will decline."
> "The disintegration of Black families is a major cause of poverty."
> "It's not really race anymore; it's all about class."

If you have ever discussed race relations with friends or family members, you have likely heard these and similar thoughts. Frequently heard from public commentators, these ideas are widely held although they may be incorrect, or, at the very least, incomplete and misleading.

None of these popular explanations of racial inequality can be quickly dismissed. As with most complex topics, there may be a grain of truth in some of them, but that bit of truth dissolves within a broader view of race in society.

Regarding the first statement, we do need to let old prejudices fade away, but racial prejudice is only one part of a larger problem. Although overt expressions of prejudice have been on the decline, events such as the mass shooting of worshippers in a Black church in Charleston in 2015 or Donald Trump's claim that Mexicans are rapists and criminals show that overt prejudice and racism are still frightening and disturbing realities. At the same time, as we have seen in chapter 2, prejudice (or an individual's racist attitude toward another individual) is not the sole cause of racial inequality (Golash-Boza 2016).

With regard to the second statement, there is no doubt that U.S. society is becoming more diverse (see figure 6.1). Furthermore, the increased visibility of multiracial people does change the dynamics of racism, but the seeds of racial inequality lie deeper than people's identities. The increase in multiracial identities only makes our understanding of race and racism more complex and nuanced. The growth of multiracialism has not seriously eroded the underlying bedrock of racial problems in America.

As for the third statement, blaming family background for the problems that beset so many people of color assumes, often explicitly, that people do not succeed because something is wrong with their moral and cultural values. Although it is common to blame the alleged moral failings of some people for not "making it," such rationales are poorly supported by careful research. The connection between

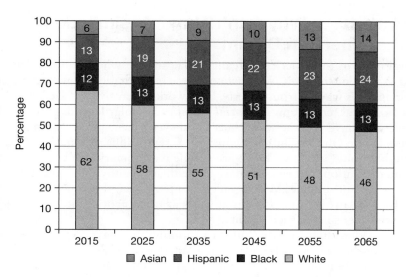

FIG. 6.1 Race and Ethnicity as a Percent of the U.S. Population, 2015–2065

As you can see, White Americans will no longer be a numerical majority in the not-too-distant future. (Note that the graph does not indicate who identifies as multiracial.) Do you think that this demographic change in the composition of the U.S. population will change how people think about race? What changes in a structural analysis of racial inequality will be needed?

Source: Brown, Anna. 2015. "Key Takeaways on U.S. Immigration: Past, Present, and Future." Pew Research Center. (http://www.pewresearch.org/fact-tank/2015/09/28/key-takeaways-on-u-s-immigration-past-present-and-future/.)

culture and social structure is also the subject of heated debate in the social sciences. Although cultural attitudes and values cannot be ignored, to rest an explanation of complex social phenomena solely on culture is misleading. Simply put, culture is a manifestation of racial inequality, not a root cause.

Finally, with reference to the fourth statement, **class,** that is, the system of differential access to economic, social, and political resources, is indeed significant in shaping opportunities for all racial and ethnic groups. This does not, however, mean that race no longer matters. As you will see later in this chapter, both race and class together shape people's odds of success. Attributing cause to only one of them overlooks the complex interaction between race and class.

Ample research and theory exist to test and examine whatever ideas people hold about racial inequality and ethnic success. Theory is not just some abstract or hypothetical way of thinking. Theory provides explanations of observable facts. When a theory no longer suffices to explain a phenomenon that has been carefully observed, the theory must, at least, be revised. Theories also try to answer big questions, such as the one in this chapter: Why do some racial and ethnic groups succeed while others fail? We explore this important question through the presentation of sociological theory about race and ethnic inequality.

We Made It . . . Why Can't They? Assimilation and the American Dream

A central tenet of the American dream is that anyone who tries hard enough can succeed in the United States. Whether coming into the nation from another country or working one's way up from poverty, hard work is perceived as the key to success, or in sociological terms, upward *social mobility*. Popular legends extol the virtues of people who have become wildly successful even when starting from modest origins. People like Oprah Winfrey, Venus and Serena Williams, and Bill Gates come to mind. No doubt about it: These are people with remarkable talent whose hard work and dedication to their craft have made them wealthy. Such cases, though, are the exception, not the rule. Most people end up in much the same class where they began (Isaacs, Sawhill, and Haskins 2008). Far more people with great talent and intelligence never soar to such heights.

The fact that many White, European immigrants have experienced upward mobility over time leads many to think that anyone can make it through hard work and cultural adaptation. Indeed, the ideal of upward mobility is one reason so many immigrants find coming to the United States so appealing. The relative success of White European immigrants over time, though, has become a standard by which other immigrant groups are frequently judged, even though each immigrant group has faced different historical and contemporary conditions. New immigrants are often scorned for not adopting American culture and instead holding on to their own cultural values . . . as if changing their cultural frame is all that is needed to succeed. How do groups become integrated into society? To answer this, we turn to a brief examination of assimilation theory.

The Assimilation Model

The idea that cultural values shape socioeconomic success has a firm grip on American minds, guiding people's thinking about how groups become part of this society. The ideal of the United States as a melting pot[1] where different groups come together and form a single culture has long been part of the American dream.

The process by which ethnic groups are incorporated into this single dominant culture is called **assimilation**. Assimilation is typically thought to involve the gradual dissolution of previous ethnic identities as groups take on the cultural and social habits of the new society (Alba and Nee 2003).

For a long time, the **assimilation model** was the standard for how sociologists and others conceptualized the process of immigrant incorporation. Assimilation was thought to progress as immigrant groups came to be more culturally similar to the host society, especially in the second and third generations. Assimilation was also thought to occur through **acculturation**, that is, the adoption by incoming groups of the language, values, and norms of the host society.

Understanding Immigrant Incorporation

As the U.S. population has become more ethnically diverse, scholars have revised traditional assimilation theory to recognize the complex and different ways that

[1] The chapter opening photo shows an event at the Ford English School—established in 1914 by Henry Ford to teach immigrant workers American values and language—where workers in native dress enter a "melting pot" and emerge "Americanized."

groups become part of a new society. Older thinking about assimilation now has a somewhat negative connotation by suggesting that new immigrants must give up their culture if they are to be incorporated into American society.

Current thinking about immigrant incorporation examines the complex processes involved in the incorporation of new groups. Several ideas guide new research on the process of assimilation:

- Assimilation is not a one-way process.
- Immigrants can maintain an ethnic identity even while assimilating into a new society.
- Immigrant groups vary in the degree to which they are integrated into society.
- How different groups are welcomed into a host nation is influenced by relationships between nations.
- Immigration is shaped by macro-structural conditions, but also by the decisions that individuals and families make in the context of their own lives.
- Some groups become racialized through the process of immigration.

Assimilation is not a one-way process.

An ethnic group may lose some of its unique cultural forms over time, but its presence also changes the society it enters (Alba and Nee 2003; Alba 2012). Mexican Americans, as an example, may enter U.S. society and adopt some of its cultural patterns (language, cultural taste, and so forth), but they will likely also maintain some distinctly Mexican cultural values and behaviors. Furthermore, as groups become incorporated into their new society, the society itself may adopt some of the cultural characteristics of the new group.

Immigrants can maintain an ethnic identity even while assimilating into a new society.

This can happen to differing degrees. Immigrant identity involves a complex process of "practices, beliefs, and behaviors that are subject to constant readjustment and reorganization" (Massey and Sánchez 2010:23–24). Immigrant identity is thought to remain strongest in the presence of an ongoing flow of immigrants that replenishes strong immigrant identification (Jiménez 2010).

Immigrant groups vary in the degree to which they are integrated into society.

The degree of integration depends on the particular social and economic conditions at the time of group entry, as well as the skills and resources that immigrants bring with them (Brown and Bean 2006). Immigrants seldom come from among the poorest people in the nation of origin, because it takes resources to move. Currently, for example, almost one-third of foreign born workers (30.8 percent) are employed in management, professional, and related occupations (U.S. Bureau of Labor Statistics 2015d).

How different groups are welcomed into a host nation is influenced by relationships between nations.

That welcome varies along with the economic, political, and military conditions in the host and sending countries (Rumbaut 1996). The immigration of Cubans into the United States in the 1960s, for example, occurred in the midst of the Cuban Revolution, when the Cuban government nationalized American industries on the island. Most of those who initially fled to the United States during the Cuban Revolution were professionals and other middle-class workers for whom the United States held an open-door policy. Anticommunist sentiment in the United States kept the door more open for Cubans than for other groups; the U.S. government also provided support that enabled many Cubans to do quite well in their new country (Pedraza 1996).

Immigration is shaped by macro-structural conditions, but also by the decisions that individuals and families make in the context of their own lives.

This has been demonstrated in research (Massey and Sánchez 2010). Although immigration involves social structural processes, it is important to remember that people make decisions about their lives in the context of larger social forces. Political refugees have to make difficult decisions to leave their home nations, often disrupting families and communities. Such was the case when Syrian refugees have had to flee to Europe and the United States as the result of war and violence in their country. In such cases "push" factors are more important than the "pull" that other immigrants may feel when seeking new opportunities (Pedraza 1996).

Some groups become racialized through the process of immigration.

Many immigrant groups come from nations where race does not mean what it does in the United States, and they find themselves to be thought of in racial terms once they enter the country. For example, Latinos from various ethnic backgrounds have not traditionally been considered a "race," but some of them experience becoming "blackened," especially if they work in low-wage, service-oriented jobs. Racial profiling, for example, is now leading to high rates of detention and deportation of Latino and Black immigrants (Aranda and Vaquera 2015). Groups are more likely to become racialized during periods of intense **nativism** by the dominant group, that is, when dominant groups begin to favor policies that favor the interests of those already here. Ironically, in the United States strong nativism exists at the same time that the nation extols itself as a nation of immigrants (Kibria, Bowman, and O'Leary 2014).

In sum, assimilation is not a simple linear path that always leads to upward mobility and integration into a new society. Immigrants experience different trajectories, including those who experience downward, not upward, mobility upon arrival (Gans 1992; Jiménez 2010; Waters 2000). As one example, many Vietnamese, Korean, and West Indian immigrants who were highly educated professionals in their home nations find themselves working largely in low-wage service occupations, such as in nail salons and other personal services, in the United States (Kang 2010).

The processes that differentiate patterns of integration for diverse groups are referred to as **segmented assimilation** (Portes and Zhou 1993). Segmented assimilation tells us that immigrants may be integrated into some parts of society, but not others. The social, economic, and cultural resources people bring with them influence chances for assimilation, as does how groups are perceived and received in the host society.

Structural barriers such as poor schools in immigrant neighborhoods or discrimination in the labor market create barriers for immigrant success. Immigrants who become racialized are even less likely to find success. As an expert team of sociologists studying immigration have concluded, "Children of Asian, black, mulatto, and mestizo immigrants cannot escape their ethnicity and race, as defined by the mainstream. Their enduring physical differences from whites and the equally persistent strong effects of discrimination based on those differences . . . throw a barrier in the path of occupational mobility and social acceptance" (Portes, Fernández-Kelly, and Haller 2005:1006).

The linkage between race and ethnicity as social constructs reminds us that like race, ethnicity is a social boundary. The two interweave such that race constructs ethnicity and ethnicity can construct race. The boundaries between the two are fluid and emergent, depending on social and historical conditions (Kibria, Bowman, and O'Leary 2014). Although a black-white divide has long characterized American society, the increasing presence of new immigrant groups changes the boundaries of what both race and ethnicity mean and how they influence diverse group experiences in an unequal society.

A Structural Perspective on Racial Inequality

By now you know that racism is not just about individual attitudes. Rather, it is built into the very structure of society. But you are bound to misunderstand why racial inequality still exists if you do not understand the larger context from which it comes, that is, the institutionalized social practices that have produced and sustained **racial stratification**. Racial stratification is a hierarchical arrangement in society by which different racial groups have differential access to economic and social resources, power, and perceived social worth. Certainly, individual attitudes are partially to blame for the persistence of inequality, but they are a manifestation of underlying institutional structures.

The riots that shook the city of Baltimore in the spring of 2015 provide an example. The nation watched as angry, mostly young Black men and women—many of them in their teens—threw rocks at police, looted stores, and burned cars in the streets. Triggered by the death of a young Black man, Freddie Gray, while he was in police custody, the riots were a symbol of many of the racial problems that the nation faces. Youth unemployment, crime and violence, police brutality, and urban blight, to name a few, are problems that plague not only the city of Baltimore, but also many of our nation's other cities and their communities.

When the riots occurred, some people called the rioters "thugs," as if the disruptive behavior reflected the rioters' misplaced values. The stereotype of young Black people as criminally motivated resonated easily with much of the general public, even while African American leaders in the community called in unison to halt the rioting, calling for peace and nonviolence. The riots beg the question of what conditions generate such behavior (also see LEARNING OUR PAST). Instead of simply blaming individuals, how can we explain what would frustrate people to the point that they would resort to such behavior?

Answering this question requires a structural analysis of racial stratification—how it came to be and why it persists. Several key points anchor a structural analysis of racial stratification. They are:

1. Racial inequality is systemic and cannot be understood simply by looking at individual attitudes and actions.
2. Racial stratification distributes resources (both material and socio-cultural) unequally and in patterned ways.

3. The past matters in shaping the present.
4. The advantages and disadvantages that accrue to different groups in a system of racial stratification are cumulative.
5. State policies play a role in buttressing racial stratification.
6. Racial inequality is anchored in the macro structures of society, but experienced at the micro level of society.
7. Dominant groups have a tendency to blame the victim for racial inequality.
8. Racial stratification overlaps and intersects with other systems of inequality, particularly class and gender.

Let us examine each.

LEARNING OUR PAST

Urban Riots

During the 1960s, riots like the one that shook the city of Baltimore in 2015 erupted in cities around the nation. Urban riots occurred in cities as diverse as Los Angeles; Detroit; Newark, New Jersey; Wilmington, Delaware; Hartford, Connecticut; Chicago; and others. In each city, people were killed and injured, property was destroyed, and hostilities flared. Perhaps presaging the events of five decades later, in each of these urban riots, police behavior was the spark that lit the anger of frustrated communities.

What did we learn from the 1960s riots that can help us explain riots like the one that occurred in Baltimore in 2015? Following the 1960s riots, President Lyndon Johnson appointed the National Advisory Committee on Urban Disorders, known as the Kerner Commission. The Commission was charged with determining the cause of the riots and recommending policies for change. The Kerner Commission report, published in 1968, became a nationally best-selling book.

The Kerner Commission concluded that the underlying cause of the riots was white racism and Black frustration with the lack of economic opportunity. As the report stated, "White racism is essentially responsible for the explosive mixture which has been accumulating in our cities since the end of World War II" (Kerner Commission 1968). The Kerner Commission and subsequent research on urban riots identified various determinants of urban riots, including:

- Pervasive discrimination and segregation in employment, education, and housing
- Black migration into cities and white exodus, thus producing massive and growing concentrations of Black poverty and deteriorating facilities, services, and unmet human needs
- Segregated, poor Black neighborhoods, where there was little opportunity for young people, combined with crime, drug addiction, bitterness, and festering resentment against White society
- White fear over the riots, especially among Whites who had little contact with Black people (Jeffries and Ransford 1969)
- The Black community's general tendency—although most of the rioters were young people—to defend and justify the rioters' actions as a reasonable response to realistic evils (Sears 1969)

In sum, urban riots such as those in the 1960s, as well as more recent ones, are the outward symptoms of deeper social realities (Lee 1968). Have conditions changed since the 1960s in our nation's cities? If so, how? If not, how not? What does this suggest for the potential for more urban violence?

Systemic Racism

Racial stratification refers to a system of power and the unequal distribution of resources. This means that racism is a *system* of racial hierarchy, not just a collection of individual attitudes and behaviors. Individual attitudes and actions are no doubt important, but they have developed within institutions that have been founded and maintained to create, enhance, and defend white property. In this sense, racism as an attitude is not just "tacked on" but is endemic to the whole institutional structure of society. Of course, institutions change over time. Some of the explicit acts of racism of the past are no longer with us, but, as we will see, racism is still very present . . . both at the individual and institutional level. At the institutional level, it is ever-evolving and changing.

Sociologist Joe Feagin defines institutional patterns of racial inequality as **systemic racism.** He writes that systemic racism is "centrally about the creation, development, and maintenance of white privilege, economic wealth, and sociopolitical power over centuries" (Feagin 2014:14). Feagin continues, "Systemic racism includes the complex array of anti-Black practices, the unjustly gained political-economic power of whites, the continuing economic and other resource inequalities along racial lines, and the white racist ideologies and attitudes created to maintain and rationalize white privilege and power" (Feagin 2014:6).

As Feagin argues, systemic racism creates *unjust impoverishment* for people of color and *unjust enrichment* for Whites. This may seem inflammatory, as if Whites are somehow undeserving or not working for what they have earned. An individual's work ethic is not really the point. The point is that institutionalized racial inequality is a system that provides advantages and disadvantages that are not always obvious, nor necessarily intentional, but that nonetheless benefit White people over others, although to different degrees.

White privilege is often taken for granted because its advantages are not usually recognized by those it benefits. The advantages of white privilege are not equally distributed within the White population, but they are nonetheless real (see LIVING WITH RACISM). As shown in chapter 4, Peggy McIntosh (1983) calls white privilege an "invisible backpack," a bundle of tools, roadmaps, passes, and so forth that help clear the path that White people take in society.

White people often question the existence of white privilege, a common reaction especially among White people who see themselves as disadvantaged relative to others. White blue-collar workers, for example, may think they have no privilege at all. In fact, they may think that others are gaining advantages *because of* their race or their gender. The fact is that white privilege is not distributed equally throughout the White population, because the system of racial stratification also intersects with systems of class and gender stratification. Still, even though White people may experience inequality and a precarious economic status, they do not experience racism nor, among men, the sexism that structural inequalities produce.

You can test the presence of white privilege with a simple exercise based on the so-called **racial tax** (see student exercises at the end of this chapter). The racial tax is the antithesis of white privilege, the extra burden that people of color experience as they go through their daily lives. Both the racial tax and white privilege are part of the pattern of systemic racism.

LIVING WITH RACISM

For me, ignoring race and racism has never been an option. Even when it would have been easier to turn away, there were too many forces and circumstances pulling me back, compelling me to look at the matter square in the face—in *my* face. Although White Americans often think we've had few first-hand experiences with race, because most of us are so isolated from people of color in our day-to-day lives, the reality is that isolation *is* our experience with race. We are all experiencing race, because from the beginning of our lives we have been living in a racialized society, in which the color of our skin means something socially, even while it remains largely a matter of biological and genetic irrelevance. Race may be a scientific fiction—and given the almost complete genetic overlap between persons of the various so-called races, it appears to be just that—but it is a social fact that none of us can escape no matter how much or how little we may speak of it. . . . Race can be a falsehood, even as racism continues to destroy lives and, on the flipside, to advantage those who are rarely its targets.

Source: Wise, Tim. 2011. *White Like Me: Reflections on Race from a Privileged Son.* New York: Soft Skull Press.

It is usually easier for White people to think of racism as producing disadvantage for others. Rarely do White people think about the advantages that systemic racism gives them. Not only are White people rarely taught to recognize white privilege, but they also do not typically think about how to change it. As long as white privilege goes unacknowledged, its everyday power persists.

The Distribution of Resources: Racial Stratification

The second point in a structural theory of racial inequality is that economic, cultural, and social resources are distributed unequally by race. You do not have to look very hard to see this. A mere glimpse at data on economic levels, educational attainment, and other social indicators quickly reveals racial disparities on virtually every measure of socioeconomic well-being (see table 6.1). A persistent income gap, differential unemployment rates, levels of educational attainment, rates of arrest and imprisonment, access to political power—even how long you live—are indicative of the consequences of racial inequality.

The various outcomes of racial stratification are shown in table 6.1 and examined in subsequent chapters, but a few highlights include the following:

- Hispanic children are more than twice as likely to be poor as White children; Black children, three times as likely (Proctor, Semega, and Kollar 2016).
- Even with the relatively recent expansion of the Black middle class, the gap between Black and White family income today is *the same* as it was in 1972 (Proctor, Semega, and Kollar 2016).
- Unemployment among Black men is routinely twice the national unemployment rate (U.S. Bureau of Labor Statistics 2016a).
- Asian American poverty is higher than poverty among Whites (Proctor, Semega, and Kollar 2016).

TABLE 6.1   Racial Stratification: Key Indicators

	White, not Hispanic	African American	Hispanic	Asian American	American Indian
Median Income $	62,950	36,898	45,148	77,166	36,252[a]
Poverty Rate %	9.1	24.1	21.4	11.4	29.2[a]
Unemployment Rate %	4.6	9.6	6.6	3.8	6.1[a]
Arrest Rate (per 100,000 people in that population group)	380	2207	966	1.2	2.1
Bachelor's or higher degree, aged 25 and older (2013) %	30.7	27.5	12.9	50	8

Sources: National Center for Educational Statistics. 2014. *Digest of Educational Statistics 2014*. Washington, DC: U.S. Department of Education. (https://nces.ed.gov/PUBSeARCH/pubsinfo.asp?pubid=2016006.); U. S. Bureau of Labor Statistics. 2016. *Employment and Earnings 2015*. Washington, DC: U.S. Department of Labor. (https://www.bls.gov/opub/ee/2015/home.htm.); Federal Bureau of Investigation. 2016a. *Crime in the United States 2015*. Washington, DC: U.S. Department of Justice. (https://ucr.fbi.gov/crime-in-the-u.s/2015/crime-in-the-u.s.-2015.); Proctor, Bernadette D., Jessica L. Semega, and Melissa A. Kollar. 2016. *Income and Poverty in the United States*. Table A-1: Households by Total Money Income, Race, and Hispanic Origin of Householder: 1967–2015. Washington, DC: U.S. Bureau of the Census. (https://www.census.gov/content/dam/Census/library/publications/2016/demo/p60-256.pdf.)

Note: All data from 2015 unless otherwise noted.

[a]Data from 2013.

Despite the fact that such disparities are heavily documented in research, they remain largely invisible to many. As we will see in a later section of this chapter, many people find it easier to blame people for their own failures instead of thinking about the systemic racism that is part of our social structure. Why do such patterns persist? To answer that question, we must look at other features of a structural analysis of racial inequality.

The Past Shapes the Present

Past practices and policies reverberate in the inequality that we see today. This is not as simple as thinking that slavery directly caused modern racism or that the annexation of Mexico is the reason for Mexican Americans' current socioeconomic status. While these events matter, it is the ongoing effect of past practices that has allowed some groups to move forward while others have been held back.

For example, how and when a group entered U.S. society really matters. Don't forget that White European groups arrived voluntarily; African Americans arrived in chains. Mexican Americans were annexed as the result of war. Additional European immigrants arrived around the turn of the twentieth century, as the U.S. economy was expanding. Industrialization provided jobs, even for those who lacked an advanced education.

Recall from the previous chapter that, as White immigrants were entering the United States, Chinese and Japanese laborers were being forcibly removed from the

The invention of the washing machine was accompanied by a campaign to oust Chinese workers from a niche in the labor market. As you can see in this 1886 advertisement, racism, nationalism, and xenophobia intersected to exclude Chinese workers.

workplace (see photo). They were, in fact, completely excluded from entering the country once their labor was no longer needed. And, as White Europeans were gaining a foothold in the U.S. economy, African Americans, though newly freed from slavery, were being subjected to the ravages of Jim Crow racism. Segregated into separate schools, separate housing, and separate public facilities, African Americans, especially in the South, were denied opportunities for economic and social advancement. Even in the North, African Americans who had moved to seek work found themselves shoved into predominantly Black urban ghettoes and sometimes viciously excluded from labor unions.

Other developments in the twentieth century also stymied the advancement of people of color. In the 1930s, for example, the federal New Deal was implemented to alleviate the effects of the Great Depression. Policies enacted under the New Deal provided some relief from the grinding poverty that marked Black life in the South. Enacted during the Franklin D. Roosevelt administration, the policies were color-blind in principle but ended up differently impacting Black and White citizens. The Social Security Act of 1935 denied benefits to domestic and agricultural workers—the very occupations that employed the majority of Black men and women at the time. As a result, if you were Black in the 1930s, despite the best intentions of federal policies of assistance, you did not receive the same benefits Whites received (Katznelson 2005).

In sum, the point of looking to the past to understand racial inequality is not to locate present conditions solely in the past but to see the impact of past decisions and actions on racial inequality in the present. Once you do so, you will see, in the sobering words of comedian Jon Stewart, how the past has "left us with a gaping racial wound that will not heal" (Duchon 2015).

Accumulating Advantage and Disadvantage

People denied opportunities in the past simply start from a different place in the present. Even when obstacles have been removed, such as through the passage of civil rights legislation, past practices mean that groups have a particular challenge just catching up. President Lyndon Johnson captured this well in a famous commencement address delivered at Howard University in 1965. Johnson said, "You do not take a person who, for years, has been hobbled by chains and liberate him, bring him up to the starting line of a race and then say, 'You are free to complete with all the others,' and still justly believe that you have been completely fair" (Johnson 1965).

Johnson's words are reflected in the concept of the **sedimentation of racial inequality**, which refers to the fact that "structural disadvantages have been layered one upon the other to produce black disadvantage and white privilege" (Oliver and Shapiro 1995:51). Discrimination and racial segregation in the past have prevented people of color from accumulating assets to the same extent as White Americans. How so?

A great example comes from the federal GI Bill, passed in the aftermath of World War II. Historians now claim that the GI Bill was the single most important factor in creating America's middle class. It provided returning veterans access to low-cost home mortgages, business loans, and educational benefits. Specifically, under this bill, if you bought a new house in the newly developing suburbs in the 1950s, you could get a very-low-interest loan, perhaps even without making a down payment. This was a huge boon both for the housing market and for those who purchased "starter" homes that appreciated over the years. This benefit gave those who had even modest means some degree of financial equity—an asset that they could then pass on to the next generation or possibly reinvest.

Following World War II, the GI Bill gave returning veterans support for attending college. It is estimated that 48 percent would not have been able to attend without the help of the GI Bill. Yet racial segregation in the nation's colleges and universities meant that this advantage was not equally enjoyed by returning Black veterans.

Who benefitted? African Americans and other people of color certainly were among those who fought in World War II and were entitled to the benefits of the GI Bill. But systemic racism prevented people of color from being able to access the opportunities that this important legislation provided. One major obstacle was the decision to administer the benefits of the GI Bill in a decentralized way, thus putting its administration in the hands of local officials who in many localities supported segregation and made it difficult, if not impossible, for Black veterans to access the benefits of this legislation.

Racial discrimination in the housing market also prevented veterans of color from acquiring the same benefits that Whites received. Restrictive covenants written into deeds commonly prevented people of color from buying homes in predominantly White neighborhoods. Other discriminatory practices by banks and real estate agents kept people of color out of newly forming suburban neighborhoods in which even buying a small home—a modest financial asset—would pay off over future generations. Denied this possibility, disadvantage accumulated over time for persons of color.

The GI Bill also provided unprecedented access to higher education. Yet when it was passed, educational institutions were still highly segregated. In the North, African Americans made up a tiny proportion of students in colleges that were using highly selective criteria for admission. Black veterans in the South were still formally excluded from White institutions of higher education. The GI Bill did provide a boon for enrollment in historically black colleges, but segregation in education remained a fact of life.

The end result was that a colorblind benefit like the GI bill—in the context of systemic racism—prevented veterans of color from attaining the same upward mobility so many White veterans experienced. People of color fell behind the starting line. Although the GI Bill did foster the growth of a small Black middle class, its advantages accrued mostly to the white middle class, producing what Ira Katznelson has called "affirmative action for whites" (Katznelson 2005). Generations of White people benefited from this policy, even though the descendants of World War II veterans might not readily recognize the advantage it provided. As sociologists Melvin Oliver and Thomas Shapiro write, "Every circumstance of bias and discrimination against Blacks has produced a circumstance and opportunity of positive gain for Whites" (1995:51). That is how the *sedimentation of racial inequality* works.

State Policies Make a Difference

You can see in the example of the GI Bill that state policies matter in furthering or reducing racial inequality. Note that the GI Bill was a federal program open to all veterans, no matter their race. On the face of it, the program seemed to provide opportunities for Black, Latino, and Native American veterans to seek more education, better housing, and perhaps open a small business. Faced with open and legal segregation though, people of color were excluded by a seemingly colorblind policy that nonetheless left people of color "cemented to the bottom of society's economic hierarchy" (Oliver and Shapiro 1995:5).

Other state-based policies also contributed to this disadvantage. We do not normally think of the current interstate highway system as racist. Everyone uses it, no one is denied access to it, and it exists due to a huge outlay of federal dollars. We now take for granted that the interstate highway system lets us move relatively easily and quickly from state to state and coast to coast. Begun in the 1950s, the system was designed to reduce city traffic, increase interstate commerce, and facilitate the movement of people, mostly White, from the burgeoning, mostly White suburbs to city jobs. The result was a sharp increase in the number of automobiles, population change with Whites in the suburban ring of cities and people of color in the cities proper, and a shift in the balance of power between cities and suburbs (Sherman 2014).

Whom did the interstate highway system serve best? It strained the transportation budgets of cities and was also built in ways that walled off Black and Latino urban neighborhoods. In many cases, Black and other ethnic neighborhoods were actually destroyed as homes were demolished to make way for highways. Often people of color were cut off from transportation networks that provided access to jobs and the more economically vital parts of the city (Sherman 2014). Once again, policies of the federal government opened doors for some and closed them for others.

Racism at Every Level

A structural perspective on racial inequality locates racial inequality in the macro-structure of society. That is, the roots of racial inequality lie in society's institutions—the economy, the political system, and so forth. Yet, even with racial inequality anchored at the macro level, it is manifested at different levels of society.

Sociologist Evelyn Glenn delineates this by identifying three levels at which processes of racial inequality appear: *social structure, representation*, and *micro-interaction*. Social structure refers to the "rules regulating the allocation of power and resources" in society. Micro-interaction includes the norms, etiquette, and spatial rules that orchestrate social interaction across racial boundaries. The representational level refers to the "symbols, language, and images that express and convey racial meanings" (Glenn 2002:12). You can also think of these three levels as:

* the institutional level
* the ideological level; and,
* the interaction level.

The education arena provides a brief example. At the institutional level, a large amount of racial segregation marks the nation's schools and colleges. White men hold the most institutional power by being those most likely to hold positions of leadership, especially in the most prestigious institutions. Racial disparities also persist in educational attainment and in the quality of schools. Being able to attend the very best schools also reproduces racial inequality because those with the most prestigious educational credentials are those most likely to achieve high socioeconomic status.

At the ideological level, the images, ideas, and ideals that are taught in schools implicitly or explicitly promote racial exclusion. For example, how are people of color seen in schoolbooks? Although representations of people of color have improved a lot in recent years, stereotypes continue to disparage people of color, as we saw in chapter 3. What you don't see can be just as damaging as what you do see (Tatum 1997). For example, limited images or histories of people of color in textbooks teach all of us that somehow people of color do not matter much or that they are inferior, marginal, and different—reflections of racial inequality at the level of ideology.

At the level of interaction, race shapes how different groups are treated in schools and how students interact with each other. Latino and Black boys, for example, tend to be labeled early on as "troublemakers." The label alone can be enough to produce behavior that funnels Latino and Black boys into the "school to prison pipeline" (Ferguson 2000; Stromquist 2012; Noguera and Hurtado 2011).

Racial inequality exists at every level of society, underscoring the importance of change at all levels: how people interact; what they think and believe; and how resources and positions of influence are distributed. You will see, in the chapters on social institutions that follow, how these different levels of inequality are played out in different settings, such as work, education, health care, and criminal justice.

Blaming the Victim

Most people, especially those in the dominant group, find it easier to blame racially unequal people and groups for their own failure than to acknowledge the structural roots of racial inequality. Blaming the victim is a strong narrative in American culture—a narrative that makes individuals responsible for their own outcomes, no matter what structural barriers or assists they might face (Ryan 1971).

Individualism is a strong cultural ideal in American society. A culture of individualism gives people unprecedented freedom, but it also obscures the realities of structurally based group inequalities. You see evidence of this tendency in public opinion polls. White people are more likely to see a level playing field for all than people of color are. For example, in national polls asking if discrimination is still to blame for Black Americans' inferior jobs, income, and housing, only 15 percent of Whites say discrimination is mostly to blame; 83 percent of Whites say it is "something else" (Gallup 2013). Although this national survey did not probe to find out what "something else" means, the odds are that respondents blamed Black people's values and attitudes to a great extent.

Nowhere is the tendency to blame people for their own plight more apparent than in public understandings of poverty. Structural inequality is by far the main reason poverty is as high as it is in the United States (see chapter 7). People repeatedly say that poverty is the result of deficient family values, poor parenting, lack of ambition, or an absence of the work ethic, among other shortcomings. Even the very name of the federal law that now shapes federal assistance to the poor reflects this assumption. Titled the Personal Responsibility and Work Opportunity Act, this federal policy (so-called welfare reform; also see chapters 3 and 7) names "personal responsibility" as the trigger point for poverty (Greenbaum 2015). Unless the narrative of blaming the victim ceases to exist, people will continue to deny that racism is real and will overlook continuing practices of discrimination and the impact of past practices on the reproduction of racial inequality.

Intersecting Inequalities: Race, Class, and Gender

Anyone who has experienced the pernicious effects of racial inequality knows how all-consuming the experience of racism can be. Race has a social and economic impact all its own, but race also intersects with the influence of other social factors, including social class, gender, age, sexual preference, and nationality, among others.

The scholarship that examines the intricate connections between different social factors, especially class, race, gender, and sexuality, is **intersectional theory**. It took a feminist revolution and the work of women of color for most people to begin seriously analyzing how race, class, gender, and sexuality interrelate (Baca Zinn and Dill 1996). As a second wave of feminism developed in the 1960s and 1970s, women of color criticized the feminist movement for ignoring them. A new and more complete way of understanding the experiences of diverse groups of women emerged. Now intersectional analyses of race, class, gender, and sexuality have amassed a wide swath of research in every field of study.

The basic insight of intersectional theory is that race, class, and gender operate simultaneously in shaping the experience of all people (Andersen and Collins 2016; Crenshaw 1989; Collins 1990). The point is not to compare and rank oppressions or to try to discern whether race or class or gender is the most important feature of one's life. Rather, the point is to understand how race, class, and gender are together embedded in a *matrix of domination* in society (Collins 1990). Race, class, and gender, interwoven into the social structure of society, operate in overlapping and interconnected patterns of power and inequality—together shaping all people's lives.

Of course, at any given moment, a given person might feel the influence of one social factor more than another. A Black man stopped by the police in an affluent neighborhood will certainly feel the salience of his race most prominently at that moment. The fact that he is a man, however, is just as important as race in shaping his overall life chances. Likewise, a Latina who is sexually harassed while walking down the street will keenly feel her gender, but her identity as Latina actually merges both her gender and racial-ethnic identity, probably along with her class and age.

Intersectional theory also teaches us that race, class, and gender are each manifested differently, depending on the others. Masculinity, for example, may be expressed differently if one is Latino and poor versus Black and middle-class or White and poor. Likewise, being a woman is manifested differently depending on one's class and race position. Intersectionality means that we have to understand the unique and complex ways that people are located in a system of overlapping inequalities. In the above example of a Black man stopped by the police, the fact that he is a Black man of a particular class status is what matters as a whole.

By understanding the interconnections of race, class, and gender, we also garner a more complete view of how society is organized and how we live our lives, depending on our social location. The social facts of race, class, and gender are not isolated one from the other. Each is manifested differently depending on its configuration with others (Andersen and Collins 2016). For example, White women are disadvantaged by virtue of their gender, but advantaged by virtue of their racial status. In chapter 7 you will see in more detail how intersectionality plays out in the social and economic status of different groups.

What's Class Got to Do with It? The Race-Class Connection

People often say it is class, not race, that best explains the fact that so many people of color have lower socioeconomic status than do most Whites. Certainly, class is relevant, but does class obliterate the influence of race? The fact is that class and race matter together in shaping people's life opportunities, and they combine in particular ways at different times. We can see this by taking a long-range view of how race and class have been conjoined in different periods of U.S. history.

In an important analysis of racial inequality, William Julius Wilson (1978) divides U.S. history into three broad periods that he argues are key to understanding the shifting connection between race and class. Wilson links transformations in the significance of race to key political-economic transitions in U.S. history. Through this long-range lens, Wilson points to large-scale transitions that currently shape the connection between race and class.

The three distinct periods that Wilson identifies have shaped the life chances of African Americans. Each characterizes a different **political economy**, which is the linkage between systems of power and economic systems at given points in time. The periods are:

1. the pre-industrial economy
2. the industrial economy
3. the post-industrial economy

The pre-industrial economy in the United States marks the period of slavery. Although slavery existed only in the South, the nation's entire economy was dependent on a slave-based system. Under slavery, racial power was absolute, lying solely in the hands of the White aristocracy. Racial oppression was conscious, deliberate, and explicit—a system of racial power that continued even beyond the end of slavery, especially with the advent of Jim Crow, legally mandated racial segregation. Even though masked by white paternalism, state policies were explicitly racial. Although in the pre-industrial period there was minimum physical distance between racial groups, there was maximum social distance.

The industrial period, roughly from the beginning of the twentieth century through World War II, is marked by the growth of industrial labor. Manufacturing, not agriculture, became the economic driver. During this period, race relations were marked by more overt racial and class conflict, especially between White and Black workers, but also between Whites and others. White workers tried to neutralize Black competition in the labor force while managers used race to try to divide the interests of the working class. During this time period, Blacks also fled the South as best they could both to escape the ravages of Jim Crow and to seek new job opportunities. The result was the emergence of an urban, but segregated, Black population.

In the post-industrial period (roughly post–World War II through the present), the nation's economic base shifted from manufacturing to the service industries. That is, manufacturing jobs declined while those based on service work increased. This transition has been fueled by automation and the use of technology, but also by the rise of a global economy where manufacturing jobs have been largely relocated overseas, where labor is cheaper.

Wilson argues that this political-economic transformation has had huge and deleterious effects on Black Americans and other people of color. In the post-industrial period, he argues, class has increasing significance in shaping the life chances of people of color, including recent immigrant groups. In an industrial economy people (especially men) could find relatively decent jobs in manufacturing without being highly educated or having advanced technological skills. But without such skills and training in the post-industrial economy, people get stuck in low-wage service work—or they have no work at all. Chronic unemployment and poverty are the result, forming an **urban underclass** consisting of people (mostly of color, but also the white working class and poor) at the absolute bottom of the economic system who are largely unable to overcome the barriers posed by structural realignments in the political economy. In this context, class and race intermingle in shaping people's life chances. Furthermore, racial tensions are then driven by these social structural transformations. When you add contemporary patterns of immigration to the mix, race and ethnic relations become highly volatile.

In sum, in our post-industrial period, race does not alone determine life chances, as would have been true in earlier periods of time. Yet, class and race are still deeply intertwined, meaning you cannot claim that the influence on people's well-being is simply one or the other. Race and class together form a structure of opportunity that has profound effects on the life chances of various groups.

What about Culture? The Culture-Structure Debate

Throughout this chapter, you have read some of the common reasons people give for racial inequality. Many of these commonsense explanations blame the culture of the disadvantaged for their lack of success. "If people would only try harder" or "if parents would just raise their children right" is commonly heard in conversations about the causes of inequality—*ifs* that are routinely leveled at people of color.

Does culture have a role in explaining social and economic outcomes? This is a hotly debated question among political commentators, policy makers, and scholars. Understanding this debate—and deciding what is true—first requires another look at the concept of culture, on the one hand, and that of social structure, on the other.

Culture refers to the total way of life of a given society or group of people. Culture includes many things—both material objects and ideas such as values, norms, habits, perceptions, attitudes, and so forth. These different ideas are the mental frames that people use to understand and interpret the world they inhabit (Small, Harding, and Lamont 2010). Culture provides, then, a shared outlook and modes of behavior that are the lived world of people in society (Wilson 2009, 2010a; also see chapter 3 of this volume).

Social structure, on the other hand, refers to practices in society, often abstract, that influence people's behavior and outcomes in life. Social structure includes behavior, such as discrimination, and institutional practices, such as laws, policies, and various procedures that shape how we behave and where we end up. Social structure also comprises the large-scale changes in society—demographic, economic, political, and so forth—that have adverse effects on different groups (Wilson 2009).

When people point to culture as a cause of racial inequality (or other forms of inequality), they are usually using culture to refer to the attitudes, values, and behaviors of the disadvantaged—as if people's cultural outlook prevents them from succeeding. There is, however, "considerable evidence of the widespread adoption of mainstream values among the poor" (Small, Harding, and Lamont 2010:14).

The research evidence is that people who are poor want to work, want to marry, and want to have the resources of a comfortable life, but find their quest to do so thwarted (Edin and Kefalas 2005).

There is also ample evidence in the research scholarship of the existence of certain unique cultural attitudes and behaviors among the urban poor, even when they also share the values of the dominant culture (Venkatesh 2006). Elijah Anderson's ethnographic research (1999), for example, details how people in poor, racially segregated neighborhoods value "street smarts," and act accordingly in an elaborate set of cultural-meaning systems and behaviors. Anderson and others are quick to point out, however, that developing a "code of the street" is a necessary adaptation for living in safety; for men, it also has to do with a display of masculinity otherwise denied by the dominant culture (hooks 2003; Majors and Billson 1993). As with other cultural forms, the "code of the street" shows how people in challenging situations develop innovative and creative social practices and social structures even without the cultural resources that dominant group members will have. Hip-hop culture is another example; it is a highly innovative set of practices (in language and body movement) and values that emerged from the street, even though it is now quite mainstream (Morgan and Fischer 2010).

Note, then, that culture is an *adaptation to social structural conditions*—poverty, segregation, denial of opportunity—and not a thing in and of itself, even though it can take on a life of its own. Although a distinct culture may exist among the disadvantaged, it is intricately entangled with social structure. Culture is not a causal determinant of poverty or racial inequality; it only shoulders the blame for the effects of social structure.

When culture is invoked as an explanation for racial inequality, typically the focus is on the culture of the disadvantaged. But the influence of the *dominant culture*—its values, norms, and attitudes—is just as important (Wilson 2009). We have already seen that racism in the dominant culture is a powerful force that shapes social outcomes for different groups. In addition, the dominant culture can rely on **cultural capital**, which refers to the knowledge and resources that advantaged groups get by virtue of their location in society. The best schooling, influential social networks, style of speech, knowledge of elite culture, and other non-material assets form the cultural capital that enables people to experience economic mobility and to pass their advantages on to subsequent generations. Ignoring the influence of the dominant culture while targeting culture as an explanation for racial inequality is missing the elephant in the room.

In the end, debates about culture and structure have to be attentive to the larger social forces that produce cultural habits and outlooks. The culture-structure debate is usually stated as an either-or proposition. Cultural explanations usually get the most attention from policy makers (Wilson 2009). But culture and structure are two sides of the same coin; both are connected to the concept of race in society. Cultural explanations resonate with the value of individualism that is deeply rooted in U.S. society, but a sole focus on culture blunts attention to potential structural changes that could actually alleviate racial inequality.

Conclusion

A structural analysis of racial inequality shows that it is "neither fixed nor timeless" (Hobbs 2014:74). Such a conclusion can be read as pessimistic about the possibilities for social change because the system seems so entrenched. A structural analysis, though, also provides hope, because inequalities that evolve from structural factors can be changed if the structures are transformed. Throughout the course of U.S. history, people of color and their allies have organized to resist the structural oppression that racial inequality produces. These actions are examined further in chapter 12.

The important thing to see now is how racial inequality has its roots in institutional practices. The manifestation of racism at the institutional level can be seen in every one of the institutions of society—work, family, education, health care, criminal justice, among others—subjects to which we will turn next.

Key Terms

acculturation, 124

assimilation, 124

assimilation model, 124

class, 123

cultural capital, 141

intersectional theory, 138

nativism, 126

political economy, 139

racial stratification, 127

racial tax, 129

sedimentation of racial inequality, 133

segmented assimilation, 126

systemic racism, 129

urban underclass, 140

Critical Thinking Questions

1. You are discussing race with a friend who says, "If people would just try harder, they would succeed. That is proven by the experience of immigrant groups." Having read this chapter, what would you now say?
2. How is blaming the victim consistent with American cultural values? How is it not? What does your answer suggest for changing this common response to racial inequality?

Student Exercises

6.1: Using the concept of the "invisible backpack" of white privilege, make your own list of white privileges in everyday life. If you can, compare your list to those that people from a different racial group make. How can such an exercise help us reduce the effects of racism? You can also expand this exercise to develop lists of other forms of privilege, thus developing an *intersectional analysis* of privilege.

6.2: If you can, do this exercise in a group that includes both White people and people of color. Each person gets one point for each item that he or she can answer as "true." Once completed, you will very likely find that the number of points White people get far exceeds the number of points people of color get. These differences in the everyday experiences of Whites and people of color are a good illustration of how systemic racism is played out in the everyday experiences of people *even when they have every intention of not being racist.* White privilege prevails for some, while others pay a "racial tax."

1. I can take a job in an organization with an affirmative action policy without people thinking I got my job because of my race.
2. I can look at the mainstream media and see people who look like me represented in a wide variety of roles.
3. I can go shopping most of the time pretty well assured that I will not be followed or harassed.
4. If my car breaks down on a deserted stretch of road, I can trust that the law enforcement officer who shows up will be helpful.
5. I have a wide choice of grooming products that I can buy in places convenient to campus and/or near where I live as a student.
6. I never think twice about calling the police when trouble occurs.
7. The schools I have attended teach about my race and heritage and present them in positive, affirming ways.
8. I can be pretty sure that if I go into a business or other organization (such as the university) to speak with the "person in charge," I will be facing a person of my race.
9. I rarely feel that I am being singled out because of my racial-ethnic identity.
10. When I graduate from college, employers will evaluate me based on my skills and accomplishments.

Challenging Questions/Open to Debate

Some argue that class has become more important than race in determining the life chances of people of color. Do you agree or disagree? Does your answer change when considering groups other than African Americans?

Economic Inequality

Work, Class, and Poverty

As long as poverty, injustice and gross inequality exist in our world, none of us can truly rest.
—Nelson Mandela

OBJECTIVES

- Describe the significance of income inequality for people of color

- Explain why wealth is important in understanding racial inequality

- Define and discuss economic restructuring as it shapes the status of people of color

- Analyze the status of people of color in the workforce

- Compare and contrast different explanations of racialized economic inequality

- Discuss how race affects the likelihood of poverty and current social policies to address poverty

Signs of race and economic inequality are all around us. If you go into any major city, you will see homeless people—many of them African American—on the streets. Who lives in the wealthiest sections of the city? Who maintains the gardens and lawns in those exclusive homes? Drive through a highway construction site and take note of the workers' race and gender. Are White men doing the skilled labor while people of color, and perhaps some White women, stand and hold the stop signs? For that matter, who works in what jobs on your college campus?

These observations will tell you a lot about the topics covered in this chapter: how race shapes income and wealth inequality, and the experiences of people of color in the workplace. People from many different groups, including White people, suffer from unemployment, low wages, and blocked opportunities while income inequality is on the rise in the nation. Economic inequality falls disproportionately on the nation's racial and ethnic minorities, a fact that is especially evident in the high rates of poverty among people of color.

We begin with two hypothetical scenarios that reveal some of the workings of racial and economic inequality. Imagine two men whom we will name John Page and Jordan Henderson. Both work as midlevel managers in a local bank. John lives in a nearby suburb and owns a home worth about $250,000. He and his wife still make monthly payments on their mortgage, but they can afford it with their two salaries. Their payments are also affordable because John's parents helped them out with a substantial down payment when they bought the house. John's parents have recently retired and sold the home where John grew up. Because their home had appreciated over time, they were able to pay cash for the smaller home in the retirement community where they now live. John is glad that his parents are financially comfortable and that their health is good enough that they can travel and do other things they enjoy. He is also relieved that his parents' retirement community provides assisted living and nursing care for when his parents will likely need more care. For now, his parents enjoy the many activities that the community includes: a pool, gym, game rooms, and other amenities.

Jordan makes the same salary as John. The two men also have the same job benefits (health insurance partially supported by the bank, a retirement fund, two weeks of paid vacation, and some sick days allowed each year). Both John and Jordan consider themselves middle-class and, by most people's understanding of middle-class, they are. Jordan recently bought a house, but he could not afford to live in John's neighborhood. In fact, he had had to pick up a second part-time job to save enough for a small down payment. His monthly payment is about the same as John's but his house is only valued at $150,000. Jordan also uses part of his salary to support his aging parents, both of whom have health problems. It is clear that his parents will both need full-time nursing care soon, and Jordan is really worried about how he will pay for it. He hates the idea of putting them in one of the nearby nursing homes—depressing places with a lot of old women just sitting in the hallways in wheelchairs—but he cannot afford anything better. Unlike John, whose two children will soon be off to college, Jordan has no idea how he will pay the in-state tuition of the nearby college for his children. He is very afraid of increasing his debt.

Two families, both middle-class, and two very different life situations: These scenarios could describe any number of families, but in this case, John's hypothetical family is White and Jordan's is Black. Of course, there are White families in each of these situations, just as there are Black and Latino families who are not struggling but living a comfortable middle-class life. But overall, race is highly significant in shaping how well individuals and families fare and how well they can manage common life situations, much less emergencies such as a health crisis, an accident, or a job layoff.

The scenarios above provide an important sociological lesson about the significance of race, along with class, in understanding people's lived experiences. The scenarios also teach us a lesson about the significance of both income and wealth in shaping people's life chances. As we saw in the previous chapter, the economic standing of different racial-ethnic groups in the present is shaped by the cumulative effects of the past. In the scenarios above, the fact that John's White family had resources that could be passed on to the next generation puts John in a more advantageous position relative to Jordan, even though both are earning exactly the same income now. Key to understanding their different life situation is the distinction between income and wealth.

Income Inequality: The Difference Race Makes

Income is the money brought into a household over a given period from various sources, such as earnings and investment dividends. In 2015, **median income** for all households in the United States was $56,516. A median is the midpoint, that is, half the population has higher income; half, lower. Of course, what a particular income means depends on many things such as family size, region of residence, special needs, and, as we will see, whether one has any other sources of financial security.

Perhaps an income of about $56,000 sounds like a lot to you, but what does it actually provide? Economists estimate that a family living on a median income might own a home but have many years left on the mortgage. The parents probably drive a used car and have older versions of smartphones and other electronics. If they take a family vacation, they probably stay close to home, possibly staying with relatives or friends. They have no luxuries and only a small savings account, if any. The children are certainly not wearing the most recent fashionable labels (Rose 2014). Is this a middle-class lifestyle? Certainly not, at least if middle-class status is judged by what you see in televised sitcoms or dramas, which display images of middle-class comfort that are unattainable on a median income.

The reported median income of $56,616 is for all U.S. households. By adding in race and ethnicity, the picture changes. White non-Hispanic and Asian American median incomes are the highest. Hispanic and African American households fare the worst, as you can see in figure 7.1. Except for Asian Americans, the only families that actually reach the level of national median income are married-couple families with two earners present. You also must be careful in interpreting Asian American income because this broad category includes Asian American groups whose median incomes are substantially different. (You can learn more about income and various social characteristics by exploring the topic on the webpage of the U.S. Bureau of the Census, http://www.census.gov.)

Factors other than race, such as gender, age, and region of residence also predict household income. A caution is needed here, however. You will commonly hear that the income gap between women and men is about 20 percent. That is accurate when

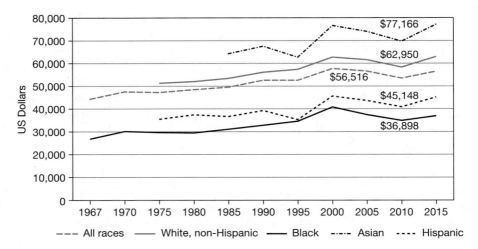

FIG. 7.1 Median Income, 1967–2015

Source: Proctor, Bernadette D., Jessica L. Semega, and Melissa A. Kollar. 2016. *Income and Poverty in the United States:2015*. Table A-1: Households by Total Money Income, Race, and Hispanic Origin of Householder: 1967–2015. Washington, DC: U.S. Bureau of the Census. (Also available at https://www. census.gov/content/dam/Census/library/publications/2016/demo/p60-256.pdf.)

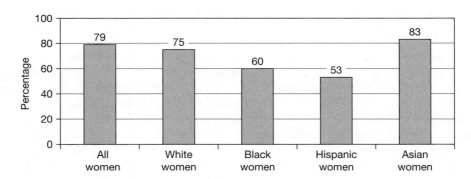

FIG. 7.2 Women's Income as a Percent of White Men's Income (Year-Round, Full-Time Workers)

Source: Proctor, Bernadette D., Jessica L. Semega, and Melissa A. Kollar. 2016. *Income and Poverty in the United States: 2015*. Table A-1: Households by Total Money Income, Race, and Hispanic Origin of Householder: 1967–2015. Washington, DC: U.S. Bureau of the Census. (Also available at https://www.census.gov/content/dam/Census/library/publications/2016/demo/p60-256.pdf.)

looking at *all* women compared to *all* men, a big change from 1970 when it was 58 percent. But the gender income gap changes when you add race and compare different racial-ethnic groups of women to White men. For example, even when working year-round and full-time, Hispanic women earn only 34 percent of what White men earn with both working year-round and full-time, as you can see in figure 7.2.

Later in this chapter we will look at why the racial gap in income persists. For now, it might surprise you to know that the income gap between African American and White households now is *exactly the same* as it was in 1967: 58 percent, as you see in figure 7.1. The Hispanic-White income percentage (at 72 percent) has barely changed since 1972 (when it was 74 percent), the first year that Hispanics were separately identified in the federal income data (Proctor, Semega, and Kollar 2016a). Even with the growth of the black and Hispanic middle classes, the income gap between Whites and other groups remains persistent and substantial.

Income is surely important in determining one's well-being. Volumes of research over the years have shown that income is highly correlated with such things as physical and mental health, victimization by crime, political values, and even how well one scores on standardized tests (Andersen and Taylor 2017). Income is clearly important, but even more telling about one's relative economic well-being is wealth—or lack thereof.

Race, Wealth, and Debt

Wealth, different from income, is the monetary value of all of one's assets minus outstanding debt. This is also known as one's *net worth*. The significance of wealth lies not only in the resources it provides, but also in the fact that it can accumulate over time and be transmitted to subsequent generations. It works like frequent flier miles: The more you have, the more you can get.

While the racial income gap is large and unchanging, the racial wealth gap is even greater. On average, Whites actually have *twelve times* the wealth of Black Americans and *ten times* as much as Hispanics (McKernan et al. 2015). Another way to put this is that for every dollar saved by White Americans, African Americans have 12 pennies; Hispanics, 10 pennies (see figure 7.3).

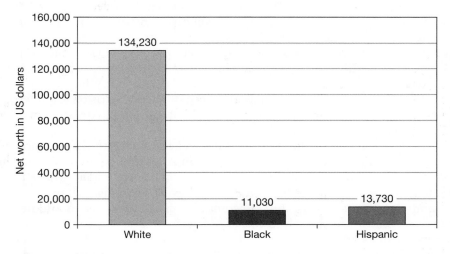

FIG. 7.3 The Wealth Gap

Source: McKernan, Signe-Mary, Caroline Ratcliffe, C. Eugene Steuerle, Emma Kalish, and Caleb Quakenbush. 2015. *Nine Charts about Wealth Inequality in America.* The Urban Institute. (http://datatools.urban.org/Features/wealth-inequality-charts/.)

The wealth gap is partially caused by income inequality. Higher incomes obviously make it possible to save more. Differences in earnings over a lifetime also add up. Indeed, the wealth gap between African Americans and Whites grows as the two groups age. To illustrate: When they are in their thirties, White Americans have three times the wealth of Black Americans, but by age sixty, White Americans have eleven times as much (McKernan et al. 2015).

Employment patterns also influence how much one will have saved in a retirement account. Currently, 68 percent of all workers do not have an employer-sponsored retirement plan. Only half of all employers now offer retirement plans, a decline since 1999 when two-thirds of employers did so. White workers are more likely to be working for employers who provide retirement plans; 63 percent of Whites have such a benefit, compared to 34 percent of Hispanics, 49 percent of Asians, and 58 percent of African Americans (Shin 2015). Without such a plan, retirees have to rely on Social Security income (which is affected by one's lifetime earnings); they might also have to continue working or face the possibility of poverty.

Most people's primary source of wealth, even when modest, is home ownership. Home ownership for Hispanics has improved somewhat in recent years, but for African Americans it has worsened. Both Blacks and Hispanics, however, are less likely to own homes than are Whites—even when they are at the same income level. In 2013, 69 percent of White families owned their own home, compared to 45 percent of Hispanics and 43 percent of African Americans (McKernan et al. 2015). Black and Hispanic families are also more vulnerable to losing their homes through foreclosure. Research also finds that when people of color move into an integrated neighborhood, it often "turns" minority. Home values then decline (Flippen 2004).

The other side of wealth is debt. Because Whites in general have more assets than people of color, they are able to manage higher levels of debt, especially in the form of home mortgages. Looking only at credit card debt, studies actually find little difference in the debt carried by White, Black, and Hispanic Americans, but, when you consider mortgage debt along with other debt payments, Blacks and Hispanics spend a higher portion of their monthly income on debt payments (53 percent for Black Americans, 56 percent for Hispanics, and 47 percent for Whites; De'Armond and Zhu 2011). Student loan debt has also been dramatically rising for all groups, but the average debt from student loans is highest among African Americans (McKernan et al. 2015).

Without an understanding of racial differences in wealth, you cannot fully understand the dynamics of racial inequality in America. Even in the Black and Hispanic middle classes, the wealth gap means there are racial differences in what it means to be middle-class. One might have a good income, own a home, and send children to college, but substantial racial differences in middle-class lifestyles can still prevail. Middle-class African Americans, for example, still have an earnings gap of seventy cents to the dollar compared to middle-class Whites, but for every dollar of wealth held by the White middle class, middle-class Blacks have only fifteen cents. Wealth matters because its absence makes it more difficult to achieve the dreams that people have for their children (Oliver and Shapiro 2006).

Growing Inequality and Economic Restructuring: What's Race Got to Do with It?

The differences reported here in income and wealth have long been true, but they exist now in a context of growing inequality among all Americans. For most people in the bottom half of the income distribution, income has been quite flat in recent years. For those at the top, income has increased. Equally telling is the distribution of wealth: Just 10 percent of the population hold two-thirds of all wealth in the nation (Rose 2014). The United States is rapidly becoming a more unequal society than at any other time in the past.

Inequality in any society or group may be assessed by what is known as the **Gini coefficient,** a measure of income distribution in a given group or society. Measurement ranges from zero to one; zero indicates that there is no inequality, and one indicates that one person holds all of the income. Sweden, one of the most equal societies in the world, has a Gini coefficient of .27 while the United States has one of .41—the highest among the industrialized nations (World Bank 2015).

The Gini coefficient can be used to compare the degree of inequality between nations, but it can also be used to measure the degree of inequality *within* particular groups. It seems from limited current research that inequality among Whites is increasing, while African Americans have seen less change (Schneider 2013). Income inequality is known to contribute to poor health as well as other adverse outcomes for people. The impact of growing income inequality, however, may actually be somewhat higher for the most advantaged groups—likely because the disadvantaged are already feeling the brunt of inequality (Subramanian and Kawachi 2006). This can help explain some of the anger and frustration of the white working class whose sense of disenfranchisement can be expressed as racism, such as when its members blame people of color rather than understanding how the system of inequality works against many White people too.

The inequality we are witnessing is happening in the midst of massive **economic restructuring,** that is, socioeconomic changes that are fundamentally altering patterns of employment and work. Economic restructuring includes four major components: deindustrialization, the information technology revolution, globalization, and demographic change (Andersen and Taylor 2017).

Deindustrialization is the shift that began at the end of World War II and has moved the nation away from a manufacturing-based economy to a service-based economy. The transition from manufacturing to service continues to change the work people do and the opportunities that work brings. You see this shift in the large numbers of workers who have been displaced from jobs in such areas as steelwork, coal-mining, and other manufacturing industries. Job loss has been especially prominent in so-called Rust Belt states, such as Ohio, Pennsylvania, and West Virginia, among others, where work was traditionally dominated by these blue-collar jobs. Promises to bring back such jobs likely influenced the election of Donald Trump as president, but the reality is that the decline of such jobs is the result of longtime structural changes, which makes it unlikely that such jobs will come back in any significant way.

In a manufacturing-based economy, most workers produce goods. In a service-based economy, most jobs involve either direct services (such as medical care, childcare, repair work, and so forth) or the transmission of information (as by lawyers, teachers, and scientists, on the higher end, as well as insurance processors, fast-food workers, and office clerks, on the lower end).

At the end of World War II, about 40 percent of all jobs in the United States were manufacturing jobs. Seven decades later, fewer than 20 percent of jobs are in manufacturing, and the number continues to decline. Job growth is also almost entirely in the service sector (Lee and Mather 2008; U.S. Bureau of Labor Statistics 2013). Manufacturing exists: Goods are still produced, but they are more typically produced abroad where labor is cheaper.

At the same time, the **information technology revolution** has drastically changed the workplace. Information technology now permeates just about every part of the occupational system. At the high end, workers need strong skills and complex training. At the low end, jobs have become more automated or perhaps even been turned over completely to robots or other sophisticated information technology. In all parts of the labor force, however, people are likely working with computers: Even if they are not designing information systems, they are tapping or clicking on screens to order food, buy products, or process information.

Another part of economic restructuring is **globalization,** referring to the increasing economic linkage between different nations. Although the economic system has long involved global trade, manufacturing production has shifted to parts of the world where labor is cheap, even while consumption expands in the more affluent nations. Parts of the production process, as well as the provision of services, are increasingly outsourced to other parts of the world. A transaction initiated from your smartphone might be handled by someone on the other side of the globe. Furthermore, the odds are that the clothes you wear, the toys you own, and even the foods you eat are produced in another part of the world.

Demographic change, that is, change in the characteristics of the population, is also transforming the workplace. Workplaces are now more diverse than ever (Frey 2015). One of the biggest changes is the increased presence of women in the labor market and a decrease in the labor force participation rate of men. Hispanics and Asians are the fastest growing groups in the workplace; African Americans are projected to be about 14 percent of the workplace by 2050, compared to 11 percent now. Non-Hispanic Whites, who were 70 percent of the workforce as recently as 2005, are expected to be only about 50 percent by 2050. Among women, African American women have always worked. Their labor force participation continues to be higher than that of other women, although the employment gap between White and Black women has closed in recent years (U.S. Bureau of Labor Statistics 2016a; Lee and Mather 2008).

Altogether, economic transformation has had a huge effect on all groups, especially for those who have historically relied on manufacturing jobs for decent pay and relatively steady work (Chen 2015). In a manufacturing economy, a person with only a modest amount of education could still get work that might support a family, especially if in a unionized workplace. Now, jobs are more likely found in the service sector of the economy. Without advanced education and strong skills, people are likely to end up in low-wage service work—the part of the labor market where people of color predominate.

Moreover, in a service-based economy, technology changes so fast that many skills quickly become obsolete. Workers who are best able to survive in such a market must be nimble, that is, armed with education and the technological skills to survive in such a competitive workforce.

For people of color, these transformations have resulted in high rates of joblessness and the emergence of an urban underclass (also see chapter 6). The formation of the underclass—composed largely of Black Americans, Latinos, Asian Americans, immigrants, and impoverished Whites—has produced an array of social problems that, as we will see, have arisen from a state of permanent, structurally caused joblessness (Wilson 1978).

It is not just the underclass, however, that is affected by these changes. Economic restructuring has also prompted the decline of the traditional working class, leaving many people feeling left behind and no longer attached to the contemporary economy. Without understanding the structural roots of economic restructuring, many White working-class people feel resentment toward racial minorities, as if the success of some people of color is robbing White people of their opportunities. This racial resentment has certainly driven some of the right-wing political movements of recent years that the nation is witnessing (Hochschild 2016).

Race and the Workplace

Every day, millions of Americans get up and go to work. Every day, millions do not. Work ties you to society. Without work, the social bond between you and society is loosened. As a result, people are likely to experience various forms of distress, such as depression and poor physical health. In their alienation from ordinary social bonds, they may turn to crime or violence.

Work is part of a nation's economic institutions—institutions that, as we see, are based on racial inequality. You need not look far to see the consequences. Who works where in your community? Are immigrants clustered in certain occupations? Are young men of color just hanging out on street corners during working hours for other people? When you shop for groceries, whom do you see doing what work? Observing everyday life in this way reveals a lot about how race and ethnicity are structured in the labor market.

What you will be observing is the **racial division of labor**, that is, how race shapes who does the different tasks in society. The racial division of labor is cross-cut by several factors, including gender, age, and immigrant status, among other social variables. As one example, women of color tend to be clustered in occupations where most of the other workers are other women of color. Of course, there are many exceptions to this pattern. In professional jobs, for example, women of color will likely be present but underrepresented. A given woman of color may be one of a few in, for example, an academic department. Race and gender as well as age are intertwined in the division of labor—a salient point in intersectional theory (Andersen and Collins 2016; see chapter 6). The entanglement of race and gender inequality also creates quite different outcomes in people's earnings (see figure 7.4).

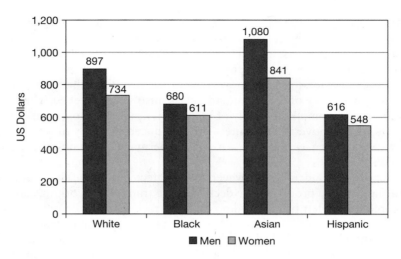

FIG. 7.4 Median Weekly Earnings, 2015

Source: U.S. Bureau of Labor Statistics. 2016a. *Employment and Earnings 2015.* Washington, DC: U.S. Department of Labor. (https://www.bls.gov/opub/ee/2015/home.htm.)

Occupational Segregation

The feature that best describes the racial division of labor in society is **occupational segregation**, which refers to the pattern by which different groups of people are niched into certain occupations—based on such worker characteristics as race, gender, age, and so forth. Data on the distribution of people of color and Whites in the workplace reveal clear patterns of such segregation.

You can see in table 7.1 that there are significant differences in where different racial-ethnic groups are employed. Whites are more likely to be in management positions compared to Hispanics. Asians are less likely to be in natural resources, construction, and maintenance jobs than others, although more likely than others to be in professional jobs.

You have to be careful in interpreting these data, however, as the categories reported by the U.S. Department of Labor are quite broad and include a diverse range of jobs. The professional category, for example, includes such jobs as physicians, teachers, social workers, nurses, and entertainers—jobs with quite different pay, prestige, and influence. Racial representation also varies within particular professions. African Americans, for example, are 10 percent of all professionals, but 6 percent of physicians, 5 percent of postsecondary teachers, and only 1 percent of environmental scientists. They are 22 percent of social workers, 12 percent of registered nurses, and 17 percent of lab technicians (U.S. Bureau of Labor Statistics 2016a).

In another example, the category of "natural resources, construction and maintenance" includes such diverse jobs as sorters of agricultural products (where Hispanics are 54 percent of the total workforce), electronic power line installers (Hispanics are 11 percent), and drywall installers (Hispanics are 62 percent; U.S. Bureau of Labor Statistics 2016a).

TABLE 7.1 Occupational Distribution 2015 by Percentage of Population in Occupational Categories

	White	Black	Hispanic	Asian
Management	17.0	11.3	9.3	17.3
Professional	22.7	19.1	12.2	33.9
Sales and Office	22.6	23.7	21.1	19.9
Service	16.2	24.8	24.9	16.1
Natural Resources, Construction, Maintenance	10.2	5.7	16.3	3.1
Production, Transportation, and Material Moving	11.4	15.4	16.1	9.6

Source: U. S. Bureau of Labor Statistics. 2016a. *Employment and Earnings 2015.* Washington, DC: U.S. Department of Labor. (https://www.bls.gov/opub/ee/2015/home.htm.)

Gender and race together shape occupational segregation. As one example, women are 95 percent of all childcare workers; 37 percent of these workers are women of color (Smith and Baughman 2007). Childcare and other occupations where women of color are overrepresented are among the lowest paid jobs (Catanzarite 2003; Branch 2011).

Since the passage of the Civil Rights Act in 1964, efforts to desegregate the workforce have had some success. When this bill was passed by Congress, White men had a near total hold on the best jobs. Since then, desegregation efforts have made some difference, but studies show that desegregation occurs only when there is organized pressure for change, such as from social movements, union activism, judicial rulings, and the federal government. Without that, progress stalls (Stainback and Tomaskovic-Devey 2012).

Unemployment and Joblessness

Employment patterns also reveal the persistence of racial discrimination and inequality in the workplace. Perhaps even more telling is the high rate of unemployment, especially among African Americans and, to a somewhat lesser extent, Hispanics.

The **unemployment rate** is calculated as the percentage of people in a given population who are "officially" out of work. Note that the unemployment rate undercounts the actual number of people truly out of work. To be included in the official unemployment rate, a person must have been actively looking for work in the period measured (usually the last four weeks), be available for work, and have no other employment during the period measured. Discouraged workers or those who, for any reason, are not known by local officials will not be included in the official unemployment rate.

The unemployment rate counts numbers of persons who are unemployed, but not necessarily all those who have experienced **structural unemployment**, which refers to job loss that results from an entire industry shutting down or the permanent disappearance of a particular kind of job. The closing of a steel plant produces

Whenever the national unemployment rate is announced, you can predict with great certainty that African American employment will be at least double the national rate.

structural unemployment, as does the automation of certain kinds of jobs. Whole communities can be decimated under such circumstances, and workers who are affected by structural unemployment can have even longer periods of unemployment than others, as their skills may be outmoded.

Joblessness, then, can actually exceed the official unemployment rate. Of course, people who work "under the table" are also not included in the unemployment rate, nor are those who are *underemployed*, that is, those working in jobs for which they are overqualified, such as the barista in a local coffee shop who holds a master's degree or the immigrant Uber driver who holds a college degree. Yet, even with its limitations, the unemployment rate gives us a good picture of how the economy is working for people.

Whatever the national unemployment rate, you can quite accurately predict the Black unemployment rate from it. The Black unemployment rate has been and continues to be at least twice that of the overall rate, sometimes more. You can see this in figure 7.5 by comparing the unemployment rates for Black, Hispanic, Asian, and White American women and men.

Even more startling is the high rate of unemployment among minority teens (counted by the Department of Labor as those between sixteen and nineteen years of age; see figure 7.6). Unemployment for young, less educated men is also different now than it was in the past, primarily because it does not typically result from job loss but from the inability of these men to find stable work (Wagmiller and Lee 2014).

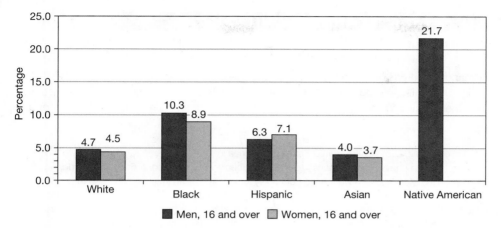

FIG. 7.5 Unemployment Rate, 2015

Note: Native American rate comprises both women and men and is based on the 2012 rate.

Source: U.S. Bureau of Labor Statistics. 2016a. *Employment and Earnings 2015*. Washington, DC: U.S. Department of Labor. (https://www.bls.gov/opub/ee/2016/home.htm); Stegman, Erik, and Amber Ebarb. 2013. "Sequestering Opportunity for American Indians and Alaska Natives." Center for American Progress. (http://www.americanprogress.org.)

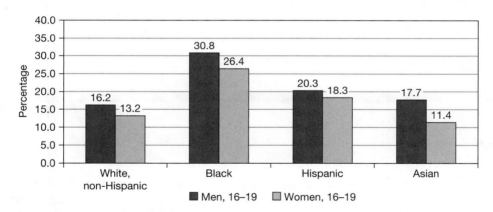

FIG. 7.6 Teen Unemployment Rate, 2015

Source: U.S. Bureau of Labor Statistics. 2016a. *Employment and Earnings 2015*. Washington, DC: U.S. Department of Labor. (https://www.bls.gov/opub/ee/2016/home.htm.)

Unemployment among young people is especially problematic because young people are likely entering the labor force for the first time. If they are unable to find work, they may become discouraged and alienated from the labor market—a phenomenon that can lead to illegal activity. If the national unemployment rate matched the level seen for African Americans and Hispanic teens, we would declare ourselves in a major economic depression.

LEARNING OUR PAST

The *Bracero* Program

The *bracero* ("manual worker") program brought close to five million Mexican workers to the United States starting in 1942 until the program officially ended in the late 1960s. Many Mexican Americans today can trace their origins to this program, as captured in the following narrative of the son of a bracero worker:

> My Dad, Celedonio Galaviz, came to the United States of America in 1951. He came to [participate] in the Bracero program. He didn't have enough money to make the journey from Jalisco to the [U.S.] border so my Grandmother (on my Mom's side) gave them a cow. They looked at it as an investment . . . so they sold the cow for 80 pesos which was [a lot] of money in that time, and used the money to make the long trip to the U.S. He had 2 contracts with the . . . program. The first time he went to Texas, the second time to California. He . . . faced racial discrimination in Texas, like having to use the back entrance at restaurants to eat and drinking out of a water hose. . . . He didn't mind or complain much, he was just glad to be working and making money to help support his family in Mexico. He tells about a time when they were asking all the short men to line up on one side. But they left him out, so [he] step[ped] in line with the short men. Until they noticed him and made him get back in line with the other men. He questioned them and they said that all the short men were going to pick . . . celery, strawberries . . . and that the taller men were going to pick lemons . . . he was 6 ft. tall. By the time he came to California he was known as a hard worker and was asked to return to work . . . when his contract expired. He was sponsored to come here and work by his boss. He got his Green card, and later his . . . citizenship. He sent for his family, all seven of us in 1965. He used to say[,] "I don't have a lot of money to leave you, but what I do leave you is a land where you can do or be anything you want." We all made good in the United States and are thankful to our Mom and Dad for bringing us to this land of opportunity.

Source: Galaviz, Sal. N.d. "The Promised Land." Bracero History Archive, Item #3227. Retrieved November 17, 2015 (http://braceroarchive.org/items/show/3227).

The Immigrant Labor Force

Historically, immigration flows have been tied to the needs of labor. Laws, policies, and practices have been routinely used throughout history to bring in immigrants when there was a need for more workers (see LEARNING OUR PAST). When immigrant labor was no longer needed, restrictive policies pushed them out of the labor force and, often, simply out of the country—and they were barred from reentering.

Despite exclusionary policies and the hostilities that so many immigrant groups have faced over time, immigrants remain a vital part of the U.S. labor force. Currently, there are 25.7 million foreign-born workers in the United States—16.5 percent of the total plus about eleven million undocumented workers who do not show up in official data, but who provide essential labor that supports much of the nation's agricultural, industrial, and service output (see LIVING WITH RACISM). Among foreign-born workers are some of the lowest-paid workers, but also some of the most highly educated and professional workers. In recent years,

LIVING WITH RACISM

An Undocumented Farm Worker

I'm Odilia Chavez, a 40-year-old migrant farm worker based in Madera, California, the heart of the fertile Central Valley. I'm also a single mother of three: My 20-year-old eldest son came and joined me in 2004, crossing with a coyote [a smuggler of immigrants into the United States]. My son is now at the university, studying political science. The younger two were born here—American citizens.

I grew up in Santiago Yosondua, Oaxaca, in southern Mexico. I went to school through third grade, my dad was killed when I was 11, and we didn't even have enough food to eat. So I went off to work at 12 in Mexico City as a live-in maid for a Spanish family. I'd go back each year to Oaxaca to visit my mom, and the migrants who'd come back from the United States would buy fancy cars and nice houses, while my mom still slept on a mat on the floor in our hut. A coyote told me he could take me to the United States for $1,800. So I went north in 1999, leaving my four-year-old son behind with my mother. I was 26.

We crossed through the desert into Arizona, hiding from the border patrol. I finally arrived in Madera in March of 1999, and I moved into a boarding house for migrant farmworkers. I'd never worked in a field. It was really hard at first—working outdoors with the heat, the daily routine. But I've certainly learned. In a typical year, I prune grapevines starting in April, and pick cherries around Madera in May. I travel to Oregon in June to pick strawberries, blueberries and blackberries on a farm owned by Russians. I take my 14-year-old daughter and 8-year-old son with me while they're on their summer break. They play with the other kids, and bring me water and food in the field. We'll live in a boarding house with 25 rooms for some 100 people, and everyone lines up to use the bathrooms. My kids and I share a room for $270 a month.

On all the harvests, men and women work side-by-side doing the same job, and women work just as fast as the men. I've been harassed one time: when a boss who drove us out to the field every day wanted to hug me, and said he wouldn't charge me the $8 a day for the ride if I'd go out with him. (Most of us don't have driver's licenses, so the contractors organize rides to work.) I left the job. In California, especially in Fresno and Madera counties, there's an abundance of farm jobs. So you don't have to do one you don't like. . . .

I've seen on the news that some Congress members or American citizens say undocumented workers are taking their jobs. We're not taking their jobs. In the 14 years I've been here, I've never seen an American working in the fields.

Source: Chavez, Odilia. 2013. "Farm Confessional: I'm an Undocumented Farm Worker." Written and translated by Lauren Smiley. *Modern Farmer* (http://modernfarmer.com/2013/11/farmworker-confessional/).

foreign-born workers have also been more dispersed geographically than would have been true in the past when immigrants were mostly located in the largest urban areas.

Currently, men who are foreign-born are more likely to be employed than their native-born counterparts. Foreign-born women are less likely than native-born women to work, especially if they have young children (U.S. Bureau of Labor Statistics 2015c). The places in which foreign-born people work, though, reflect clear patterns of ethnic segregation. As you can see in table 7.2, foreign-born men are more likely than native-born men to be employed in natural resources,

TABLE 7.2 Occupational Distribution of Native- and Foreign-Born Workers, by Percentage by Gender

	Men		Women	
	Foreign-born	Native-born	Foreign-born	Native-born
Manufacturing, business, and financial operations	11.5	18.4	11.9	15.7
Professional	17	18.6	22.3	28.7
Service	17.3	13.5	32.1	19.2
Sales and office	12.4	17.3	22.5	30.9
Natural resources, construction, and maintenance	22.4	15.2	1.8	0.8
Production, transportation, and material moving	19.5	17.0	9.6	4.8
Total	100	100	100	100

Source: U.S. Bureau of Labor Statistics. 2016b. *Labor Force Characteristics of Foreign-Born Workers Summary.* (https://www.bls.gov/news.release/forbrn.nr0.htm.)

construction, and maintenance, as well as production, transportation, and material moving. Among women, foreign-born women compared to native-born women are less likely to be in professional occupations, sales, and office work but more likely to be in natural resources, construction, maintenance, production, and transportation work, and material moving work.

Immigrants enter a structure of inequality in the United States in which their participation in the workforce is shaped by several factors, including their own level of education, the composition of their families, employers' practices, and historical context, including the political-economic relationship between their home nation and the United States (Kibria, Bowman, and O'Leary 2013).

Immigrants use various strategies to situate themselves in the labor market. Some form **ethnic enclaves,** that is, niches where there is a clustering of particular immigrant groups in a given occupation or industry (Kibria, Bowman, and O'Leary 2013:62; Wilson and Portes 1980). Nail salons, ethnic food restaurants, and small grocery stores, among other establishments, are evidence of the presence of ethnic enclaves throughout the United States. As ethnic enclaves help immigrants cope with the discrimination they face in the general population, they add to the rich diversity of the U.S. public.

Despite immigrants' contributions to the U.S. economy and our dependence on immigrant labor, numerous myths drive how immigrant workers are perceived (see "Myths about Immigration"). The fact is that if immigrants, including those who are undocumented, were to leave, the U.S. economy would suffer, and so would all of the people who depend on immigrants' services. Yet U.S. immigration policy remains in a quagmire, caught between the interests of employers, reluctance and disagreement among politicians, and strong divisions in public opinion about how the policy should be formulated (Pew Research Center 2015d).

Ethnic enclaves are common in many urban areas. They provide an economic niche in which immigrants can enhance their social and economic capital.

MYTHS ABOUT IMMIGRATION

Myth: *Most immigrants are poor.*
Fact: Immigrants are a mix of professional workers, academics, and those who fill low-wage service jobs. Typically, the poorest members of the population in a sending nation cannot afford to migrate (U.S. Bureau of Labor Statistics 2015d; Liosa 2013).

Myth: *Immigrants take jobs away from Americans.*
Fact: Immigrants make many contributions to the U.S. economy, and there is no correlation between immigration and unemployment rates. Immigrant entrepreneurs also create jobs for Americans (American Immigration Council 2015).

Myth: *Immigrants increase the crime rate.*
Fact: Foreign-born people have a much lower crime rate than native-born people. Stereotypes in the media of immigrants engaged in criminal activity target immigrants for abuse in the criminal justice system (Stansfield et al. 2013; Longazel 2013; Rumbaut 2009b).

Myth: *Immigrants don't pay taxes but take advantage of U.S. benefits.*
Fact: Immigrants, including undocumented workers, pay the same taxes and Social Security as U.S. citizens. Immigrants are not eligible for welfare or food stamps unless they have been permanent legal residents for five years. Fewer than 5 percent of all immigrants receive welfare, food stamps, or unemployment benefits (Massey 2005; American Immigration Council 2015).

Debates about and perceptions of immigration are strongly linked to understandings of race. The **race-immigration nexus** refers specifically to the linkage between race and immigration, including how social institutions, ideology, and social practices frame immigration and end up reinforcing racial ideas (Kibria, Bowman, and O'Leary 2013). Immigration policies that define some immigrants as "good" and others "bad" support and reinforce ideas about other racial minorities. For example, stereotyping Asian Americans as a "model minority" supports implicitly (and sometimes explicitly) a stereotype of Black Americans as unwilling to work. In this way, beliefs about immigrants, though often racist in and of themselves, also reproduce racial thinking about other groups.

Explaining Racial Economic Inequality

Clearly data on economic inequality reveal huge differences between racial-ethnic groups. The question remains: Why? Several different approaches provide answers; they include: overt discrimination, human capital, and the split labor market.

Overt Discrimination

Although it is now against the law, racial discrimination—both overt and covert—continues to be a significant factor in the life chances of people of color. That discrimination still exists can be documented via **audit studies,** experiments that use actors or other simulations to reveal when discrimination occurs and with what frequency (Feagin 2014). For example, researchers might send two applicants, different in race or ethnicity but identical in terms of prior experience, educational level, and grooming to a job interview. The goal of such a project is to document the extent to which discrimination occurs when race or ethnicity is the only distinguishing factor between two applicants. Audit studies can also be applied to gender discrimination and, potentially, other forms of discrimination.

In one widely cited example of an audit study, the researchers generated four identical job resumes that differed only in the names of the applicants. They then sent the four resumes to 1,300 online job advertisements. Two resumes used names that "sounded white"—Emily and Greg. The other two used names that "sounded black"—Lakisha and Jamal. The researchers found that "Greg" and "Emily" were far more likely to receive callbacks for an interview than were "Lakisha" and "Jamal," despite their identical backgrounds. Applicants who were "White" had to send ten resumes to get one callback, whereas "Black" applicants had to send fifteen resumes to get one callback—a 50 percent racial gap (Bertrand and Mullainathan 2004).

In another important audit study, the researchers submitted 9,400 randomly generated resumes to online job advertisements. They submitted identical resumes to each advertisement, but used names that were distinctively female and male and, presumably, "white" and "black." In the "female" category were presumably White "Clare" and "May" and presumably Black "Ebony" and "Aaliyah." Similarly, there were two presumably White males, "Cody" and "Jake," and two presumably Black males, "DeShawn" and "DeAndre." In all other characteristics, including college education, the "applicants" were identical. The researchers found greater evidence of racial discrimination in those jobs that involved customer interaction. In general, Black applicants got 14 percent fewer callbacks, but when customer interaction was involved in the job, Black applicants were 28 percent less likely to get a callback. Furthermore, the researchers found that discrimination *increased* when applicants were matched on the highest qualifications (Nunley et al. 2015; Vedantam 2015).

These studies reveal a fact that many White people continue to deny: that racial discrimination is alive and well in the job market. You can sometimes infer discrimination by observing only outcomes, such as differences in income, but courts in recent years have been reluctant to use measured outcomes as proof of discrimination. Often courts want to see *intent* to discriminate, something much harder to prove. Also, people may not directly intend to discriminate but hold implicit biases that have shaped their decisions about hiring and promotion. Audit studies provide a method that researchers use to show the presence and frequency of discrimination.

Human Capital

Human capital refers to the individual characteristics of workers. Such things as level of education, skills, prior experience, and individual factors like age, marital status, and parenthood are called human capital variables because they can and do influence labor market outcomes. For example, simply having a degree from a more selective university—a human capital variable—influences employment outcomes. Research shows, however, that Black graduates of the most selective institutions only do as well as White candidates from less selective universities (Gaddis 2015).

Clearly, race matters even when human capital has an influence. Human capital has an influence on people's success in the labor market, but it cannot explain the full degree of racial inequality. No doubt, getting a good education, acquiring job skills and training, and developing a good work record are important, but other factors are also at play. Having networks that can lead to a job, for example, really matters, as demonstrated in research. In one example, sociologist Deirdre Royster studied Black and White working-class men who were equally matched, particularly in having a high school education and a stable residence. Even with these comparable human capital variables, the White men in her sample were better able to find working-class jobs because of the "invisible hand" of referrals from those already in White job networks (Royster 2003).

A Split Labor Market

Split labor market theory analyzes the workforce as divided into two primary sectors: the *primary labor market* and the *secondary labor market*. There is also an informal underground economy where earnings are illegal or "under the table" (Venkatesh 2006).

The primary labor market has relatively high wages, job benefits, opportunities for advancement and, generally, rules of due process that regulate how employees are treated. Although economic restructuring is also affecting the primary labor

Because of the low minimum wage in the United States, large numbers of employed people still find themselves living perilously close to or in poverty.

market, these remain the best jobs. Even in the primary labor market, however, changes mean that few people can count on staying in the same job or with the same employer over a lifetime.

The secondary labor market, on the other hand, has low wages, little opportunity for advancement, few, if any, job benefits, and little formal protection for workers. Fast-food workers, cleaners, and various other service jobs are typical of the secondary labor market. Workers have little say in how they do their work and may be subjected to the whims of employers. Women and people of color are generally most likely to work in the secondary labor market.

Each of these explanations of inequality at work provides some perspective on racial inequality in the labor market. At the heart of each are connections between racial inequality and other forms of inequality, such as gender, ethnicity, immigration status, and age. Although no one explanation of economic inequality is complete, together they provide compelling reasons, especially in the context of structural transformations of the workplace, for why so many people lack the resources to live the American dream they may hold dear.

Poverty: America's Basement

For being one of the most affluent nations in the world, the United States has a shockingly high degree of poverty. As shown in figure 7.7, the high rate of poverty among Hispanic, Native American, and African American people is a national disgrace.

In 1944, while studying U.S. race relations, Swedish economist Gunnar Myrdal identified the poverty-stricken underclass as "America's basement" (1944:49). Since then, poverty has declined somewhat (from 19 to 13.5 percent of all people), but not as much as one would hope in an otherwise prosperous nation.

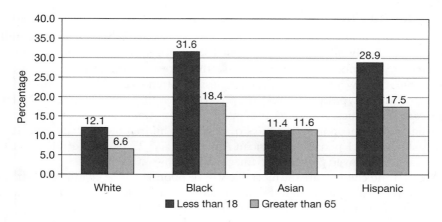

FIG. 7.7 Poverty Rate by Race and Age, 2015

Source: Proctor, Bernadette D., Jessica L. Semega, and Melissa A. Kollar. 2016a. *Income and Poverty in the United States: 2015*. Table B-2: Poverty Status of People by Age, Race, and Hispanic Origin: 1959–2015.Washington, DC: U.S. Bureau of the Census. (Also available at https://www.census.gov/content/dam/Census/library/publications/2016/demo/p60-256.pdf.)

Living in poverty is experienced in different ways. It might mean depending on a food bank for meals or living on the street or in a homeless shelter. It might mean skipping meals to be able to pay for a child's school supplies or depending on public assistance for infant formula. It probably also means being judged by others as a failure because our nation generally views poor people with disdain.

Measuring Poverty

However poverty is experienced, there is an official way of measuring it. The federal government calculates the **poverty line** based on a formula established in the 1930s by the U.S. Department of Agriculture (USDA). The USDA took the price of a low-cost food budget and multiplied by three, assuming that food was one-third of a family's budget. That amount, adjusted each year for the cost of living, defines the official poverty line: $24,267 for a family of four in 2015.

Can you see some problems with this measurement? Unlike in the 1930s when the measure was established, housing now consumes a much larger proportion of the typical family budget. The official poverty line also does not account for regional differences in the cost of living, nor does it include any accounting for necessary out-of-pocket expenses, such as childcare, medical expenses, work-related expenses (such as transportation and uniforms), and so forth. Moreover, anyone whose income is just a dollar or so above the official poverty line is excluded from the poverty rate.

Because of these problems with measuring poverty, many researchers have suggested new ways of measuring poverty, including measures that would account for various noncash benefits, such as food stamps, tax credits, and subsidized housing. To date, however, the federal government has not changed the official measure of poverty, possibly because by doing so, as experts estimate, the reported rate of poverty would likely increase by about 1 percent (Mattingly and Varner 2015).

Who Are the Poor?

Under the current method of calculating poverty, in 2015 there were 43.1 million people officially living in poverty—a full 13.5 percent of the U.S. population. The majority of the poor are White, because they are the largest proportion of the total population. White poverty, nonetheless, is often overlooked because of popular social stereotypes that associate poverty with people of color. Still, African Americans, Hispanics, American Indians, and Asian Americans experience distressingly high and disproportionate rates of poverty. Children of color are especially at risk: A shocking 31 percent of African American and 29 percent of Hispanic children now live in poverty (Proctor, Semega, and Kollar 2016a).

Women and children are the most likely to be poor, as can be vividly seen when you look at poverty rates in different family structures. Regardless of race, female-headed households (that is, households with children and no husband present) have the highest rates of poverty (see figure 7.8). Among Black and Hispanic households, poverty rates for female-headed households are especially high. In all households headed by persons over age 65, women are more likely to be poor than men, a fact explained by a number of factors, including a lower level of Social Security. Because Social Security

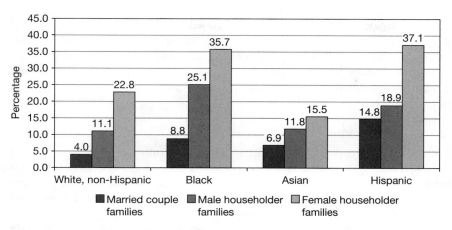

FIG. 7.8 Poverty Rate by Family Structure, 2015

Source: U.S. Bureau of the Census. 2015b. *Age and Sex of All People, Family Members, and Unrelated Individuals Iterated by Income-to-Poverty Ratio and Race, Detailed Poverty Tables.* Table POV-02. Washington, DC: U.S. Bureau of the Census. Retrieved December 30, 2016 (http://www.census.gov/data/tables/time-series/demo/income-poverty/cps-pov/pov-02.2014.html).

payments are based on lifetime earnings, women—and especially women of color—receive lower income from this source (U.S. Bureau of the Census 2015b).

Too many people in the United States live in **deep poverty**, formally defined as living on less than $3,000 a year. Deep poverty has actually increased since the mid-1990s. As with all poverty, the majority of those in deep poverty are White, but Hispanics and Black Americans are disproportionately living in deep poverty (10.5 percent of all Hispanics, 12.5 percent of all Blacks, and 4.4 percent of all Whites; Edin and Shaefer 2015). People living in such deep poverty include those who are unemployable, the long-term unemployed or underemployed, those who are severely underpaid, and people who are "casualties of poverty," that is, people overcome by the accumulation of catastrophes that poverty can bring. A serious illness or accident, for example, may mean having to leave the workforce. Without health insurance, bills can pile up, possibly even leading to eviction and, eventually, homelessness. Especially for those with limited financial means, problems can cascade, resulting in deep, perhaps permanent, poverty (Gans 2014; Desmond 2016).

Poverty is problematic enough when it affects a particular family or household, but it is even more problematic when it becomes **concentrated poverty**, involving entire neighborhoods. Concentrated poverty is defined as when 40 percent or more of those in a given census area live below the federal poverty line. Concentrated poverty has become especially pronounced since 2000, and has more than doubled for non-Hispanic Whites, although Hispanics and Black Americans are still the most likely to reside in areas of concentrated poverty (Jargowsky 2015; Kneebone 2014). For anyone living in such conditions, concentrated poverty has terrible effects for the whole neighborhood: higher crime rates, more violence, less family stability, and greater likelihood of other social problems.

Why Does Poverty Occur? The Structure-Culture Debate

If we are to reduce poverty, we have to understand why it occurs. The causes and consequences of poverty are many, but can be summed up in two frameworks: social structural explanations and cultural explanations. As you saw in the previous chapter, there is an ongoing debate, both in the public and in the scholarly research, about the relative influence of each.

Structural Explanations

All of the social structural trends we have been examining—economic restructuring, joblessness, and structural unemployment—contribute to high rates of poverty among different groups. High rates of unemployment for minority men are surely a major cause of poverty. For women, unemployment is important, but employment can also cause poverty for women, given their low wages.

Low-wage work simply does not lift someone out of poverty. Simple arithmetic will show you this: If you are employed full-time (forty hours per week, fifty-two weeks of the year) at the federal minimum wage (currently $7.25), you will not earn enough to rise above the federal poverty line. In fact, this income barely brings you to 50 percent of the poverty line. Some states and municipalities, sensitive to this concern, have raised the minimum wage but even with a raise to fifteen dollars per hour, proposed by many, earnings would only bring you up to the federal poverty line.

Structural causes of poverty can be direct, as in the case of unemployment. But they can also be indirect (Wilson 2010). Economic and political policies that appear to be race-blind have strong, adverse effects on those groups who are the most vulnerable. Economic restructuring to a high-tech, global economy, for example, benefits highly skilled workers who are less subject to job displacement than are less-skilled workers. Racial discrimination of the past means that less-skilled workers are more likely to be people of color, although White working-class people are also vulnerable to the same changes. The bifurcation of the labor force that is resulting from economic restructuring is one of the most significant, even though indirect, causes of poverty among the "truly disadvantaged" (Wilson 1993).

Structural explanations of poverty also connect to *intersectional theory*. The simple fact that women of color and their children are the most likely to be poor reveals that gender inequality *in combination with race* is a significant cause of poverty. Low wages, lack of affordable childcare, and welfare policies put women of color in some of society's most impoverished situations. Social structural perspectives on poverty must take into account gender inequality as well as race.

Cultural Explanations: Blaming the Victim

If social structural causes are so critical in understanding poverty, does culture matter? A national culture of judging the poor as somehow undeserving permeates public understanding of the causes of poverty. This is typified in Congressman Paul Ryan's assertion that inner-city men do not learn the value of a culture of work (Blow 2014). Ryan's view is a common one, despite much sociological evidence to the contrary.

Sociologist Victor Chen argues that, rather than the absence of a culture of work, a *culture of judgment* is a defining feature of our time (Chen 2015). Such a judgmental national attitude blames the poor for their own plight, as if they enjoy being dependent on so-called government handouts—handouts that are actually far less generous, when available at all, than the stereotype of the poor suggests.

Stereotypes about "welfare queens" are rampant in American culture, as is the assumption that the family structures of poor minority people are to blame for poverty. Many routinely and vigorously assert that people of color are poor because of their presumed reliance on public assistance, the absence of fathers in the family, and poor parenting. People often assert these claims with absolutely no knowledge of or experience with people of color who actually live in poverty. The belief is strong enough that, even with evidence to the contrary, people will insist that it is true. Such claims are even built into policies that promote marriage as the best solution to women's poverty—policies that completely overlook the risks that marriage can bring, such as domestic violence.

Research evidence has consistently shown that stereotypes about the connection between culture and poverty are just not true. Researchers have shown that the poor want to work, share the same values as the middle class, and do not condone such things as teen pregnancy, father absence, and welfare dependency (Kaplan 1996; Greenbaum 2015; Edin and Kefalas 2005). Yet, even with this evidence the tendency to blame the poor is glued to the public imagination, leaving us with little political will to establish social policies that could actually alleviate poverty.

The Safety Net . . . Full of Holes

The idea that poor people do not want to work is now embedded in federal programs to assist those in need. The movement for "welfare reform" culminated in the Personal Responsibility and Work Reconciliation Act (PRWRA) passed by Congress in 1996. The very title of the law presumes that a lack of "personal responsibility" is the basis for need. The law requires that recipients of the very limited aid that is available must work.

The PRWRA abolished the original welfare program—Aid to Families with Dependent Children (AFDC), a program that was established in 1935. The initial beneficiaries of AFDC in the 1930s were mostly White women and their children. The program grew and by the 1960s it had become largely identified with Black women. The public withdrew its support and became downright hostile as people leveled accusations of "welfare dependency" and made presumptions about the promiscuity of Black women (Gordon 1994; Gordon and Batlan 2011; Quadagno 1996). These attitudes culminated in the passage of welfare reform in 1996.

The new welfare law created the current welfare program known as Temporary Assistance to Needy Families (TANF, pronounced "TAN-if"). There are several provisions under TANF:

- Adults receiving TANF are required to work for two years after they start receiving aid. If they are not working, they must participate in community service. The rules about work are complex and vary from state to state, but those receiving TANF must do either paid or unpaid work.

- Opportunities to seek further education or job training are strictly limited.
- There is a two-year limit on the receipt of welfare assistance at any one time and a lifetime limit of five years. States can exempt people from the five-year time limit, but exemptions cannot exceed 20 percent of the total caseload. Some states have made this even more restrictive, such as in Arizona, where there is a one-year lifetime limit.
- Unmarried teen parents must stay in school and live at home or in an adult-supervised setting; pregnant women must identify the biological father of the child through a paternity test.
- Anyone ever convicted of a drug felony is banned for life from TANF (and food stamps).
- Specific requirements vary from state to state, but can (and usually do) include "family caps," that is, there is no additional funding available to a recipient who subsequently has another child.

The various provisions of TANF reveal the beliefs that poor women only have children to get bigger welfare checks, that the poor enjoy being dependent, and that need is caused by irresponsibility and a refusal to work. Funding for TANF comes from block grants given to individual states based on their level of AFDC spending in 1994. The funds provided are capped to certain maximums, limiting federal funding for spending on welfare and pushing welfare expenditures to state budgets—budgets already strained for other reasons. As noted in chapter 3, payments under this program are quite small and have shrunk by about 20 percent in recent years.

What has been in the impact of welfare reform? Politicians tout the success of welfare reform because the welfare rolls have shrunk since the passage of the PRWRA. What else might be expected, though, with such a restrictive program? Serious research on the impact of welfare reform finds that those who have left welfare often just disappear from the system. They are less likely, for example, to report poor health, get cash assistance from any source, or have decent transportation to work. These conditions can make consistent work patterns nearly impossible (Powers, Livermore, and Davis 2013; Silva 2013). Research also finds that welfare leavers are now less likely than under earlier welfare programs to seek more education (Dave, Corman, and Reichman 2012). Despite its intent to help people become self-sufficient, a decline in TANF support is not associated with an increase in self-sufficiency (Aratani, Lu, and Aber 2014; Katz 2012).

Stereotypes about welfare abuse still dominate the public discourse about welfare. In any population, of course, there will always be a few who take advantage of the system, but the wholesale blame of poor, typically minority, people for their circumstances has punched holes in an already fragile safety net. Consequently, the United States is one of the least generous of the Western industrialized nations in its support for those in need.

Conclusion

It is impossible to overstate the importance of racial differences in economic well-being. Surely money is not everything, but the lack of money lies at the heart of many other problems. In the chapters to follow, you will see a significant relationship between economic well-being and other measures of well-being, such as health, educational attainment, criminal activity, and so forth. Were the nation to make a commitment to lessening the economic inequality between racial-ethnic groups, we could also go a long way toward reducing racial-ethnic tensions.

Key Terms

audit studies, 162
concentrated poverty, 167
deep poverty, 167
deindustrialization, 151
demographic change, 152
economic restructuring, 151
ethnic enclaves, 160
Gini coefficient, 151
globalization, 152
human capital, 162
income, 147

information technology
   revolution, 152
median income, 147
occupational segregation, 154
poverty line, 166
race-immigration nexus, 162
racial division of labor, 153
split labor market, 164
structural unemployment, 155
unemployment rate, 155
wealth, 148

Critical Thinking Questions

1. In what ways is economic restructuring, coupled with growing income and wealth inequality, affecting you and your family? Be as specific as possible in your answer.
2. Using the federal poverty line for a family of four ($24,267 in 2015), develop a monthly budget based on expenses for everything you think you would need to support yourself and your family of four (two adults, two children). Use the actual cost of housing, food, and so forth in your locale. What can you afford and not afford? How would you make ends meet on a poverty-level income?

Student Exercises

7.1: Identify a job you have had. What was the racial and gender composition of the job? What were the wages? Were there job benefits? Was there a formal career ladder or opportunity for advancement? What protections did workers have? Would you describe it as being in the *primary* or the *secondary labor market*? Why? Is this a job you can imagine having for your entire life?

7.2: Look around your community and identify an *ethnic enclave* that you might see. Who lives or works there? Take some time to interview one of the workers there. What is the person's background (education, national origin, time in the United States, skills)? How long has the person been working in this place? Has he or she had other opportunities or not? What does your interview tell you about immigrant experiences and ethnic enclaves?

Challenging Questions/Open to Debate

An employee of a business organization sends an e-mail to a friend in which the employee makes racially offensive remarks. The employee accidentally sends the e-mail to a colleague who happens to be Latina and who is deeply hurt by what is said. She complains to the head of human resources. Should the employee who sent the remarks (who is otherwise a highly performing member of the organization) be fired? Why or why not?

CHAPTER 8

Bringing It Home

Families and Communities

If you're tired of hearing about racism, just imagine living with it.
—Jon Stewart (2014)

OBJECTIVES

- Describe racial-ethnic diversity among families
- Identify how racism shapes myths about racial-ethnic families
- Understand how the historical treatment of racial-ethnic groups has shaped family structures
- Explain the elements of a structural perspective on racial-ethnic families
- Describe the connection between racial inequality and care work
- Identify key trends that are shaping racial-ethnic families
- Analyze current social policies about family and the impact of these policies on racial-ethnic groups

In the fall of 2015, two books about America's families became national best sellers. One, *Between the World and Me* by Ta-Nehisi Coates, passionately describes the tough neighborhoods in Baltimore where he grew up. The other, *Unfinished Business* by Anne-Marie Slaughter, details the challenges that more privileged families face in balancing family and demanding professional careers. Two books, written by two highly accomplished people; one writer, Black, and the other, White. Each book is written as a letter to the author's children.

Both books chronicle the challenges that different families face under very different family circumstances. Coates's book vividly depicts the challenge of growing up in a neighborhood wracked by poverty and racism. Yet he has risen to national prominence, in large part through the support of his family and community. Slaughter's book details the stress of trying to balance a professional career and family responsibilities in a society where there is little institutional support for working parents. Taken together, these books show the very different realities faced today by our nation's families, but they also show the need for community support systems and institutional changes that would assist all kinds of families.

Families are often described as the bedrock of society. Families are supposed to be "havens in a heartless world" (Lasch 1977), in which children are nurtured, adults find solace and comfort, and people care for their elders. The family is idealized as a *private sphere*, that is, a site in society where love and intimacy are the norm and people are shielded from the harsher realities of the *public world*. Some families achieve this ideal; many do not. Either way, the family ideal obscures the social forces that pummel families, often making family life anything but ideal.

All families are influenced by social, historical, and cultural changes, but there are particular effects of such realities for racial-ethnic minority families. Simply trying to raise children in a world where parents need to buffer children against the harms of racism provides a unique challenge for parents. The economic status of people of color, especially high rates of poverty and the reality of low-wage work, make providing basic care uniquely challenging for people of color. Furthermore, the separation of family members because of immigration or high rates of incarceration means that racial-ethnic families have to cope with losses that other families are less likely to experience.

All the while, people of color have to endure the punitive social judgments that routinely disparage, misunderstand, and misjudge minority families. Much maligned, racial minority families have borne the brunt of blame for the nation's social problems. Nonetheless, minority families have also been a source of strength and resilience, including, or perhaps especially, during times of great turmoil and trouble. Understanding racial-ethnic families is thus central to understanding the social dynamics of race and racism.

What Do Families Look Like? Diverse Family Forms

The U.S. Census Bureau uses specific terms to count and describe family structures in the United States. The census starts by counting everyone living in a unit as a **household;** the person who owns or rents the unit is termed the **householder.** Within the broad category of household are **family households** and **nonfamily households.** Family households are those with at least two members who are related by birth, marriage, or adoption. Nonfamily households are those where persons are living alone or where nonrelatives share the household, such as roommates.

Given this terminology, you can use the census data to describe the different living arrangements of America's families. You can also compare families according to race and other social characteristics (such as age, income, and region of residence). Remember that the census also uses particular terminology to describe different racial and ethnic groups.

As you can see in figure 8.1, there is significant diversity in family structures among different racial-ethnic groups. Among both White non-Hispanic, Asian, Native Hawaiian/Pacific Islander, and Hispanic households, about half are married couples. Among Black and American Indian/Alaska Native households, a smaller percent are married couples. The relatively low number of husband-wife households in these groups is partially explained by the large number of never-married people in each population.

Female-headed households are increasingly common in all groups. Female-headed households are especially common among African Americans, with 21 percent of African American households headed by mothers with no partner present. Similar patterns prevail among Hispanic and Native American/Alaska Native households (Vespa 2013; U.S. Bureau of the Census 2016a). From a sociological perspective, the point is not to make moral judgments about these different types of household and family formation, but to understand the social conditions that influence each.

Ties That Bind, Bonds That Break: Marriage and Divorce

You can see in figure 8.2 that there are significant differences in the marital status of different racial-ethnic groups. Marriage in all groups is a fragile relationship, one that can be disrupted by any number of issues both personal and societal. The likelihood of marriage is also conditioned by a number of factors, including attitudes toward marriage, but also the availability of partners. Because of rising inequality, young people may have limited financial resources and thus be less likely to enter marriage (Furstenberg 2014). Many low-income women also place motherhood before

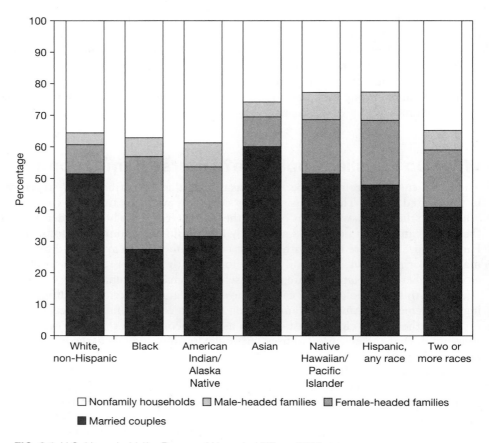

FIG. 8.1 U.S. Households by Race and Household Type, 2015

Source: U.S. Bureau of the Census. 2016a. *America's Families and Living Arrangements:2015.* Table C3. Living Arrangements of Children under 18 Years and Marital Status of Parents, by Age, Sex, Race, and Hispanic Origin and Selected Characteristics of the Child for All Children: 2015. Washington, DC: U.S. Bureau of the Census (https://www.census.gov/hhes/families/data/cps2015C.html.)

marriage because they may see motherhood as providing them a more secure identity than they would get from a male partner. Researchers have found that, contrary to much public opinion, low-income women of color place the same high value on marriage that others have, but they find it difficult to achieve the financial security that people usually want before they marry (Edin and Kefalas 2005; Kefalas et al. 2011).

Divorce, too, is influenced by one's social location in society. Asians and Hispanics are the least likely to be divorced, and White and Black Americans are the most likely. The many causes of divorce include differences in cultural attitudes. Shared cultural attitudes, then, may be one reason for the low rates of divorce among Hispanic households and Asian households. The prevalence of divorce among low-income couples, however, shows the strain that economic struggle can place on families.

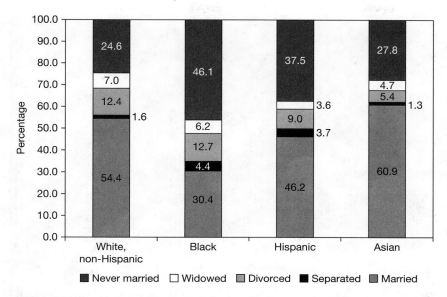

FIG. 8.2 Marital Status by Race and Ethnicity of the U.S. Population, 2013

Note: Some bars may not total 100 percent due to rounding.

Source: Stepler, Renee, and Anna Brown. 2016. *Statistical Portrait of Hispanics in the United States, 1980–2013.* Age/Gender/Marital Status/Fertility, Table 10. Pew Research Center. Retrieved January 6, 2016 (http://www.pewhispanic.org/2016/04/19/statistical-portrait-of-hispanics-in-the-united-states/#current-age).

How Children Live

Data on different family experiences are especially striking when you look at the living arrangements of children in the United States. Among White children, 75 percent live with both parents. Among African American children, one-third live with both parents; Hispanics, 60 percent; and Asians, 82 percent (U.S. Bureau of the Census 2016a). Divorce, separation, and spousal absence are some reasons, but the biggest factor is the decline in marriages for women who have children.

The birth rate has fallen since 1966 for all racial-ethnic groups, including teenagers. Contrary to popular belief, the birth rate for unmarried teens has also fallen, dramatically so for Black and Hispanic unmarried teens (Hamilton et al. 2015).

Multigenerational Households and Grandparents

Two other changes that are noticeably affecting families are an increase in the number of multigenerational households and the number of grandmothers raising grandchildren. *Multigenerational households* are those that include three or more generations. Such households are especially common now among Black Americans, Native Americans, Asian Americans, and Hispanics, where about 10 percent of households in each group are multigenerational compared to about 4 percent for non-Hispanic Whites (Lofquist 2012).

Multigenerational households have become more common especially among people of color and, most particularly, for new immigrant groups.

Multigenerational households are also more likely to include someone who is foreign-born, that is, an immigrant. Although there is nothing inherently wrong with such multigenerational arrangements, multigenerational households are more likely than others to be in poverty. People often develop flexible kinship ties as a buffer against poverty and economic dislocation.

There is nothing new about having grandparents help raise children, but recently the number of children living in grandparents' homes has increased substantially, doubling since 1970. While grandparent-maintained households are still a small proportion of the family population, the increase is especially pronounced among African Americans and Latinos. Fourteen percent of Black and Asian children live with a grandparent, compared to 12 percent of Hispanic children and 7 percent of White, non-Hispanic children. Sometimes there is a parent present, but 28 percent of Black children live with a grandparent and no parent present, compared to 24 percent of White children, 12 percent of Hispanic children, and 3 percent of Asian children. Studies find that this is a considerable source of stress, especially when the grandmother is younger and not married (Ellis and Simmons 2014).

Race and Same-Sex Couples

Only recently has the U.S. Census included data on same-sex couples (both married and unmarried). This has made it hard to show trends over time, at least until now. What we do know is that there is not much difference by race in the proportion of same-sex households. What is different is that same-sex racial-ethnic minorities are

Social stereotypes imagine gay and lesbian families to be largely rich, White couples, but the truth is that there is more racial diversity among LGBT families than among heterosexual married families.

more likely than other same-sex couples to be raising children. Interracial and interethnic relationships are also more common among same-sex couples than among opposite-sex couples (Gates 2012). This may be because same-sex couples tend to be more highly educated than opposite-sex couples and thus more liberal in their attitudes. Do not assume, though, that same-sex couples in any racial group are only found among higher-income earners. One of the myths about same-sex couples, men especially, is that they are all rich.

These facts about American families are quite different from what many people believe to be true. Various myths cloud our understanding of contemporary families, particularly myths about racial and ethnic families. Images of Tiger Moms, Black matriarchs, Latino mothers, and absent fathers abound in popular culture and, as we will see in the next section, generate misleading ideas that too often also frame social policies otherwise meant to help families in need.

Mythologizing Families: Racial Beliefs about Families

Despite the diversity in family forms, there is a persistent idea that a two-parent, married, heterosexual couple with a male breadwinner and a stay-at-home mother is best for all concerned (Baca Zinn, Eitzen, and Wells 2015). Although fewer than 20 percent of all families match this ideal, the *family ideal* has a firm grip on cultural beliefs about families.

The persistence of the family ideal means that families that deviate from this presumed norm are imagined as somehow dysfunctional and unstable, as if they condone teen pregnancy, do not value marriage, and are misguided in how they raise their children. Racial and ethnic stereotypes infiltrate this ideal as minority families get blamed for numerous social problems in society (Baca Zinn, Eitzen, and Wells 2015). As with other stereotypes, the truth about family life is obscured by misleading and false assumptions.

One example is the Tiger Mom myth about Asian families. The Tiger Mom stereotype portrays Asian American families—mothers in particular—as overly strict in their childrearing with an unrelenting emphasis on academic achievement (Chua 2010). It may be necessary to concede a small bit of truth in this stereotype in that Asian culture has traditionally emphasized children's obedience to their elders and strict discipline (Lee and Zhou 2004), but the "Tiger Mom" image reflects sweeping overgeneralizations about all Asian mothers. In reality, Asian American women are more complex than the stereotype suggests. Studies also show that young Asians are highly aware of the stereotypes about them. Young Asians do report feeling pressure to do well in school, especially in science. In general, young Asian students have higher educational achievement than other groups, but high-pressure parenting also has negative consequences for them, such as when parents perceive socializing as having an adverse effect on grades and thus discourage their children from doing so (Hanson and Gilbert 2012; Yi 2013).

Stereotypes of Latino families, to cite another example, depict them as strongly family-centered and rooted in *machismo*. There is, however, more variation among Latino families than the stereotype suggests. Machismo is often misunderstood as a simplistic expression of male dominance and authoritarianism, but in reality, machismo is a more complex value that is anchored in traditional concepts of honor among Latino men (Mirandé 1997; Baca Zinn 1982). Understanding machismo in other than narrow stereotypes means developing a more complex analysis of how masculinity among Latinos has been shaped and constrained by the subordinate position that Latino men have within society (Zambrana 2011).

Familism within the Latino community has traditionally been associated with a very strong attachment to family—an attachment that is thought to be stronger than individual identity. As in the case of machismo, to overgeneralize about familism among Latinos is to oversimplify the complexity of Latino families and communities. Latinos tend to have more frequent family interaction and a strong sense of attachment to family, but traditions also change with economic and social transitions in society and within Latino communities. Among Chicanos, for example, research finds that there is some decline in close-knit kinship as new generations encounter different social conditions. (Rochelle 1997; Zambrana 2011). Measured by such things as proximity to family members, co-residence, and financial support, familism also tends to decline as socioeconomic status rises (Zambrana 2011).

While it is difficult for families to maintain *traditional* family forms when society around them is changing, there is little doubt that kinship networks are still important and a considerable source of social support among Latinos (Hartnett and Parrado 2012; Sarkasian and Gerstel 2012; Gerstel 2011). But it's just as clear that strong family networks are important in providing social and emotional support and in fostering educational and economic success in all families, not just Latino families.

African American families are also subjected to numerous social myths, a primary one being the myth of Black **matriarchy**. A matriarchy is a society in which women hold power. The myth of Black matriarchy typifies Black women as holding all the power within Black families. This stereotype is also used to explain various social problems in Black communities, as if Black women emasculate their men, keeping them from forming strong family attachments (Moynihan 1965). There is no doubt that African American women have had to be strong and assertive to survive in a racist world, but translating this into the idea of powerful Black women who emasculate Black men is a gross racial stereotype that completely distorts the relative powerlessness of Black families, and Black women in particular.

You may recall an image of a Black mother during the 2015 Baltimore riots—a mother who chased her teenage son down the street, punching him and yelling, "Don't become another Freddie Gray"—a reference to the young man who was shot and killed by the police in Baltimore, precipitating the riots. The video of the mother went viral on social media and the mother made numerous appearances on national media. One media outlet heralded her as the "mother of the year." To many White Americans, the mother's behavior was laudable, but the popular image also implied that urban violence would be curtailed if only Black families exercised more discipline. In this regard, the image of the mother merely reproduced a stereotype of an "angry Black woman."

Stereotypes of Native American families are also rooted in misconceptions about Native cultures. Traditional family forms among Native Americans are as diverse as the many tribal nations that make up the Native population (Glick and Han 2015; Walls and Whitbeck 2012). Romanticized ideas of Native American families as living a peaceful, bucolic existence belie the reality that many Native families face intense social pressures, not the least of which is a history of isolation, exclusion, and invisibility.

In sum, beliefs about racial-ethnic families, at least as held by outsiders, rarely reflect the realities of family life within these different communities and groups. Families are never as simple as common stereotypes suggest. Yet, stereotypes, as we have seen throughout this book, have a hold on how people tend to think about other groups. In the absence of other information, stereotypes easily take root and blossom, often to the detriment of actually helping families.

Families in the Making: Diverse Histories of Family Formation

People experience their families as a network of personal relationships, but those relationships are shaped by larger histories that extend beyond individual lives. As argued before in this book, the past shapes the present. This is as true for family structures as for other social institutions.

Family experiences for all groups in the United States have been dramatically transformed by the history of industrialization and, more recently, changes in the economic structure of society. Coercive labor and the disruptions incurred by economic displacement have especially influenced the families of people of color (Glenn 2002). Whether the families of Japanese agricultural workers, Chinese railroad workers, Black slaves, or Mexican miners, minority families have faced an onslaught of practices that have separated them, robbed them of resources, and deprived them of the rights enjoyed by other families. In the face of racial and ethnic oppression, families have typically had to be resilient and build their own support systems.

The process of industrialization in Western society has profoundly influenced family formation among diverse racial and ethnic groups. Prior to industrialization, households were the primary site for economic production. Whether small-scale farming or large plantations, work was performed largely in households where women's labor—both slave and free—was vital to the economy (Dill 1988). With industrialization and the emergence of factories, goods were produced outside of the home. The new organization of industrial labor separated paid labor from the home and created a wage-based economy that devalued women's unpaid labor in the home. Home became idealized as a refuge from work—at least for those in the more privileged classes. During this transition, White women had few legal rights, but they were glorified as having their proper place within the family. Women of color were given none of this honor, although their labor has been critical to economic production.

Under slavery, African American families had no rights—including the right to marry and form families. Slaves could not marry nor were their children their own. Rather, slave children were the property of slave owners and could be given as property to others, as frequently happened. One such example is Ona Judge, a slave of George and Martha Washington. When threatened with being given away to Washington's daughter, Ona Judge Staines ran away and lived to the age of seventy-five as a fugitive from slavery (Dunbar 2017).

Under slavery, Black families were separated according to the needs of the slave-owning class. There is a belief that slavery weakened family ties, but research on slavery shows that slaves constructed kinship ties however they could and maintained a belief in marriage as a long-term commitment. Children born outside of marriage were accepted as family. Even though not formally recognized in law, marriage ceremonies between slaves were frequent. Furthermore, kinship networks functioned as a source of resistance to oppression, making family a vital part of the path toward African American freedom (Dill 1988; Gutman 1976; Genovese 1972).

Since slavery, economic inequalities of race have denied the role of breadwinner to African American men. Black men's low wages and high rates of unemployment and, now, incarceration, have meant that Black women have had to work out of economic necessity to support their families.

Like Black slaves, Chinese Americans earlier in U.S. history were denied the right to form families. Except under a few special circumstances, Chinese women were denied entry to the United States, even while their spouses worked to build the nation's infrastructure. Chinese immigrant men would use what they earned in the United States to support families in China, but the only Chinese women who were allowed to enter the United States in the early twentieth century were merchants' wives. Split households became the most common family form for Chinese Americans. Not until 1965, when the Immigration and Nationality Act lifted immigration quotas (see chapter 5) were Chinese families able to reunite in the United States (Dill 1988).

In the American Southwest, the U.S. conquest of Mexican lands uprooted families and forced many Mexican men into labor camps. Sometimes women and children could accompany men to the labor camps, but not always. When men had to leave families to find work, they would leave behind female-headed households, a form of family that prevailed in Chicano communities in the mid-nineteenth century. Much of the history of Chicano families and, now, Latino immigrant families is marked by constant disruption as people migrate to find work (Baca Zinn, Eitzen, and Wells 2013; Dill 1988).

These examples show the influence of larger structural forces on family experiences. Similar patterns affect other groups as well—groups whose family histories are shaped by economic dislocation, exclusionary social policies, and widespread social changes. The next section details the components of a structural analysis of family experiences.

Structuring Families: Structural Diversity Theory

This brief history of racial-ethnic families illustrates that social and economic changes drive the formation and character of racial-ethnic families. **Structural diversity theory** identifies those forces that shape families, both historically and currently. This perspective includes several major points adapted from the work of Maxine Baca Zinn (2010; also see Baca Zinn, Eitzen, and Wells 2015):

- Racial patterns in family formation are rooted in the inequality of work and labor.
- Race intersects with class and gender in shaping diverse family structures.
- Families are formed through both social structure and human agency.
- Racial representations of families attempt to justify existing hierarchies of domination and subordination.
- Families can be sites of resistance against racial and other forms of oppression.

Racial patterns in family formation are rooted in the inequality of work and labor.

Families are hardly immune to the patterns of labor that have marked the experiences of racial-ethnic groups throughout U.S. history. Inequality in the opportunity structures people encounter strongly influence the structure and well-being of families. Something as basic as whether men can find work will determine whether they are even perceived as "marriageable" (Wilson 1993). Unemployment or persistent low wages can plague families, making it difficult to hold them together. This is certainly true for all families, but given the economic inequalities for racial-ethnic groups, it is especially true for racial-ethnic minority families.

The economic interests of employers also shape family life. For example, having strong families may threaten employers who want workers to be most loyal to their jobs, not their families (Dill 1988). Indeed, most work organizations treat people first as workers, not as family members. Now global capitalism is also producing a new family form: **transnational families**, in which family members are dispersed not just across regional but also national borders.

Race intersects with class and gender in shaping diverse family structures.

This point, taken from intersectional theory, asserts that race, class, and gender together shape different family experiences. Even within the same racial-ethnic group, family experiences will differ depending on social class. You also saw in the previous chapter that female-headed households are far more likely to be poor than other households, a fact that is true in all racial-ethnic groups, but is especially pronounced for African American and Latina households. This fact is a vivid illustration of the intersection of gender, race, and class in shaping family life.

Likewise, the intersection of race, class, and gender means that women's and men's experiences in the family are different depending on their race, gender, and class status. Thus, there are significant differences among men in their ability to support families. Gender roles within families are also manifested differently depending on one's race and class.

Families are formed through both social structure and human agency.

Clearly social structures and processes, both historical and contemporary, shape family experiences. This book has emphasized the importance of social structures in all matters pertinent to race relations. Still, social structures do not exist without the specific actions of people, that is, *human agency*. Both dominant and subordinate groups take actions that affect family life. The actions of dominant groups have tremendous power to influence families, such as through the creation of policies that deny federal funding to poor women seeking abortions. Subordinated groups also engage in behaviors that help them adapt to family stresses. Such behaviors that can be essential to survival, such as sending one's children to other caretakers when work obligations demand it. There are countless examples of coping behaviors—many of them positive, but others not—that let family members adapt to their situation. Simply put, we cannot fully understand families without acknowledging the influence of both social structure and human agency.

Racial representations of families attempt to justify existing hierarchies of domination and subordination.

Each of the social myths about racial-ethnic families that we examined above is an ideological construction. Ideologies are systems of beliefs that attempt to justify the existing status quo. The representation of racial-ethnic minority families as somehow dysfunctional is an example. For instance, the belief that minority families are pathological can thwart attempts to make effective change by blaming families for their own plight. In this way, existing racial inequalities are maintained. Such beliefs are too often embedded in social policies that have a deleterious effect on racial-ethnic minorities.

Families can be sites of resistance against racial and other forms of oppression.

Most typically, the families of people of color are depicted in terms of social problems. What gets overlooked from this stereotype is how families nurture and sustain people even in the face of racial oppression. Teaching children how to cope with racism and ethnic prejudice is one way that families prepare their members to resist the assaults of racial inequality (Elliott and Aseltine 2013). As sites of resistance, families also provide a counterbalance to the dominant narrative that describes people of color as a social problem or as culturally deviant.

In sum, structural diversity theory emphasizes that family structures and processes are part of the overall racial structure of society. Within their families, people of color have rarely been given the same degree of legal or social protection that other families have. Indeed, families of people of color are far more likely to be scrutinized by the state—by police, social welfare agencies, school systems, and the like. The watching eyes of so many state agencies can make it seem that social problems, such as violence and substance abuse, are more common among the families of people or color. These problems, however, may not be as visible in White, middle-class and elite families. No doubt, the pressures that family members experience because of racial inequality can lead many to problematic behavior, but family social problems can usually be traced to social causes, not just individual motivations.

Caring across the Life Course

Care work is a relatively new term used to describe the labor that people do to sustain life, including such things as childcare, cleaning, and cooking. Care work is also known as **reproductive labor**, a concept originally developed by Friedrich Engels (1884), a colleague of Karl Marx, to analyze the work people do to maintain and reproduce the labor force. *Care work* or *reproductive labor* emphasizes that this work is indispensable to the economy, both historically and now.

Care work has traditionally been unpaid and most commonly done by women in the privacy of the home in the form of housework and childcare. Now, however, more care work is paid labor, although it is still somewhat invisible and often taken for granted. It is most frequently the work of women of color who are found in "back rooms"—cleaning, cooking, and throwing out the trash—but it can also include work like that done by social workers, therapists, and so forth. Especially as White women have increasingly moved into paid labor, women of color are providing much of the care work, working as nannies, cleaners, and personal care aides (Glenn 1992). Their care work is done both in public sites and in private homes. Because of the hidden nature of so much care work, it is hard to estimate who does it, how much they do, and how much they earn. Estimates are that there are more than twenty million nannies, housecleaners, daycare workers, home care aides, and social workers, among other care workers (Duffy 2011).

Care work is organized through a gender and race division of labor that positions women of color and recent immigrant women in low-wage jobs. In fact, the presence of care work at the bottom of the labor market is a large contributing factor to race, gender, and class inequality in society. As you saw in the previous chapter, various forms of care work are among the lowest paid and least regarded occupations. Care work done in private homes is also often "under the table," meaning that taxes and Social Security are not paid and the work carries no job benefits, such as health insurance, sick leave, or vacation. The privately negotiated nature of such work also puts tremendous discretion in the hands of employers, who are often women themselves and, as studies show, are often capable of treating care workers as if they are invisible and have no lives of their own (Rollins 1986; Romero 2002, 2012).

Racial attitudes shape different conceptions of care work, depending on who does it. Done by White, bourgeois women, care work is typically glorified as "women's special role," as if the work is some sort of spiritual calling. When associated with women of color, care work tends to be perceived as menial labor requiring little skill or job training (Roberts 1997b). This racialized perception is also apparent in varying concepts of stay-at-home moms. Middle-class White stay-at-home moms are praised; poor women of color who stay home to care for their children are stigmatized as lazy welfare cheats.

Conceptions of care work are thus entangled with the racialization of occupations. Parenting is a deeply social activity, one that has specific racialized and gendered meanings. Think about what it means to say "to mother." What comes to mind? Most likely you associate mothering with nurturing care. When you hear "to father," do you only imagine the biological act of conceiving a child? More than likely. Motherhood and fatherhood are deeply social concepts and, as such, also carry the racial baggage that burdens a racially unequal society.

Racially Controlling Images of Motherhood

Feminist author Adrienne Rich (1976) has posited that motherhood is an institution. This means that motherhood is a complex system of social behaviors organized into a social structure. For women of color, motherhood is a racialized and gendered institution because it is entangled with these forms of inequality. Mothering practices are shaped by both race and gender, as are how people perceive mothers and how mothers perceive themselves, as described earlier in the discussion of the Tiger Mom stereotype for Asian American mothers. Numerous researchers have shown that African American mothers encourage a stronger sense of independence in their daughters than do White mothers. All mothers use various strategies to keep their children safe (Ridolfo, Chepp, and Milkie 2013), but women of color also have to "socialize children for survival" (Collins 1990). Regardless of class or race, all mothers feel they have to shield their sons and daughters from harm, but gender, class, and race shape mothers' perceptions of the harms their children face and the strategies they use to try to protect them (Elliott and Aseltine 2013).

Concepts of motherhood are also colored by race. Motherhood is glorified in White middle-class families, but deeply stereotyped for the families of people of color. Black motherhood is typified by various controlling images, including that of the "mammy" (Collins 2000). Women of color are well aware of these controlling images and have to negotiate a path through stereotypes of themselves as welfare dependent, on the one hand, and "strong Black women," on the other (Dow 2015). Latina mothers are stereotyped as all-caring and consumed by the mothering role; Jewish mothers, as guilt-inducing. All such stereotypes derive from simplistic concepts of women's more complex mothering identities.

When women of color define their own notions of motherhood, themes of resilience and sharing emerge. Sharing mothering is a long-standing practice within Black communities, noted in the concept of **othermothers** (Collins 2000), the term for those who raise children other than their own. Economic necessity and other realities of Black women's participation in the labor force mean that someone other than the biological parent may have to care for children. The presence of Marian

Robinson, former first lady Michelle Obama's mother, in the White House was an example of this practice.

Mothers now have to navigate new conceptions of motherhood, because a culture of "intensive parenting" has taken hold (Villalobos 2014). This intensive parenting is an impossible ideal that adversely affects all parents (Slaughter 2015) but puts particular stresses on women of color (Elliott, Powell, and Brenton 2015). Studies find that parenting stress is significantly lower among Whites and American Indians than among Black and Hispanic parents (Nam, Wikoff, and Sherraden 2015).

The Myth of the Absent Black Father

Fatherhood also carries racial meanings, meanings that are entangled with gender and class. Black fathers, in particular, are routinely stereotyped as absent from their families, as if they do not care about their children. It is true that significant numbers of children live with only one parent (see figure 8.3), but it is also true that a significant proportion (43 percent) of Black children live with their father, whether he is the only parent in the household or not (U.S. Bureau of the Census 2016a). This fact is often overlooked by those who cling to common stereotypes of father absence.

Studies of Black, low-income fathers show the difficulties they face in trying to support children. Some walk away or do not admit to being a father, but more fathers than the stereotype suggests "do the best they can" to support their children. Many are determined to be involved in their children's lives, and they provide intermittent support when they can, but fatherhood often comes after a brief relationship with, and involving little commitment to, the mother. The odds of sustaining a relationship are weakened when there is not a strong attachment to the mother (Edin and Nelson 2013).

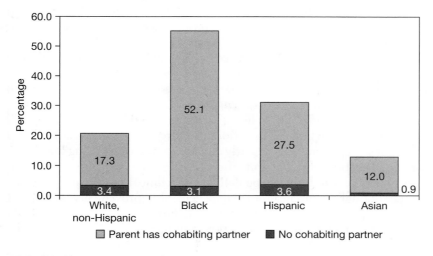

FIG. 8.3 Children Living with One Parent, 2012

Source: Vespa, Jonathan, Jamie M. Lewis, and Rose M. Kreider. 2013. *America's Families and Living Arrangements: 2012*. Washington, DC: U.S. Bureau of the Census. (Also available at http://www.census.gov/content/dam/Census/library/publications/2013/demo/p20-570.pdf.)

Stereotypes of low-income fathers blame their cultural values for any absence from their children's lives, but the disconnection of fathers is as much the result of economic and class-based factors as of cultural values per se. In fact, social class erases many of the differences that exist between Black and Latino fathers and others (Newman and Messengill 2006).

Nonetheless, it is true that Black American households are more likely than those in any other group to have female heads of households, as we have seen in figure 8.1. The term *absent,* however, has taken on a pejorative meaning, especially for Black families, as if men are not present at all in the life of the family (Coles and Green 2010). This pejorative idea assumes a particular standard of family by which all other families are judged, even when we know that family forms vary across racial-ethnic groups. What takes minority fathers out of the household are very often economic factors and the high rate of incarceration of Black and Latino men. Research finds that when fathers are separated from their children, they do experience a great sense of loss (Coles and Green 2010).

Eldercare

You can tell a lot about a society by how it treats its elders. By that standard, the United States is not doing very well. The aging population is a growing share of the total U.S. population and is expected to continue growing as the Baby Boomer generation ages. Although racial-ethnic diversity is most pronounced in the younger generation, the share of older people (those more than sixty-five years old) who are racial-ethnic minorities is also expected to increase, comprising 25 percent of the U.S. older population by the year 2050 (Yang and Levkoff 2005; Frey 2015).

Who cares for the elderly? American society typically leaves individual families on their own to figure out how to care for elder parents. High-quality institutional care is expensive. Even middle-income families are likely to find that high-quality care is out of reach of their budgets. As a consequence, individual family members, usually women, provide eldercare.

There are significant racial differences in how eldercare is provided. Generally, Whites are more likely than racial-ethnic minorities to reside in nursing homes. But, African Americans, Hispanics, and Asian Americans now make up a growing percentage of nursing home residents (Feng et al. 2011; Li et al. 2015). At the same time, the number of White nursing home residents is in decline.

As in society as a whole, segregation, not integration, is the norm in nursing homes. Racial segregation is particularly a problem because nursing homes with the greatest concentration of racial and ethnic minorities have more limited financial resources and are more likely to be deficient in clinical treatment, personal care, and safety. Although researchers note some general improvements in the quality of care, racial disparities in the quality of nursing home care remain (Akamigbo and Wolinsky 2007; Konetzka and Werner 2009; Smith et al. 2007; Howard et al. 2002; Li et al. 2015).

For all racial groups, however, the predominant form of eldercare is home-based care. Traditionally, Latinos and Black Americans have held family caregiving, and thus eldercare, as an especially strong value. Different cultural beliefs continue to shape people's experiences with home-based eldercare. Black Americans and

Mexican Americans report stronger obligations to support aging parents than do White Americans (Fingerman et al. 2011; Evans, Coon, and Belyea 2014).

Ironically, Black families have fewer resources to provide care for aging parents, because of the economic differentials that exist across racial groups, even though the Black elderly generally have greater care needs than do Whites. Although they provide more care in the home, Black women report it to be less of a burden than do White women (Conway, Jones, and Speakes-Lewis 2011).

Changing Trends for Racial-Ethnic Families

Families are not immune from social changes in the society at large. Population changes alone are changing America's families and will be creating new challenges for meeting the needs of both the nation's older population and the growing number of young people. At the same time, increased racial and ethnic diversity, changes in the number of interracial marriages, and the influence of immigration patterns will likely affect family experiences in the years ahead.

One of the biggest changes facing the nation is population change. The nation's youth will increasingly be composed of people of color, particularly Asian and Hispanic youth. Demographers predict that the number of White youth will continue to decline for years to come (Frey 2015). At the other end of the population distribution, White people will remain the largest share of the aging population. As they die, the nation's population will tilt toward being populated by more people of color.

Still, in the immediate future, the number of White seniors will increase substantially, largely because of longer life expectancy. Moreover, the senior population is predicted to increase much more than will the number of people in the labor force—that is, those who generally provide the support for both the young and the old. The older group, mostly White, will then be competing for social and economic resources with the younger group, mostly people of color. This could produce a strong generational divide in what one commentator has called a great divide between "the gray and the brown" (Brownstein 2010, cited in Frey 2015:35). How families will adapt to these changes remains to be seen.

Loving across Racial Lines: Interracial Dating and Marriage

Another change affecting families and race relations is the increasing number of interracial marriages. Interracial marriage was at one time completely illegal, both between Whites and Blacks as well as between Whites and other groups (see LEARNING OUR PAST). In the mid-nineteenth century, for example, fearing a threat to "racial purity," California outlawed marriage between White and Chinese people and between Whites and so-called Malays, a term referring to Filipinos (Takaki 1989).

Only relatively recently in our nation's history did the U.S. Supreme Court rule on bans against interracial marriage. The deciding case involved a couple, Mildred Delores Jeter Loving (a Black woman also descended from Rappahannock Native Americans) and Richard Loving (a White man). The Lovings were married in 1958 in Washington, DC. When they returned to their hometown in Virginia, the police

LEARNING OUR PAST

Laws against Interracial Marriage

Beginning in the 1600s, various states passed laws that prevented freed Black slaves from marrying Whites. Having such a relationship—or even the suggestion of one—could, until very recently, get you murdered. Until the Supreme Court ruled such bans against interracial marriage unconstitutional, a lot of effort went into preventing both sexual and marital unions, not only between Whites and Blacks, but also between Whites and other groups. Early in Maryland's history, for example, a White woman who married a Black man would then be considered a slave.

Prior to *Loving v. Virginia,* thirty-nine states enacted antimiscegenation laws, that is, laws preventing interracial marriage. The specifics of such laws varied state to state; some not only prohibited marriage between Whites and Blacks, but also between Whites and "Indians," referring to Native Americans; "Hindus," south Asians; "Mongolians," a racist term that lumped together Chinese, Japanese, and Koreans; and "Malays," Filipinos.

Section 20-54 of the Virginia Code stated: "It shall hereafter be unlawful for any white person in this State to marry any save a white person, or a person with no other admixture of blood than white and American Indian. For the purpose of this chapter, the term 'white person' shall apply only to such person as has no trace whatever of any blood other than Caucasian; but persons who have one-sixteenth or less of the blood of the American Indian and have no ot[*sic*] her non-Caucasic blood shall be deemed to be white persons."

Source: Volpp, Leti. 1999. "American Mestizo: Filipinos and Antimiscegenation Laws in California." *UC Davis Law Review* 33(4):795–835.

raided their home in the middle of the night and charged the couple with violating the Virginia law that prohibited interracial relationships. Nine years later the Supreme Court ruled that laws prohibiting interracial marriage were unconstitutional (*Loving v. Virginia,* 1967).

Now, interracial marriages are a small, but growing, percentage of all marriages (see figure 8.4). To illustrate: In 1970, less than one percent of marriages were interracial. Even more telling was that at that time, only one-quarter of Americans approved of interracial relationships (Lee 2015). Now, 10 percent of marriages are interracial and over one-third of Americans (37 percent) say different races marrying each other is a good thing for society (Wang 2015).

Crossing interracial boundaries can still be difficult because doing so "involves steep asymmetries of power and resources" (Alba and Foner 2015a:1). Even now, with changing attitudes about interracial relationships, interracial couples still encounter significant opposition from family and friends, even though discomfort with interracial relationships can be expressed in subtle ways (Childs 2005; Dalmage 2000).

Studies of online dating sites illustrate how constricting racial boundaries can be. People seem to generally choose internet dates based on appearance. Researchers who have analyzed online dating sites have observed that Whites are especially likely to choose those who appear to be White and Blacks select dates mostly with

Interracial marriage, though still somewhat rare, is increasing in frequency and has long been thought to be an important part of reducing racial and ethnic prejudice in society.

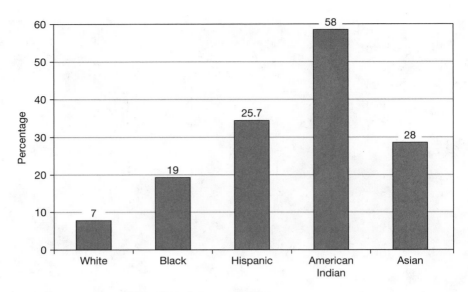

FIG. 8.4 Intermarriage Rate by Race/Ethnicity, 2013

Note: Hispanic data are from 2010.

Sources: Wang, Wendy. 2012. *The Rise of Intermarriage: Rates, Characteristics Vary by Race and Gender.* Pew Research Center. Retrieved January 6, 2017 (http://www.pewsocialtrends.org/2012/02/16/the-rise-of-intermarriage/); Wang, Wendy. 2015. "Interracial Marriage: Who Is 'Marrying Out?'" Pew Research Center. Retrieved January 6, 2017 (http://www.pewresearch.org/fact-tank/2015/06/12/interracial-marriage-who-is-marrying-out/).

people who appear Black. Latinos who themselves look "white" also select other Latinos who look "white." Race and gender combinations also influence choices made on online dating sites. White men are more likely than other men to select Asian women, but they generally exclude Black women as potential dating partners. White women, on the other hand, tend not to select Asian men (Feliciano, Robnett, and Komaie 2009; Feliciano and Robnett 2014).

Patterns of race and gender are also apparent in who marries whom (see figure 8.5). Perceptions of marriageability are shaped by both race and gender. Latinos are twice as likely to intermarry as are Black Americans. Asian females are more likely to intermarry than are Asian men. Black men are more likely to intermarry than are Black women (Lee 2015). Almost two-thirds of all interracial marriages are White-Black marriages, over two-thirds of which are Black husbands with White wives. Latino intermarriage has been increasing, most frequently with non-Hispanic Whites.

Among immigrants, foreign-born people are less likely to intermarry than are native-born people. Still, one in six of all marriages now involve immigrants; half of these involve immigrants marrying native-born partners. Again, racial boundaries are significant. Immigrants considered to be White are more likely to marry native-born partners while Black immigrants are far less likely to cross this color line (Lichter, Qian, and Tumin 2015). It appears that the social construction of race penetrates even our most intimate decisions.

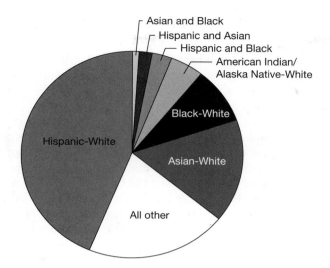

FIG. 8.5 Multiracial Marriages in the United States, 2010

Source: Frey, William H. 2015. *Diversity Explosion: How New Racial Demographics Are Remaking America.* Washington, DC: Brookings Institution Press.

Also on the rise are transnational marriages, that is, marriages in which each partner comes from a different country. Transnational marriages are most common where there has been a cultural tradition of arranged marriages. In such cultures, dating may be associated with sexual promiscuity. Parents coming from such traditional cultures may exert enormous pressure on the second generation, especially daughters. Some parents might believe that marrying outside one's ethnic group will bring great dishonor to the family and weaken the maintenance of ethnic identities and culture (Kasinitz et al. 2008; Pyke 2014).

Certain social structural conditions also influence the likelihood of intermarriage. Increased migration, the ease of global transportation and communication, and, of course, changed attitudes all produce more exposure between groups and the possibility for romantic attachments to develop. The likelihood of interracial marriage is also shaped by cultural preferences and various constraints, such as marriage laws or social controls imposed by families. In other words, proximity makes intermarriage more likely (Qian and Lichter 2011; Rodríguez-Garcia 2015).

Many believe that as more people date, fall in love, and marry across racial-ethnic lines, the barriers between race and ethnic groups will disappear. Interracial marriage has long been seen as the ultimate measure of racial integration (Gordon 1964). Despite this belief, intermarriage does not necessarily reduce racial and ethnic prejudice. Indeed, Whites may find themselves "colorized" by an interracial marriage. Children of mixed-race marriages involving a White and a Black parent also tend to be defined as Black even if that is not how they self-identify (Rodríguez-Garcia 2015). Interracial dating and marriage do, however, bring about an understanding among White people of the salience of race, making them more aware of and attentive to racism (Vasquez 2014).

Families and Immigration: A Two-Way Street

As we have seen, immigration is transforming the racial and ethnic makeup of the U.S. population. Immigration also brings new cultural forms, including changes in family structures and values. Even while families are changed by the immigration experience, they are critical to the immigration process, as they provide networks and support systems for new arrivals.

Over time, immigration policy has constructed how families develop and survive. Family reunification has been a central theme of immigration policy, albeit in restricted ways. Depending on the economic interests of dominant groups, only certain family members have been allowed admission. Thus, while immigration policy has altered the racial-ethnic composition of the United States, it has also restricted what counts as a legitimate family (Lee 2013). Families themselves often use more expansive concepts of family to include **fictive kin** (Stack 1974), that is, those individuals who are part of an extended family network but are not biological kin.

Currently, two-thirds of immigrants enter the United States through family reunification policies. The United States is unique in this way because in other industrialized nations migration is mostly driven by employment needs, not family concerns. Of course, employment figures in U.S. immigration patterns, but the focus on families is a much stronger feature of U.S. immigration policy (Lee 2013).

Immigrants use family networks as a way to settle in and to seek work, but in doing so they also reconstitute family structures and roles. Immigration, for example, can change existing gender roles in families. Men who migrate without their wives may take on more household work and childcare. Both men and women rely on extended family networks for care (Hondagneu-Sotelo 2007). In other words, family structures have to be fluid as they adapt to new situations. This is true when migration is across national borders, but it can also be true during internal movement as family members seek work where they can find it.

Within immigrant families, children are particularly vulnerable, especially when immigration is illegal (Dreby 2010; Bean, Brown, and Bachmeier 2015). Undocumented families and their children live with the constant threat of deportation and separation from family members. Even when born in the United States, children in undocumented families fare worse in educational achievement (Pyke 2014). Young people's inability to get green cards also hampers access to good jobs. Their educational and employment disadvantages, however, disappear when the parents are able to obtain legal status.

Race is central to family experiences as immigrants encounter a new culture. New racial identities may be imposed on immigrants even though they may never have been considered a "race" in their homeland. Just as race shapes immigrants' experiences however, so do immigrants shape the concept of race (Pyke 2014).

Immigrants are shifting the color line in the United States, moving the nation away from a traditional Black-White divide to a far more complex racial structure, one that deeply affects families. Who people marry, how they define themselves, how others see them, and what resources a given family may have are all shaped by the shifting conceptions of race in the United States. For immigrants, as well as others, race shapes every dimension of family life, including "immigrant identities, family structures and living arrangements, who marries whom and who is likely not to marry at all, where families reside and children go to school, levels of educational attainment, marital and nonmarital fertility, the kind of jobs people do and how much they earn, exposure to crime, access to healthcare, and how long people live" (Pyke 2014:194). In short, families are on the front lines of the nation's racial challenges.

Families and Social Policy

"Family values" has been a recent rallying cry for fixing social problems in society. The assumption seems to be that if people would only embrace "traditional family values," our nation's problems would be solved. This is reflected in often-heard statements that if people would just raise their children right or if men would assume their responsibilities as fathers, then families would not be "broken" and people would not fall into a cycle of poverty, substance abuse, and crime. Fixing the family and not the society, according to this logic, is the solution to our nation's troubles.

Such arguments have framed many of the social policies designed to help families, especially poor, minority families. Welfare policy embeds this assumption in its very title, focusing on "personal responsibility." Current family policies also stress the importance of marriage. Under both the Bush and Obama administrations, the federal government spent billions of dollars on marriage promotion campaigns. Marriage promotion campaigns provide support groups and workshops mostly to low-income couples to help them improve their relationships. Although marriage counseling can be helpful to some couples, it hardly addresses what causes so many low-income minority couples to break up: economic stress (Greenbaum 2015). Some of our family policies even punish people rather than help them when they are unable to support their children. Putting fathers in jail for not paying child support, for example, does little to help men find decent jobs so they can support their children. (Of course, there are those who are irresponsible, who walk away from family responsibilities, and who spend money frivolously rather than paying child support.)

Are we, though, really doing enough to help families whether or not they would benefit from a marriage promotion campaign, that is, whether or not they fit the traditional family ideal? Obviously, families would be better off when there are two incomes, but is it a given that a parent and children are necessarily better off with the other parent in the home as well?

Current cultural and policy assumptions about the need for male breadwinners can be traced back to the influence of the infamous Moynihan Report. The Moynihan Report was issued in 1965 under the Johnson administration and still reverberates in national family policies. In perhaps its most widely quoted passage the report states, "At the heart of the deterioration of the fabric of Negro [sic] society is the deterioration of the Negro [sic] family" (Moynihan 1965:5). Moynihan singled out female-headed families as producing a "tangle of pathology," arguing that the reversal of men's and women's roles in the family was a root cause of poverty in the Black community.

We have seen that Black poverty and unemployment are higher than for other groups. Black children are also more likely than others to live in single-parent families. But it was Moynihan's conclusion that poverty was caused by the structure of Black families, and not by economic inequalities, that set off a firestorm of criticism. Moynihan placed the blame for racial inequality *within* Black families, specifically those headed by Black women. He assumed that the solution to Black American inequality was to reinstate men as heads of household.

Moynihan ignored a great deal of social science research on the resilience of minority families as well as the fact that single-parent families typically emerge in societies where men are absent because of war or incarceration (Gans 2011). Moynihan also ignored U.S. policies over the years that have separated and torn apart families. Arguing that people of color should strive to be in traditional families is particularly ironic given that national policies have specifically denied this family form to so many racial-ethnic minorities over the years. Laws against intermarriage, barring family members from entering the country, disregarding citizenship rights for children born in the United States, and other policies have denied certain groups ideal conditions in which to form strong families. That people have done so despite these structural barriers is a sign of family strength, not pathology.

Conclusion

What all families need are economic policies that lift families out of poverty and provide jobs that pay a living wage—to women as well as men. Simply paying the nation's care workers wages that reflect the value of this essential work would go a long way toward assisting American families (Slaughter 2015).

Also needed are more generous family-leave policies, more and higher quality childcare, and less racially unequal institutional care. Compared to other industrialized nations, the United States is quite stingy when it comes to family support policies. Paid maternity leaves, more vacation time, and strong social assistance programs all tend to be more generous in other nations. At the core of family social policies should be recognition of the diverse forms of contemporary families, including the nation's racial-ethnic minority families. Family policies that rely on old notions of a family ideal simply cannot meet the different needs of today's men and women and their children.

Key Terms

care work, 185

familism, 180

family household, 175

fictive kin, 194

household, 175

householder, 175

matriarchy, 181

nonfamily household, 175

othermothers, 186

reproductive labor, 185

structural diversity theory, 183

transnational families, 183

A Critical Thinking Question

Federal policy has tended to promote marriage as a way to address the high rate of poverty among female-headed households. If you were you advising the Congress on such policies, what would you say?

Student Exercises

8.1: Using the website of the National WIC Association (http://www.nwica.org/wic-basics), look up the provisions in your state for poor women and their children under the Special Supplemental Nutrition Program for Women, Infants, and Children (known as WIC; pronounced "wick"). What percent of children in the state you selected are "food insecure"? What is the average food benefit under the WIC program? How would you determine whether this is adequate to meet children's needs?

8.2: Oral history is a method often used to recover the experiences of family members. Older family members are especially invaluable for recalling the historic events and family events that have shaped the family in the present. Conduct an oral history with one of the older members of your family. What specific historical events are most important in this family? Was race or ethnicity important in this family's background? What kind of work did members of different generations do, and who took care of the family? If possible, in a multiracial/multiethnic class, compare and contrast the oral histories that you collect and discuss the influence of race and ethnicity on the experiences of diverse families.

Challenging Question/Open to Debate

Should the government promote marriage through such things as tax incentives, limitations on assistance to single parents, marriage promotion marketing campaigns, and the like?

CHAPTER 9

Race and Place

Residential and Educational Segregation

A child miseducated is a child lost.
—attributed to President John F. Kennedy

OBJECTIVES

- Describe patterns of racial segregation in housing
- Discuss changing patterns of racial segregation in schools
- Explain different reasons for the racial gap in educational achievement
- Analyze the impact of social policies on racial segregation

Marsha is a young girl who lives in a middle-class neighborhood outside of Washington, DC. Both of her parents work full-time and commute into the District to work. Marsha attends public schools and earns good grades. Her parents expect Marsha to go to college. They have saved as much money as they can to pay the tuition, room, and board. If they need to, they can borrow money at a reasonable interest rate, based on the equity they have built up in the house they bought some years ago. They live in a neighborhood where the value of their home is now more than what they initially paid.

Another young girl, Cassandra, also earns good grades. She and her mother, a single parent, live inside the District. Cassandra's mother works in a local nursing home. She often has to pick up extra shifts to make ends meet. When she does, Cassandra stays with her aunt, but she has to take a bus after school to her aunt's neighborhood. If her mother works late, Cassandra spends the night with her aunt and takes the bus back to school the next morning. Cassandra's mother, like Marsha's parents, dreams of sending Cassandra to college, but she has no idea how she will pay for it. She has a very small savings account, but most of her income goes to meeting basic expenses. Now she has a substantial outstanding balance on her credit card, which she had to use when Cassandra's grandmother became ill and needed medical supplies not covered by her health insurance.

Here are two families, each with their own challenges, and two young girls, each working hard in school and dreaming of a good life ahead. Most likely you imagined Marsha as White, Cassandra as Black. In some ways, their race does not matter because each scenario could describe people from different racial backgrounds. The odds are, however, that more White families are in Marsha's family's situation while more Black families face Cassandra's situation. Taken together, these cases reveal some of the dynamics of racial inequality in housing and education.

Sociologist George Lipsitz has written, "Relations between races are relations between places" (2011:6). Two of those places are where people live and where they go to school. Housing and education, the subjects of this chapter, are key components of racial inequality in society. They are the places where people live day-to-day but they are also places that are highly segregated by race.

Think about this: Do you live in a place with open space, nice views, good transportation, easily accessible shopping, and good schools nearby? Are the nearby homes and apartments well kept? Is your neighborhood safe? Who lives near you? As a high school student, were you challenged in school? Were the school facilities well equipped with current books, science labs, and other resources? What racial-ethnic groups were in your classes?

Answers to these questions will tell you a lot about racial segregation in the United States, especially if you compare your answers to someone from a different racial-ethnic background. If you are Black or Latino, chances are that you went to a school that was predominantly populated by students of color. If you are Asian American, you likely went to a more integrated school. If you are White, you might have gone to a racially integrated school, but the odds are that you had a better school than most schools with a predominantly minority enrollment.

Housing and education have been on the front lines of the movement for civil rights, and with good reason. Some of the key victories of the civil rights movement have involved policies intended to address racial segregation in housing and in schools. Indeed, many of the legal cases that now define racial equality under the law have come about because of housing and education. The **Fair Housing Act of 1968** prohibits discrimination in housing. Prior to that, the landmark Supreme Court case ***Brown v. Board of Education*** (1954) ruled school segregation unconstitutional. Yet now, more than six decades later, residential and educational segregation by race remain a stubborn reality of American life. By some measures, both types of racial segregation are actually growing, with serious consequences both for people of color and for White people. We start by looking at residential segregation.

Living in Separated Spaces: Housing and Residential Segregation

Residential segregation is the pattern by which different racial and ethnic groups live apart from one another. Residential segregation is significant, not because there is anything necessarily wrong with people living near people like themselves, but because racial segregation is highly correlated with people's social and economic resources. Residential segregation is related to the quality and value of housing, the likelihood of exposure to crime and violence, access to transportation, the quality of schools, and countless other measures of well-being.

The start of this commnity garden in the lower ninth ward of New Orleans is typical of the community effort that brings people together to create nurturing spaces even in the poorest neighborhoods.

Even one's physical health is impacted by residential segregation (also see chapter 10). People living in racially segregated, low-income, disadvantaged neighborhoods typically have less access to the healthiest and freshest food. In such neighborhoods, there are fewer supermarkets than in better-off places. Small neighborhood stores where food is more expensive are more likely in racially segregated, low-income neighborhoods (Walker, Keane, and Burke 2010). Racial minorities' neighborhoods are also twice as likely to have fast-food chains, food sources known to be linked to poorer health (Cannuscio et al. 2014; Block, Scribner, and DeSalvo 2004).

Racially segregated neighborhoods also exacerbate existing economic disadvantages. Low-income, minority neighborhoods are dotted with payday lenders, pawn shops, and other places that charge exorbitant fees, leaving people with the fewest resources actually paying more for what they need (Lipsitz 2011). If that were not enough, the dominant society heaps negative social judgments on people in such neighborhoods. Residents there are less valued by the dominant society, no matter their actual character, values, and ideals.

Simply put, place matters, and race shapes place. As an example, Black families, even when they earn five times more than low-income White families, are more likely to live in neighborhoods where many people are poor. Few middle-class White families face such conditions. Racial segregation is also particularly hard on children. Racial minority families with children are actually even more segregated than families without children (Orfield 2013).

Has the nation made progress in reducing racial segregation since the historic antisegregation decisions of the 1950s and 1960s? In some ways, yes, but in other ways, no, as we will see in the next section.

Chocolate Cities, Vanilla Suburbs?[1] Changing Patterns of Residential Segregation

Measuring segregation is not an easy matter, but even a glimpse at where people live reveals that the United States is a quite segregated nation. Many of the nation's largest cities are now "majority-minority," that is, most of their population is Black, Latino, and Asian, with a large part of the White population living in the suburbs and outer fringes of the city. At the same time, downtown areas are becoming quite racially and ethnically diverse. Some White people, especially younger ones, are now moving into cities, attracted by walkable neighborhoods, cultural resources, and some decline in the crime rate (Semuels 2015b). Although cities are becoming diverse, how integrated or segregated are they?

This is a complex question. By some measures, residential segregation has declined across the nation since the 1960s, especially that between Black and White Americans. However, the complexity of residential patterns arises from the influx of immigrants and the increasing diversity of the population. Segregation patterns also vary significantly in different regions and between different groups. For example, in recent decades Black-White segregation has declined overall, while Latino and Asian populations have become more isolated from Whites (Logan and Stults 2011; Rugh and Massey 2014).

---

[1] This term was first coined by Reynolds Farley et al. (1978).

How much segregation is detected depends to some extent on how it is measured. Some measures account for the *distribution* of populations; other measures calculate the *isolation* of groups (or lack of exposure) from each other. These are not necessarily the same thing.

The extent to which two groups are *distributed* across a given place—a city or a school system, for example—is represented by the **index of dissimilarity**. This index, which can range from zero to one hundred (or sometimes zero to one), shows how many people of a given group would have to move in order to reach an even distribution of groups in the area being examined.

It takes quite sophisticated quantitative analyses to calculate the index of dissimilarity for various cities and regions. Generally speaking, however, analysts agree that an index of sixty or greater is indicative of a high degree of racial segregation (Rugh and Massey 2014). You can see in table 9.1 the indexes of dissimilarity for select cities in the United States, including the nation's ten largest cities. As you can tell, by this measure our cities remain highly racially segregated.

TABLE 9.1 How Segregated Are the Nation's Cities? Index of Dissimilarity for Select U.S. Cities, 2010

This table includes the ten largest cities in the United States with select others—Atlanta, Boston, Miami, and Seattle—added. The index of dissimilarity, as indicated in this example, measures the extent to which the groups shown are separated from Whites, measured in units of census tracts. The index can range from 0 to 100, with 100 meaning perfect segregation. An index of 65 or higher is generally interpreted as indicative of a high degree of racial segregation.

	Black	Hispanic	Asian	American Indian
Atlanta	83.5	64.5	64.5	63
Boston	75.8	60.4	46.7	61.2
Chicago	69.5	61.4	51.9	63.5
Dallas	71.5	65.3	49.5	45
Denver	67.4	59	40.2	48.1
Houston	71.5	61.5	49.9	46.5
Miami	80.3	45.6	40.8	63.8
New York	85.3	69.5	54.1	75.5
Philadelphia	80.6	67.3	57.9	70.6
Phoenix	54.4	60.0	32.6	53.4
San Antonio	53.5	52.6	33.6	43.7
San Diego	63.6	61.1	51.5	39.8
San Jose	44	55	49.6	39.6
Seattle	64.2	41.7	52.5	46.1

Source: Social Science Data Analysis Network. N.d. "CensusScope—Segregation: Dissimilarity Indexes." CensusScope. (http://www.censusscope.org/segregation.html.)

Note: Data in each case include the city only, not the full metropolitan area, which would include suburban areas. In most, but not all, cases, the index of dissimilarity is slightly lower in the metropolitan area than in the city per se.

The index of dissimilarity only measures the *distribution* of groups in a given area. For example, if a given city is 70 percent Black and Latino and all of its neighborhoods are 70 percent Black and Latino, then the index of dissimilarity would not reveal segregation because each neighborhood reflects the racial composition of the city. What if, however, most of the White population in this city lived in its suburbs? Common sense would tell you that this is a very segregated city. Social scientists then use additional measures to assess the degree of *isolation* or *exposure* that groups have to each other.

Measures of isolation find that the segregation between Latinos and Whites and between Asians and Whites in recent years has actually *increased* even while the index of dissimilarity between these groups has been relatively steady. The isolation of Blacks has actually declined rapidly in recent years, but only because of their greater exposure to other people of color. The exposure of Blacks to Whites has hardly changed over the past two decades. To illustrate, sociologists have found that in 1990 the average Black person lived in a neighborhood that was 34 percent White; by 2010, this had increased only slightly to 35 percent (Rugh and Massey 2014; Reardon and Owens 2014; Logan and Stults 2011). In general, the highest segregation in the United States is that between the Black and the White populations. There is relatively low segregation between Asians and Whites, with Hispanics falling in the middle (Lichter, Parisi, and Taquino 2015).

How segregated the nation is by race depends, however, on where and how you look. Since 1990, the racial segregation of neighborhoods has declined, but when you look at whole metropolitan areas, segregation, especially between Blacks and Whites, has increased significantly. Suburbs have become more diverse, but many Whites keep moving farther out of cities. Many metropolitan areas, such as Chicago, Detroit, and Milwaukee, continue to have very high degrees of racial segregation (Lichter, Parisi, and Taquino 2015).

In many places segregation is so extreme that scholars refer to it as **hypersegregation**, a phenomenon that occurs when nearly all of the residents of a given area are of the same group (Massey and Denton 1998). Researchers find that the number of hypersegregated metropolitan areas has decreased since 1970, but there has been little change since in the degree of hypersegregation. By 2010, one-third of Black metropolitan residents lived in hypersegregated areas (Massey and Tannen 2015).

Hypersegregated areas are typically characterized by *concentrated poverty*; as described in chapter 7, these are areas where 40 percent or more of the population is poor. This means that even people who are not poor but live in such areas are surrounded by poverty. Concentrated poverty declined in the 1990s when the economy was booming and social policies countered some of the trends toward segregation, but since then it has more than doubled (Jargowsky 2015a). You can see in table 9.2 that Blacks and Hispanics, even when they are not poor, are the groups most likely to live in high-poverty neighborhoods.

Concentrated poverty is particularly acute in the Midwest and Northeast, areas that have been particularly hard hit by the decline in manufacturing jobs. In Syracuse, New York, for example, two-thirds of the city's poor Black and Hispanic people live in areas of concentrated poverty. Other areas of the nation are not immune, however. Half of the Black poor in Fresno, California, live in neighborhoods of concentrated poverty, as do half of the Latino poor in McAllen-Edinburg,

TABLE 9.2 **Neighborhoods with Concentrated Poverty, 2009–2013**

Percentage of population living in high-poverty neighborhoods nationwide by race/ethnicity, age, and poverty status.

		AGE				
		0–5	**6–11**	**12–17**	**Adults**	**All Ages**
TOTAL	Poor	16.5	15.6	14.7	13.8	14.4
	Nonpoor	2.7	2.4	2.5	2.8	2.7
WHITE	Poor	6.2	5.2	4.6	8.2	7.5
	Nonpoor	0.9	0.7	0.7	1.2	1.2
BLACK	Poor	28	26.6	25.2	24.2	25.2
	Nonpoor	7.9	7.6	8	9.3	9
HISPANIC	Poor	18.1	17.9	17.6	16.9	17.4
	Nonpoor	5.3	5	5	5.9	5.7

Source: American Community Survey 2009–2013 data posted by The Century Foundation, as cited in Jargowsky, Paul A. 2015a. "Architecture of Segregation: Civil Unrest, the Concentration of Poverty, and Public Policy." New Brunswick, NJ: The Century Foundation. Rutgers University. (http://apps.tcf.org/architecture-of-segregation.)

Texas. In such neighborhoods, police-community tensions are high, unemployment is rampant, and schools are often failing (Jargowsky 2015a).

Quantitative measures of segregation are telling, but they cannot account for the actual degree of interaction that groups might have with each other even in integrated spaces. A given neighborhood, for example, might be well integrated, but Black, Latino, and White neighbors rarely visit each other's homes, do things together, or share personal details about their lives. One illustration of this is found in the history of the American South where little physical distance existed between Black and White people, but maximum social distance was the norm (Grigoryeva and Ruef 2015). Even in racially integrated neighborhoods in the early twenty-first century, residents' perceptions of how integrated the neighborhood actually is also vary by race; there is often segregation block by block (Rich 2008, 2009).

With the expansion of the Black and Latino middle class, many African Americans and Latinos have moved into suburban areas (Lacy 2007; Pattillo 2007, 2013). Still, middle-class Black Americans, on average, live in poorer neighborhoods than Whites (Pattillo 2005).

When people of color move into predominantly White areas, they encounter what sociologist Elijah Anderson has termed **white space**, that is, areas in which Black people perceive themselves to be "typically absent, not expected, or marginalized when present" (2015:10). When people of color enter white space, they likely feel uncomfortable, as if the place is "off limits." White people, on the other hand, rarely perceive the same thing, instead imagining white space to be neutral or simply unremarkable. This concept underscores the fact that racial segregation and integration are not simply about numbers. *Segregation and integration are*

LIVING WITH RACISM

Black People in "White Space"

Elijah Anderson is a distinguished sociologist on the faculty at Yale University. Author of many books and widely cited for his scholarship on race and ethnicity, as a Black man he nonetheless experiences racial harassment upon entering what he calls "white space." He writes:

> Several years ago, I vacationed in Wellfleet, Massachusetts, a pleasant Cape Cod town full of upper-middle-class white vacationers, tourists, and working-class white residents. During the two weeks that my family and I spent there, I encountered very few other black people. We had rented a beautiful cottage about a mile from the town center, which consisted of a library and a few restaurants and stores catering to tourists. Early one weekday morning, I jogged down the road from our cottage through the town center and made my way to Route 6, which runs the length of the Cape from the Sagamore Bridge to Provincetown. It was a beautiful morning, about 75 degrees, with low humidity and clear blue skies. I had jogged here many times before. At 6 a.m., the road was deserted, with only an occasional passing car. I was enjoying my run that morning, listening to the nature sounds and feeling a sense of serenity. It seemed I had this world all to myself. Suddenly a red pickup truck appeared and stopped dead in the middle of the road. I looked over at the driver, a middle-aged white man, who was obviously trying to communicate something to me. He was waving his hands and gesticulating, and I immediately thought he might be in distress or in need of help, but I could not make out what he was saying. I stopped, cupped my hand to my ear to hear him better, and yelled back, "What did you say?" It was then that he made himself very clear. "Go home! Go home!" he yelled, dragging out the words to make sure I understood. I felt provoked, but I waved him off and continued on my way.

Source: Anderson, Elijah. 2015. "The White Space." *Sociology of Race and Ethnicity* 1(1):10–21.

fundamentally social constructs that involve not just who is present and who is not, but also how people relate to and perceive one another. See LIVING WITH RACISM for an illustration.

How Does Segregation Happen?

How have we become such a segregated nation? There is no single reason. Many White people think that racial segregation is a choice that people of color make, but the truth is that social structural factors—both past and present—cause racial segregation and the racial disparities found in housing today.

Discrimination is certainly one cause of residential segregation. Audit studies (see chapter 7), for example, find that about 20 percent of the time White homeseekers are favored over others in terms of being shown homes and getting more favorable terms for home financing. With regard to people of color, real estate agents have been known to employ **steering**, that is, directing potential homebuyers away from neighborhoods that are predominantly white. Agents may do so unintentionally or simply by thinking that this would be the buyer's choice. Nonetheless, steering has been shown to be a common practice even now that likely reflects *implicit bias* (Kwate et al. 2013; Turner and Ross 2005).

Discrimination can also occur even when the practices that produce it are seemingly colorblind. Individuals, for example, might behave in ways they believe will help protect the value of their property, such as not allowing the development of affordable housing in their neighborhood. Or, communities might pass zoning ordinances that disallow the construction of multiple-unit dwellings. These and other apparently well-intended actions have discriminatory outcomes, even if there is no thought given to the consequences for people of color.

In other words, discrimination is not always intentional nor is it readily detected. Fair housing laws prohibit discrimination, but proving that discrimination has occurred is not easy. Antidiscrimination laws put the burden of proof on individual victims who may not even be aware of it while it is happening. Also, victims of discrimination have to know their rights and have the resources and willingness to pursue a claim of discrimination. Consequently, even with antidiscrimination laws and policies in place, discrimination can continue unabated.

Another phenomenon that shapes racial disparities in housing is the dynamic of neighborhoods "turning" when people of color move in. It is well documented that property values are lower in areas where there are high proportions of people of color (Anacker 2010; Pattillo 2013). If a neighborhood starts to change from mostly white to including more minorities, people living there may see their property values start to fall. This initial decline can start a vicious cycle as more White people move out, thus causing further deterioration in the value of homes. Those who stay will find their assets dwindling. Even studies that control for the characteristics of the housing units and the education, occupation, income, and marital status of residents have shown that housing appreciates more slowly in predominantly Black and Latino neighborhoods compared to White neighborhoods (Flippen 2004; Kim 2000; Denton 2001).

Practices of lending institutions are also a major reason for racial disparities in housing. Analysts have concluded that an "unequal system of housing finance (among other racial and class discriminatory practices) has indelibly shaped the geography and demography of metropolitan areas, creating clear patterns of uneven development marked by disinvestment that has disadvantaged central cities and advantaged suburbs" (Pattillo 2013:513).

One way this has happened is through **redlining**, a practice from the 1930s that rated different areas in terms of their worthiness for mortgage lending. Areas that were heavily minority were typically redlined, making it nearly impossible for people to get mortgages in these areas. The practice was deemed illegal under the Federal Housing Act of 1968, but there is ample evidence that the practice continues, perhaps not so explicitly, but similarly in terms of the availability of mortgage credit (Badger 2015). Such practices make is less likely and more expensive for minority borrowers to finance a home.

Another practice that has contributed to racial disparities in housing is **predatory lending**, which became especially apparent in the Great Recession of 2008 and the resulting housing foreclosure crises. Predatory lending refers to the practice of financing very high-risk loans and doling out **subprime mortgages** with little review of people's ability to pay. The practice was the main reason for the economic crisis starting in 2008. Although the recession affected most Americans, African Americans were much more likely than other groups to be prey to such practices (Rugh, Albright, and Massey 2015).

Approving a subprime mortgage—a housing loan that has higher interest rates than the prime lending rate—is almost the reverse of redlining: Instead of denying people loans, granting subprime mortgages makes it much more expensive to borrow money, which also increases the risk of default. Numerous studies show that Latinos and African Americans have been far more likely to receive higher-cost and higher-risk loans, thus lowering their disposable income and putting them at greater risk of foreclosure (Rugh, Albright, and Massey 2015).

Most Americans' single most important asset is their home. Any threat of losing one's home has drastic consequences. The foreclosure crisis that accompanied the recession of 2008 had strong racial dimensions. Even after controlling for income, borrowers' creditworthiness, and home values, researchers have concluded that racial segregation was a major predictor of the foreclosure crisis. Many Americans were hurt by this crisis, but the cost to Black Americans has been especially substantial. Specifically, research has found that Black Americans have paid an additional 5 to 11 percent in monthly mortgage payments, collectively losing millions in home equity (Rugh, Albright, and Massey 2015; Rugh and Massey 2010).

The Consequences of Residential Segregation

You can see that the impact of racial segregation has substantial consequences. Lipsitz summarizes the impact this way: "Relegating people of different races to different spaces produces grossly unequal access to education, employment, transportation, and shelter. It exposes communities of color disproportionately to environmental hazards and social nuisances while offering Whites privileged access to economic opportunities, social amenities, and valuable personal networks" (Lipsitz 2011:6).

Indeed, the impact of racial disparities in housing is hard to underestimate. At the individual level, people separated from each other are less likely to develop friendships or know each other well enough to refute racial stereotypes. Even in racially integrated neighborhoods, racial norms and patterns of interaction may prevent people from knowing each other. As seen earlier, social distance may be greater than physical distance. White residents might also dictate the norms of the neighborhood by, for example, controlling homeowner associations or intervening in residents' daily practices, such as pet care, lawn care, style of décor, and so forth (Mayorga-Gallo 2014).

For people of color, the disadvantages that come from housing inequality also create disrupted lives. For renters, eviction disproportionately affects African Americans and, to a lesser extent, Latinos. Black women actually experience the highest incidence of eviction (Desmond 2016; Pattillo 2013). Frequent moving also disrupts children's education, although, on the positive side, children who move from poor areas to higher-income areas end up with better educational achievement than those who remain in poor areas (Orfield 2013).

Residential segregation also has a huge impact on the education of the nation's children. Because residential segregation is so deeply tied to school segregation, where a family lives shapes access to a good education. Having poor schools in a neighborhood can discourage people from moving there even if they desire an integrated neighborhood. Thus, poor schools help produce residential segregation, and residential segregation produces poor schools (Frankenberg 2013). Either way, given its connection to educational segregation, residential segregation stifles the achievement of students of color. We thus turn to the topic of race and education.

Learning in Unequal Places: Schooling in a Racially Unequal Society

Perhaps we would not care quite so much about residential segregation if it were not so closely tied to educational outcomes. The fact is the vast majority of schools that serve children of color, especially low-income children of color, are inferior to those serving Whites. Poorer facilities, lower test scores, higher dropout rates, and fewer college-preparatory courses all mark schools in segregated Black and Latino areas (Darling-Hammond 2010, 2004).

Segregation and Re-segregation: The Aftermath of *Brown*

Frederick Douglass wrote, "Once you learn to read, you will be forever free." Having been born a slave, Douglass knew the cost of not having an education. Slaves were seldom allowed to learn to read. Many did so nonetheless, knowing that literacy was a way to gain freedom. Yet throughout U.S. history, racial inequality in education has prevailed (see LEARNING OUR PAST).

LEARNING OUR PAST

Interview with Teacher/Civil Rights Activist Julia Matilda Burns, 2013

The U.S. Library of Congress holds a number of oral histories that were taken as part of its Civil Rights History Project. In this interview, Julia Matilda Burns describes her experiences as a young girl in the 1950s being educated in all-Black schools. Mrs. Burns went on to become a schoolteacher as well as a civil rights activist in Holmes County, Mississippi. At the time of the interview, Mrs. Burns was seventy-six years old, and she reflected on the encouragement teachers gave her while she was a young student in the segregated schools of Mississippi.

My major influence that I can recall was my tenth grade English teacher. Very smart lady, very smart, and she just had a liking for people who wanted to do something. And I guess she could see in me what I could not see in myself, and she suggested to me that I should go to college and major in English. And that's what I did. And I think about her continuously now . . . what an impact that was on my life. . . . You know, tenth grade children, they don't think about their future. . . . they're just having a good time. . . .

During that time, teachers took an interest in children's well-being and their future. All the way through high school, there was some teacher telling you what you ought to do, or what you should do. And those teachers even visited the families in the community and told the parents, "Your child did this, your child did that." And believe it or not, you know, if it's good, the parent will work with it. If not, the parent would try to correct it.

Source: Civil Rights History Project. 2013. Julia Matilda Burns oral history interview conducted by John Dittmer in Tchula, Mississippi. Video. Library of Congress. (https://www.loc.gov/item/afc2010039_crhp0073/.)

Until 1900, almost half of all Black adults in the United States were unable to read or write (National Center for Educational Statistics 2015a). Literacy rates among Black Americans improved over the twentieth century as young children were able to get at least a basic education, even if in segregated schools. American Indian children in the late nineteenth and early twentieth centuries were forced into so-called Indian schools—to give up their own cultural ways and become acculturated into the dominant culture, as required by the U.S. government. In the western United States, Chinese students were denied entry into the public schools until 1905, when the Supreme Court required the state of California to extend public education to the children of Chinese immigrants, few as they were because of the Chinese Exclusion Act of 1882.

Segregated schools were deemed lawful by the U.S. Supreme Court in the 1896 decision **Plessy v. Ferguson**. The decision enshrined the principle of "separate but equal" into U.S. constitutional law. Homer Plessy was a mixed-race man, a Creole, from Louisiana who was arrested in 1892 for sitting in the "white" section of a railroad car, thus violating the Separate Car Act that had been passed in Louisiana in 1890. A coalition of civil rights organizations challenged his arrest, ultimately taking his case to the U.S. Supreme Court. But in 1896 the Supreme Court ruled that "separate but equal" was constitutional in all public facilities, schools included. *Plessy v. Ferguson* ushered in the infamous period of Jim Crow segregation, legitimating racial segregation in virtually every area of life and including the now-infamous separate bathrooms for "white" and "colored," separate water fountains, separate seating areas on public buses and, most especially, the separation of children in public schools.

Activism by people of color continued to challenge legally authorized racial segregation throughout the twentieth century, culminating in the landmark *Brown v. Board of Education* decision in 1954. Eight years prior to the *Brown* decision, a federal Court of Appeals in California had ruled in *Mendez v. Westminster* that the separate schools for Mexican Americans in California were unconstitutional, striking down segregation for children of Mexican, Asian, and Indian descent (Foley 2005). Thurgood Marshall, the African American attorney who argued the *Brown* case before the Supreme Court and later became the first African American Supreme Court justice, participated in the *Mendez* case, which no doubt influenced his argument in the *Brown* decision (Blanco 2010).

Brown v. Board of Education combined four cases involving segregated schools in Kansas, South Carolina, Virginia, and Delaware. In Virginia, a sixteen-year-old student initiated the case when she organized a school walkout to protest segregation. In the state courts, only the judge in Delaware ruled segregation to be illegal. Presenting the case to the Supreme Court, Thurgood Marshall, supported by the National Association for the Advancement of Colored People (NAACP), argued that segregation harmed Black children. Looking back on it now, the argument could have been more broadly framed, showing the harm done by segregation to all of society. At the time, however, research focused on the damage to Black children that racial inequality produced. It was the first time social science evidence was used to support an argument before the Supreme Court.

In its unanimous decision, the Supreme Court ruled that separate schools were a violation of the rights of equal protection guaranteed to all citizens under the

The effort to desegregate Little Rock Central High School in 1957 required military escorts to protect the nine young Black children who enrolled in the school. Resistance from White citizens was so severe that Arkansas governor Orval Faubus closed all of the Little Rock high schools for an entire school year to avoid further integration of the schools.

Fourteenth Amendment to the U.S. Constitution. Asserting that education is the most important function of local and state governments, the Court concluded that "the doctrine of 'separate but equal' has no place . . . in the field of public education" and that "separate educational facilities are inherently unequal" (U.S. Supreme Court 1954).

Despite such a strong Supreme Court ruling, the *Brown* decision did not change things overnight. Following *Brown*, many Whites fiercely resisted desegregation. School boards, especially in the South, did all they could to skirt desegregation.[2] In Arkansas, the governor simply closed the schools altogether to avoid desegregation. In Virginia, the governor and the legislature created policies they actually had the nerve to title "Massive Resistance." Such policies made it nearly impossible for Black students to enroll in White schools and allowed schools to close if ordered to desegregate (Blackside 1987; Daugherty 2015).

---

[2] As just one example, the author of this book, a White woman, was a student in Georgia public schools in the 1960s. Not until her senior year of high school in 1966 did her school admit any Black students. Even then only four Black students were admitted to a senior class (and no other classes) of about 130. This token desegregation came solely as the result of court orders, following insistence by activist Black citizens.

Intense policing in schools, especially those populated largely by Hispanic and Black students, has become so pronounced that some schools resemble prisons rather than learning environments.

White parents also fled from public schools, especially in the South. New private schools were created for Whites—schools that came to be known as "segregation academies" ("Segregation Academies and State Action" 1973). Although the Supreme Court had ordered schools to desegregate "with all deliberate speed," it took years before school districts actually complied with court-ordered desegregation—and then only following continued pressure from civil rights organizations and, eventually, the federal government (Reece and O'Connell 2016; Clotfelter 1976; Moye 2005).

Schools finally opened completely to students of color between the 1960s and the mid-1970s. But even as late as 1968—fourteen years after the *Brown* decision—81 percent of Black students in the South still attended majority black schools (Orfield 2001). Civil rights groups persistently mobilized throughout the South to bring pressure on southern school districts and colleges to desegregate. Only after great reluctance to do so did the federal government ultimately step in. By the mid-1960s, the walls of segregation started to crumble, and by the mid-1970s, numerous court-ordered desegregation plans were implemented, despite ongoing protests by many White communities in the North as well as the South. There was, though, significant progress during this time period, as hundreds of schools throughout the nation desegregated (Reardon and Owens 2014; Orfield 2013).

Experts do not agree on exactly how much segregation has changed. For one thing, segregation differs by region, in different kinds of institutions, and for

TABLE 9.3 Percentage of Students in 90–100 Percent Minority Schools, per Region

	Black		Latino	
	Percent attending majority-minority schools:	**Percent change, 1968–2011**	**Percent attending majority-minority schools:**	**Percent change, 1968–2011**
South	34.3	−56	41.5	+23
Border states[a]	41	−32	20	N/A
Northeast	51.4	+20	44.2	+0.5
Midwest	43.2	−26	26.2	+285
West	34.4	−32	44.8	+283

[a]"Border states" were slave states (Maryland, Delaware, Missouri, and Kentucky) that bordered northern free states. They did not secede during the Civil War.

Source: Orfield, Gary, and Erica Frankenberg. 2014. *Brown at 60: Great Progress, A Long Retreat, and an Uncertain Future.* Los Angeles: Civil Rights Project/Proyecto Derechos Civiles, University of California–Los Angeles.

different racial-ethnic groups. Asians, for example, are generally less segregated than Latinos and African Americans. In addition, as with residential segregation, how much segregation is found depends on how it is measured. Like residential segregation, educational segregation is also detected either in terms of *dissimilarity* (distribution across an area) or *isolation* (separation of groups from one another). What experts agree on is that the isolation of students of color—Black Americans and Latinos, in particular—has increased significantly since about 1980 (Orfield and Frankenberg 2014; Reardon and Owens 2014; Logan and Stults 2011).

The concentration of people of color within a city coupled with white flight to the suburbs means that students of color can be isolated from White students, even when their distribution in a particular school district matches their representation in the city population. Isolation indexes, on the other hand, show that students have very little exposure to other racial-ethnic groups when Whites leave the city proper in substantial numbers. This is precisely what has happened.

Even with some studies showing a decline in segregation, as measured by the index of dissimilarity, Black and Latino students are, in general, much more isolated from White students than in 1980 (Logan and Stults 2011). Since 1980, the proportion of Black students attending majority Black schools has also risen dramatically. And as you can see in table 9.3, large numbers of Black and Latino students attend so-called majority-minority schools that are 90 percent or more Black and Latino. In 1980, only one-third of Black students attended such schools (Reardon and Owens 2014; Orfield 2013; Orfield and Frankenberg 2014). Table 9.3 also shows that the likelihood of this attendance pattern varies by region of the country.

Nationwide, the typical Latino student attends a school that is 57 percent Latino. Latinos are also now more segregated in schools than are Black students (Orfield and Frankenberg 2014). With the number of Latino students growing, their

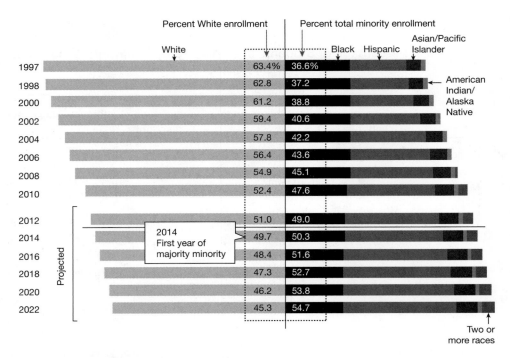

FIG. 9.1 Majority-Minority Public Schools in 2014

Source: Krogstad, Jens Manuel, and Richard Fry. 2014. "Dept. of Ed. Projects Public Schools Will Be 'Majority-Minority' This Fall." Pew Research Center. (http://www.pewresearch.org/fact-tank/2014/08/18/u-s-public-schools-expected-to-be-majority-minority-starting-this-fall/.)

segregation is predicted to increase unless there is a major shift in educational policies (see figure 9.1).

You can see these patterns of segregation by looking at typical classroom experiences. Figure 9.2 shows the racial composition of schools, based on nationwide data. From this information, you can conclude that the typical White student attends school with 72.5 percent White students, 8.3 percent Black students, 3.9 percent Asian students, 11.8 percent Latino students, and 3.5 percent Native American or multiracial students. Moreover, Black and Latino students are far more likely to be in schools with large proportions of Black and Latino students, while Asian students are likely to be in more diverse school settings. Thus, there are stark differences in the exposure of different groups of students to each other, with Blacks, Asians, and Latinos much more likely to be intermingled than are others, especially Whites (Orfield and Frankenberg 2014).

Since 1980, the walls of segregation have been reconstructed. By the mid-1970s, massive desegregation had taken place in the South, primarily because of so much oversight by the federal courts. Now, however, Black students in the South are as segregated as they were in the late 1960s (Orfield and Frankenberg 2014), although not as strictly segregated as they were prior to *Brown*, when racial segregation was absolute. Efforts to desegregate have completely stalled. Several court decisions have

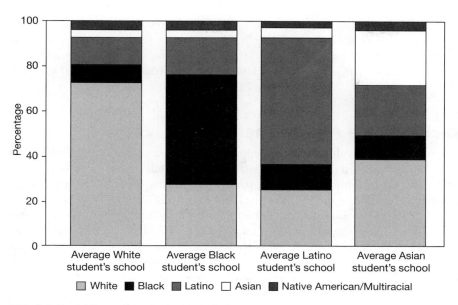

FIG. 9.2 Racial Segregation in the Nation's Schools, 2011–2012

Source: Orfield, Gary, and Erica Frankenberg. 2014. *Brown at 60: Great Progress, A Long Retreat, and an Uncertain Future*. Los Angeles: Civil Rights Project/Proyecto Derechos Civiles, University of California–Los Angeles.

also supported the termination of many of the desegregation plans of earlier years. The result is that most of the gains of the post-*Brown* era have been lost as schools are now re-segregating (Orfield 2013).

Students are segregated not only by race and ethnicity, but also by social class. Rising inequality has shaped how neighborhoods are populated, thus affecting the composition of schools (Reardon and Owens 2014). Poverty is also clearly linked to school segregation. Nationwide, in schools with a majority of minorities, most of the students—two-thirds by most estimates—are poor. In predominantly White schools, on the other hand, typically only about one-third of students are poor. Moreover, segregation by socioeconomic class has notably increased since the 1970s (Reardon and Owens 2014).

Finally, even when schools are statistically integrated, there is often segregation within. In other words, a school may be numerically balanced in terms of the percentages of different racial-ethnic groups, but internal segregation means that they follow different paths—both educationally and socially. White students are more likely to be placed in college-prep courses, AP courses, and honors curricula, while students of color are more likely to be tracked into different classes. These patterns can result in highly segregated schools even when teachers and parents value racial integration (Lewis and Diamond 2015; Lewis, Diamond, and Forman 2015; Tyson, Darity, and Castellino 2005). Consequently, even when schools desegregate, "racial inequality [remains] embedded in organization structures and processes" (Lewis and Diamond 2015:86).

The cost of school segregation is high. As Gary Orfield, a national expert on schools and re-segregation, puts it, "Segregation feeds stratification, inequality, and the denial of opportunity" (2013:44). Young people of color, as a result, suffer from a continuing achievement gap on various measures of educational attainment.

Race and the Achievement Gap

No one doubts the value of a good education. A good education can lead to opportunities that would be otherwise unattainable. Indeed, the belief in education as a path to upward mobility is a strong part of the American Dream. Yet every day we see evidence of failure in U.S. schools. News of failing students, discontented teachers, dilapidated schools, and inadequate school resources frequent the headlines. At the heart of these concerns are huge racial disparities—disparities so stark that commentator Jonathan Kozol calls them the "shame of the nation." Kozol even goes so far as to say that the nation operates *apartheid schools*—a reference to the different education children of color receive relative to White children (Kozol 2006, 2012). The result is the racial **achievement gap**.

Race and Educational Outcomes

The achievement gap refers to racial differences in educational opportunity, learning, and achievement. The achievement gap is extensively documented and indicated by various measures. The gap matters for individual students, because having a good education is increasingly important for success in the current economic structure, that is, the best jobs demand the skills a well-educated person is expected to be able to develop. Education also matters for society as a whole, because the nation needs not just the scientific skills but also the critical thinking and social intelligence that education promises to deliver. Without a well-educated citizenry, the nation simply cannot compete efficiently in the increasingly global and technological economy.

In fact, the United States is losing ground in educational stature relative to other nations. Compared to other economically developed nations, especially Europe and Asia, the United States is falling behind, now ranking in the lower third of student scores on standardized international math and science tests. Furthermore, our nation's poor performance is largely explained by the gap in White and Asian versus Black and Latino test scores (Darling-Hammond 2010). In other words, were the nation to close the racial achievement gap, it would not only benefit students of color but would also improve our educational standing relative to the rest of the world. As Linda Darling-Hammond, a renowned education scholar, puts it, "It is our continuing comfort with profound inequality that is the Achilles heel of American education" (2010:8).

Differences in educational achievement are the subject of much highly detailed and telling research. On numerous measures, Black and Latino students lag behind White and Asian American students. Some progress has been made, however, and many students of color have been successful in the nation's schools. The racial gap in achievement also closed substantially from the 1960s into the 1980s as schools

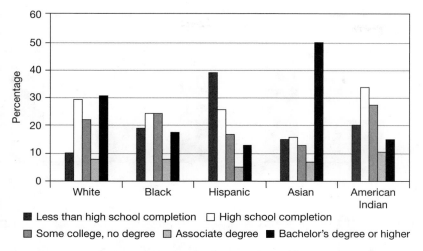

FIG. 9.3 Educational Attainment by Race/Ethnicity, Persons Age 25 and Over, 2013

Source: National Center for Education Statistics. 2015b. *Percentage of Persons 18 to 24 Years Old and Age 25 and Over, by Educational Attainment, Race/Ethnicity, and Selected Subgroups: 2008 and 2013.* Table 104.40. Washington, DC: National Center for Education Statistics. (https://nces.ed.gov/programs/digest/d14/tables/dt14_104.40.asp.)

desegregated (Orfield 2013). Recently, however, the gap between Latinos and Whites has actually increased. Those gains made through the 1980s have started to level off, with significant gaps remaining between Black and White, and Latino and White students (Morris and Perry 2016).

Underachievement in school is the result of a complex and prolonged series of steps in which students of color are underresourced, poorly taught, overly punished, and, as a result, more likely to fail or drop out. Underachievement accounts for the large difference in educational attainment that is still present across racial and ethnic groups (see figure 9.3). What is more, the differences found in earlier education carry over into differences in student achievement in college (Byrd, Brunn-Bevel, and Sexton 2014). Black and Latino college students, for example, are overrepresented in the least selective colleges and underrepresented in the nation's more selective colleges and universities (Supiano 2015).

Measures of educational achievement are typically based on nationally standardized exams, but other measures also show the seriousness of this problem. School dropout rates show that Native American, Black, and Latino students graduate from high school less than Whites (see figure 9.4). Students of color are, in fact, overrepresented in every category that measures the achievement gap—dropout and graduation rates, school suspensions, college attendance, and others (Noguera 2008; National Center for Education Statistics 2013). The result for Latino and African American students is *subtractive schooling* (Valenzuela 1999:3), that is, an educational process that "divests youth of important social and cultural resources, leaving them progressively vulnerable to academic failure" (1999:3).

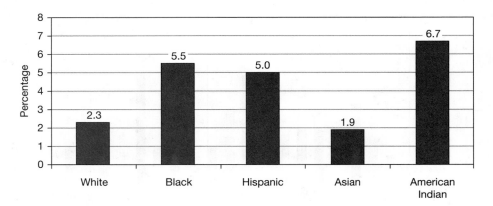

FIG. 9.4 School Dropout Rates (Percent of 9th through 12th Graders Dropping Out of Public School), 2009–2010

Source: National Center for Education Statistics. 2013. *Number and Percentage of 9th- to 12th-Graders Who Dropped Out of Public School or Jurisdiction: 2009-2010.* Table 219.50. Washington, DC: National Center for Education Statistics. (http://www.nces.ed.gov.)

Explaining the Achievement Gap

Scholars can and do document the many ways that students of color are vulnerable to poor educational outcomes. The big question is why these students are so vulnerable.

Black and Latino parents are often blamed for their children's level of achievement, because of a misconception that Black and Latino parents do not value education. Research, though, finds that average Black parents actually value education more and have higher expectations for their children than do White parents. Black parents are also just as involved in their children's education as are White parents. National data also show that Black high school students are more likely than White students to discuss grades and school issues with their parents and friends (Lewis and Diamond 2015; Harris 2011; Blau 2003). Blaming parents for the racial achievement gap simply does not hold up through research.

Others claim that students of color are influenced by an *oppositional culture.* The argument is that students underachieve because they think of school success as "acting White." Researchers have failed to find strong support for this idea, although some suggest that if this influence exists, it is more likely among Black students who are attending predominantly White high schools. Studies find overall, however, that Black students are actually very much like White students in their attitudes about grades, college attendance, and other measures of achievement (Tyson 2011; Lewis and Diamond 2015).

In general, Black students seem to have more pro-school attitudes than White students. Furthermore, high-achieving Black students tend to be the most popular. In short, there is little consistent support for the idea that students of color disdain academic success. Certainly, school cultures stratify social groups—nerds, preppies, stoners, and so forth—and all students, regardless of race, have to navigate this tricky terrain of social hierarchies and social judgments. Students of color have the additional burden of having to navigate the terrain of racism, and they are very much aware of having to do so (Carter 2007; Harris 2011; Lewis and Diamond 2015).

Blaming parents and young people of color for educational failure is a popular accusation, but the main reason for the achievement gap is inequality in schools. On virtually every measure of school quality—test scores, class size, teacher qualifications and turnover, facilities and district spending, and the presence of a college-preparatory curriculum—schools with large majorities of Black and Latino students fall below predominantly White schools (Darling-Hammond 2010; Noguera 2008; Ladson-Billings 2006).

Inequality in the schools means there are different educational opportunities for students. Teachers with strong academic backgrounds and certification produce students who achieve more. On every measure of teacher quality (certification, subject matter training, pedagogical training, experience, and college attended), schools that serve large numbers of minority students have generally less-qualified teachers. In addition, even when teachers are strong, teacher turnover in such schools is very high (Darling-Hammond 2010).

Curriculum differences in schools that serve predominantly minority students also put those students at an educational disadvantage. Students simply learn more when they have a high-quality curriculum that prepares them for college-level work, ample and current textbooks, and modern laboratory facilities and libraries. The absence of such high-quality curricula and learning environments in predominantly minority schools reverberates in the educational achievement of the students who attend these schools.

Within the same schools, **tracking**, separating students according to presumed ability, puts many students of color at a disadvantage. Much research shows that racial-ethnic minority and lower-income students are overrepresented in lower tracks within schools. At the same time, they are underrepresented in tracks that provide honors experiences, advanced placement courses, and other programs for gifted students (Tyson 2011; Oakes 2005). Being in lower tracks can also reinforce teachers' lower expectations that students of color will learn.

A final explanation for the achievement gap is the impact of school discipline. Increased policing, cameras in schools, and zero-tolerance policies have contributed to a disciplinary regime in schools that tends to criminalize any student who violates school rules (Kupchik 2010; Morris and Perry 2016). This has fallen especially hard on Latino and African American students. Studies find that many teachers tend to perceive Black and Latino youth as dangerous and threatening, thus subjecting them to more surveillance and discipline. Subjective judgments, for example, about Latino and Black youth who display a "street" style in their dress and demeanor can cast them in a negative light. Once labeled as deviant, the label sticks and punishment might come more often, in a process that has been labeled the "school to prison pipeline" (Ferguson 2000; Shedd 2015), as stated earlier (see chapter 5).

In schools, Black and Latino students are more likely to be put in detention, suspended, or expelled. In fact, Black students are seven times more likely to be punished than are White students; Latinos, twice as likely. Asian American students, on the other hand, may be viewed through the "model minority" stereotype that protects them from disciplinary action (Morris and Perry 2016; Ferguson 2000). You might conclude that differing punishments occur because Black and Latino students misbehave more. Studies show, however, that Black and Latino students are punished more *even when there is no difference in how students actually behave.* Even when Black and Latino students engage in the same behavior as White students, they are more likely to be punished. Boys, especially, engage in a broad range of disruptive behaviors at school, but African American boys are far more often referred to disciplinary authorities. The behavior of students of color is more frequently responded to with disciplinary action based strictly on subjective judgments by those in authority (Rios 2011; Skiba et al. 2002; Morris 2005).

How much of the achievement gap can be explained by the fact that students of color are also more likely to be poor? No doubt, poverty is a large part of the problem in education. When large numbers of disadvantaged students are concentrated in a school, educational achievement drops. Moreover, the concentration of low-income minority students in schools has been increasing nationwide, a function of the increase in concentrated poverty (Rothstein 2013).

With more than 20 percent of the nation's children living below the poverty line and even larger percentages of Black and Hispanic children among the poor, schools are not immune from poverty's grip. In schools with large numbers of poor children, all students—both the poor and the nonpoor—do worse. Moreover, low-income students in high-poverty schools do worse than poor students who attend more affluent schools (Darling-Hammond 2010).

Poverty alone, however, cannot account for the entire gap in educational achievement. Race and poverty are so entangled that it is often difficult to dissect the influence of one or the other. Still, race also matters in and of itself, as demonstrated through the volumes of research that show the impact of race on educational experiences. Denying that race matters in shaping educational experiences is a sure way to miss much of what happens as students progress through their education. Social class, including poverty, surely shapes the experiences of different groups of students, but without including race as part of the picture, one will not fully understand the challenges students of color face—at all levels of education.

When schools fail children, they rob them of the social and cultural capital that enables success. **Social capital** refers to the access people have to networks and relationships that bolster their progress in life. *Cultural capital* refers to the noneconomic assets that one holds often by virtue of education. Cultural capital includes not only one's knowledge, but also what are referred to as soft skills: speech patterns, general demeanor, social networks, and etiquette, to name a few. Just like money, cultural capital is an asset in that it provides people with a form of power and access to the dominant culture. Without it, one remains an outsider.

Social and cultural types of capital are both enhanced by a high-quality education. Each provides a toolkit that helps people navigate their way through society. Education, of course, imparts skills—reading, critical thinking, calculating skills, and so forth—but social and cultural capital are just as valuable, albeit more subjective. When functioning well, schools impart social and cultural capital as well as knowledge, but schools tend to reward students who already bring certain kinds of cultural capital into the schools with them (Lewis and Diamond 2015). Such factors as educated parents, early reading, and exposure to the arts all can give students a leg up even before they enter school. Although we think of schools as great equalizers, they in fact tend to reproduce any inequalities that exist before students begin their formal education.

The reasons for the racial achievement gap are many, and they overlap, making policy solutions particularly complex. Explanations of the achievement gap include many levels of analysis—the social structure of the schools, patterns of social interaction, and the beliefs and perceptions that teachers and students have of racial-ethnic groups. These parts of the achievement gap, as educational specialists conclude, "mutually reinforce each other and collectively generate different educational trajectories" (Lewis and Diamond 2015:167).

Succeeding Against the Odds: Race and School Success

Studying the racial achievement gap reveals the enormous social forces that are impeding educational attainment for students of color. The harm done to the nation's children is great in terms of lost potential, both to individual children and to society as a whole. No doubt, the forces of racial inequality in the schools contribute to the stubborn persistence of an underclass and to the nation's ability to compete in the new global economy. But what if we think about education in a different way and ask not just what impedes the education of minority youth, but also how students of color succeed?

Shaun Harper, an education professor, has done just that. Harper conducted a national study of African American college men, interviewing them on forty-two different college campuses around the United States. His focus on Black men is especially important because they make up one of the most disadvantaged groups in terms of high school completion, college attendance, and college graduation. By focusing on successful men, Harper challenged what he calls a *deficit perspective*; he developed a framework that identifies how students of color find their way to success even in the context of a racially unequal landscape.

Harper found that achieving Black men had parents who consistently held high expectations for their sons' education, even if the parents were not themselves college-educated. Parental influence alone was not enough, however. Influential teachers, beginning in early schooling, also ensured that the young men had the information, resources, and support needed to succeed in school. These three things—*information, resources,* and *support*—are critical throughout students' educational paths.

Information can be as basic as understanding what courses are needed in high school (or earlier) to be competitive in college admissions. It can also mean understanding the college admissions process and potential funding sources. Resources include financial support, but also such things as the availability of books, test preparation, and other crucial educational materials. Support could also refer to financial support, but critically, it also means the support of peers, teachers, and community leaders. Finally, the students in Harper's research had to be able to respond to the racism they encountered in college (or school) through engaging in productive social networks, not just getting angry (Harper 2012).

Harper's research is consistent with what many other scholars have found about student success. Support from family, peers, and teachers is critical, but individual resources are not enough. Research on Latinas, as one example, finds that being successful in school means carving paths that provide mentoring support and information, while also maintaining a positive identity of oneself as Latina and forming group ties that affirm Latina identity (Barajas and Pierce 2001). Such identity work can be especially critical when students of color enter educational institutions that are culturally structured as middle-class White environments. Learning how to navigate such environments is a key part of student success (Stephens et al. 2012). Teachers and others can help by creating classroom experiences that promote what scholars call *identity safety*, that is, classroom environments that empower students of color by acknowledging racial realities and using student diversity as a teaching resource, not a handicap (Steele and Cohn-Vargas 2013).

Ensuring the educational success of students of color is not simply a matter of individual identities or individual relationships. Schools have to structure resources to help students of color succeed. Such practices can cultivate success for students of color and, in so doing, will likely enhance educational paths for all students.

Conclusion

Since the days of Jim Crow segregation, there has been much progress in reducing residential and educational segregation, even if major problems remain. Progress is being challenged, though, by retrenchment in the courts, weak enforcement of existing policies, and in the attitude that we no longer need racially based interventions.

Key decisions by the U.S. Supreme Court have limited possible remedies for school desegregation. For example, the Supreme Court ruled in *Bradley v. Milliken* (1974) that school systems were not responsible for desegregation across district lines unless they had intentionally discriminated. Discrimination is now rarely so explicit. A series of such cases has meant that court-ordered desegregation efforts have declined, evidenced by the re-segregation of the schools.

National educational policy has also tended to make individual schools or school districts responsible for change. Teachers often shoulder the blame. How schools are funded also robs poorer districts of the resources to create better schools. In other nations, education is usually funded centrally. In the United States schools rely on local taxes, meaning that low-income areas simply have fewer resources to build better schools. Although there is not a perfect correlation between funding and school quality, there is a strong association (Darling-Hammond 2010).

Fair housing policy includes a wide range of programs that are designed to eliminate discrimination and reduce segregation. These include targeting predatory lending practices, reporting landlord abuses, and monitoring cases of discrimination. Federal housing policy has shifted from densely packed large public housing units to voucher programs designed to disperse people rather than concentrate them into dense high-crime areas. In principle, housing voucher programs reduce concentrated poverty, but the concentration of poor people in inner cities has meant that such programs have had a negligible impact (DeLuca, Garboden, and Rosenblatt 2013). Also, better-off communities, when faced with the possibility of affordable housing coming into their area, often organize to prevent it, arguing that it will affect their own property values (Semuels 2015b).

Public attitudes also shape the nation's response to segregation. A large majority of the American public say they would prefer to live in a community made up of a mix of different races (Pew Research Center 2008), but few actually live in such communities. Further, more than three-quarters of White Americans say that Black children have as good a chance as White children to get a good education (Gallup Editors 2014). Inconsistency in the beliefs and actions of so many White Americans confirms what Malcolm X famously said: "America preaches integration and practices segregation." The strong assumption that change should be colorblind and not race-specific when race still matters thwarts attempts to continue the nation's work toward desegregating neighborhoods and schools (Darby and Saatcioglu 2014).

Author Bryan Stevenson has stated, "Social distance can breed contempt" (Stevenson 2015). His statement reminds us that racial segregation breeds misunderstanding, stereotypes, and accusations of blame leveled against society's most vulnerable. Without a renewed societal commitment to ending the segregation that divides us, we fail a significant portion of the national citizenry, including failing a commitment to the nation's children. A renewed value placed on integration, not individualism, would go a long way to ending the segregation that the Civil Rights movement fought so hard to overcome.

Key Terms

achievement gap, 216

Brown v. Board of Education (1954), 201

Fair Housing Act (1968), 201

hypersegregation, 204

index of dissimilarity, 203

Plessy v. Ferguson (1896), 210

predatory lending, 207

redlining, 207

residential segregation, 201

social capital, 220

steering, 206

subprime mortgages, 207

tracking, 219

white space, 205

Critical Thinking Questions

1. Review the two opening scenarios in this chapter. Given what you have learned in this chapter, what would you predict about the educational path of the two young girls? What would help to make both successful in their educational dreams?

2. What does it mean to say that education reproduces the inequality already found in society at large?

Student Exercises

9.1: Go to Census Scope (http://www.censusscope.org) and click on the segregation tab. Navigating the information on this web site, report on the segregation indexes for an area of your choosing. Does segregation in this area differ for different racial-ethnic groups? Given what you might know about this particular area, what do you think explains the segregation patterns? Give a report on which groups are the most segregated in the city you have chosen.

9.2: Using table 9.3 as an example, construct a table that gives an approximation of the racial composition in your high school. Would you describe your high school as integrated, segregated, or hypersegregated? What factors in your community explain this?

Challenging Questions/Open to Debate

Many of the gains made in closing the achievement gap from the 1960s into the 1980s came as the result of race-conscious desegregation efforts. Since then, schools have re-segregated and courts and school districts have largely lost what gains were made. Should race-conscious efforts to desegregate the schools be re-implemented, or should the nation allow race-blind policies to govern education?

CHAPTER 10

It Gets to You

Health Care and the Environment

*All communities and persons across this nation should live
in a safe and healthful environment.*
—President William Clinton

OBJECTIVES

- Detail some of the indicators of health disparities by race and ethnicity
- Explain the reasons for persistent health disparities
- Identify different dimensions of institutional racism in the health care system
- Analyze the link between racism and reproductive health
- Define and explain environmental racism

In the winter of 2016, a federal emergency was declared in Flint, Michigan, because the city's water was contaminated with lead. City residents were warned not to drink the water. By then, however, local officials already knew about the water's lead contamination and city residents had been drinking it for more than a year without knowing it. Large numbers of the city's children were found with high levels of lead exposure, a condition very damaging to their long-term physical health and social development. Adults exposed to lead also may develop various illnesses such as kidney ailments, abdominal pain, and decline in mental functioning. According to engineering experts, not one neighborhood in the city of Flint had safe drinking water.

Angry residents demanded the resignation of the state's governor and the city leadership because of their disregard for the health and safety of Flint's residents. About two years before, the city's manager, in a cost-cutting measure, had switched the water source from clean water supplied by Lake Huron to the Flint River. Residents immediately started complaining about the color, smell, and taste of the water, but no change was made—other than raising the price. City officials also found unacceptable levels of coliform bacteria in Flint's water, and so they pumped extra chloride into the system. The water then became so highly corrosive that it caused lead to leach from the supply pipes into home plumbing, basically poisoning city residents.

Flint has a population near one hundred thousand people, 55 percent of them African American and another 9 percent other people of color. Prior to the water crisis, Flint had already been devastated by the closure of several major automobile plants. Unemployment in Flint is twice that of the rest of the nation. In Flint, 42 percent of the population lives below the poverty line—more than 2.5 times the poverty rate in Michigan and almost 3 times that of the nation as a whole (U.S. Bureau of the Census 2016c).

As this crisis unfolded, people all over the country questioned whether state and local leaders would have been so blasé about such a public health crisis had it occurred in a mostly White, more affluent city. The poisoning of Flint's residents calls to mind an ongoing national problem: racial disparities in the health of the nation's people.

It Makes You Sick: Race and Health Disparities

There are many indicators of racial and ethnic differences in health and wellness. On virtually every measure, racial-ethnic minorities in the United States have poorer health than Whites. As you will see below, racial disparities are found in higher rates of mortality, early onset of disease, and greater severity and consequences of disease. Furthermore, health disparities for people of color have persisted over time and at all levels of income and education (Williams and Mohammed 2013).

You can see this to some extent by answering a simple question: Did you get a good night's sleep last night? Being short on sleep is highly associated with an increased risk of early mortality, but how well you sleep is also associated with your racial, ethnicity, gender, and occupational status. If you are Black, you are quite likely to be short on sleep compared to Whites and Latinos. Among both Blacks and Latinos, being short on sleep increases with higher professional status. For Whites, the reverse is true: Whites are shorter on sleep when in lower-status roles. Black women professional workers have the least sleep of all. White women professionals are the least likely to be short on sleep (Jackson et al. 2014). These facts may surprise you, but they point to the significance of race and social class in predicting an important measure of good health.

You would expect that with some improvement in the socioeconomic status of racial minorities, health disparities would be declining. In a few instances, they are, but with some health conditions, disparities have actually increased. As an example, in 1950, Black and White Americans had comparable death rates from heart disease and cancer. Now African Americans have higher death rates from these two diseases than do Whites (National Center for Health Statistics 2015). Black women are also still more likely to get breast cancer at an early age and are diagnosed at later disease stages (Dean at al. 2014). The sections below examine some of the evidence of health care disparities, including a discussion of the reasons for such inequalities.

Race: A Matter of Life and Death

Starting with the simple reality of your **life expectancy**—the average number of years that people born in a particular year can expect to live—race and ethnicity matter. Life expectancy in the United States has increased for all groups over time, but significant differences remain based on both race and gender, as you can see in figure 10.1. Women in every racial-ethnic group live longer than their male counterparts, but African American men have the shortest life expectancy of all (National Center for Health Statistics 2015).

You can also see in figure 10.1 that Hispanics actually have a longer life expectancy than do White non-Hispanics—a phenomenon referred to as the *Hispanic*

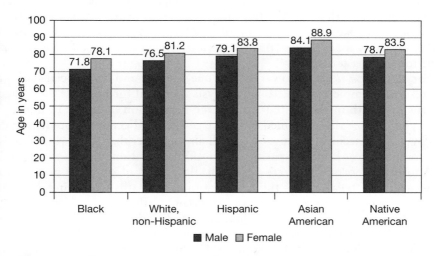

FIG. 10.1 Life Expectancy in the United States by Racial Group, 2014

Note: Native American and Asian American data from the 2010 census; all other data from 2014.

Source: Arias, Elizabeth. 2016. "Changes in Life Expectancy by Race and Hispanic Origin in the United States, 2013–2014." NCHS Data Brief 244 (April), Figure 3 and Figure 4. Hyattsville, MD: National Center for Health Statistics. Retrieved January 19, 2017 (https://www.cdc.gov/nchs/data/databriefs/db244.pdf).

paradox (Markides and Eschbach 2011). You would think that Hispanic life expectancy would be more comparable to that of African Americans, given the similarity in their socioeconomic status. It appears that one reason for the longer life expectancy of Hispanics is their lower rate of smoking (Lariscy et al. 2016), but experts do not yet have a complete understanding of this paradox.

The timing and cause of death is also somewhat predictable based on race. **Death rate** (also called the *mortality rate*) is calculated by measuring the number of deaths in a given population, relative to the population size, in a given period of time. Death rates are often adjusted by age to account for the different age distribution within racial-ethnic populations. To provide an example: The age-adjusted death rate for all diseases in 2013 for non-Hispanic Whites was 747.1 per 100,000 in the population but higher for African Americans at 860.8 per 100,000. For other groups, the death rate was lower: Native Americans/Alaska Natives, 591.7; Hispanics/Latinos, 535.4; and for Asian and Pacific Islanders, 405.4 (National Center for Health Statistics 2015).

In addition to the overall death rate, the major causes of death for different populations are also shaped by race and ethnicity. African Americans have higher rates of death than do Whites for all of the leading causes of death (heart disease, cancer, stroke, diabetes, and homicide; National Center for Health Statistics 2015). In fact, experts have estimated that about one hundred thousand Black people die prematurely each year. Were there no racial disparities in health, Black people would not die so young (Williams and Mohammed 2009, 2013; Kung et al. 2008).

Patterns of death vary for different diseases but are strongly based on people's social status. Native Americans, for example, have lower death rates from heart disease and cancer compared to Whites and African Americans, but are more likely to die from motor vehicle accidents. Latinos also have lower death rates from heart disease and cancer than do Whites, but have higher death rates from influenza. Asian Americans have the best health of all. You must be careful interpreting this, however, because the category "Asian American" includes many different groups, as is true for Latinos as well.

For all groups, health also varies with one's gender and one's social class status. As a result, a complex intersectional analysis is critical for understanding detailed patterns of health in the United States. One illustration of this is in figure 10.2, where you can see the combined influence of race and gender is predicting death rates by various accidental causes. You will also see later that social class is a significant component of health disparities in the U.S. population.

Another important indicator of the health status of different populations is **infant mortality**, measured as the number of infant deaths—counting those under one year of age—in a given year per one thousand births. In fact, infant mortality is commonly used as an indicator of a nation's well-being.

Infant mortality is quite low in the United States compared to other nations of the world (5.0 per 1,000 births in 2015). But, infant mortality among African Americans and Native Americans gives a more disturbing picture of the nation's health. Infant mortality for African Americans in 2015 was 10.9; for American Indians, 8.4. These rates of infant mortality are comparable to those in some of the world's poorest nations, such as Botswana and Brunei (Central Intelligence Agency 2015).

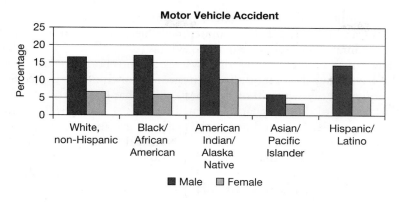

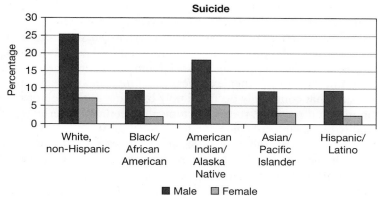

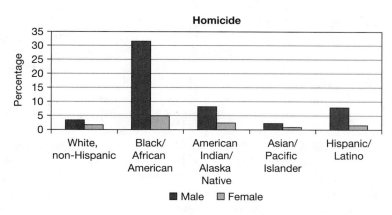

FIG. 10.2   Death by Motor Vehicle Accident, Suicide, and Homicide: The Significance of Gender and Race

Source: National Center for Health Statistics. 2015. *Health, United States, 2014: With Special Feature on Adults Aged 55–64.* Hyattsville, MD: U.S. Department of Health and Human Services. (http://www.cdc.gov/nchs/data/hus/hus14.pdf.)

Among Latinos in the United States, overall infant mortality is actually quite low, but it varies in different Latino populations. Puerto Ricans in the United States have a higher infant mortality rate than do Whites (6.9 per 1,000 births), but other Latinos have lower infant mortality than Whites. Latinos born outside of the United States also have lower infant mortality than those born within the United States. No one has yet figured out why, although experts think that having strong ties to one's community is part of the explanation (Viruell-Fuentes et al. 2013). No doubt, poverty also plays a role. The good news is that, for all groups, infant mortality rates have declined significantly since the 1980s (National Center for Health Statistics 2015). This is an indication that the nation can do more to reduce infant mortality.

Feeling the Burden: Stress and Hypertension

Everybody knows what stress is. Whether studying for exams, working long hours, or just feeling frazzled by too much to do—everyone feels stress at one time or another. Chronic stress, though, can produce **hypertension**, a condition of elevated blood pressure. Elevated blood pressure is a physiological fact, but physicians know that blood pressure varies depending on social and environmental conditions. You might have, at one time or another, experienced *white coat syndrome*, the elevation in blood pressure that commonly occurs simply by going to the doctor's office. Such an elevation in blood pressure, though, is typically fleeting. Hypertension based on racial inequality can be life-changing.

African American men and now Mexican-origin men are the two groups most likely to live with uncontrolled hypertension. Even comparing Black and White poor men, Black men have blood pressure that is 57 percent higher than that for Whites (LaVeist 2005; National Center for Health Statistics 2015). African Americans even maintain higher levels of blood pressure than Whites while they are asleep (Smith, Ruiz, and Uchino 2000). Why?

One answer is that racism itself is a source of stress. Constantly being on the alert for potential insults or other microaggressions wears people down. Medical researchers have concluded that racial differences in stress not only exist but are the key factor linking racial status to poor health.

Simply put, cumulative exposure to stress from racism is detrimental to one's health. In studies of exposure to stress, researchers consistently find that African Americans, men especially, have a higher prevalence of stress and more accumulation of different stresses than do Whites. Latinos born in the United States also have prevalence rates and patterns of stress similar to African Americans. Foreign-born Hispanics are more similar to White Americans in their stress profiles. Financial and relationship problems are the most prevalent forms of stress. There is little doubt that experiencing multiple sources of stress is correlated with poor physical and mental health (Sternthal, Slopen, and Williams 2011).

Race and Risk: Alcohol, Substance Abuse, and Accidents

Behaviors such as smoking, drinking, and drug abuse are all known health risks, and they have a racial dimension. Without actual data, racial stereotypes prevent some people from knowing who engages in what risks. Contrary to stereotypes, for example, American Indians are *less likely* to be heavy alcohol users than are Whites. Whites are actually the group most likely to report current use of alcohol. And on college campuses, African American, Latino, and Asian students are much less likely to be binge drinkers compared to White students (National Center for Health Statistics 2015; Substance Abuse and Mental Health Services Administration 2014).

Patterns of illegal drug use also vary by race and ethnicity. The use of illegal drugs is highest among Native Hawaiians and Pacific Islanders, lowest among Asian Americans. Usage varies, however, depending on the substance. Marijuana and the misuse of prescription drugs are the most common forms of substance abuse among all people, but Hispanics and Asians are least likely to have used marijuana in the past year. Whites, Hispanics, American Indians, and those who identify as multiracial are the groups more likely to be misusing prescription drugs (Substance Abuse and Mental Health Services Administration 2014).

What explains these differences? It is easy to attribute risky behaviors to individual factors, but individual behaviors have a social context. For example, there is some evidence that young people of color are less likely to drink because they perceive (and rightly so) a greater risk if they are seen as being out of control. Among African Americans and Latinos, having a strong religious faith also seems to deter drinking. The use of illicit drugs also depends on their availability and expense (Keyes et al. 2015; Holt et al. 2015; Stevens-Watkins et al. 2012). Others argue that factors such as a strong feeling of belonging in a racial or ethnic community lessen the abuse of illegal substances. This does not mean that substance abuse is not a problem among minority populations. It is only to say that social context is an important part of explaining differences in risk-taking behavior.

You can also see the influence of social factors in patterns of accidental death in figure 10.2. Homicide is the fifth leading cause of death for African American men, the only group for whom this cause of death is among the top ten causes of death. Death from HIV/AIDS is also shockingly high for African American men, who are eight times as likely to die from HIV as are Whites. Hispanics are twice as likely as Whites to die from HIV (National Center for Health Statistics 2015). Health, no doubt, is a physiological reality, but understanding that reality requires a social, not just a physiological, analysis. Given the centrality of race to social context, race must be part of this understanding.

Race Weighs In: Obesity and Eating Disorders

When former first lady Michelle Obama launched a national effort to reduce obesity, she touched a nerve in the American public. Only 30 percent of the American population lives within what the National Institutes of Health defines as a *healthy body weight*—a measure of your weight relative to your height. As with other health measures, there are substantial differences in body weight because of race, ethnicity, and gender, as you can see in figure 10.3. Black women and Mexican-origin men are the least likely to have a healthy body weight. Black and White women, along with White, non-Hispanic men, are most likely to be overweight or obese. Poverty also influences weight: People living below the poverty line are less likely to be a healthy weight (National Center for Health Statistics 2015).

Being overweight is only one part of the problem. Eating disorders such as anorexia and bulimia are also associated with racial-ethnic identities. The beauty ideal for women in American culture is one of a thin—often *extremely* thin— woman. Women who internalize the extreme as an ideal are those most likely to

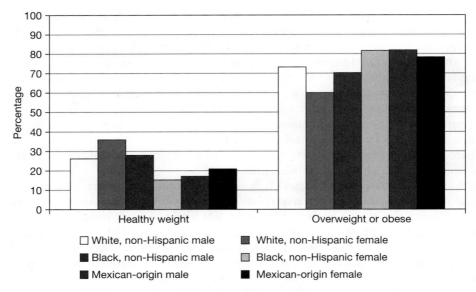

FIG. 10.3 Weight in America: Healthy Body Weight and Overweight, by Race and Gender

Source: National Center for Health Statistics. 2015. *Health, United States, 2014: With Special Feature on Adults Aged 55–64.* Hyattsville, MD: U.S. Department of Health and Human Services. (http://www.cdc.gov/nchs/data/hus/hus14.pdf.)

develop eating disorders as they strive for this unhealthy look. For women of color, though, different cultural ideals that value larger women may mediate against disordered eating. White women are more likely to become anorexic and/or engage in extreme weight loss.

Now, however, more women of color are developing eating disorders in the form of anorexia and bulimia. Why? Studies find that eating disorders are more likely for women of color when they identify with the dominant white cultural ideal. In other words, White women are more at risk for eating disorders when they overly identify with a "culture of thinness." Women of color, on the other hand, are more likely to be at risk for eating disorders when they have low levels of ethnic identity—that is, when they adopt the white ideal of beauty, not the ideals traditionally specific to their own group (Cotter et al. 2015; Gordon et al. 2010; Shuttlesworth and Zotter 2011).

Immigrant Health

Given the high rate of immigration in the United States, health researchers are increasingly interested in immigrant health. In the United States, 69 percent of Asians and 40 percent of Latinos are foreign-born. Foreign-born people generally have better health outcomes than do their counterparts in the United States. Yet, the longer an immigrant remains in the United States, the worse the person's health becomes. Why? Experts explain this as the result of geographic isolation, residential segregation, and the decline in socioeconomic status that tends to follow immigration.

To date, most studies of immigrant health have focused on Latinos. Research shows that Latinos born outside the United States, in general, have less heart disease, cancer, and other illnesses than do U.S.-born Latinos. This may be in part because those in the best health are those most likely to make the migration journey, but it is also partially explained by the fact that Latinos are a younger population than other groups. Still, compared with U.S.-born Latinos, foreign-born Latinos generally have fewer health problems (Consuelo Nacional de Población 2008; Centers for Disease Control and Prevention 2015).

Despite public myths that immigrants abuse the U.S. health care system, the fact is that immigrants underutilize health care services. Per capita health care expenses are far less for Latino immigrants than for U.S.-born Latinos. Latino immigrants have lower expenditures for emergency room visits, hospitalization, and prescription drugs, with one exception: children. Expenses for emergency room visits by Latino immigrant children are higher than for U.S.-born Mexican children, even though immigrant children use the emergency room less often. This is explained by the fact that Mexican immigrants wait longer to seek treatment and thus are sicker once they go to an emergency room (Mohanty 2006).

By far, however, the greatest problem for Mexican immigrants in the United States is their lack of health insurance. Estimates are that half of the Mexican immigrant population in the United States has no insurance coverage. Without insurance, people are especially vulnerable when they get sick or injured (see figure 10.4).

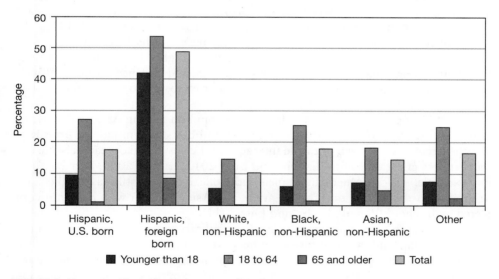

FIG. 10.4 Persons without Health Insurance (2013)

These data were compiled in 2013. You can see that people of color are less likely to have health care coverage than White, non-Hispanic, people. The Affordable Care Act did, however, significantly increase coverage for all groups, especially people of color. Changes in federal policies are, thus, likely to have a differential impact on certain groups. Who is most likely to be affected by any reductions in health care coverage?

Note: The White, non-Hispanic, 65 and older rate is 0.4 percent, so it is so small as to not be seen.

Source: Pew Research Center. 2015e. "Persons without Health Insurance, by Age, Race, and Ethnicity, 2013." Statistical Portrait of Hispanics in the United States, 1980–2013. Washington, DC: Pew Research Center. (http://www.pewhispanic.org/2016/04/19/statistical-portrait-of-hispanics-in-the-united-states/ph_2015-03_statistical-portrait-of-hispanics-in-the-united-states-2013_current-35/.)

Why Do Racial Health Disparities Persist?

Documenting health care disparities is one matter, explaining them, another. There are several reasons for racial health disparities, but two primary explanations are: (1) the connection between race and class; and, (2) the persistence of racial residential segregation.

The Race-Class Connection

One of the most important questions about health disparities is the relationship between race and social class. Are the disparities that we see primarily the result of the lower socioeconomic status of racial-ethnic populations? To some extent—perhaps a large extent—yes, but race and class both have effects of their own. Class and race are, in fact, so entangled that it can be difficult to parse out the influence of each one.

In general, people in poor households, regardless of race, have poorer health and less access to high-quality health care. Various indicators of health are certainly tied to social class status. National surveys, for example, examine a broad range of health care quality measures, including access to preventive care, treatment for acute illnesses, chronic disease management, and the quality of health care settings, such as in doctors' offices, emergency rooms, dialysis centers, nursing homes, hospices, home health care services, and so forth. No matter what measure of health you use, poverty matters (Centers for Disease Control and Prevention 2014).

Poverty is without question very hard on people's health. Poverty brings higher rates of teenage pregnancy, higher levels of stress, higher infant mortality rates, lower birth weight babies, and greater risk of crime and violence—all indicators of health. Concentrated poverty brings even greater exposure to environmental hazards, which then produce poor health outcomes.

Given that concentrated poverty is more common among African Americans and Latinos, you can see that poverty, race, and class intermingle in producing health outcomes. But even with the interaction of class and race, each also has an independent effect on health (LaVeist and Isaac 2012, LaVeist 2005; Barr 2014). As one example, African American women with college degrees still have higher rates of infant mortality than do White, Latina, and Asian women who have not completed high school (Pamuk, Fuchs, and Lutz 2011).

Perhaps even more poignant is a study of military veterans that has found that Black, Hispanic, and multiple-race veterans have poorer health and higher levels of activity limitations once they return home from military service. Why? Class status explains some of this pattern, but so do military experiences. Black, Latino and multiple-race soldiers, even accounting for social class, are exposed to greater harms during military service (Sheehan et al. 2015).

No doubt, social class is a significant correlate of whether you have good health or bad, but race matters in and of itself. One way to see this is through the impact of racial segregation on health outcomes.

The Consequences of Segregation

Racial segregation also has serious consequences for people's health. Indeed, racial segregation is one of the major reasons for racial health disparities.

Residential segregation is strongly associated with various measures of health. The social isolation that results from segregation, for example, is known to affect the health of African Americans. Studies of Latinos also show that those in the most highly segregated Latino neighborhoods have relatively little access to medical specialists and, thus, poorer health outcomes (Dinwiddie et al. 2013; Collins and Williams 1999; White and Borrell 2011).

In general, people living in racially segregated neighborhoods also have less access to facilities that promote good health. This includes quality health care services and the presence of nearby stores that sell healthy food. Such stores are rarer in segregated minority neighborhoods.

Many studies have documented that residential segregation is related to a variety of negative health outcomes: preterm births, stress, and the likelihood of specific diseases. The linkage of residential segregation to crime also creates health risks because of the greater likelihood of violence (Kramer et al. 2010; Mendez, Hogan, and Culhane 2014).

Highly segregated cities are also bad for White people's health, although not to the same extent as for Black and Latino residents. Segregated cities also harm White people's health because such cities tend to have characteristics that harm everyone. Exposure to pathogens, congestion, and higher crime rates, to name a few such features, mean that everyone's well-being is compromised. Specialists have concluded that were living conditions to be more equal, racial health disparities would likely diminish (LaVeist et al. 2011; Collins and Williams 1999).

Institutional Racism and the Health Care System

People of color's reduced access to quality health care and treatment in the health care system in general are major reasons for their poor health outcomes. As one example, see LIVING WITH RACISM. Large disparities with regard to care for people of color have been well documented (Institute of Medicine 2012). There have been recent improvements, most notably in greater health insurance coverage since the passage of the Affordable Care Act in 2010 (addressed in more detail below). Whether these improvements will persist with changes in this federal law remain to be seen. On various other measures, however, disparities of care remain, especially for African Americans and other people of color (National Center for Health Statistics 2015).

Institutional racism in the health care system is clearly part of the problem. Institutional racism shows up in the inadequate delivery of health care to people of color, as well as in the bias that health care providers are likely to hold. Overall, people of color, especially if they are poor, receive less costly and less intensive medical care. Among women, for example, Whites are the most likely to get mammograms; Latinas, the least likely (Institute of Medicine 2012). Racial-ethnic minorities underutilize health care services in general, a pattern partially explained by socioeconomic status, but also by the fact that people of color are less likely than Whites to have a regular source of care. Numerous studies have found that health care providers also treat people of color differently. For example, racial-ethnic patients are subjected to longer waiting times in emergency rooms because of the stereotypes held by emergency room staff (Lara-Millan 2014).

LIVING WITH RACISM

The Immortal Life of Henrietta Lacks

At a once unmarked grave in rural Virginia there is now a memorial to a largely unknown Black woman whose death has since saved countless numbers of lives. Henrietta Lacks was a tobacco farmer in rural Virginia, part of an extended family descended from slaves. In 1951, Henrietta Lacks went to Johns Hopkins Hospital in Baltimore for what she felt as a knot in her abdomen. Hopkins was the closest hospital to her that would treat Black patients. She was diagnosed with cervical cancer and died a few months later at the age of 31 after experiencing terrible pain as the cancer metastasized throughout her body.

Unbeknownst to Lacks's family, doctors cultured some of her cancer cells when she died. For reasons still unknown, other people's cancer cells lived only for a few days, which prevented their use in biomedical research, but Henrietta Lacks's cells lived on, allowing scientists to put the cells into mass production. The *HeLa cells*, named in her honor, have become the basis for groundbreaking research on cancer and countless cancer treatments over the years.

Her story has been largely unknown; until the early twenty-first century, her family knew nothing about how her cells influenced the development of biomedical research. Sharing the proceeds of her best-selling book, *The Immortal Life of Henrietta Lacks*, journalist Rebecca Skloot created the Henrietta Lacks Foundation that provides financial support to people in need, including members of Lacks's family because they have contributed to so much scientific research even without their knowledge or consent.

Source: Skloot, Rebecca. 2010. *The Immortal Life of Henrietta Lacks*. New York: Crown Books; also see the Henrietta Lacks Foundation website, http://www.henriettalacksfoundation.org.

Studies have also documented that Black, Hispanic, and Asian patients, especially children, are less likely to be given pain medications for things like broken bones. One such study showed that Black children being treated for appendicitis in hospital emergency rooms are far less likely than White children to be given pain medication (Goyal et al. 2015). Another study of emergency rooms has found that Black patients are 60 percent less likely to get pain medications even for the same reported levels of pain as are other people (Fleegler and Schechter 2008). Researchers explain these differences as resulting from bias on the part of health care providers—bias that may be unintentional but exists nonetheless.

We've Got You Covered: Health Insurance

One piece of good news about race and health is the increase in the number of people covered by health insurance since the passage in 2010 of the **Affordable Care Act (ACA)**, informally referred to as Obamacare. Prior to the passage of the ACA in 2010, 50 million Americans (17 percent of the population) had no health insurance. Twenty percent of African Americans and one-third of Hispanics had no coverage (DeNavas-Walt, Proctor, and Smith 2010). Only four years following passage of the

It is increasingly common for people with limited health care options to use emergency rooms for routine and sick care, as was true for this four-month old child and her mother. This results in both overcrowding and long wait times in the nation's hospitals.

law, the number of uninsured Americans had dropped to 10 percent of the population, with the gaps in coverage among Whites, Blacks, Asians, and Latinos also closing (see figure 10.4; Smith and Medalia 2015). Whether these trends will continue, however, is questionable as the Trump administration and the U.S. Congress have threatened to repeal Obamacare.

Even with the ACA fully in place, people of color are still less likely to be covered by health insurance (either private or public) than White Americans. Hispanics have the highest rate of noncoverage, followed by Native Americans, Black Americans, and then Asian Americans. Much of this gap is explained by the fact that White Americans are more likely to have coverage through employers, whereas people of color are more likely to need federal and state-based health coverage, including Medicaid. Adults are generally less likely to be covered than children, mostly because of children's Medicaid eligibility (Kaiser Foundation 2016).

Poverty and immigration status explain much of the gap in insurance coverage, but significant shares of the uninsured are also those who recently immigrated. Undocumented workers are excluded from Medicaid coverage, and there is a five-year waiting period for Medicaid even for those who have entered legally (Kaiser Foundation 2016).

TABLE 10.1 Representation of People of Color in Select Health Care Occupations, by Percentage

	Black	Hispanic/Latino	Asian American
Physicians/surgeons	5.5	5.6	21
Physician's assistants	6.4	5.9	11.3
Physical therapists	6.7	4.6	12.5
Therapists	9.7	13.1	2.4
Registered nurses	11.8	6.7	8.2
EMTs/Paramedics	7.7	8.4	1.2
Licensed practical nurses	27	9.9	5.0
Nursing home/home health aides	35.9	15.4	4.5
Personal care aides	23	18.2	7.9

Source: U.S. Bureau of Labor Statistics. 2016a. *Employment and Earnings 2015*. Washington, DC: U.S. Department of Labor. (https://www.bls.gov/opub/ee/2016/home.htm.)

Health Care Workers

One of the problems for the treatment of racial-ethnic minorities in the health care system is the status of people of color as workers in this system. You can see in table 10.1 that, relative to their proportion in the overall population, Black Americans and Latinos are highly underrepresented in the higher status jobs in health care (as, for example, physicians, physician's assistants, and therapists), but overrepresented in the most low-status and poorly paid health care jobs (such as work as home health aides and personal care workers). Why does this matter?

Having more minority providers seems to enhance the care that patients receive. African Americans and Latinos are less likely than Whites to think their physicians care about them (Sewell 2015). People are also more likely to utilize health care services when their physicians are of the same race. Whites and Asian Americans are far more likely than African Americans, Blacks, and Native Americans to be treated by physicians of their same race. Having a matched-race physician also reduces the bias that people of color experience (Sacks 2013).

Care and Cultural Competence

Evidence such as that above shows that good health is not solely about access, but also about what happens once you enter a health care facility. Stereotypes, attitudes, and *implicit biases* (also see chapter 2) can all affect people's health. For example, minorities are more likely than Whites to receive discourteous care which can then affect health outcomes (LaVeist, Nuru-Jeter, and Jones 2003; Kwate and Meyer 2011).

Much empirical evidence shows that White medical care workers tend to hold negative implicit racial biases and explicit racial stereotypes. These implicit biases can persist even when people's explicit racial attitudes are colorblind. In the end, institutional racism can operate even without people consciously intending to discriminate (van Ryn et al. 2011).

As people have become more aware of the power of implicit bias and health disparities, there has been a movement to educate health care workers in the ability to both recognize and understand cultural differences that can exist between care workers and their patients. This is called **cultural competence**, and it involves care workers becoming aware of one's own cultural particularities, as well as having the capacity to recognize, value, and work with cultural differences (White with Chanoff 2011).

With an increasingly racially diverse and multicultural society, cultural competence has become increasingly important in the training of those who will be working in health care settings. Cultural competence does not come easily and, in most cases, has to be learned, because people have a tendency to assume a more ethnocentric point of view. Yet cultural competence is crucial to patients' well-being and recovery from illness. Being able to communicate, to empathize, and to explain health care treatment across cultural differences can mean the difference between life and death.

Cultural competence acknowledges that a patient's beliefs about health and decisions about treatment may be based upon the patient's cultural background. It is increasingly important for medical/health care staff to be alert to cultural factors, especially when working with underserved populations, in our multiracial society. Indeed, it is also critical when working on global health care (Dy and Purnell 2012).

Up Close and Personal: Race and Reproductive Politics

Reproductive politics refers to the linkage between systems of power and life's most intimate matters, such as birth control, abortion, and pregnancy. Since race is pervasive in society, it intrudes into these personal areas as well. Throughout the history of racism in America, racism has robbed people of color of reproductive rights. Social attitudes and explicit social policies have determined whether, how, and when people of color are able to reproduce. Although some of the extreme abuses of the past have ended, they still resonate in contemporary reproductive politics.

Eugenics

Eugenics refers to practices that purport to improve the human race by controlling the reproduction of people deemed to be "inferior" or somehow genetically compromised. Historically, eugenics movements have stemmed from notions of racial superiority and inferiority and have kindled some of the most horrendous acts of violence in human history. Eugenics formed the ideological backbone that resulted in the annihilation of Jewish people during the Nazi Holocaust, because Nazis believed Jews to be unfit and biologically inferior to the so-called Aryan race (see chapter 1). Throughout U.S. history practices like forced sterilization, medical experimentation, and outright annihilation have also marked the history of Native Americans, Latinos, and African Americans.

LEARNING OUR PAST

The Infamous Tuskegee Syphilis Study

The Tuskegee syphilis experiment is a notorious case of medical abuse. Starting in the 1930s and continuing into the 1970s, the U.S. Public Health Service deliberately withheld treatment from four hundred Black men who were recruited as research subjects in a study of the advanced stages of syphilis.

All of them, mostly sharecroppers from around Tuskegee, Alabama, were told they were getting free government health care. They were never told that they had syphilis and were given no treatment at all. Instead, the men were carefully observed so that physicians could see how the late stages of syphilis progressed.

Some of the men received occasional aspirin for headaches, but none was given penicillin, a drug that physicians knew could have saved the men's lives. Doctors watched as many of the men died from the untreated disease, which at the time they were told was "bad blood," a common umbrella term that comprised various ailments such as exhaustion and anemia.

Not until 1972 was this horrendous experiment revealed to the public, when whistleblowers leaked the story to the press. At that time, only a small number of the men were still living. The Tuskegee experiment then became the impetus for federal regulations that now require informed consent and voluntary participation in all research, medical or other. In 1997 President William Clinton issued a formal apology to the African American community for this horrendous abuse of federal power and unethical medical practice.

How could such a thing happen? The Tuskegee experiment can only now be understood in the context of the extreme racism and stereotyping of Black men and sexuality that was rampant at the time. The disregard by the federal government for Black lives also reverberates in much of the distrust that many African American citizens still feel toward federal health programs.

Sources: Jones, James H. 1993. *Bad Blood: The Tuskegee Syphilis Experiment*. New York: Free Press; Reverby, Susan M. 2009. *Explaining Tuskegee: The Infamous Syphilis Study and Its Legacy*. Chapel Hill: University of North Carolina Press.

Eugenics movements typically claim that inferiority is rooted in the biological character of the targeted group. Such claims are based on *pseudoscience*, that is, ideas that claim to have scientific grounding but are in fact completely groundless as scientific fact. Over time, however, a great deal of effort has been put into pseudoscientific practices, such as measuring the skulls of Black criminals to try to explain crime as a function of brain size. True science, however, has often been developed using people of color as research subjects, often without consent or with incomplete information. LEARNING OUR PAST provides one such case study. Strictly with regard to reproductive politics, however, is the development of the birth control pill that, in the late 1950s, was tested on Puerto Rican women in Puerto Rico (Briggs 2002).

Reproductive Control and Forced Sterilization

Regulating the reproduction of people of color has been a central theme in the history of racial oppression (Roberts 1997a). At times, regulation has meant encouraging reproduction, such as during slavery when slave owners encouraged breeding of slaves to increase the unpaid labor force. At other times, women of color have been denied the right to bear children, such as through forced sterilization and other birth control policies that discouraged reproduction.

For example, during the 1950s and 1960s, backed by U.S. interests in economic development, various programs promoted *contraception* for Puerto Rican women (Briggs 2002). In addition, Puerto Rican women on the island were routinely coerced into sterilization, a procedure that became so common that it was called *la operación.* Women were often not informed that the procedure was irreversible and, as a result, by the late 1960s a full one-third of Puerto Rican women of childbearing age had been sterilized (Gutiérrez 2008; Roberts 1997a).

Sterilization abuse has been part of Native American history, too. In the early 1970s a government investigation found that physicians at Indian Health Services had sterilized large numbers of Native American women without their consent. Native women could be threatened with losing their health care access if they did not consent. In many cases a doctor would perform a sterilization procedure without a woman's consent while she was having, for example, a needed appendectomy. For their part, physicians working for the Indian Health Service were exempt from the usual medical practices of required consent. From 1960 to 1980, when these practices were rampant, there was, not surprisingly, a steep decline in the Native American birth rate (Lawrence 2000).

To this day, Black and Hispanic women in the United States are still more likely to be sterilized than are White women (see figure 10.5). For some women, this is a choice, but in the context of past abuses, it is easy to wonder under what circumstances women face this decision and how well informed they are about its consequences.

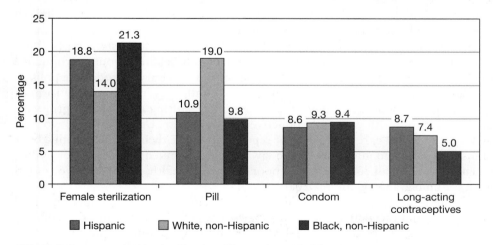

FIG. 10.5 Contraceptive Use by American Women (age 15–44)

What factors do you think explain the different patterns of contraceptive usage depicted in this graph?

Source: Daniels, Kimberly, Jo Daugherty, and Jo Jones. 2014. "Current Contraceptive Status among Women Aged 15–44: United States, 2011–2013." NCHS Data Brief 173 (December), Figure 1. Hyattsville, MD: National Center for Health Statistics. Retrieved January 19, 2017 (https://www.cdc.gov/nchs/products/databriefs/db173.htm).

Policies regarding federal funding for reproductive health are also telling. Federal policy prohibits the use of public funds for abortion, except in a few states where state funds, not federal funds, can be used. This law, passed in Congress in 1978 and known as the Hyde Amendment, primarily affects Medicaid and thus is particularly restrictive for women who rely on government assistance for their reproductive health. Sterilization, on the other hand, is fully covered by Medicaid, although there is a thirty-day waiting period between giving consent and having the procedure. This rule is intended to protect women on public assistance from the past abuses of forced sterilization; more advantaged women, however, are not usually subjected to the same notification requirement.

Race Beliefs and Contemporary Reproductive Politics

Although eugenics is now highly discredited, its impact can still be seen in some of the contemporary politics of contraception and birth control. Past practices have made some radical Black activists suspicious of any form of birth control that is promoted by federal or state agencies, believing that it constitutes a form of genocide. On the other side, some White supremacist groups fear that Whites will be outnumbered by people of color even though differences in birth rates between racial-ethnic groups are relatively small in the United States.

Reproductive politics continue to be influenced by racial beliefs. Black and Latino women are stereotyped in the dominant culture as "breeders"—an attitude reflected in the assumption that poor women of color have children only to increase their welfare payments. This attitude, though never based in fact, has been encoded into law, such as in federal "family cap" policies that deny federal aid to recipients if they have another child (also see chapter 7). The revised federal welfare policy of 1996 also provided a cash reward to some states that successfully limited out-of-wedlock births to women receiving Temporary Assistance to Needy Families (Gutiérrez 2010). Such policies reveal the extent to which racial stereotypes about reproduction continue to frame national policy and debates about reproductive rights. Anti-immigrant sentiment is also part of contemporary reproductive politics. Immigrant women and men face a number of challenges in seeking any form of health care. Even for legal immigrants, constantly shifting policies and programs deter access to health care—reproductive and otherwise. Undocumented workers may avoid seeking care out of fear of repercussions for them or their family. Lack of insurance, limited information, and laws that have limited health care for undocumented workers all contribute to a poor climate of health, reproductive or otherwise, for immigrants (Gutiérrez 2010).

Contemporary reproductive politics are a dense tangle of competing social movements and racial and gender ideologies. Usually lost in the midst of competing arguments and passionately felt political opinions about reproduction is the actual reproductive health of women of color. They, especially the poor among them, are subjected to inadequate information, inadequate resources, and lack of access to high-quality reproductive health. Yet they have been consistently manipulated by policies that allow them neither the freedom to have children nor the freedom to decide not to. Only in this context can you begin to understand what reproductive freedom would really mean for people of color (Joffe and Parker 2012; Roberts 1997a).

Racism in the Air You Breathe: Environmental Racism

The poisoning of the water in Flint, Michigan, called public attention to the strong connection between racial inequality and environmental pollution. The pattern reflected by the situation is known as **environmental racism**, by which racial-ethnic minorities are disproportionately exposed to environmental wastes and other hazards (Brulle and Pellow 2006). This means that toxic waste facilities and other pollutants are more likely to be located in neighborhoods that are largely populated by people of color. Even something as basic to one's health as having adequate plumbing facilities is known to be associated with racial inequality. American Indians and Alaska Natives, for example, are less likely to have basic plumbing facilities than other groups (Gasteyer et al. 2016).

Environmental racism has a class dimension to it as well. These same patterns of pollution are also found in poor and working-class White neighborhoods. But people of color are disproportionately affected by environmental hazards (Schulz et al. 2016).

Environmental racism also includes a policy dimension, namely, that there is less enforcement of environmental regulations in areas populated by people of color. Additionally, people of color are underrepresented in leadership positions in environmental organizations, even though people of color have taken an active role in organizing movements against environmental racism. In sum, environmental racism is "any policy, practice, or directive that differentially affects or disadvantages

When it was revealed in 2015 that the drinking water in Flint, Michigan, was contaminated, residents demanded the resignation and arrest of Governor Rick Snyder for knowingly allowing Flint's residents to drink it.

(whether intentional or unintended) individuals, groups, or communities based on race or color" (Chavis, cited in Bullard 1994:497).

Siting Waste

The evidence of environmental racism is substantial. Most studies that document this pattern tend, however, to be based on local studies. National studies are more difficult to do because of the complexity of mapping such a large area and correlating sites with population data. The most comprehensive national study to date has found that African Americans and Hispanics disproportionately live within one mile of toxic waste facilities (Mohai and Saha 2007). Comprehensive assessments of risk at a national level also show that Blacks and Latinos are more likely than Whites to be exposed to higher levels of nitrogen dioxide gas and other toxic substances. Further, these racial differences persist, even controlling for various social and economic characteristics of individuals and households (Kravitz-Wirtz et al. 2016).

Various other local studies have also shown that large percentages of people of color live in areas where there are higher levels of toxic waste and releases. The National Association for the Advancement of Colored People has found, for example, that a huge proportion of African Americans (80 percent) live within thirty miles of a coal-powered plant, a fact that may explain the much higher rates of asthma found among African American children (Brulle and Pellow 2006).

A number of facts have become clear from studies of environmental racism:

- Areas with a large percentage of non-White residents have higher levels of toxic release in the air (Arora and Cason 1998; Kim, Campbell, and Eckerd 2014; Bullard 2008).
- Compared to White Americans, African Americans are more likely to live near landfills, airports, and oil refineries (Centers for Disease Control and Prevention 2013).
- Immigrants are more likely than nonimmigrants to live in places with high levels of pollution (Mohai and Saha 2006; Pellow and Brehm 2013).
- Hispanics have a greater likelihood of working in occupations where rates of injury or death are highest (Byler 2013).
- Latinos are more likely to be exposed to pesticide poisoning because of their work as farm and garden laborers (U.S. Bureau of Labor Statistics 2015b).
- More than 70 percent of African Americans compared to 58 percent of Whites live in counties that are in violation of federal clean air laws and standards (Payne-Sturges and Gee 2006; Russell 2011).

Intent or Innocence?

The facts above show the vast disparities in exposure to toxic environmental hazards. Researchers who study environmental risks have concluded that exposure to toxic substances is "a pathway through which racial inequality literally gets into the body" (Sampson and Winter 2016:279). Why does environmental racism occur? Is it because polluters deliberately discriminate against people of color and poor people? Does class explain toxic waste dumping more than race? Is dumping just a matter of market forces because it is cheaper for companies to situate landfills, toxic waste dumps, and other pollutants in less economically valuable neighborhoods? Do polluters avoid neighborhoods where people have more resources to resist environmental degradation? All of these questions drive different explanations of environmental inequity.

Here's what we know: Both race and class are significant in explaining patterns of pollution, but class alone is not a sufficient explanation. Race and class are entangled, but race also has effects of its own. Research on toxic waste dumping has concluded that factors uniquely associated with race explain much of the location of hazardous waste facilities (Mohai and Saha 2007). Housing discrimination, racial steering, and the factors associated with racial residential segregation all contribute to environmental racism.

There is also a bit of the "chicken and the egg" conundrum in considering environmental racism. Do disadvantaged groups move to areas where properties are already cheaper because of environmental conditions, or do property values decline once a neighborhood becomes predominantly populated by people of color? Both are probably true, but the end result is that racial disparities exist (Sze and London 2008). Market forces also operate in this dynamic. Companies that produce toxic products select places where land and labor are cheaper. The fact is that such places, regardless of the actual intent of corporate leaders, tend to be the places where racial-ethnic minorities live. These populations also are less likely than others to have the resources to leave (Been and Gupta 1997). Even if companies intentionally engage in such behavior, it is very difficult to prove intent to discriminate in the courts if people sue polluters.

Finally, the NIMBY ("not in my backyard") phenomenon comes into play: Financially better-off communities have more resources to resist pollutants in their neighborhoods than do others. Even with the mobilization of people of color and others through the environmental justice movement, seldom do less-advantaged communities have the political power to fight corporate power.

The Environmental Justice Movement

Environmental justice is "the principle that all people and communities are entitled to equal protection of environmental and public health laws and regulations" (Bullard 1996:495). The environmental justice movement took shape in the 1970s and 1980s when residents in different communities organized against risks they identified in their communities. Typically, environmental justice initiatives are locally focused, organized by residents, and often led by women. Fundamentally, the environmental justice movement comprises a vast network of only loosely affiliated organizations, most of them grassroots organizations that stem from residents' concerns about a specific environmental hazard (Brulle and Pellow 2006; Pellow 2007).

Although many environmental justice organizations are locally based, they generally share a common outlook that individuals have the right to be protected from environmental degradation. The environmental justice movement typically targets actions to address the disproportionate risks that people of color and the poor face from environmental hazards. Leaders in the movement have also argued that the burden for proving harm done should be shouldered by those who produce the harm, including large corporations. Because it is so difficult to prove intentional discrimination by polluters, movement leaders have also argued that the standard

Advocates for environmental justice have been an important voice in pointing out the dumping of toxic waste and the presence of pollution in predominantly low-income, race- and/or ethnicity-based residential communities.

of proof should be the differential impact of dumping, not intent per se (Pellow and Brulle 2007).

The deterioration of the earth's resources is cause for worry for all people of the world. The risks are clear, and the fate of the world depends on how well we address this critical issue. Even though environmental degradation and climate change affect us all, part of the solution has to be recognizing and addressing the specific effects on people of color—both in the United States and around the globe.

Climate Change: Are We All in It Together?

A final dimension of environmental racism is the differential impact of climate change on people of color—both nationally and abroad. Two points are clear: (1) even though climate change threatens life for us all, people of color suffer differential risks; and, (2) people of color contribute less to climate change (Takeuchi et al. 2016; Roberts and Parks 2007).

To the first point: The effects of climate change and other forms of disaster are not equally experienced. Although the consequences of such things as hurricanes, tornadoes, floods, and now climate change can devastate entire communities, people of color are disproportionately vulnerable (Tierney 2007; Klinenberg 2002). Hurricane Katrina in New Orleans in 2005 is one telling example. Although

Katrina's devastating impact was felt by many groups of people, low-income African Americans were far more likely to die or, if they survived, to be displaced from their homes (Weber and Peak 2012).

Experts point out that people of color are typically the first to feel the long-term effects of air pollution, extreme heat, drought, food and water shortages, storms, and floods. Furthermore, when disasters occur, people of color and the poor in general have the fewest resources to deal with such crises. In the aftermath of a disaster, such things as an increase in energy costs will also have a disproportionate burden on those who are already struggling.

To the second point: Ironically, those most affected by climate change are also those least likely to contribute to it. The most disadvantaged and marginalized populations generally use less carbon-based fuel, thus contributing less to the development of climate change than other groups. In a more specific example, Native Americans whose lands have been deforested have not been those whose practices contribute to climate change. They have seen much in the way of natural resources extracted from their lands—leaving the land barren—and little remuneration (Harlan, Pellow, and Roberts 2015).

Conclusion: Health and Social Policy

Health disparities based on race, ethnicity, and class have been stubbornly persistent. Although there have been some improvements, such as in extended life expectancy and greater health insurance coverage, many of these disparities are not going away (Institute of Medicine 2002, 2012; Agency for Healthcare Research and Quality 2015). To understand health disparities, you have to see them in the broader context of racial inequality. This context, however, can also show you how disparities can be reduced.

People tend to think that improved medical treatment and new technologies of care are the best conduits to better health. No doubt, medical advances matter, but a unique experiment also shows the importance of addressing the broader social context if we are to improve the health of people of color. In a clever experiment, medical researcher Stephen Woolf and colleagues compared the number of lives saved by medical advances compared to those saved by equalizing Black and White mortality rates through such causes of poor health as environment and lack of access to medical care. They found that for every life saved by biomedical advances, five would be saved by eliminating the discrepancy in mortality rates between African Americans and Whites. The medical researchers concluded, "Achieving equity may do more for health than perfecting the technology of care" (Woolf et al. 2008:S26).

We have seen that economic inequality has much to do with the disparities in evidence. At the same time, residential segregation explains a significant portion of the racial health gap. You can conclude from this that reducing the income/wealth gap between Whites and people of color, while also addressing the different dimensions of racial segregation, would go a long way to reducing racial health disparities.

Key Terms

Affordable Care Act (ACA), 236

cultural competence, 239

death rate, 228

environmental justice, 245

environmental racism, 243

eugenics, 239

hypertension, 230

infant mortality, 228

life expectancy, 227

reproductive politics, 239

Critical Thinking Questions

1. Why is residential segregation such a strong predictor of racial health disparities?
2. What evidence do you see of the connection between race and reproductive politics? Use a current news report as evidence of your claims.

Student Exercises

10.1: Pay a visit to your local emergency room and make a count, as best you can, of the number of people there and the racial-ethnic composition of the waiting people. Then look up the percentage of people of color in the population of your city, county, or state. Is the proportion of the population of people of color in the ER waiting room representative of the population of the area? Why or why not?

10.2: Examine the chart in figure 10.5. What differences do you see in contraceptive use, comparing women of different racial-ethnic backgrounds? How do you explain what you see?

Challenging Question/Open to Debate

Imagine you are the owner of a company that generates toxic waste from your production process. You are under pressure by your Board of Directors to cut costs, so you look for and find a run-down area of a nearby community where you can dispose of the toxic material. As it turns out, the nearby residents are about 85 percent African American and Latino. If you dispose of the waste there, does this make you a racist?

CHAPTER 11

Justice and Injustice

Race and Crime

Where justice is denied, where poverty is enforced, where ignorance prevails, and where any one class is made to feel that society is an organized conspiracy to oppress, rob and degrade them, neither persons nor property will be safe.
—Frederick Douglass

OBJECTIVES

- Report the difference in perceptions and facts about race and crime
- Explain how crime statistics are influenced by the social construction of race
- Understand who is most likely to be victimized by crime

- Detail the facts about immigration and crime
- Evaluate the impact of institutional racism within different elements of the criminal justice system
- Explain the social structural components that connect race and crime

Imagine a society where there are three groups of citizens, each group supposedly identified by the color of their skin: the Greens, the Blues, and the Purples. There are laws in place in this society that give equal protection under the law to all people regardless of the color of their skin. The overwhelming majority of the Green, Blue, and Purple people are law-abiding citizens. Yet, the Green and Blue people are far more likely to be arrested and to be held in the society's prisons. The Purple people hold most of the power in society, especially in the courts and law enforcement.

Were you to encounter this society, what would you think about why so many Blues and Greens are in prison? Is there something wrong with them and their families and communities, or are they just targeted more by the police, even if Purples engage in the same behavior? Why does the system of justice not work the same way for the Blues and Greens as it does for the Purples?

This is also a society where Green and Blue people worry about whether their children, particularly their sons, will be shot by the police, even if the young people are not doing anything wrong. A little swagger or an edgy attitude toward the police can get a young man shot. As a result, most of the Greens and Blues—even if they have never committed or been convicted of a crime—believe the system is stacked against them. There is a great deal of evidence that they are right. At the same time, the Purple people are generally fearful of the Greens and Blues, as if they will be victimized by them, even though the odds are greater that Green and Blue people will be victims of crime.

You have surely guessed that this is an allegory—albeit abbreviated—of crime and justice in the United States. Racism has a major role in the United States in the likelihood of crime by different racial-ethnic groups, the likelihood of arrest and conviction of crime, and the now widely known mass incarceration of African American and Latino men and, increasingly, women.

The connection between race and crime is a heated subject in U.S. society, the stuff of TV dramas, political campaigns, and daily conversation. The subject polarizes people, with one side crying that the police are racist, the other side decrying "black criminality" (Bobo 2015).

Nearly every aspect of crime and justice in the United States involves race, a fact that has become increasingly obvious with the emergence of the Black Lives Matter movement. This movement developed in the aftermath of numerous highly publicized police shootings of Black men and the suspicious deaths of several Black people while they were held in police custody for minor crimes (such as failing to signal for a lane change while driving, as was the case for Sandra Bland).

In the heat of public discussions about race and crime, it is often difficult to perceive the truth, but some facts about race and crime in the United States provide a glimpse of the problem:

- African American men are six times more likely to be imprisoned than White men; Hispanic men, twice as likely (Carson 2016).
- Seventy percent of those who have now been found wrongfully convicted, based on DNA evidence, are people of color—mostly African Americans, but also Hispanics and Asian Americans (Innocence Project 2016).
- Native American women are twice as likely as Black and White women to be victims of rape; Hispanic and Asian women, the least likely to be rape victims (Planty and Krebs 2013).
- Fear of crime is greatest among people of color, and with good reason: People of color are those most likely to be victimized by crime (Hicks and Brown 2013; Truman and Langton 2015).
- Half of all Americans think that immigrants make crime worse, despite the fact that immigrants are actually less likely than native-born Americans to commit crime (Pew Research Center 2015b; Ewing, Martinez, and Rumbaut 2015).

This chapter examines the connection between race and crime, including information on who is most likely to be victimized by crime, to commit crime, and to be incarcerated. Throughout the chapter you should be asking yourself about the influence of institutional racism on the criminal justice system. We begin with an examination of public perceptions of crime and their basis in reality.

Race and Crime: Myths and Realities

Tune in to the local evening news on any given night in just about any city, and you will very likely see images of violent crime—perhaps murder, arson, armed robbery, or assault. More often than not, the perpetrator will be a person of color, probably African American or Latino. If you were to base your understanding of crime on what you see in the local news, you would think that the United States is a crime-ridden society. You would probably also conclude that Black Americans and Latinos are more prone to crime than other groups. You would also probably think that crime is rising in America.

In truth, violent crime has actually been on the decline in recent years, although the frequent reporting of the increased murder rate that has occurred in a few cities leads people to think that violent crime is on the rise everywhere. Although Black Americans are more likely to be arrested for crime than are White Americans, questions remain about whether this is because African Americans actually commit more crime or are just policed more. Further, despite crude stereotypes about immigrants as criminals, the truth is that immigrants are actually less likely to commit crime than are native-born citizens. African Americans are also more likely to be crime victims than are White Americans (Truman and Morgan 2016).

Even in the face of such information, research studies show that racial-ethnic minorities are more likely to be shown in the media as crime suspects instead of as victims. In addition, African Americans are much more likely to be shown as linked to violence than are White people, even though the majority of violent crime is actually committed by Whites (Gruenewald, Chermak, and Pizarro 2013; Bjornstrom et al. 2010). And since 9/11, the most common media images of Muslims cast them as terrorists and as people to be feared (Rivera 2014).

Crime gets more attention than any other subject in local news reporting, unless there is some sort of weather emergency. Not surprisingly then, a large majority of the U.S. public (70 percent) think that crime is rising, despite the fact that violent crime has generally been on the decline since the 1990s. Violent crime has not reached the levels experienced near the end of the twentieth century (see figure 11.1; Federal Bureau of Investigation 2016a; McCarthy 2015).

Race and crime in the media may provide entertainment, but they also reinforce controlling images of people of color. They also depict how the justice system works in a distorted manner. Crime dramas, for example, show clients being well represented by attorneys who are locked in battle against each other. In fact, most criminal cases are settled quickly through plea-bargaining. Attorneys may barely know their clients as they rush to get cases through the court docket (Barak, Leighton, and Cotton 2015). Yet, manufactured media images lead people to believe that the system of justice is neutral and fair. It is then easy to conclude that anyone prosecuted by it must have done something wrong.

Research also shows that racial bias—both implicit and explicit—is linked to how people perceive crime. Those holding the highest degree of racial bias are more likely to see crime as increasing. They are also more likely to explain crime in individualistic terms, that is, by understanding crime solely as a consequence of individual behavior without comprehending the societal context in which crime occurs and is punished (Callanan 2012; Drakulich 2015).

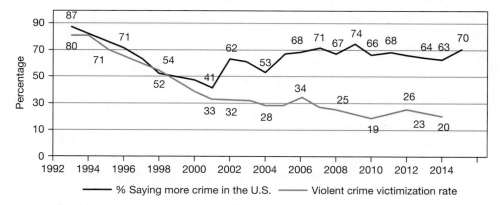

FIG. 11.1 Perception versus Reality: Crime and Perception of Crime

Note: Violent crime includes murder and non-negligent manslaughter, rape, robbery, and aggravated assault.

Sources: McCarthy, Justin. 2015. "More Americans Say Crime Is Rising in the U.S." Princeton, NJ: The Gallup Organization; Federal Bureau of Investigation 2016a. *Crime in the United States 2015*. Washington, DC: U.S. Department of Justice. (https://ucr.fbi.gov/crime-in-the-u.s/2015/crime-in-the-u.s.-2015.)

The bottom line is that public perceptions of the connection between race and crime are seldom based in fact, but result instead from the social construction of race and crime by the mass media. Graphic displays of violence are common in the media; they provide strong imagery that helps generate advertising revenues as media corporations compete for audiences (Iyengar 2010). Just imagine how people might think differently about crime if the media narrative shifted from associating people of color with criminality to focusing on the victimization of people of color by the history of racism.

Counting Crime: The Social Construction of Racial Categories

National data on crime come from two primary sources: the FBI's **Uniform Crime Reports** and the Department of Justice's **National Crime Victimization Surveys**. Uniform Crime Reporting (UCR) provides data on crimes reported, crimes cleared, and persons arrested. Police departments collect these data and forward the information to state and federal authorities. Seven types of offenses committed are then used to create the **crime index**: murder/non-negligent manslaughter, rape, robbery, aggravated assault (with a weapon), burglary, larceny/theft, and motor vehicle theft. Only murder, rape, robbery, and aggravated assault are included in the *violent crime rate*.

Supplementary UCR information addresses murder victims, offenders, and incident characteristics. Keep in mind that UCR data include only those crimes that come to the attention of police agencies. People who can hide their crimes are excluded from the crime statistics. Also, police departments vary in how and whether they report victims' and perpetrators' race, ethnicity, and other characteristics.

The National Crime Victimization Survey (NCVS) is conducted annually, based on a representative national sample of U.S. households. These data are the primary source of information about nonfatal violent and property crimes, as based on victims' self-reports. The survey results are then reported by the Bureau of Justice Statistics and made available online to the public, as are data from the Uniform Crime Reports. The NCVS includes data on various crimes, but unlike the Uniform Crime Reports, it also collects information on domestic and intimate partner violence.

Both UCR and the NCVS provide invaluable information about crime and its victims, but there are limitations to both forms of data. For example, the Uniform Crime Reports only include those crimes where an arrest has taken place. Unreported crime goes undetected. The Victimization surveys are based on self-reports by crime victims and thus can be unreliable. Neither format includes corporate crime. As a consequence of official crime data ignoring corporate crime, it becomes easy to infer that such crime is not as harmful as other crimes. In truth, the impact of corporate crime on people's lives can be enormous—even greater than that from street crimes.

Even more problematic in official crime statistics is how race and ethnicity are defined and categorized. Starting in 1933, the Uniform Crime Reports included three categories for race: White, Black and "Other." Today there are five categories for "race" in UCR data: White; Black; American Indian and Alaska Native;

TABLE 11.1 Arrests for All Crimes in Crime Index, by Race and Ethnicity, 2015

	Total Arrests Race	White	Black or African American	American Indian or Alaska Native	Asian	Native Hawaiian or Other Pacific Islander	Total Arrests Ethnicity	Hispanic or Latino	Not Hispanic or Latino
Number:	**8,248,709**	5,753,212	2,197,140	174,020	101,064	23,273	**6,546,220**	1,204,862	5,341,358
Percent distribution:	**100**	69.7	26.6	2.1	1.2	0.3	**100**	18.4	81.6

Note: Individual percent distribution figures do not total 100 due to rounding.

Source: Federal Bureau of Investigation. 2016a. *Crime in the United States 2015*. Washington, DC: U.S. Department of Justice. (https://ucr.fbi.gov/crime-in-the-u.s/2015/crime-in-the-u.s.-2015.)

Asian; and Native Hawaiian or other Pacific Islander. Where are the Latinos, you might ask? And why don't these categories match those provided by the U.S. Census Bureau?

"Mexican" was added as a category in the Uniform Crime Reports in 1934 but then dropped in 1941. Between 1980 and 1985, a separate category for Hispanics was created, but the designation was then dropped. Beginning in 2013, the Uniform Crime Reports started to again include Hispanic/Latino arrests in a separate category (Gabbidon and Greene 2016; Walker, Spohn, and Delone 2012). In other words, UCR data treat race and ethnicity as distinct categories.

Table 11.1 is from the Uniform Crime Reports and shows how UCR tallies arrests separately by race and ethnicity. You can see that ethnicity is reported apart from race, making comparisons with Latinos/Hispanics and other groups difficult, to say the least. Some local agencies do not even collect information on ethnicity, so you can see that the number of total arrests is not the same for "race" groups and for "ethnic" groups. Moreover, fluctuations in how Hispanics have been categorized over time make it virtually impossible to study long-term trends, that is, *longitudinal analyses* (Walker, Spohn, and Delone 2012; Gabbidon and Greene 2016).

Data on Native Americans in the Uniform Crime Reports are also obscured by the fact that Native Americans fall under a complex array of jurisdictional legal entities. Not all tribal police agencies send arrest data to UCR, so Native American arrests may be undercounted. In the current NCVS, Native Americans are counted as "other" along with Alaska Natives; Asians, Native Hawaiians, and other Pacific Islanders; and, persons of two or more races. This is hardly a reasonable way to understand crime for such diverse groups.

The NCVS is also problematic in how race and ethnicity are counted. The NCVS has included racial categories since 1973. Originally, the categories were White, Black, and Other (Asian/Pacific Islanders, American Indians, Aleuts and Eskimos). Hispanics were not included as a separate category until 1977. Now the NCVS reports on Whites, Blacks, Hispanics, and "others," depending on how respondents self-identify.

In sum, how agencies categorize race and crime is fraught with problems. Racial and ethnic categories are inconsistent—both over time and from agency to agency. As a result, measuring the association between race and crime is flawed—but as this information is disseminated, it still shapes people's thinking about the connection between race and crime.

The racial and ethnic categories in these reports also reify race and ethnicity as if they were fixed categories when, in fact, as you have learned, they are social constructions. Racial and ethnicity identity in victimization data is based on self-reports, but forced into the categories given in the surveys. Arrest data from the Uniform Crime Reports might just as easily be based on how a police officer checks a box as on how a person self-identifies.

One consequence of the complexity of how crime is tabulated and recorded is an overwhelming emphasis on African American crime. As you review the data included here on crime and crime victimization, keep the imperfections in the official statistics in mind while noting that these sources remain the best available national information on crime. Scholars often collect their own data, adding to the richness of what we know, but the official data remain the only source for general patterns in crime commission and victimization. At the heart of these crime statistics lurks the issue of race as a social construction.

Race, Violence, and Victimization

The problematic nature of crime statistics notwithstanding, there is little doubt that victimization by crime is higher for people of color—and certain people of color at that (see figure 11.2). African Americans and Hispanics are the most likely to

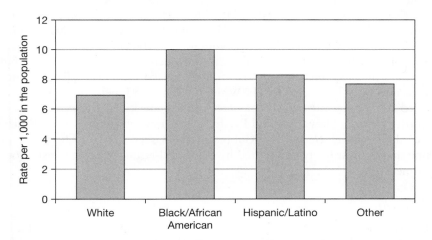

FIG. 11.2   Violent Crime Victimization by Race and Ethnicity, 2015

Note: "Other" includes American Indians, Alaska Natives, Asians, and Native Hawaiians and other Pacific Islanders.

Source: Truman, Jennifer L., and Rachel E. Morgan. 2016. *Criminal Victimization, 2015.* Washington, DC: Bureau of Justice Statistics. (https://www.bjs.gov/content/pub/pdf/cv15.pdf.)

be victimized by serious violent crime, that is, rape, sexual assault, robbery, and aggravated assault. At the same time, however, victimization by crime for all groups, including people of color, has actually declined in recent years, with the exception of rape and serious intimate partner violence. In every racial-ethnic group, men are more likely than women to be crime victims, except in the case of rape (Truman and Morgan 2016).

Age also has a great deal to do with the likelihood of crime victimization. People between eighteen and twenty-four years of age are the most likely to be victimized by crime. Household income is also a factor in predicting crime victimization. Generally speaking, people in the lowest income brackets are most likely to be victimized by crime. Such data must be interpreted with caution, however. Among other things, when the category of "Other" appears in such statistics, it usually includes groups with very different experiences (Asians, Native Americans, Alaska Natives, Pacific Islanders, and people identifying as mixed race). The category "Hispanic" includes Cubans, Puerto Ricans, and Mexicans, and many other groups, all varying in their social and economic circumstances (Truman and Morgan 2016).

Research on victimization by crime has tended to focus on crimes such as homicide, rape, and armed robbery, but what if we changed our concept of victimization? Official statistics on crime victimization overlook certain actions that could well be construed as crime. One example is the theft of Native American land by White settlers. Another is the manipulation of the housing market by Wall Street investors, which victimized millions of people during the recession of 2008 and caused countless economic losses. Such information is not found in official crime statistics (Barak, Leighton, and Cotton 2015). While official crime statistics can reproduce racial narratives that blame people of color for the vast majority of crime, other forms of crime are overlooked.

Crime victimization data also teach us that crime victims and perpetrators tend to be of the same race and ethnicity. Black-on-Black crime, for example, is far more common than Black-on-White crime or Black-on-Latino crime (Stowell, Martinez, and Cancino 2012; Cancino, Martinez, and Stowell 2009). American Indians make up the group most likely to be victimized by someone of a different race, but the majority of crimes against Indians are still committed by other Indians. Almost all violent crime by White offenders is White-on-White; 91 percent of Whites killed are killed by Whites, 80 percent of Blacks killed are killed by other Blacks, and two-thirds of Asian, Hawaiian, and Pacific Islander crime victims are victimized by those of their own race/ethnicity (Gabbidon and Greene 2016). The one example of crime that is most likely committed by one racial-ethnic group against another is hate crime.

Hate Crime

The United States has a long and gruesome history of **hate crime**, most notably in the history of lynching (see LEARNING OUR PAST). Beginning in 1990, the federal government started collecting data on hate crime, now included in the FBI's Uniform Crime Reports. Hate crime is formally defined as crime that includes evidence of prejudice based on race, religion, sexual orientation, ethnicity, disability, gender, and gender identity. Hate crime can be directed against individuals, but it also includes crimes against property, such as the desecration of mosques and temples.

LEARNING OUR PAST

Vigilante Justice—Lynching and African American Trauma

In the face of contemporary concerns about race and crime, it may be easy for some to forget the vigilante justice that terrorized African American communities through much of U.S. history. Through much of the late nineteenth and twentieth centuries, even the smallest perceived violation could result in death as White mobs lynched and murdered thousands of Black men, mostly—but not exclusively—in the American South.

The Delta Oral History Project conducted interviews from 1995 to 1996 with African Americans in the Delta region of Mississippi. Many of their narratives recall the fear, trauma, and terror that were constant under this form of vigilante justice. The following is an excerpt of such a narrative, by Dr. L. C. Dorsey, who grew up in Sunflower County, Mississippi:

> There was a tremendous amount of fear in the community and in almost every house of this faceless group of people who arrived at your home at night, on horses and in cars, to drag you out and kill you for any little infraction of rules you didn't always know about. People worried tremendously about their sons and the menfolk in their families. People worried that if a white man looked at a black girl, and they tried to keep them in the background because they couldn't protect them. They couldn't protect their wives and stuff. What you remember about it was the fear, that there was no way to be protected. . . . It was all this fear that these people had of white folk, that they would come and get you in the middle of the night and kill you. I understood the fear so strongly that it wouldn't even let them [the adults] talk our loud.

Source: Dorcey, Dr. L. C. 1996. Interviews by Owen Brooks and Kim Lacy Rogers, Winstonville, Mississippi, February 27; reprinted in *Trauma and Life Stories: International Perspectives*, 1999, edited by Kim Lacy Rogers, Selma Leydesdorff, and Graham Dawson. New York: Routledge.

Hate crime statistics vastly underestimate the extent of the problem, because the only hate crimes that appear in official data on crime are those reported to the police, classified as such, and then passed on to the FBI. The data we do have, however, provide significant information about these patterns of crime victimization.

Racially motivated behavior is the most common form of hate crime (see table 11.2). African Americans are the most likely objects of hate crimes; they are victimized way out of proportion to their representation in the overall population. Anti-Jewish hate crime and hate crimes directed against gay men are the next most common forms (Federal Bureau of Investigation 2016b). Hate crimes against Muslims are also becoming more frequent, as was witnessed in the aftermath of the presidential election of Donald Trump, whose campaign ignited a surge in anti-Muslim violence (Potok 2016).

The FBI does not categorize data according to victims' immigrant status. Even if they did, undocumented immigrants would likely be reluctant to report crimes against them for fear of deportation. Experts note, however, that hate crimes against Hispanic-identified people have increased in recent years, suggesting that anti-immigrant hate crimes have become more frequent (Langton, Planty, and Sandholtz 2013).

TABLE 11.2 Hate Crime in the United States, 2015

Hate crime based on:	Number of reported incidents:
Race	3,310
Religion	1,354
Sexual Orientation	1,053
Disability	74
Gender	23
Gender Identity	73

Source: Federal Bureau of Investigation. 2016b. *Hate Crime Statistics 2015*. Washington, DC: Federal Bureau of Investigation. (https://ucr.fbi.gov/hate-crime/2015/resource-pages/hate-crime-2015-_summary_final.)

Hate crimes are often committed not just by hateful individuals, but by organized movements, such as white-supremacy movements (Levin and Nolan 2016). Such movements emerge under particular social and historical conditions, particularly when dominant groups perceive a racial threat to their status in society. White people who hold "entrenched beliefs about their rightful position in society" (Durso and Jacobs 2013) may come to think that gains for racial-ethnic groups are coming at the expense of White people. Many have argued that this is exactly what mobilized so many White people to vote for Donald Trump in the presidential election of 2016. The surge in hate crimes and the increased activity of white-supremacy groups in the aftermath of Trump's election to the presidency are evidence of this phenomenon. Movements based on hatred threaten the safety and well-being of targeted groups.

Immigration and Crime: Rhetoric and Fact

When Donald Trump called Mexican Americans "rapists" and "criminals" during the presidential campaign in 2016, he tapped a nerve within parts of the U.S. public. Immigrants have had a long history of being demonized as criminals: At the beginning of the twentieth century, Irish immigrants were stereotyped as prone to gang violence. Italians have been depicted as mobsters, as if all were part of the Mafia. Mexican and South or Central American immigrants, especially men, are stereotyped as violent "macho" men. Despite the rhetoric, the fact is that crime is lower among immigrants than among other population groups (Longazel 2013; Rumbaut and Ewing 2007).

Public opinion surveys show that a large segment of the American public think that immigrants are more likely to engage in crime. Half of Americans also think immigrants are making crime worse (Pew 2015b). There is, however, little connection between perceptions of immigrant crime and reality.

Numerous studies have found that *crime is lower for immigrants*—of all ethnicities—than for native-born people, including those in the same ethnic group.

Claims that immigrants are criminals are false, although such claims were made frequently at rallies during Donald Trump's presidential campaign. The fact is that recent immigrants are *less likely* to commit crime than other groups.

Among Mexican immigrants, as one example, crime rates are lower for immigrants than for Mexican Americans born in the United States. Native-born Hispanics are actually seven times more likely to be imprisoned than are immigrant Hispanics (Rumbaut and Ewing 2007). Similar patterns hold for Asian immigrants. Even among high school dropouts, immigrant rates of imprisonment are lower than for native-born dropouts.

What is true is that the longer immigrants remain in the country, the more likely they will be involved with crime. First-generation Americans, that is, immigrants, are 45 percent less likely to commit violent crimes than are second- and third-generation Americans of the same ethnicity. Furthermore, this pattern holds for Hispanic, White, and Black immigrants. Contrary to popular belief, a higher concentration of immigrants within a neighborhood is also associated with lower rates of violent crime (Sampson 2008). In other words, it is the experience in the United States, not immigration per se or ethnic identities, that creates criminal behavior (Sohoni and Sohoni 2014; Stansfield et al. 2013).

Several studies also show that increased levels of immigration are actually related to a decline in lethal violence. Put another way, as immigration has increased in recent years, violent crime has actually decreased (Ousey and Kubrin 2014). The fact is that immigrants are far more likely to be victims of crime than offenders (Martinez 2014; Martinez and Valenzuela 2006). A better predictor of crime than immigration per se is social disorganization within communities (e.g., an absence of community organizations, churches, and watch groups). Immigrant communities tend to produce strong social bonds; thus, crime rates in such communities tend to be lower (Emerick et al. 2013; Martinez 2014).

Criminal Injustice: Race and the Administration of Justice

Until recently, African Americans were the largest minority group in the United States, but they have now been surpassed by Latinos. As 13 percent of the U.S. population, African Americans are overrepresented in virtually every indicator of criminal justice—in victimization by crime, in the likelihood of arrest, and as prisoners in local jails and state and federal prisons. When convicted, African Americans are also likely to receive longer sentences than others, often even for the same crimes that the others commit. They are also far more likely to be given the death penalty and make up almost half of all death row inmates (Snell 2014; Spohn 2015).

Hispanics, although closely matched in socioeconomic status to African Americans, do not fare quite so badly, although Hispanics are now a growing share of the imprisoned population. The imprisonment rate for Hispanic men is nearly one-third less than that for African American men, but it is over twice that of White men (Carson 2016). Hispanics are also disproportionately arrested for crime relative to their numbers in the population (Federal Bureau of Investigation 2016a; Truman and Morgan 2016).

There are widely held misperceptions about race and crime, but there is substantial evidence that race plays a significant role in the execution of justice—or, as many would say, *injustice* in the United States. In the midst of widespread public fears about race and crime, it is easy to overlook the fact that 70 percent of all arrests are of White people. Whites are also arrested for two-thirds of all rapes and commit most of the white-collar crime in the United States (Federal Bureau of Investigation 2016a). Still, relative to their size in the population, African Americans and Latinos are a disproportionate number of those caught in the criminal justice system. Why?

Do African Americans and Latinos commit more crime or are they just targeted more by the criminal justice system? We will examine this question in the last section of this chapter; first we have to examine the different steps in the administration of justice. You will see that racial discrimination persists though every step of the criminal justice system, starting with the likelihood of arrest (see figure 11.3) all the way through the administering of the death penalty. Although racial discrimination is not as overt as it was years ago, when, among other things, African Americans were formally excluded from serving on juries and could be lynched for the mere hint of violating a social norm, extensive evidence of institutional racism remains in the system of justice.

Policing and Social Control

Racial stereotypes portray young Black and Latino men as suspicious and potentially dangerous. As a consequence, Black and Latino males get enhanced scrutiny

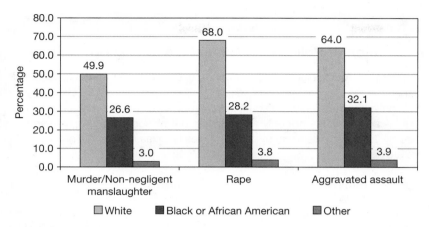

FIG. 11.3 Percent Distribution of Arrests, 2015

Note: "Other" includes American Indians, Alaska Natives, Asians, and Native Hawaiians and other Pacific Islanders.

Source: Federal Bureau of Investigation 2016a. *Crime in the United States 2015.* Washington, DC: U.S. Department of Justice. (https://ucr.fbi.gov/crime-in-the-u.s/2015/crime-in-the-u.s.-2015.)

from a young age from various authorities. Ample research finds that Black and Latino boys are more likely to be suspended, put in detention, or expelled from school, even as early as middle school. Being labeled early as a troublemaker has long-term consequences (Ferguson 2000; Rios 2015, 2011).

Sociologist Victor Rios calls what happens to Black and Latino males **social death**—a process by which they lose their humanity. Rios writes that male Latino and Black youths experience social death by being "rendered as criminal suspects not just by police but by schools, community centers, social workers, merchants, community members, and even family members. By the time that these young men become young adults, their lives have been policed, punished, and dehumanized by various institutions" (Rios 2015:60). Rios, now a highly successful academic scholar, describes his own early experience with police in his community in LIVING WITH RACISM.

The result of such intensive policing is that by age eighteen, about one-third of Black men have experienced at least one arrest, compared to 22 percent of White men. As young people enter their twenties, the racial gap in arrest rates grows: Nearly half (49 percent) of Black men have been arrested at least once by age 23, compared to 38 percent of White men (Brame et al. 2014).

The routine suspicion with which Black and Latino men are viewed is also familiar to adult minority men. Black men and many Latinos can report many personal experiences of being stopped for questioning for "driving while Black" or "driving while Brown." With some frequency Black men, regardless of social class, are stopped by police for "being in the wrong neighborhood," even if the neighborhood is their own!

These situations are examples of **racial profiling**, that is, the practice of using race—and race alone—as a criterion for stopping or detaining someone on suspicion

LIVING WITH RACISM

The Routinization of Police Harassment—A Young Boy's Story

Dr. Victor Rios is a distinguished sociologist who studies race, crime, and juvenile justice. His book, *Punished: Policing the Lives of Young Black and Latino Boys* (New York: New York University Press, 2011), examines the criminalization of minority youth in their routine encounters with police and state agencies. He knows his subject well—not only as a scholar, but as someone who as a young boy was routinely hassled by the police. His account of those times is a classic example of the policing of minority youth. Here are his words:

> Growing up I experienced constant police harassment and brutality, making me normalize police violence in my community. I personally had my face stomped to the cement by the police at age fifteen. My younger brother had been dragged out of a car through the window and beaten at age fourteen by a gang of notorious police officers who called themselves "the Riders." When we filed complaints with the Oakland Police Department or talked to lawyers for help, we were ignored. It seemed that there was nothing we could do about unsanctioned police violence, that no one cared, and that there were no avenues for getting the word out.

Source: Rios, Victor M. 2015. "Police, Punished, Dehumanized: The Reality for Young Men of Color Living in America." Pp. 59–80 in *Deadly Injustice: Trayvon Martin, Race, and the Criminal Justice System*, edited by Devon Johnson, Patricia Y. Warren, and Amy Farrell. New York: New York University Press.

of having committed a crime (Andersen and Taylor 2017). Racial profiling is a well-known and highly common phenomenon, evidenced in one way by studies that have examined the frequency of motorists being stopped, ticketed, and searched. Black Americans are pulled over for traffic stops by the police more often than Whites. Although there are only small differences in whether Black and Hispanic drivers are ticketed once stopped, compared to Whites, Blacks and Hispanics are three times more likely to be searched (Langton and Durose 2013). Studies have also shown that Black Americans are four times more likely than Whites to experience the use of force during encounters with the police; Hispanics, twice as likely (Hyland, Langton, and Davis 2015).

Traffic stops are annoying to anyone but can be especially frightening if you are a person of color. For Black and Latino citizens, a police encounter can be deadly. Trayvon Martin, Eric Garner, Michael Brown, and Freddie Gray: These became household names when the public became aware of the deaths of these young African American men at the hands of police. There will likely be others by the time you read this book. Young Black men are twenty-one times more likely to be shot by police than their White counterparts (Gabrielson, Jones, and Sagara 2014) and the issue of police brutality is a serious public concern, although of fair greater concern to African Americans than to Whites and Hispanics, as indicated in national opinion polls. White Americans are more likely to think that the police use deadly force only when necessary, whereas African Americans are more likely to think that the police use deadly force too quickly and are treated too leniently when they do kill (National Opinion Research Poll 2015). Reliable information about shootings by police is hard to get because police departments are the only place where such records are kept, if they are kept at all. What we know is that the victims of police

Protests against the all-too-common shootings by police of Black and Hispanic people have sparked greater awareness of racial profiling

shootings have almost always been young, usually, but not always, men, and commonly shot while fleeing or resisting arrest or perhaps just showing some "attitude." The shooters are mostly White officers, but Black officers have killed, too.

Racial bias has much to do with the likelihood that a police officer will shoot someone. Various controlled experiments have shown that *implicit racial bias* increases the likelihood that someone will shoot even an unarmed target when that target is African American. Scientifically tested in laboratory settings, these findings have serious implications for actual police behavior. A police officer may have to make a quick decision to shoot or not shoot a suspect. Implicit bias that he or she may not even be aware of can trigger the officer's response (Eberhardt et al. 2004). Such research findings are now being used in training programs for police officers in an effort to reduce unwarranted police shootings.

Getting Tough on Crime: Racial Disparities in Sentencing

Under the Reagan administration in 1980, the nation began a crusade to "get tough on crime." The result, as we will see, was a dramatic increase in imprisonment. Sentencing policies were also changed. Prior to the "get tough" movement, judicial officials had more discretion than they do now in sentencing decisions. The new, more punitive approach, based on explicit social policies such as mandatory sentencing for drug offenses and the infamous "three strikes, you're out" policy, reduced judicial discretion. The result was a swelling of the nation's prison ranks (Gabbidon and Greene 2016).

Even if there is some relaxing of these policies, which seems highly unlikely given the law-and-order approach of the Trump administration, patterns of racial disparities in sentencing appear. Research shows that Black and Hispanic offenders are more likely than Whites to be incarcerated after arrest. Discrimination in sentencing means that Black and Latino offenders often receive longer sentences for the same crime when committed by their White counterparts. Factors such as severity of the crime, the offender's employment status, a prior record, and even the region of the country have a role in sentencing, too, but an offender's race matters in and of itself (Spohn 2015).

Racial minorities are also given longer sentences for minor crimes such as drug offenses. Some research shows than Hispanics receive even harsher sentences than do African Americans—at least in regions where they are the majority population (Ulmer and Johnson 2004). People of color who victimize Whites are also sentenced more harshly than when the victim is of the same race (Spohn 2015). As concluded by a national review of current research on sentencing, "There is compelling evidence that those who murder Whites, and particularly Blacks who murder Whites, are sentenced to death and executed at disproportionately high rates" (Spohn 2015).

The research on racial disparities in sentencing is complex and often highly nuanced, but the end result is that Black men convicted of crime serve 7 percent more time than White non-Hispanic men (Bradley and Engen 2016). In the face of such data, it is little wonder than that nation's jails and prisons are bulging. As Michelle Alexander has noted, "The fact that more than half of the young Black men in any large American city are currently under the control of the criminal justice system (or saddled with criminal records) is not—as many argue—just a symptom of poverty or poor choices, but rather evidence of a new racial caste system at work" (Alexander 2010:16).

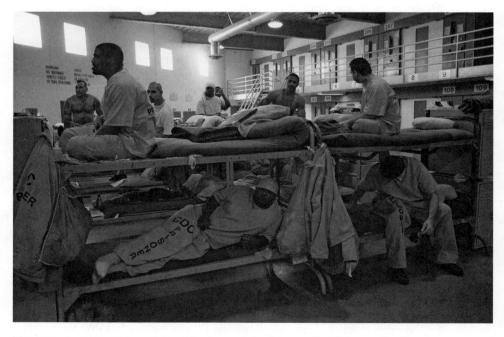

Mass incarceration of Hispanic and Black people has been called "the new Jim Crow" (Alexander 2010).

Mass Incarceration

The most obvious indication of this new racial caste system is the nation's prison system. The emergence of more punitive criminal justice policies has created a new social problem: the **mass incarceration** of people of color. Some argue that the problem of mass incarceration is now greater than the problem of crime per se (Coates 2015). The impact of mass incarceration falls not just on incarcerated individuals, but also on families, communities, and society as a whole.

The United States now has the highest imprisonment rate of any nation in the world. The United States holds one-quarter of the world's prisoners, while having only 5 percent of the world's population. The increase in imprisonment in the United States has been dramatic since the mid-1970s when a "War on Drugs" was declared. From the mid-1970s to the mid-1980s, the U.S. incarceration rate doubled and then doubled again over the next ten years. By 2015 the nation's imprisonment rate had reached 690 per 100,000 people (Kaeble et al. 2016), although imprisonment rates have fallen somewhat in very recent years.

People of color are a hugely disproportionate number of those in prison: 60 percent of those imprisoned are members of only 30 percent of the U.S. population. One in three Black men and one in six Hispanic men can expect to go to prison in their lifetime (see figures 11.4 and 11.5; Kerby 2012). Race is the most important single factor in explaining these high rates of incarceration, which exist at a time when the actual crime rate has declined (Campbell, Vogel, and Williams 2015).

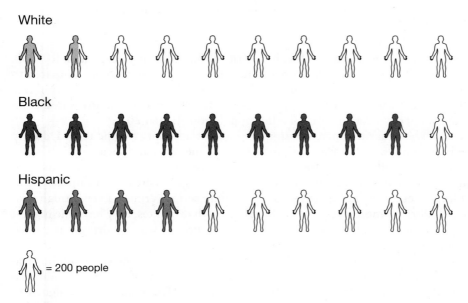

FIG. 11.4 Men and Women behind Bars, 2015

Number of White, Black, and Hispanic men and women in prison in 2015 per 100,000 U.S. residents age 18 or older

Source: Carson, E. Ann. 2016. *Prisoners in 2015*. Washington, DC: Bureau of Justice Statistics. (https://www.bjs.gov/content/pub/pdf/p15.pdf.)

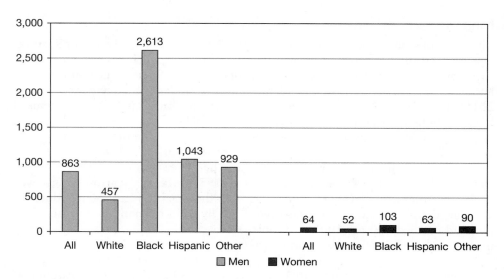

FIG. 11.5 Imprisonment Rate in State and Federal Prisons, 2015

Number of White, Black, and Hispanic men and women in prison in 2015 per 100,000 U.S. residents of all ages

Note: The overall rate is not the sum of the separate group rates. This is because a rate is per the number in a given population, and each of these groups has a different total population.

Source: Carson, E. Ann. 2016. *Prisoners in 2015*. Washington, DC: Bureau of Justice Statistics. (https://www. bjs.gov/content/pub/pdf/p15.pdf.)

The mass incarceration of African Americans has been unprecedented. In 1980, for example, 5.5 percent of Blacks had a history of felony conviction, compared to 2.1 percent of the adult population overall. By 2010, the U.S. felony conviction rate for Blacks had risen to 18.3 percent, with rates over 20 percent in many states, compared to 6.4 percent for the overall adult population (Uggen 2016).

It may seem that the increase in imprisonment accounts for the recorded drop in the crime rate. But the relationship between crime rates and incarceration is not as clear as you might think. Most experts attribute the increase in imprisonment to social policies that stemmed from the "War on Drugs." Increases in imprisonment occur largely because of drug arrests and not more serious crimes. Even though people of color are no more likely to sell illegal drugs than Whites, they have the highest arrest rates for drug offenses. What was to have been a war on drugs has turned into a war on young Black and Hispanic men.

John Ehrlichman, the former chief domestic advisor for the Nixon administration, reported that the War on Drugs was a specific policy of the Nixon administration (when mass incarceration started to expand). The policy was designed to neutralize the antiwar left and Black people, who had grown increasingly radical in the 1970s (see chapter 12). In Ehrlichman's words, "We knew we couldn't make it illegal to be either against the war or black, but by getting the public to associate the hippies with marijuana and blacks with heroin, and then criminalizing both heavily, we could disrupt those communities" (Ehrlichman, cited in Baum 2016).

What has evolved from the War on Drugs was the creation of a **carceral state**, defined as a society in which concerns about security are widespread and prisons become a mechanism for social control of a population. Increased surveillance of public places, high rates of imprisonment, and fear of crime also permeate such a society. It is clear that in the United States, the consequences of a carceral state are worse for poor and minority men (Western 2014, 2007; Western and Muller 2013).

The Spillover Effect: The Social Consequences of Mass Incarceration

Imprisonment leaves a permanent mark. Post-release, those who have served time find themselves banished from many of the basic rights of citizenship. The consequences for both individuals and whole communities can be devastating. Analyst Christopher Uggen (2016) calls this the **spillover effect,** the consequences of imprisonment that profoundly affect the lives of former prisoners and the people around them. Even with a clean record, a former prisoner will find it very difficult to find work. In most states, felons lose the right to vote, and in many places, they cannot receive public assistance.

The likelihood of employment after prison falls especially hard on Black men, as shown by Devah Pager in her widely cited studies of employment, race, and former prisoners. Pager developed a clever research design utilizing role-players who posed as ex-convicts looking for work. Her fake job seekers included both Black and White men, some with a criminal record, the others not. They all used the exact same script in looking for work. The results of her study reveal the great extent to which both race and ex-con status influence the likelihood of employment. All of the ex-cons, Black and White, in her study received fewer callbacks for interviews than those with no record. But most interesting was her finding that Black men who were *not* ex-cons were less likely to be invited back for job interviews than Whites who were ex-cons. In other words, the effect of race alone actually exceeded the effect of incarceration (Pager 2007; Pager and Pedulla 2015; Phelps and Pager 2016).

Once released from prison, former prisoners (who may be in their prime working years) face severe material hardship. A comprehensive study of former prisoners has found that more than half are unemployed, two-thirds receive public assistance, and many have to rely on female relatives for financial support and housing. Their disadvantage leaves former prisoners among the least socially integrated in society. "Material insecurity combined with the adjustment to social life outside prison creates a stress of transition that burdens social relationships in high-incarceration communities" (Western et al. 2015:1512).

The spillover effect also impacts families and communities. For children alone, the consequences of having a parent in prison are tremendous. One million Black children now have a father in jail. More than half of the Black fathers in prison report being the family breadwinner. Sixty-two percent of Black children have a parent who has gone to prison, compared to 17 percent of Hispanic children and 15 percent of White children (Coates 2015).

Communities are affected by the spillover as well. Having large numbers of ex-offenders in a given place has negative effects for the whole community; for one thing, it raises the unemployment rate of the area. High rates of incarceration also lessen the availability of marriageable men. Fewer marriageable men means more female-headed households and, thus, higher rates of poverty. A cycle of poverty is generated—not because of people's values, but because of unemployment and a family's reliance on a woman's lower wages.

The National Research Council has also concluded that the costs of mass incarceration to the nation are significant, outweighing the benefits of a "get tough on crime" approach (Travis, Western and Redurn 2014). It is true that some White, rural communities have lobbied for and benefitted from having prisons located in their community as a boost to employment. But, more generally, the expansion of prisons, costing over $80 billion per year, uses up funds that could otherwise be spent on education and other social services to help poor, minority communities. The cost of mass incarceration to the nation's people of color cannot be overestimated.

Death Row and Wrongful Conviction

Debates about capital punishment in the United States have long included discussions of the impact of racial discrimination. The United States is the only Western democracy that still utilizes the death penalty. The constitutionality of the death penalty has been challenged repeatedly over the years in a complex series of cases before the U.S. Supreme Court. In 1972 the Supreme Court ruled in *Furman v. Georgia* that the death penalty was unconstitutional. The decision rested on the lack of uniformity from state to state in determining whether a penalty of death was warranted. Only four years later, in *Gregg v. Georgia*, 1976, the Court reversed itself, with a slight majority of the Justices ruling that state statutes had eliminated the procedural disparities found earlier in the determination of death penalty judgments. Legal scholars and some of the Supreme Court justices nonetheless argued that the administration of the death penalty carried with it great race and class bias (Walker, Spohn, and Delone 2012).

In 1987, the death penalty was constitutionally tested again when Warren McCleskey, a Black man in Georgia, was sentenced to death for shooting and killing a White police officer. In his petition to the Court, McCleskey argued that there was racial discrimination in death penalty cases. He based his appeal on research that found that murder defendants were more likely to receive the death penalty when the victim was White. In a highly controversial decision, the Supreme Court ruled in *McCleskey v. Kemp* that no racial bias was specifically found in the McCleskey case. Warren McCleskey was executed in the electric chair in 1991.

Current constitutional law allows capital punishment, although it is questionable whether the Supreme Court will eventually determine that capital punishment constitutes cruel and unusual punishment. People debate the death penalty on various grounds, especially moral ones. Public opinion about the death penalty is divided along racial lines. Nearly two-thirds (63 percent) of White Americans favor the death penalty. Half of Hispanics (52 percent) support it, but only 40 percent of African Americans do (Pew Research Center 2015b). Several states have now repealed the death penalty based on various concerns, including racial discrimination.

TABLE 11.3 Prisoners on Death Row, by Number and Percentage, 2016

	Number	Percentage
White	1,230	42.3
Black	1,214	41.8
Latino	380	13.1
Native American	27	0.9
Asian	53	1.8
Unknown at the time	1	.03

Note: Percentages do not total 100 due to rounding.

Source: Fins, Deborah. 2016. *Death Row U.S.A. Summer 2016*. Baltimore: NAACP Legal Defense and Educational Fund, Inc.

Although race per se has not been the main argument in recent challenges to the death penalty, descriptive data certainly suggest that racial discrimination is still a factor in rulings for the death penalty. By the end of 2013, almost three thousand prisoners were on death row in the United States, 46 percent of whom were Black (see table 11.3), far out of proportion to their numbers in the general population. Both the number and proportion of death row prisoners who are Black has been fairly constant since 2000. California, Texas, and Florida account for almost half of those on death row, even though those three states combined only contain between one-quarter and one-third of the U.S. population (Snell 2014).

Research on racial discrimination in death penalty cases shows that "race continues to be a significant factor in the administration of capital punishment" (Poveda 2009:566). Racial disparities in judgments for the death penalty seem to be higher in cases where the evidence is less clear. In other words, there is less racial difference in death penalty decisions in the most aggravated and clear-cut cases. In cases that are not so clear-cut, racial disparities are higher (Baldus, cited in Barak, Leighton, and Cotton 2015:278). Various factors other than race are related to death penalty decisions, including whether the defendant has adequate legal counsel, race of the victim, and the accused's prior record. Scholars debate the extent to which race itself plays a role when there is a death-eligible trial, but the large percentage of people of color on death row certainly suggests that race matters.

Equally disturbing are cases of wrongful conviction. Seventy percent of the exonerations that have occurred as the result of DNA evidence are people of color, two-thirds of whom are African American (Grimsley 2012). One of the main reasons for wrongful conviction is eyewitness testimony, notoriously unreliable as evidence and certainly influenced by racial bias. A very large portion of the cases of Black prisoners being exonerated after serving a prison sentence are those in which White eyewitnesses identified a Black person as the culprit.

Even though the number of cases where wrongful conviction has been proven is small, research indicates that the combination of race of the defendant and race of the victim is a significant factor in wrongful convictions (Harmon 2004). Death penalty cases and wrongful convictions are two more ways that racial injustice pervades the criminal justice system. As sociologists have concluded, the "white racial framing" of Black men is central to discrimination against them in the criminal justice system (Free and Ruesink 2012; Feagin 2013).

Explaining the Race-Crime Connection

This chapter has shown the extent to which racial inequality seeps into the system of justice. What remains is explaining why crime is higher by some groups and how racial inequality is central to that pattern. Are people of color, African Americans in particular, more likely to commit crime? If so, why? Or are people of color just more likely to be identified by the criminal justice system, labeled early as delinquent, and then trapped in an unjust system?

These may seem like simple questions, but they are not. You have already seen how official statistics distort how race and crime are reported. Throughout this chapter, you have also seen how race influences the administration of justice. Even considering these facts, though, crime rates are still higher for some groups than others. The question is why. There are plenty of people in every race and ethnic group who engage in criminal behavior. Understanding criminal behavior—and then developing policies to reduce it—requires as a basis an understanding of the conditions and contexts in which crime is most likely to occur.

Criminologists debate various theories about crime, the particulars of which are too nuanced to report here. But one thing is certainly true: "Crime and crime control are inseparable from the changing reality of inequality, hierarchy, and power" (Barak, Leighton, and Cotton 2015:2). Based on criminological theory, several points can be made to frame a theoretical and social structural analysis of the connection between race and crime (Barak, Leighton, and Cotton 2015):

- Crime has both objective and subjective dimensions.
- Criminal behavior is shaped by the actions and decisions of individual actors, but those actors operate within a social environment.
- Human beings develop cultures in response to social conditions, but cultures alone do not explain criminal behavior.
- The economic system blocks opportunity for some, while providing greater advantage for others, producing conditions ripe for criminal behavior.
- Systemic inequality pervades the administration of justice.

Crime has both objective and subjective dimensions

The subjective dimensions of crime include the perceptions and fears that people hold, many of which are generated by media narratives that distort the actual truth about crime. Subjective beliefs also shape what is considered crime and what is not. Dominant beliefs about crime also reinforce racial inequality by labeling people of color as criminals, potentially increasing the surveillance and social control over minority populations.

According to **labeling theory**, once a person or group is identified as "criminal," the label sticks and it is then difficult for the person to shed it. Dominant groups also have greater power than others to apply labels, especially on the most disadvantaged. Labeling theory helps explain the cycle that emerges when people of color are identified early on as troublemakers, punished, and potentially pushed into more misbehavior. Once identified as deviant or criminal, the person so labeled then finds it difficult to escape the system of social control. Victor Rios calls this cycle **hypercriminalization,** "a process by which an individual's nondeviant behavior and everyday interaction become treated as risk, threat, or crime and, in turn, have an impact on his or her perceptions, worldview, and life outcome" (Rios 2015:63). Hypercriminalizing young people of color then produces what Rios calls a system of constant *punitive social control.*

Criminal behavior is shaped by the actions and decisions of individual actors, but those actors operate within a social environment.

Understanding the social context of crime does not ignore or excuse the criminal behavior of individuals, but it locates the cause of such behavior in social factors, not in individual attitudes or beliefs. Environmental factors such as family instability, crowding, concentrated poverty, and residential segregation shape the behaviors of people living in such contexts. While it is easy to simply blame individuals for bad behavior, that behavior can often be understood in the context of social disorganization. For example, when social bonds are loosened (such as from chronic unemployment), crime and other forms of antisocial behavior can result from strong feelings of alienation from the dominant society (Emerick et al. 2014).

Human beings develop cultures in response to social conditions, but cultures alone do not explain criminal behavior.

Some attribute high levels of crime by people of color, men especially, to a subculture of violence, as if people's values and cultural norms were the basis for criminal behavior. As you can see in figure 11.6, such a view is common—more so among White Americans than Black Americans (Thompson and Bobo 2011). When whole communities are segregated from mainstream institutions and deprived of the resources needed for success, subcultures can develop, particularly as forms of resistance. Sociologists have long argued that when people are unable to achieve the goals established by the dominant society, they may find illegitimate means to achieve success (Merton 1938).

Urban ethnographer Elijah Anderson (1999) has studied the culture of poor inner-city communities and what he calls the *code of the street.* The code of the street is a set of behaviors and attitudes that develop in poor, inner-city, Black neighborhoods. The code is a survival strategy that provides people with respect in a context where they are otherwise devalued. The code is also a means of protection against potentially aggressive and violent behavior. Seen in this way, being "cool," "tough," and "streetwise" is a mode of self-defense. But these behaviors and attitudes are often interpreted by outsiders (including, possibly, the police) as threatening, disrespectful outcomes.

Acknowledging that particular cultural forms may develop in underprivileged communities does not, however, provide an adequate understanding of criminal

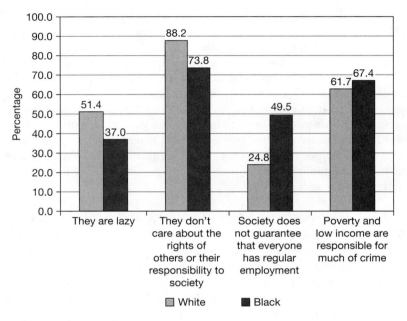

FIG. 11.6 Beliefs about Why People Commit Crime: The Racial Gap

Source: Thompson, Victor R., and Lawrence D. Bobo. 2011. "Thinking about Crime: Race and Lay Accounts of Lawbreaking Behavior." *Annals of the American Academy of Political and Social Science* 634:16–38.

action. Cultures emerge in the context of social structures as people adapt to the conditions they face. As with individualistic explanations, explanations that rely solely on culture overlook the social structures that deprive people of sound economic, political, and social opportunities.

The economic system blocks opportunity for some, while providing greater advantage for others, producing conditions ripe for criminal behavior.

In chapter 7 we saw the problems associated with the very high rates of unemployment among minority young people. Structural unemployment, little opportunity for economic advancement, and the isolation of young people of color in residentially segregated and poor neighborhoods produce the urban underclass (Wilson 1987). Individuals' minds and cultural values are not the source of this problem.

Much, though not all, of the urban underclass is young people of color, the group most likely to be apprehended and held in the criminal justice system. Black male joblessness in particular is, then, one of the prime reasons for high rates of crime. As put by sociologists Robert Sampson and William Julius Wilson, who have extensively studied such neighborhoods, "Patterns of residential inequality give rise to the social isolation and ecological concentration of the truly disadvantaged, which in turn leads to structural barriers and cultural adaptations that undermine social organization and hence the control of crime" (Sampson and

Wilson 1995:38). Although Sampson and Wilson note the role of culture in urban crime, they argue that it is the social structure of blocked opportunity that produces criminal behavior.

Systemic inequality pervades the administration of justice.

Patterns of inequality not only produce criminal behavior, but shape how the system of justice operates. This chapter has shown how each step of the criminal justice process engages racial inequality. Racial discrimination within the criminal justice system is usually not overt, but it is nonetheless systematic. Factors such as the ability of people to pay for sound representation, to post bond, or to return to good jobs following incarceration are all conditioned on a person's available resources.

Despite the idea that justice is said to be blind, systematic racial discrimination "occurs at all stages of the criminal justice system, in all places, and at all times. That is to say, there is discrimination in arrest, prosecution, and sentencing (stages); in all parts of the country (places); and without any significant variation over time" (Walker, Spohn, and DeLone 2012:29).

Conclusion

At the turn of the nineteenth century, based on his detailed study of the city of Philadelphia, the great sociologist W. E. B. Du Bois wrote, "Crime is a phenomenon of organized social life, and is the open rebellion of an individual against his social environment" (Du Bois 1899:235). Du Bois might be surprised to see how much crime still plagues many of the most disadvantaged communities in our nation. For many people of color, new economic and social opportunities are unprecedented, and those successes should be remembered while also looking at the disruptive and criminal behavior of others.

The harms done to people from crime are real and cannot be denied. Yet even while acknowledging the human suffering that stems from crime, it is important to see the structural injustices that produce criminal behavior. People are quick to blame individual misbehavior for crime, but a more accurate, though complex analysis of crime shows the societal factors involved. Understanding the social structure of crime will more likely lead to social policies that will reduce both crime and the racial disparities that pervade the criminal justice system.

Key Terms

carceral state, 267

crime index, 253

hate crime, 256

hypercriminalization, 271

labeling theory, 271

mass incarceration, 264

National Crime Victimization Survey, 253

racial profiling, 261

social death, 261

spillover effect, 267

Uniform Crime Reports, 253

Critical Thinking Questions

1. What evidence do you see in your community of a *carceral state*?
2. Using one of the following as your example, describe how *institutional racism* operates in the criminal justice system: arrest rates, sentencing, incarceration.

Student Exercises

11.1: Using the tool provided by the Bureau of Justice Statistics NCVS Victimization Analysis Tool (http://www.bjs.gov/index.cfm?ty=nvat), build a table involving personal victimization by crime. You will need to select a year (or range of years) as well as a victimization type. Select race/ethnicity as your first variable and then a second variable of your choice. What does your table reveal and how would you explain what you observe?

11.2: Go to the web page of the Innocence Project (http://www.innocenceproject .com) and review the profiles provided of prisoners who have now been exonerated based on DNA evidence. Of the more than three hundred cases included, how many appear to be people of color? How many were convicted based on "eyewitness testimony?" In what ways might race influence eyewitness testimony? What other factors might influence such testimony?

11.3: Using the link to American Public Media's The Story (http://www.thestory. org/series/after-innocence-exoneration-america), listen to the narratives there of several exonerated prisoners. What do you learn about institutional racism and how it operates as you listen to the narratives of these men and women?

Challenging Question/Open to Debate: Decriminalizing Drugs

Given that the War on Drugs has been a major contributor to the incarceration of African Americans, would it be effective to decriminalize drug use in order to reduce the impact of institutional racism? Why or why not?

CHAPTER 12

The Long Search for Racial Justice

In order to get beyond racism, we must first take account of race. There is no other way. And in order to treat some persons equally, we must treat them differently.
— Supreme Court Justice Harry Blackmun

OBJECTIVES

- Relate the earliest roots of organized resistance to racial inequality
- Understand some of the key events and outcomes of the Civil Rights movement
- Contrast the philosophy and strategies of the Civil Rights movement with that of the Black Power movement
- Compare the philosophy and tactics of the Black Lives Matter movement to those of the Civil Rights movement

- Compare and contrast colorblind and color-conscious frameworks for racial change
- Debate whether the presence of a more multiracial and multicultural population in the United States will alleviate or exacerbate racial inequality.

Reverend Martin Luther King's call for creating a society where people will "one day live in a nation where they will not be judged by the color of their skin but by the content of their character" inspires the ideal of colorblindness. This ideal guides much of our nation's approach to racial justice. A legal framework of equal rights is in place and undergirded by the constitutional principle of *equal protection*, established by the Fourteenth Amendment to the U.S. Constitution in 1868. King's exhortation, given at a time of racial crisis in U.S. history, appealed to the conscience of Americans to live up to a colorblind ideal as the path to racial justice.

History has shown, however, that colorblind initiatives do not necessarily dismantle the entrenched system of racial inequality in the United States, as you have seen throughout this book. Despite the appeal of King's call, a fundamental question arises: Should we use colorblind approaches to achieve racial equality, or do we need race-conscious actions to eliminate racial injustice? This question guides the content of this chapter.

The colorblind ideal is very consistent with the American belief in individualism and personal merit, that is, the idea that people should be judged and treated based on their actions and not on their personal characteristics, such as race, class, gender, or any number of other categorizations. This is an ideal that many embrace, and it guides much of the legislation that protects civil rights for various groups. The colorblind ideal has also been the hallmark of various movements for social justice, including the Civil Rights movement.

But is this ideal enough? We have seen that even with laws in place that guarantee equal rights, racial inequality persists and is deeply embedded in U.S. institutions. Race-specific changes have also been needed in order to open doors for previously excluded groups. Desegregating education, for example, has sometimes required using explicit consideration of race to build more diverse college admissions. Now, however, race-specific policies have become highly suspect to some, in part because race has been used so perniciously in our nation's past to exclude people.

What strategies for change do we need to go forward, and how should we think about race now? These questions are especially pressing as U.S. society becomes more multiracial and multicultural. With visible racial hatred on the rise, answers to these questions are even more critical. Answering these questions is not a simple task and requires some understanding of philosophies of change that have guided the long struggle for racial justice.

The Early Road to Civil Rights

Resistance to oppression can take many forms and is shaped by forces both internal and external to particular groups. Since before the founding of the United States, indigenous people have fought for the preservation of their lands and lives. At varying points in history African Americans, Chicanos, Asian Americans, and other minorities have had to fight for their rights and protect themselves from the harms of racial oppression. Sometimes the struggle for justice has meant outright revolt; other times, more subtle forms of resistance. Under slavery, for example, African Americans challenged the authority of white supremacy through whatever means possible, sometimes by slave revolts, sometimes by running away. Everyday actions of resistance under slavery could also be as subtle as spitting in an owner's meal, feigning illness, or sabotaging a slave owner's property. The slave's ultimate form of resistance lay in not allowing a slave owner's beliefs to control his or her own mind.

Following the abolition of slavery, newly freed Black people were emboldened by the unprecedented freedoms that the period of Reconstruction provided. This freedom was soon followed by massive repression, including changes in the law as well as organized opposition by vigilante groups. By the end of the 1870s, a massive wave of retaliation had set in, beginning, some would say, with the formation of the Ku Klux Klan in 1865 and the gradual appearance of other white supremacist groups that terrorized Black communities. Scholars estimate that, at least counting those we know about, close to five thousand people were lynched between 1882 and 1968. Most but not all were African American. Less well known is the extensive lynching of Mexican Americans, mostly in the Southwest. Lynchings of Mexican Americans were often public spectacles, conducted with the collusion of local law authorities acting in accordance with the wishes of the Anglo community (Delgado 2009; Carrigan and Webb 2003, 2015; Acuña 2005).

Even under these harsh conditions, people resisted in any way they could (Carson et al. 1987). Ida B. Wells's antilynching crusade is just one example (Giddings 2009). Resistance leaders were common in communities of color, which historian Elsa Barkley Brown calls "communities of struggle" (Brown 1995). We may not now know the names of all those Black, Latino, Asian, and Native American community leaders, but their struggles poured the foundation for those who followed. With regard to the early twentieth century, historians now conclude, "A complex, powerful, and explosive cluster of human intentions was at the heart of almost all the struggles for justice, survival, defense, and transformation which were carried on by Black people as one century eroded and another began" (Carson et al. 1987:5). You could say the same about other communities of color, too.

One of the most important developments during the early twentieth century for African American people was the widespread creation of Black institutions: universities, newspapers, mutual aid societies, women's organizations, banks, funeral homes, fraternal or sororal organizations (Giddings 2007; Hughey 2011), and others. During this time, Black communities "established their own network of medical, nursing, legal training institutions, and normal schools" (Hine 2004:1065), resulting in a professional class that was later critical to the evolution of Black activism. Urban Blacks, especially in the North, developed a tradition of business ownership and professional work in the Black community (Williams 1998). These entities formed a system of parallel institutions to White society, providing safe spaces and communication networks that paved the way for what became the Civil Rights movement (Hine 2004).

The leadership that emerged from these independent Black institutions is impressive, comprising a cadre of African Americans whose dogged work was critical to civil rights organizing. There are numerous examples, one of whom is W. E. B. Du Bois, who cofounded the National Association for the Advancement of Colored People (NAACP) in 1909. The NAACP remains one of the most influential civil rights organizations. Another historic leader is A. Philip Randolph, who organized the Brotherhood of Sleeping Car Porters in 1925, the first labor union that gave Black Americans the right to organize and be recognized as part of the American Federation of Labor. There are countless African American women leaders (Mary Church Terrell, Ida B. Wells, Mary McLeod Bethune, and others) who likewise are critical in this historic struggle. For many women and men throughout this struggle leadership was more behind the scenes and, thus, less remembered and celebrated.

These people and organizations fought to eliminate discrimination, provide education for their people, and gain access to the full rights of citizenship. Latinos founded the League of United Latin Americans in 1928 to fight discrimination and provide more education for their communities. In 1930 Japanese Americans founded the Japanese American Citizenship League, based on having earlier formed various civic clubs that supported second-generation Japanese Americans (Takaki 1989). Under the leadership of Cesar Chavez, the United Farm Workers Union led a massive strike against the nation's grape industry, protesting working conditions for Chicano and Filipino grape-pickers—a strike that began in 1965, lasted five years, and brought national attention to the exploitation of agricultural laborers (Ferriss and Sandoval 1997). These and other protest actions tell a long tale of people of color acting as agents of their own history, individually as well as collectively (see LIVING WITH RACISM).

Sociologist Aldon Morris (1984) argues that these early developments provided intellectual, financial, organizational, and informational resources that were crucial in the mobilization of the Civil Rights movement. The internal strengths of the Black community provided the vision, energy, and skills that spawned civil rights organizing in the 1950s and 1960s (Carson et al. 1987). Earlier, however, even with these resources internal to the African American community, there were limits to how much people could resist. Darlene Clark Hine puts it succinctly: For Black communities in the first half of the twentieth century, "fettered by inadequate economic resources, and dogged by the ever-present specter of white violence and terror . . . the marginal and precarious status of most African Americans severely restricted the space in which they could fashion resistance" (Hine 2004:1066).

External forces, namely the two World Wars, also helped forge the path to protest. Black, Mexican, Native American, and Asian American men and women fought in both wars. When President Woodrow Wilson declared that the U.S. entry into World War I was to "make the world safe for democracy," people noticed that soldiers were fighting for democracy abroad while Black, Mexican, and other troops did not have democracy at home. Seeing this contradiction, A. Philip Randolph pressured the federal government to desegregate the heavily segregated armed forces.

LIVING WITH RACISM

A Professor, Not a Porter—Lawrence Matsuda

Social justice is rooted firmly in my life experiences and relationships. Being a minority in a white society is an issue I cannot escape. Recently I rented a luggage cart at Sea-Tac Airport in Seattle to pick up my wife's luggage at the United Airlines' carousel. While I was looking, a tall middle-aged white male approached me and pointed to his luggage on the carousel. He said, "My bag is over there." Showing no emotion, I turned and responded, "I am a professor, not a porter. I am afraid you'll have to pick up your own baggage."

Regardless of my professional accomplishments, training or status, being an Asian American in a white society has meant being mistaken for: a waiter instead of a customer in a Chinese restaurant, a porter at the airport, a shoeshine person at a hotel, a foreigner from Japan, a Korean immigrant, and countless others. It makes me angry to deal with racial stereotypes that are insensitive, personally annoying, and insulting. Although I handle each situation differently, I found any response, no response, any exchange, or any reply makes me feel debased as a human being. I wonder, "Why even bother?"

I have experienced almost all the Asian racist remarks, ethnic slurs, insults, or well-meaning comments that effectively separate me from the larger white society in the United States. My blood pressure rises, triggering the adrenaline rush, especially when the offender feels he or she has delivered an insult so creative that surely I must have never heard it before. Nevertheless, my personal racial issues are: How can I channel my anger to creative endeavors that are positive, and how can that anger and energy be used for the betterment of the human family at large? I feel strongly that how one handles the anger in response to racism is the key to having a healthy life and being a productive citizen. From the point of view of my career, these feelings generate the following questions: How have these experiences shaped my identity? My teaching style? My perceived purpose in life and my career in education? Some of these questions will be answered but most will raise more fundamental questions like: What do you believe? What do you value most? What can you do? *What do you believe?*

Source: Matsuda, Lawrence Y. 2005. "A Professor, Not a Porter." *Community and Difference: Teaching, Pluralism, and Social Justice* 261:51–75.

Thus in 1941, President Franklin Roosevelt signed an order forbidding racial discrimination in federal agencies and companies engaged in war-related work. Then, in 1948, President Harry Truman signed Executive Order 9981, compelling the armed forces to desegregate at every level. That order reads: "There shall be equality of treatment and opportunity for all persons in the armed forces without regard to race, color, religion, or national origin."

The Civil Rights Movement

The Civil Rights movement is one of the most profoundly influential developments of modern history. This movement transformed the lives of African American people in the United States and also changed the legal and social framework that has given rights to many others, including Latinos, Asian Americans, women, LGBTQ people, and people with disabilities (Andersen 2004). Inspired by Mohandas Gandhi as he led the Indian independence movement against British control, the Civil Rights movement also spawned liberation movements around the world as people of color organized to throw off colonial rule and sought self-determination. The wide reach of the Civil Rights movement makes it one of the most transformative moments in U.S. history and, indeed, world history.

Victory over years of Jim Crow segregation came in 1954 with the *Brown v. Board of Education* Supreme Court decision (also see chapter 8). *Brown* was a major triumph for the NAACP, whose attorneys, most especially Thurgood Marshall, had championed this case. In 1967, Marshall became the first African American appointed to the U.S. Supreme Court.

Brown provided a "detonating spark" (Bennett 1964:17) to the emerging freedom struggle of Black people. Of course, the struggle had not emerged overnight. As we have seen, the Black community was not asleep prior to the 1950s and 1960s (Marks 1990). "Years of legal work, various court challenges, community organizing, and wrangling with school officials, preceded this momentous decision. After all, it was not *Brown* per se that overthrew the social order of Jim Crow segregation, but the mass mobilization of Black people and their White allies" (Andersen 2004:1079). So important were the precursors to the 1950s movement that Hine has concluded that the *Brown* decision was actually the culmination, not the beginning, of the black freedom struggle (Hine 2004:1072). With *Brown* in place and the constitutional abolition of "separate but equal," there was new hope that Jim Crow segregation would be dismantled once and for all.

A Movement Unfolds

By 1955, Black people had a long history of organizational efforts, which crystallized in the summer of that year as the result of a murder. Emmett Till, a fourteen-year-old from Chicago, was visiting Mississippi, where he allegedly flirted with a White woman. This incited two White men to take him from his bed at night, severely beat him, kill him, and then dump his body into a river. His mother insisted on an open casket funeral so that the world could see how brutally her son was killed. Images of his mutilated body flashed across the nation, infuriating Black Americans and stirring the conscience of many White Americans, who could vividly see the effects of racism. Till's murder galvanized the Black community. It was only one hundred days after Till's murder, on December 1, 1955, that Rosa Parks was arrested when she refused to give up her seat on a Montgomery, Alabama, bus.

The commonly repeated story is that Rosa Parks was just too tired to move when the White bus driver ordered her to change her seat. The stereotype in this story is that of an old, passive Black woman. In truth, Rosa Parks had long been engaged in activism prior to the events of that fateful day. She was the secretary for the local branch of the NAACP, a position she had held since 1943. This was also not the first time she had refused to obey the segregation rules on the bus. She once reflected, "My resistance to being mistreated on the buses and anywhere else was just a regular thing with me and not just that day" (Carson et al. 1987:38). Through Rosa Parks, the NAACP found the opportunity they had been looking for to challenge segregation in Montgomery.

Montgomery, Alabama, was like many southern cities: Jim Crow segregation was the rule. Black and White children could not attend the same schools. Black citizens could not be buried in White cemeteries. Black Americans could not vote. Not only were basic rights of citizenship denied to Black people, but everyday actions were also governed by Jim Crow's subtle norms (so-called rules of *racial etiquette*) and by explicit social policies. A Black person and a White person could not ride a taxi together (Branch 1988), nor could such a pair play checkers on public property. In retrospect, these regulations seem ridiculous, yet they operated to maintain as complete a system of white supremacy as possible.

Buses in Montgomery were even more segregated than in other places. Some cities had a "floating line" whereby White passengers would fill in from the front; Blacks, from the back. In Montgomery, Black passengers had to pay their fares at the front door of the bus and then walk back out and in through the back door so as not to pass through the "White section" and run the risk of a Black man's legs touching a White woman's knees (Branch 1988). Within a federal military base in Montgomery, buses were integrated, but soldiers had to rearrange themselves into segregated seating patterns when the bus reentered municipal property.

Following Parks's actions, Black leaders in Montgomery called for a total boycott of the buses; it was neither the first time nor would it be the last time that a boycott would be used to protest racism. Black citizens in Baton Rouge, Louisiana, for example, had organized a bus boycott in 1953 to protest segregated seating there. In Baton Rouge, Montgomery, and most other cities in the South, Black riders made up the majority of the bus passengers. Boycotting the buses was potentially an economically crippling action against a bus company.

The Montgomery Bus Boycott lasted for an entire year. During this time, Black people in Montgomery organized their own extensive transportation network, relying on volunteer drivers who had their own cars as well as on contributions to support taxi rides. Many walked long distances to work, sacrificing time and energy for the civil rights cause. Boycott organizers demanded three things from the bus company: (1) that bus drivers treat Black riders with courtesy; (2) that the bus company employ Black drivers on mostly black routes; and, (3) that seating would be first come, first served (Robinson 1987; Branch 1988).

The boycott only ended when the U.S. Supreme Court affirmed in 1956 that segregation on the buses was unconstitutional. As this news unfolded, one Black person declared, "God Almighty has spoken from Washington, D.C.!" (Branch 1988:193). The Montgomery movement renewed feelings that change was possible if only the federal government would enforce the nation's laws. The boycott was also significant because it resulted in the rise of black leadership, most notably that of Martin Luther King Jr., but also that of less visible ordinary citizens, particularly women from the local Black colleges who mobilized to challenge segregation (Robinson 1987). As the movement unfolded, this kind of grassroots leadership was essential.

Confronting Evil: Nonviolent Civil Disobedience

Following Montgomery, a full decade of extraordinary and visible activism fueled the Civil Rights movement. Protests were locally organized, often supported by national organizations such as CORE (Congress on Racial Equality), the SCLC (Southern Christian Leadership Conference), and others, but the thrust of the movement developed from the grassroots.

Although many of the iconic leaders of the Civil Rights movement have been men, women's leadership was critical to the success of this historic movement.

For people who did not live through this time, it may be hard to imagine what it was like to witness these events unfolding. At the time, there were only three major television networks. Most Americans used these televised reports to get the evening's news. In the decade between 1955 and 1965 the public witnessed fire bombings of Black churches, demonstrators being pummeled by fire hoses, southern sheriffs refusing to allow Black people to vote, and the assassination of movement leaders, all of which brought the Civil Rights movement to the nation's attention. The violence directed against peaceful Black protesters shocked many, thus mobilizing support among some White allies.

The main strategy of the Civil Rights movement was **nonviolent civil disobedience**. The objective was to disrupt the everyday workings of segregation by refusing to obey segregation-related laws, customs, and norms. Demonstrators were specifically trained in passive resistance, such as by going limp when the police tried to arrest them or not fighting back when they were being beaten by police or angry White mobs. Nonviolent civil disobedience was also intended to deflect accusations that Black people were inciting violence, while the horrific violence of white racism was rampant.

The philosophy of the Civil Rights movement rested on an appeal to Christian values and a call for peace and understanding. Churches provided many of the organizing spaces as well as the values that guided this movement. Accordingly, resisting segregation was seen as confronting evil. The hope was to win White people's support through appeals to "brotherhood." As we will see, this philosophy of change is in distinct contrast to the more radical movement that eventually developed. The idea was that the "hearts and minds" of White Americans would change through appeals to White people's conscience, and nonviolent action was part of that plan. The demands of the Civil Rights movement were essentially three:

1. access to public facilities and services;
2. desegregation of education; and,
3. the right to vote.

One of the early struggles over education came in 1957 in Little Rock, Arkansas. Local leaders, along with the NAACP, tried to enroll nine Black students in Little Rock High School. So strong was Governor Orval Faubus's resistance that he called out the National Guard to block the students from entering. Ultimately, President Eisenhower had to call in one thousand soldiers from the 101st Airborne of the U.S. Army to restore order and protect the young Black students. Rather than comply with federal orders, Governor Faubus resisted further by closing all four Little Rock high schools for a full school year. He was not alone in doing so. In Virginia, U.S. senator Harry Byrd organized other politicians to close an entire school system and many other public schools from 1958 to 1959, also in an attempt to stall desegregation (Branch 1988; Carson et al. 1987).

Even when facing such staunch opposition to desegregation, the movement pushed on. Protests were organized in many places—far too many to detail here. In Greensboro, North Carolina, four first-year students from North Carolina A & T (a historically Black college) organized a sit-in at the local Woolworth's lunch counter in the winter of 1960. Sit-ins had been held before in other places, but the one in Greensboro captured national attention because it was the first to be nationally televised. Many students and community members joined in, and images of their protest shot across the national news media. Sit-ins then spread to at least five other states (Branch 1988; Carson 1981).

That same year, the NAACP sued to have James Meredith, a Black man, enrolled at the University of Mississippi. The University registrar refused to admit him, setting off a major crisis in the city of Oxford. It took twenty-three thousand soldiers (including the Army, Marines, and Air Force) and many casualties to stop the rioting that White students and others ignited because they objected to Meredith's enrollment. Under intense pressure from Black leaders and a total lack of cooperation from the state's governor, President Kennedy finally federalized the Mississippi National Guard to escort Meredith safely to campus in the fall of 1962 (Carson et al. 1987; Branch 1988)

Other key events also catapulted the injustice of racial segregation to the nation's attention. In Albany, Georgia, hundreds of protesters (including Martin Luther King Jr.) were arrested during a campaign lasting several months to desegregate buses and register Black voters. A campaign known as Freedom Rides started in 1961. The Freedom Rides brought Black and White riders who deliberately traveled together from northern states into the South to challenge segregated seating on the buses. During Freedom Summer of 1964 hundreds of volunteers, including White and Black students from the North, streamed into the South to work on voter registration campaigns (McAdam 1990, 1999).

Each of these and many other events kept the pressure on local municipalities and the federal government to enforce civil rights laws. Quite a few of the young people who participated and led this movement later became senior statespeople, including Representative John Lewis of Georgia, who was severely beaten on the Edmund Pettus Bridge in Selma, Alabama, when Alabama state troopers charged the crowd demonstrating for voting rights. Now known as "Bloody Sunday" because of the violence against peaceful protesters, this event was critical to the passage of the 1965 Voting Rights Act.

Many who lived through or are just learning about the events of the Civil Rights movement find the extreme violence that was served up by its opponents hard to fathom. There was a bomb blast that killed four young Black girls in Birmingham in 1963 while they were attending Sunday school. During Freedom Summer in 1964, three civil rights volunteers—James Cheney (Black), Michael Schwerner (White), and Andrew Goodman (White)—were brutally murdered while investigating a church bombing in Mississippi. In 1965 the Ku Klux Klan murdered Viola Liuzzo, another White ally, just after the famous march for voting rights from Selma to Montgomery. Countless lives were lost—children's as well as adults'—as people fought for the basic rights of citizenship.

Finally, it seemed such sacrifices had not been in vain when President Lyndon Johnson signed the **Civil Rights Act (1964)**. The law was enacted to "enforce the constitutional right to vote, to confer jurisdiction upon the district courts of the United States to provide injunctive relief against discrimination in public accommodations, to authorize the Attorney General to institute suits to protect constitutional rights in public facilities and public education, to extend the Commission on Civil Rights, to prevent discrimination in federally assisted programs, to establish a Commission on Equal Employment Opportunity, and for other purposes."

Even with the Civil Rights Act in place, local voting registrars continued to use any number of techniques to disqualify Black voters, such as literacy tests that were virtually impossible to pass. It took a second law, the **Voting Rights Act (1965)**, to prohibit such evasions. The Voting Rights Act states: "No voting qualification or prerequisite to voting, or standard, practice, or procedure shall be imposed or applied by any State or political subdivision to deny or abridge the right of any citizen of the United States to vote on account of race or color" (Pub. L. 88-352, 78 Stat. 241).

The major accomplishments of the Civil Rights movement were the dismantling of Jim Crow segregation and the assembly of an equal rights framework in the law. The movement also produced much change in the national consciousness, ushering in the belief in colorblindness. But this was not enough. Despite the progress the Civil Rights movement made, many of the major needs of the Black community remained unmet. Poverty was widespread in Black communities: In 1965, 42 percent of Black people were still poor, compared to over half in 1955. Activists argued that civil rights gave people the right to sit in restaurants, but they couldn't afford to eat out! Nor was poverty contained in the South, where the focus of the Civil Rights movement had been. In other parts of the country, Black people were still suffering the indignities of other forms of racism, as was soon to be revealed when many of the nation's cities outside the South erupted in riots.

Power to the People: The Movement's Radical Turn

Black people have never been monolithic in their political views, nor are they now (Hine 2004). From the very beginning of Black protest, different streams of thought were present. By the mid-1960s, many Black activists were frustrated by the lackluster response of the federal government to civil rights demands and the gradualism of change. There was also a growing awareness of inadequate attention to racism outside of the South. So, even as the original Civil Rights movement continued into the mid-1960s, a more radical approach was simmering.

The Student Nonviolent Coordinating Committee (SNCC, pronounced "snick") was one of the early organizations to question the civil rights approach, even while SNCC workers were deeply engaged within it. SNCC began informally when Black students organized the Greensboro sit-ins. As their work unfolded, SNCC activists worked in parts of the South usually considered by other civil rights organizers to be too dangerous or too hard to organize. But SNCC held to a philosophy of grassroots leadership: They would not impose the will of senior civil rights leaders on local residents, but would let leadership emerge from within local struggles. This way, people from the community would be able to sustain the movement when national organizations left (Carson 1981). This nonhierarchical style of organization later influenced other movements by other people of color as well as parts of the early women's movement, as we will see.

SNCC had initially adopted the nonviolent approach of other civil rights organizations, but during voter registration drives in the South, SNCC leaders became increasingly frustrated with the U.S. government's failure to more fully embrace and enforce civil rights goals. Some SNCC leaders thought that King was too willing to compromise with the White establishment. They also became suspicious of White liberals and raised questions about whether integration should be the major goal.

Over time, SNCC's leaders became more radical, demanding a more confrontational approach, and fractures developed within the Civil Rights movement. Some, such as Stokely Carmichael (who changed his name to Kwame Ture in 1969), declared the movement to be a revolution (Carson 1981), focusing less on civil rights and more on Black power. Even Martin Luther King, who is mostly remembered for his nonviolent-civil-disobedience strategy of civil rights, became more radical before his assassination in 1968, criticizing the U.S. role in the Vietnam War and focusing his actions on the economics of poverty (Branch 1988, 1998, 2006).

Whereas during the Civil Rights movement, the issue had been challenging racial segregation and the enemy was perceived as White southern racists, now the movement shifted from a focus on converting the attitudes of White people to criticizing the White power structure. SNCC also began to see the importance of organizing the poor, not just working for voting rights.[1] A new tone and direction for Black protest was emerging with a new target for change: institutional racism (Carmichael and Hamilton 1967).

At the time, society was changing faster than Black Americans were progressing. Even with civil rights protections increasingly in place, many Black people, both

---

[1] SNCC members wore blue denim coveralls to symbolize solidarity with the working class. Jeans have long since been co-opted by the fashion industry (and can be quite expensive!), and few know that they were initially inspired by SNCC's politics, as Tanisha Ford points out (2013).

rural and urban, were living in poverty. Fighting segregation in the South no longer seemed to be the only problem. Although the Black middle class was beginning to get a stronger foothold in U.S. institutions, many were unable to take advantage of the new civil rights protections to move themselves forward.

The more radical approach that was brewing within the movement came to a head in the summer of 1965 with the riot in the Watts neighborhood of Los Angeles. Precipitated by a traffic stop of a Black motorist by a White police officer, this incident fueled underlying tensions between the police and Black neighborhood residents. The Watts riot lasted six days, resulting in thirty-five deaths, more than four thousand arrests, and millions of dollars of destroyed property.

Watts was the first of many riots in cities throughout the mid-1960s. The riots highlighted that racism was not just a matter of individual conscience or prejudiced attitudes. Rather, they were interpreted as a strike against an entire system of racial injustice. "The system," as it was referred to, became deeply implicated in the ongoing presence of racism. As the Kerner Commission (established by President Johnson in 1967 to examine the causes of the urban riots) later concluded, "What white Americans have never fully understood, but what the Negro [sic] can never forget, is that white society is deeply implicated in the ghetto. White institutions created it, white institutions maintain it, and white society condones it" (Kerner Commission 1968:1).

Striking Back: Black Power and Black Pride

This new thinking turned a page in the history of Black protest and stirred political organizing within other communities of color. Whereas the Civil Rights movement sought equal treatment within society's institutions, the Black Power movement criticized those same institutions, calling for a complete overthrow of the existing power structure. Racial solidarity, not integration, was the rallying cry.

The Civil Rights movement had taught that racial injustice stemmed from White people's moral failures. The Black Power movement, on the other hand, targeted systematic and institutional racism, not just attitudinal change. Black Power leaders took their inspiration from Malcolm X, who had himself been influenced by the teachings of Elijah Muhammad and the Nation of Islam.

Malcolm X thought the Black people should throw off the chains of racism "by any means necessary," including violence if need be. His penetrating ideas spoke to the anger and frustration of Black people, especially those in poor urban areas. At times, Malcolm X argued that Black people should separate themselves from Whites so that they could be self-governing. Early on he referred to Whites as "devils," but later in his life, after traveling to Africa, he argued that Whites could become allies to Black people in their struggle for freedom.

Malcolm X was one of the first leaders to articulate a link between the struggles of African Americans and African nations. His radical ideas transformed the Black protest movement even while his radicalism brought numerous threats on his life. He was assassinated in 1965, but his speeches and his writing were widely influential, possibly even more so after his death. His autobiography, published posthumously in 1965, remains a classic, one of the most influential American autobiographies and required reading for many students.

The Black Power movement inspired a very different racial consciousness from what had come before. New meanings of "blackness" developed that were anchored

in Black pride. The slogan "black is beautiful" inspired the recognition and celebration of Black people's African roots. Growing one's hair naturally, celebrating
African arts and culture, and changing to an African-inspired mode of dress became
strong symbols of racial pride. Even what Black people called themselves changed
in the context of the Black Pride movement. No longer "Negroes," but African
Americans, Black people embraced "blackness" as a positive identity—one that was
self-generated and not imposed by White society. Black Americans also began to
see themselves as part of a **diaspora**, that is, the connection that Black people have
across the globe because of the interconnectedness of their experiences.

One of the most radical of the groups to emerge from the Black Power movement was the Black Panther Party. The Black Panthers constituted a militant group
that urged Black people to strike back at the White establishment. The Black
Panther Party's tactics were much more confrontational than those of most other
protest organizations. The Panthers thought that the nonviolence of the Civil Rights
movement did not serve Black people well. Instead, they argued that Black people
should arm themselves as protection from White brutality, especially from police
brutality, and urged Black people to create and abide by self-governed institutions.
The Black Panther Party's Ten-Point Program called for full employment, education,
housing, an end to police brutality, and the freeing of all incarcerated Black men,
among other demands.

As this more radical movement evolved, the political framework of change
analysis itself changed, and so did the response. The revolutionary approach of the
Black Panther Party was a much more aggressive and potentially violent assault on
dominant white institutions and was perceived as far more dangerous than previous movements. As racial protest gave way to Black Power, White people's support
also dissipated. Even more significantly, the federal government instigated a massive
wave of repression against radical Black activists and the Black Panther Party in
particular. A counterintelligence program called COINTELPRO infiltrated the Black
Panther Party and other radical groups. Ultimately, the Black Panther Party disin-
tegrated after the imprisonment and murder of many of its leaders (Nelson 2015).

Although short-lived and too radical for many, the Black Panther Party has had
a lasting impact on how people think about racism and how other groups have
formed protest movements. Not everyone supported the revolutionary zeal or
actions of the Black Panther Party, yet its influence and that of other parts of the
Black Power movement are still with us today. The Black Power framework produced the concept of *institutional racism* that undergirds much of the study of racism today and can be traced to thinkers like Malcolm X, whose work shaped the
philosophy of Black Power.

One of the greatest contributions of the Black Panther Party and the Black
Power movement more generally is the articulation of an understanding of the
structural roots of racism. Just as significantly, the Black Power movement changed
people's consciousness. Black people and other people of color created a strong
sense of racial solidarity that continues to influence how people self-identify, as we
will see in more detail below. Also, the Black Power movement's analysis of power
has led White people to have to confront the privilege that they hold by virtue of
the racial power structure. Although the revolution that the Black Power movement
advocated has certainly not occurred, the mind-set that the movement created still
informs thinking today.

The Many Faces of Racial Liberation

The Black Power movement had a unique influence on other people of color, who have organized around their own histories, identities, and socioeconomic locations in U.S. society. All racial-ethnic groups have had a long history of resisting their own oppression, but the Black Power movement gave new direction to resistance and "molded the consciousness" of people of color (Omatsu 2016:60).

Various other movements were inspired by Black Power. The anti–Vietnam War movement, student movements on college campuses, the feminist movement, and others heard the call issued by Black Power and developed similar analyses of their own relationship not just to institutional racism but to other forms of oppression (Escobar 1993). For example, the Gray Panthers, who obviously patterned their organization's name after the Black Panthers, developed an analysis of institutional ageism on a parallel with that of institutional racism.

Edward Escobar sums it up thus: "The Black Civil Rights Movement of the fifties and early sixties set the stage by focusing public attention on the issue of racial discrimination and legitimizing public protest as a way to combat discrimination. Native Americans, African Americans, Puerto Ricans, and Mexican Americans all took advantage of the favorable environment and developed broad-based social movements that demanded an end to racial discrimination. Women and gays, noting that they too had suffered from discrimination, also began agitating for equality. Movements launched by White college students and opponents of the Vietnam War also benefited from the general acceptance of protest" (1993:1486).

With regard to specific racial and ethnic groups, even though each one faced unique conditions and grievances, each was inspired by Black Power to articulate a new framework for understanding racial and ethnic oppression. People of color rejected what they saw as the assimilationist goals of the Civil Rights movement and forged a new identity and a political stance that emphasized collective empowerment.

The Native American assertion of Red Power is one example. Reflecting the political influence of the Black Power movement, Native Americans in the late 1960s argued that the takeover of their native lands by White colonizers and the genocide of their people linked all Native groups into a single political force. When Native Americans seized and occupied Alcatraz Island in 1969 (see chapter 5), they used arguments similar to those of the Black Power movement by insisting that the land they occupied on Alcatraz Island was theirs to reclaim.

The Black Power Movement also transformed the Chicano movement. Mexican American people had a long history of advocating for their civil rights (see LEARNING OUR PAST). Numerous organizations in the early part of the twentieth century advocated for Mexican American rights, but a new political and social identity for Mexican Americans developed under the influence of Black Power.

Many date the beginning of the Chicano movement to 1970 in East Los Angeles, when Mexican American people launched a massive demonstration—the largest they had ever mounted—to protest the disproportionately high number of Mexican Americans being killed in the Vietnam War. They created the term *Chicanismo* to affirm the ties of Mexican American people to their Mexican heritage and to emphasize their collective roots. Although *Chicano* had once been used as a derogatory term, reclaiming the word was both a mechanism for political organizing and an affirmation of cultural pride and heritage.

The Chicano movement for civil rights protested discrimination against Americans of Mexican descent. Depicted here is the end of a six-hundred-mile march from Calexico, California, to the California State Capitol in Sacramento in 1971.

LEARNING OUR PAST

Emilio Aguayo

Emilio Aguayo is a Chicano muralist in Washington State whose parents immigrated to the United States from Mexico in the 1920s. His narrative, collected as part of an oral history project at the University of Washington, details his family's experiences and also relates a classic example of immigrants' ambitions, hard work, and hopes for their children.

We're immigrants from Mexico . . . Dad crossed after working in the foundries in the railroads of northern Mexico and journeyed north. . . . He crossed into Colorado to work . . . with his uncles. Mother followed in a different way. She was separated at the death of her parents to go to live with her aunt and her family who had moved up to Colorado. My father [met my mother in Sedgwick]. . . . They were married for fifty years and eight days. . . . My father went to the eighth grade in Mexico, my mother to the fourth grade. They never had a chance for education.

Their story is the classic immigrant story, which was to go north to America where life would be better for the family. They wanted a better life and opportunity for education, which they stressed throughout their lives. . . . They always said that they would open the door to opportunity, which is education, and it was our job to push the door open and make the most of what we had.

We did farm work to augment the family income after my dad settled down and became a regular track hand for the Union Pacific in that area—a job in which he suffered discrimination because, first of all, the white section foreman told him that as long as he was foreman, he [my dad] would never be made permanent full-time as an employee, but when the man was on vacation, my dad made it. But he was still discriminated on because the man hated that he had to have him as a worker. My dad never made more than $400 a month on his salary as a track hand, but we had a large garden and cattle and pigs and chickens that augmented our semisubsistence way of living, and with that he also helped the older kids begin to go to college.

All six of us went to college, living up to my folks' American Dream that, even though they would never have an education, someday their kids would have a college education. . . .

My family was not farm workers full-time. . . . We did a lot of thinning, lot of row crop work. We did a lot of potato picking and things like that. And I remember those conditions . . . that are often romanticized as "Oh what a beautiful sunset" . . . sunrise or sunset. It's not so beautiful, it's not so romanticized when you have to go out there and do the hard, butt-busting work of picking mile-long rows of white Idaho and red russet and red Pontiac potatoes that we had to do to make extra money to make ends meet for the family. My mother also cleaned ducks and cleaned fish and took in laundry, and we did odd jobs. . . . When we wanted spending money, we mowed lawns and took care of people's lawns when they were on vacation and spaded gardens and collected hubcaps from cars off the side of the highway and empty beer bottles to sell for spending money, or sold fish. We hunted and fished in the river. And all those early beginnings bear witness to those teachings and those hard-work, working-class ethics that my parents had. Work hard and always do your best in school and get an education. Your school comes first.

Source: "Emilio Aguayo." N.d. Seattle Civil Rights and Labor History Project. (http://depts.washington.edu/civilr/ aguayo.htm.)

Likewise, Asian Americans developed a new political consciousness in the 1960s and 1970s, redefining what it meant to be Asian. A new *panethnic identity* linked the experiences of diverse Asian groups, including Japanese Americans, Chinese Americans, Korean Americans, and others (see chapter 4; Espiritu 1992). Asian Americans united around analyses of institutional oppression that paralleled the one generated by the Black Power leaders—Malcolm X and others—who had inspired them (Omatsu 2016; Louie and Omatsu 2001).

A signal event that demonstrated the new consciousness of people of color at the time was the student strike at San Francisco State University in 1968. A coalition of African American, Chicano, Asian American, and American Indian students organized the strike, which lasted for five months. The striking students demanded a new curriculum to include the history and works of people of color. They also demanded the creation of a Black Student Union, as well as more recruitment of faculty of color and more admission of students of color. Throughout college campuses in the 1960s and 1970s, students and faculty demanded more African American, Asian American, Chicano/a, and Native American Studies—curricular changes in higher education that students benefit from today in the form of ethnic and racial studies programs.

In each of these examples, rising racial consciousness and racial solidarity brought a new awareness of the connection between different experiences of racism and institutional power. People of color throughout the late 1960s and 1970s questioned how their experiences were linked and how white power influenced their situations. Even with their diverse identities, they began to define themselves as a political whole, and even the phrase *people of color* is used to emphasize groups' common experiences of institutional oppression (Omatsu 2016). Moreover, this new identity as people of color meant that racial and ethnic minorities within the United States began to see themselves as connected to the status of people of color across the globe.

The histories of these different movements show us that change takes many forms and is led by many different groups. Also, the most significant changes in race relations have occurred only because of the mobilization of people of color. What new movements will generate further social change? Will those movements work within existing institutions or against them? Do we need movements that are race-specific or more universal in their approach? These are the questions now before us.

Black Lives Matter

Contemporary movements for racial justice take some of their lessons from movements of earlier years, but they also emerge from and respond to contemporary conditions. An important example is the Black Lives Matter movement.

The Black Lives Matter movement was founded by Alicia Garza, a community activist in Oakland, California, following the 2012 acquittal of George Zimmerman. Zimmerman had been tried for shooting and killing Trayvon Martin, a seventeen-year-old Black man. After the acquittal, Garza posted what she called a "love letter to Black people" on Facebook. Upset about the disregard for and dehumanization of Trayvon Martin's life and Black people's lives in general, Garza said that she wanted to give her young son a less bleak view of Black people than that found in the mainstream media. She also wanted to give her son a sense of the possibilities that organizing Black people in a dignified way could bring (Cobb 2016). Garza was joined by her two friends, Patrisse Cullors and Opal Tometi. Cullors tweeted, "#BlackLivesMatter," and the movement was thus named.

The Black Lives Matter movement has spread through spontaneous actions throughout the nation—often, but not exclusively, on college campuses. Black Lives Matter is organized through an informally structured national network of chapters. Some Black Lives Matter actions are organized without national coordination,

Across the country, numerous groups have staged "die-ins" to protest mass incarceration and police shootings of Black and Hispanic people. Here, activists from Artists for Justice stage such a demonstration in Times Square, New York City.

because the movement relies on grassroots organizing and resists hierarchical leadership. Black Lives Matter uses similar tactics to the Civil Rights movement sit-ins by staging "die-ins" that protest police shootings and brutality against Black people. The movement sees police brutality against Black people as stemming from structural racism.

Similar to the Black Panther Party, Black Lives Matter has also adopted a ten-point program, called "Campaign Zero," to end police brutality and the militarization of the police.

You can see the influence of previous movements on the Black Lives Matter movement, but there is also a big difference. Like earlier movements, Black Lives Matter asserts that anti-Black racism permeates society and affirms the value and dignity of Black people's lives. Going beyond earlier movements, however, the Black Lives Matter movement specifically embraces queer, transgender, disabled, undocumented, and *all* Black people (see http://blacklivesmatter.com). This inclusive perspective is not intended to dilute attention to the value of Black people's lives. Rather, it is a very inclusive call for liberation.

As the Black Lives Matter movement has captured national attention, some have responded by claiming, "All lives matter." Although this expression may seem well intended, movement activists argue that such claims diminish the specific value of Black lives, therefore reinforcing colorblind racism. As one commentator has asked, "Whose color gets erased when we go blind?" (Cauce 2016). The point of Black Lives Matter is to strongly and intentionally value the lives of all Black people.

While the intent is not to diminish or devalue the lives of others, Black Lives Matter asserts the importance of explicitly and consciously valuing Black people—in all their diversity. Black Lives Matter and the response to it point to a fundamental tension in contemporary programs for change: Is colorblindness the best path to racial justice or are race-specific plans needed?

Colorblind or Color-Conscious? Frameworks for Change

There are many lessons learned from the racial protest movements of earlier years and those that are forming now. First is simply an understanding of what **activism** means. Many people tend to think that a single leader or single type of action is what guides social change. Activism, though, takes different forms and is defined by the "multiple ideas, concepts, strategies, and ideologies that [people use] to guide, organize, and direct civil rights and social justice struggles" (Behnken 2016:3).

The historical record teaches us that the struggle for racial justice involves multiple groups who take different approaches to effect change. Sometimes change comes in local settings; other times, it is on the national stage. People sometimes organize for change under some of the worst conditions imaginable. Even in such conditions, people use whatever resources they can to advocate for their rights.

Communication networks are also critical for social protest, but they often come through outlets alternative to the mainstream media. Historically, for example, the African American press played a significant role in civil rights organizing. Now, social media are an effective tool for organizing, as we have witnessed in the many demonstrations around the nation that emerged in response to the election of Donald Trump as president of the United States, including the millions of people around the world who demonstrated in the Women's March on the day following Trump's inauguration.

Coalitions are also important in racial justice movements, although they can be fragile—especially across racial and ethnic lines. There has, for example, often been an uneasy alliance between people of color and Whites (Carson et al. 1987), but White allies are needed in the struggle for racial justice. At this writing, whether the many different groups who feel demeaned by the Trump administration will be able to form a coalition of activist groups for racial and other forms of social justice remains to be seen. The fight for racial justice sometimes means working within existing institutions to effect change. Other times demonstrations and protests that are critical of dominant institutions are important. Different approaches are needed, because the goals of racial justice are many and cannot be reached through single or unidimensional solutions. It is impossible to detail all the approaches that have been taken to address our nation's racial inequality, but four basic frameworks of change are highlighted below.

Civil Rights and the Law

As the result of the activism of many people working for racial justice, a legal framework is now in place in the United States that, at least in principle, provides equality under the law. This framework started with the **Fourteenth Amendment to the U.S.**

Constitution, passed in 1868, granting *equal protection* under the law. Specifically, the Fourteenth Amendment states: "No state shall make or enforce any law which shall abridge the privileges or immunities of citizens of the United States; nor shall any state deprive any person of life, liberty, or property, without due process of law; nor deny to any person within its jurisdiction the equal protection of the laws." The Civil Rights Act of 1964 further cemented these rights by outlawing discrimination based on race, color, religion, sex, or national origin.

Many groups can thank the Black protest movement for the activism that ultimately resulted in the civil rights bill. Since its passage, this law has been interpreted as also protecting the rights of the aged and people who have disabilities. It has also been interpreted as protecting the rights of pregnant women who, for example, cannot be terminated from employment simply because of pregnancy—a practice that was common before passage of this law. LGBTQ rights have also been extended based on the meaning of the Fourteenth Amendment and the Civil Rights Act of 1964, as have the rights of religious minorities. The Civil Rights Act created the Equal Employment Opportunity Commission, which enforces federal laws that outlaw employment discrimination and protect people who file claims against retaliation by employers.

Civil rights laws are founded in *colorblind* values, which are now widely shared within the U.S. public. For instance, a majority of the U.S. public now think that it is very important for the government to treat everyone equally (General Social Survey 2016). Indeed, it is no longer socially acceptable in most places to identify oneself as a racist, so much so that large numbers of White Americans claim that they "do not see race" (Wingfield 2015). This does not mean that racism, even overtly expressed, has disappeared. Quite the contrary, as witnessed in the rise of white supremacist groups and hate crimes, especially against American Muslims following Donald Trump's election to the presidency.

Nonetheless, civil rights are a bedrock of U.S. cultural values and social policy. But are these protections enough? In principle, the Civil Rights concept means that people participate equally in society's benefits—access to jobs, education, and the right to vote—but we know this has not been achieved. Having civil rights laws on the books is one thing; realizing their promise is another.

What is more, civil rights protections require constant vigilance. In recent years, many of the rights won as the result of the Civil Rights movement have been chipped away. The Voting Rights Act, for example, lost much of its power when the Supreme Court invalidated some of its major provisions in 2013. New voter identification laws, changes in voting procedures, and various redistricting plans that states have enacted are also disenfranchising many, especially African Americans.

In sum, the civil rights framework is an important part of the move toward racial justice, but it is not enough. Civil rights laws protect individual rights, but do not necessarily transform the social and economic standing of racial and ethnic groups. Guaranteeing equal rights also does little, if anything, to reduce the poverty that is all too high among the nation's racial-ethnic minorities. Civil rights laws do not change the underlying social structural practices and patterns that continue to exclude people of color from jobs, education, good health care, and other rights. The colorblind framework of civil rights may be embraced by most, but it is not changing the status of many.

Affirmative Action

Affirmative action is the practice of remedying past discrimination by using race-conscious measures to recruit and admit racial-ethnic minorities to positions in employment and education. Affirmative action is a strategy for change that has been very effective at enhancing access to jobs and education for underrepresented groups. Because affirmative action is a race-conscious method of addressing racial inequality, it has been both controversial and misunderstood. Many myths also surround affirmative action policies and practices, so it is important to understand the background of this strategy for change.

Affirmative action can be dated as far back as 1965 when President Lyndon Johnson required all federal contractors to file plans for hiring minority employees. It was enhanced in 1969 by President Richard Nixon, who added the requirement that federal employers had to file goals and timetables for hiring minority employees. Nixon also added women as a protected class to be included in affirmative action plans. As a result, not only have many African American, Latino, Asian American, and Native American people benefitted from affirmative action, but White women have as well.

Affirmative action requires employers and higher education institutions to make extra efforts to recruit and hire women and people of color or, in the case of colleges, to admit more students of color. Employers have to demonstrate the efforts they take to ensure fairness and to target minority applicants for jobs. Prior to affirmative action it was perfectly legal to hire people without any advertisement or outreach to previously excluded groups. In higher education, federally supported institutions also have to file plans for diversifying their student body.

The first major legal challenge to affirmative action came in 1978 in the case *Regents of the University of California v. Bakke* (pronounced "BOCK-ee"). Allan Bakke was a White male who was denied admission when he applied to the University of California–Davis Medical School. At the time, the medical school had a "set aside" program, under which they reserved sixteen of their one hundred admission slots for minority applicants. Bakke sued and took his case all the way to the U.S. Supreme Court. In 1978, using the equal protection clause of the Fourteenth Amendment, the Supreme Court ruled that the campus *could not* use quotas when admitting students to medical school, but they *could* take race into account when reviewing medical applicants. In other words, race could be considered as part of an applicant's file, but quotas were unconstitutional. As of 2017 the *Bakke* decision remains the law of the land. It has been challenged a number of times, but upheld to date.

The *Bakke* decision was also upheld in a second important case involving affirmative action, *Grutter v. Bollinger*, decided in 2003. Barbara Grutter was a White woman who sued the University of Michigan Law School for not admitting her. This is a complex case, but ultimately the Supreme Court upheld the *Bakke* decision, stating that diversity in education was a *compelling state interest*. The Court ruling was based in part on social science evidence showing that all students actually learn more when they are being educated in more diverse settings. As in the *Bakke* decision, in *Grutter* the Supreme Court ruled that universities could take race in account along with other factors when making admissions decisions.

Despite the controversies surrounding affirmative action, a majority of the public supports it, although they are somewhat more likely to do so when it is applied to women than to race: 67 percent of the public support affirmative action programs for women; 58 percent, for racial minorities (Riffkin 2015).

Affirmative action programs have benefitted both White women and people of color. Its benefits, however, only accrue to those who are already well positioned to take advantage of employment and educational opportunities. Despite myths that unqualified minorities take jobs from White men under affirmative action plans, the fact is that people must be qualified for the positions they seek. In this regard, affirmative action programs have been most effective in opening access to educated and well-trained people, but they do little to alleviate poverty and other forms of inequality that are part of the system of racial stratification. Other programs are needed to accomplish that.

Antipoverty Programs

Neither civil rights nor affirmative action programs provide a solution to the poverty that permeates U.S. society, hence the need for a third approach: antipoverty policy. Job training and job creation programs that can address the massive unemployment that has produced such a large underclass are also needed.

Consider plans to raise the minimum wage as an example. People working at the lowest minimum wage standards cannot get out of poverty even by working full-time and year-round (see chapter 7). Raising the minimum wage helps, but even at a minimum wage of fifteen dollars per hour, people would barely live above the poverty line without a second income or a second job. Living wage campaigns have called attention to this problem, and some progress is being made, but there is a long way to go.

Besides, raising the minimum wage only helps those who are already working. Job training and job creation programs are critically needed for giving people the credentials to compete in an increasingly technology-based economy.

Antipoverty and job creation policies have been increasingly difficult to sustain, however, as so much of the general public is quite hostile to so-called entitlement programs. Relative to other industrialized Western nations, the United States is quite meager in its social support programs, reflecting the cultural belief in success based on individual merit. As you have seen throughout this book, though, social structures of racial inequality harm people's ability to get ahead. Without programs to lift people out of poverty, the nation will continue to face all of the problems that poverty creates. Some suggest that if we were to develop universalistic antipoverty and job creation programs instead of ones that are race-specific, political support for such programs would be more likely (Wilson 1987).

The Diversity Agenda

A fourth approach—one that has grown in its influence in recent years—is the diversity agenda. The diversity agenda refers to the variety of programs and plans that are intended to make organizations (such as workplaces and schools) more inclusive and welcoming of various groups of people. Diversity is an all-inclusive concept, referring to racial and ethnic diversity, but also including, for example, women, LGBTQ individuals, people with disabilities, and religious minorities. As the United States becomes more diverse, more people (including leaders of organizations) are recognizing how much the nation is changing, and they are developing diversity plans within organizations to address this change.

Research shows that embracing diversity has positive outcomes for the goals of a given group. As indicated in the *Grutter* case, research has shown that students learn more in more diverse settings. This does not just apply to people of color: White students also learn more when their school and its curriculum include diverse people with different experiences and perspectives (Gurin, Dey, and Hurtado 2002). In companies, having more diverse working groups has been shown to increase market size, sales, and company profits (Herring 2009). Having more diversity in groups tends to stimulate innovation and prevent people from falling into a singular or preestablished mind-set (Page 2007).

The diversity agenda prompts organizations to require training and educational seminars to reduce the *implicit bias* that we know people hold (see chapter 2). Those biases can be based on race, ethnicity, or any number of other social characteristics. Diversity workshops then attempt to reduce such bias, noting that because racism is learned, it can be "unlearned." Such work points to the importance of education in changing the information that people have about each other.

The limitation of the diversity framework is that it does not change the fundamental institutional structures that generate bias and inequality to begin with. As such, it can become what sociologists Joyce Bell and Douglass Hartmann (2007) call "happy talk." Diversity happy talk is that which celebrates and recognizes difference but does little to challenge the systemic inequality of white privilege (Andersen 1999, 2003).

You can see the challenge of diversity work in figure 12.1. Most people, White, Black, and Hispanic, think at least something more needs to be done to achieve racial inequality, but there is a significant gap between Whites and both Black and Hispanic respondents to this question. Additionally, as figure 12.2 shows, a

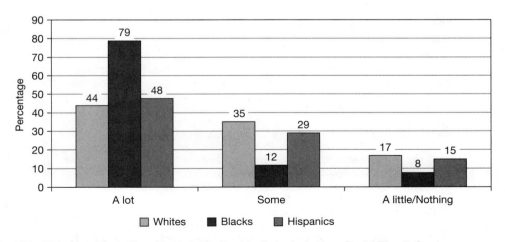

FIG. 12.1 How Much More Needs to Be Done in Order to Achieve Racial Equality?

Source: Pew Research Social and Demographic Trends. 2013. "King's Dream Remains an Elusive Goal: Many Americans See Racial Disparities," August 22. (http://www.pewsocialtrends.org/2013/08/22/kings-dream-remains-an-elusive-goal-many-americans-see-racial-disparities/.)

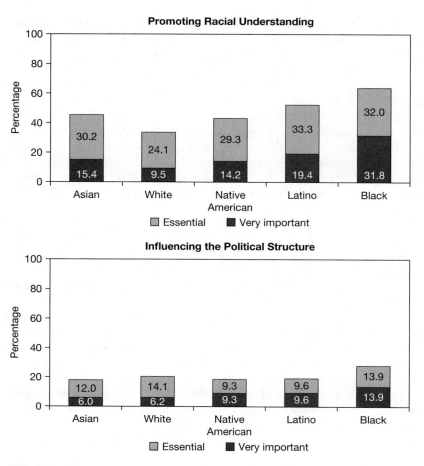

FIG. 12.2 Promoting Racial Change: Students' Perspectives

Each year the Higher Education Research Institute at the University of California–Los Angeles administers a survey to all incoming first-year students in the nation. The results allow people to gauge the attitudes of first-year students each year and how they change over time. The charts above show how the entering class of 2015 responded to questions about their personal engagement in changing race relations. As you can see, significant numbers of students thought it was important (essential or very important) to personally help promote racial understanding. A significant number also thought it was personally important to promote change in the political structure, although fewer thought this than thought that promoting understanding was important. Although you cannot see this in the graphs above, there was also a significant change from previous years in the percentage of students who thought both of these things were important, although change was greatest for Black and Latino students.

What differences do you see looking at different racial-ethnic groups' responses to these questions? What social conditions have produced the changes toward greater personal engagement that this survey has uncovered?

Source: Higher Education Research Institute. 2016. *The American Freshman: National Norms for 2015.* Los Angeles: University of California. (http://heri.ucla.edu/monographs/TheAmericanFreshman2015.pdf.)

TABLE 12.1 Race and Social Change: Frameworks for Change

	Civil Rights	Affirmative Action	Employment/ Antipoverty Policy	Antiracism; Awareness; Diversity
Focus:	Equal rights; antidiscrimination	Improvement of opportunity structures	Job creation; raising minimum wage; public assistance	Attitudinal change; education
Implementation:	Law and social policy	Employment and educational policy	Social policy; antipoverty measures; living wage campaigns	Diversity training; unlearning racism; reducing implicit bias
Who benefits:	People of color; white women; LGBTQ people; disabled people; age groups; religious minorities	Middle-class and elite people of color; White women	Poor and working-class people of color; White poor and working class	Corporations; educational institutions; non-profit organizations; individual minds
Limitations/ criticisms:	De facto segregation persists; does not address economic inequality	Does not address poverty; generates backlash	Does not address noneconomic forms of racism	Change is attitudinal, not institutional

significant number of entering college students say that promoting racial understanding is important, but fewer want to challenge the political structures that are part of racial inequality.

The problem is that change cannot be solely attitudinal. Changing attitudes and educating oneself and others are certainly necessary if we are to understand and transform the racial inequality that besets us. But, as you have seen throughout this book, attitudinal change is not enough—institutional change is essential.

Much has changed in the U.S. system of racial inequality. In many ways, people of color have opportunities now that are much better than before, but much more still needs to be done. You can see that not a single framework detailed above guides actions for social change (see table 12.1). Do we need colorblind or race-conscious strategies for change? The successes of the past tell us that both are needed. The problems associated with racism are many, and no single approach for social change is adequate in and of itself. All of them are necessary.

The New Multicultural/Multiracial Society: Where Are We Going?

As the United States becomes more diverse in its racial-ethnic composition, new questions about the future of race and ethnicity have emerged—and will continue to evolve. With a more diverse population and more people identifying as multiracial, will the meaning of race change? Given that race is a social construction, most likely. If so, will racism diminish or simply take new forms? These questions guide some of the discussion about the future of race and ethnicity in society.

The color line in the United States has historically been drawn around the division between black and white. That color line, though, formed when African Americans were the nation's largest racial minority group. Now Latinos have surpassed Black Americans as a proportion of the population (Latinos constitute 17 percent, and Black Americans 13 percent). Latinos and Asians are also expected to continue growing—with the Latino population expected to double by 2050 and the Asian population increasing by 79 percent by the same time. The White American population is expected to decline by about 6 percent by 2050 (Ortman and Guarneri 2016).

The color line is also being blurred by immigration, higher rates of racial-ethnic intermarriage, and an increase in the number of those who identify as multiracial, especially among young people (Bean and Lee 2009; Bean et al. 2009; Lee and Bean 2007, 2012). The old black-white binary that has historically defined race in the United States is no longer as sharp as it once was.

How will these major changes affect our ideas about race? Will they eradicate or blur racial boundaries? Who will be assimilated into the privileges of society? Who will be at the top and the bottom, and what will the "middle" look like?

Sociologist Eduardo Bonilla-Silva has suggested that the United States may evolve into a **tri-partite society,** that is, one that still divides people into black and white categories, but where there is a middle category that he calls "honorary whites" (2004). This would be a system of racial stratification that is more like that of Latin American and some Caribbean nations. How does he explain this?

Bonilla-Silva argues that those on the nonwhite side of the color line have shared experiences of oppression and exploitation. They have also been racialized as "black" or, in some cases, "brown." The post–civil rights era, though, has brought changes in the system of racial and ethnic inequality. Bonilla-Silva, therefore, classifies the black/brown category as "collective black."

The white category includes non-Hispanic White people but also new White immigrants, totally assimilated White Latinos, and light-skinned multiracial people. The intermediate group of "honorary whites" would include light-skinned Latinos, such as Cubans and some segments of Mexican and Puerto Rican communities, plus various Asian American groups (e.g., Chinese Americans, Korean Americans, Japanese Americans, Filipino Americans), most multiracial people, and Middle Easterners. At the bottom of this stratified system will be the "collective black," including Vietnamese, Hmong, and other Southeast Asian American groups who have low social and economic status, dark-skinned Latinos, Black Americans, new West Indian and African immigrants, and those he calls reservation-bound Native Americans (Bonilla-Silva 2004; Bonilla-Silva and Glover 2004).

At the core of this triracial system remains the fact of white supremacy. Groups who would fall into the category of white or honorary white do so mainly based on social class but also on skin tone. Bonilla-Silva argues that because of the dominance of colorblind racism, a tri-partite system of racial inequality appears to be "kinder and gentler" but is nonetheless still anchored in the dominance of White people. Whether Bonilla-Silva's projections become fact remains to be seen, but you can see evidence of this system of racial inequality emerging now. Many Asian Americans have equaled or surpassed White, non-Hispanic Americans in socioeconomic status. Certainly some middle-class and elite people of color have been highly successful, in some cases even surpassing working-class and poor Whites who see themselves as increasingly left behind. Some Latinos, depending on their national origin and social class, already define themselves as White (Forman, Goar, and Lewis 2004).

Many put their hopes in the changing perspectives and experiences of the millennial generation (those born from 1981 to about 2000). The millennial generation is the most diverse generation to date on a number of characteristics and they are thought to be more tolerant and less racist than previous generation. Is this true? Millennials, as you can see in figure 12.3, are far more accepting of interracial relationships, such as marriage between people of different racial-ethnic backgrounds, so on a personal level, they are more accepting than perhaps their parents' or grandparents' generation. But on other issues involving racial inequality, such as perceiving Black Americans as less motivated to do well, millennials are not much better than previous generations (Taylor and Keeter 2010).

Even with a more complex system of racial hierarchy, race still matters. As Jennifer Lee and Frank Bean conclude, based on the demographic and socioeconomic status of diverse groups, "Despite the increased diversity [in U.S. society], race is not declining in significance, nor is the color line disappearing" (2007:433). Group boundaries may not be as sharp as they once were, but racism is still enduring. What race and ethnicity become in the future remains to be seen, but the past shows us how, even with evolving constructions of race, race still matters—and matters a lot—in U.S. society (West 1994).

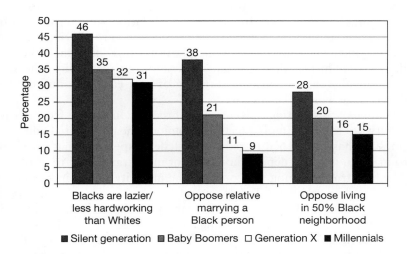

FIG. 12.3 Generational Change in White Attitudes

The "Silent Generation" includes those born between 1928 and 1945; Baby Boomers are those born between 1946 and 1964; Generation X includes those born between 1965 and 1980; Millennials are those born between 1981 and approximately 2000.

Sources: General Social Survey. 2015. Chicago: National Opinion Research Center at the University of Chicago. (http://www.gss.norc.org.); Clement, Scott. 2015. "Millennials Are Just as Racist as Their Parents." *Washington Post*, June 23.

Conclusion

It is easy to become overwhelmed by the magnitude of our nation's racial problems. It would be naïve not to take a fairly dim, perhaps pessimistic, view of the possibilities for change, but it is equally important to maintain hope. Change has indeed happened and more is possible (Killian 1971). As this chapter has shown, over the course of history the long march to racial justice has come through the actions and leadership of ordinary people, some of whom rose to prominence. Others worked more quietly, but diligently, on the ground, organizing what has in fact been a revolution in the nature of racial inequality—but an incomplete one (Killian 1968).

More than one-third of Americans now say they are worried about race relations in the United States, including half of Black Americans and one-quarter of Whites. (This survey did not include Latinos or Asian Americans.) This is a large increase even since 2014, when only 19 percent of Whites said so (Norman 2016). No doubt, media attention to shootings, threats to deport vast numbers of undocumented workers, calls to require Muslim Americans to register on a national database, the Black Lives Matter movement, and the rise of white supremacist hate crimes have shown that racism persists and is perhaps not even as subtle as people were starting to believe.

Furthermore, many of the conditions that ignited earlier protests still remain. High rates of poverty still exist not just among Black Americans, but also among Latinos, Puerto Ricans, Native Americans, some Asian Americans, and many Whites, who are, after all, the majority of the poor. High rates of unemployment, urban blight, and police brutality against people of color are all too common. While much change has occurred since the early days of civil rights, much remains to be done.

Some things are fairly certain: The U.S. population will continue to become more diverse. The public will continue to debate policies to alleviate race and ethnic inequality, including immigration policy, health care, educational access, income inequality, environmental degradation, and crime control, among others. If these topics do not fully engage an understanding of how each is connected to racial inequality, change will not be effective.

At the time of this writing, it is not clear if the nation has the federal leadership to move forward toward a more racially just union. The presidential administration begun in 2017 has threatened to reduce the federal spending that provides assistance to many in need, to deport thousands of immigrants, and to effectively ban many Muslims from entering the country. The majority of Cabinet appointments are strikingly White and male. Trump has referred to Mexican Americans as "rapists" and "criminals" and to African Americans as "living in hell." During his campaign, Trump claimed that a judge hearing a case against him could not be unbiased *because of* the judge's Mexican heritage. Trump also led the "birther" movement, claiming that former president Barack Obama was not American born. Trump's pledge to "make America great again" has seemed to many like a throwback to our troubled past when whiteness reigned, as if the movement, which Trump proclaimed to be under way, is really about making America "White again" (Blow 2014).

Yet, the history of racial protest shows us that change does not come from above. Change comes from the efforts of people who challenge existing practices and social institutions and who use education and changes in consciousness to achieve their goals. It also comes from alliances, no matter how fragile, between

White people and people of color, when White people are equipped to develop both the knowledge and the empathy to be good allies.

Among many pockets of the population, there is a clear desire to do something about racial inequality. People just do not always know how to get started. Ignoring race is clearly not the answer. This chapter's opening epigraph presents a challenge from Supreme Court Justice Harry Blackmun to a public that wants a colorblind society but does not know how to get there. Blackmun wrote the lines in his dissent in the *Bakke* case, "In order to get beyond racism, we must first take account of race. There is no other way. And in order to treat some persons equally, we must treat them differently."

Key Terms

activism, 293

affirmative action, 295

Civil Rights Act (1964), 284

diaspora, 287

Fourteenth Amendment to the U.S. Constitution (1868), 276

Grutter v. Bollinger, 295

nonviolent civil disobedience, 282

Regents of the University of California v. Bakke, 295

tri-partite society, 300

Voting Rights Act (1965), 284

Critical Thinking Questions

1. How would you compare the nonviolent civil disobedience tactic of the Civil Rights movement to the contemporary Black Lives Matter movement? Note ways that these movements are both similar and different.
2. If you could do just one thing to reduce racial inequality in the United States, what would you do and why?

Student Exercises

12.1: Identify a person who would have lived through the period of civil rights organizing. Interview the person and ask about his or her memories of that period. How did their race, social class, level of education, and region of residence at the time influence their connection to or recollections of this movement?

12.2: Watch one of the twelve episodes of the *Eyes on the Prize* video series (available via streaming and possibly in your school library). After watching, write a short essay detailing what you learned from this period of history. How have things changed since?

Challenging Question/Open to Debate

With increased racial and ethnic diversity in the U.S. population, will we create a society that is more racially tolerant and inclusive, or less so?

Glossary

acculturation process by which immigrant groups adopt the language, dress, values, and norms of the host society

achievement gap racial differences in educational opportunity, learning, and achievement

activism ideas, concepts, strategies, and ideologies that guide social change

affirmative action practice of remedying past discrimination using race-conscious measures

Affordable Care Act (ACA) policy adopted in 2010 that provided a system of health insurance exchanges and that brought health insurance to more people in the United States than ever before

anti-Semitism hatred and disparagement of Jewish people

assimilation process by which ethnic groups are incorporated into the dominant culture

assimilation model a theoretical perspective analyzing the process by which immigrant groups become integrated into host society

audit studies experiments that use actors and/or other simulations to reveal when discrimination occurs

authoritarian personality characterized by having little tolerance for difference, being rigid in judgments of others, and being highly obedient to authority

aversive racism subtle form of prejudice guided by unconscious beliefs about the inferiority of racial-ethnic groups

***bracero* program** formal agreement initiated in 1942 between the United States and Mexico that permitted Mexican citizens to work in the United States for temporary, renewable periods

***Brown v. Board of Education* (1954)** Supreme Court decision that ruled school segregation in public facilities, including schools, unconstitutional

capitalism economic system based on the pursuit of profit and private ownership

carceral state society where security spreads everywhere as a mechanism for social control of the population

care work labor that people do to sustain life, such as childcare, cleaning, and cooking

chattel system wherein human beings are the property of others for a lifetime

Chinese Exclusion Act (1882) law denying the entry of Chinese laborers to the United States

Civil Rights Act (1964) law banning discrimination in employment and creating the Equal Employment Opportunity Commission

class system of inequality by which groups have different access to economic, social, and political resources

colorblind racism idea that it is best to just ignore race and to look at people as if they are all alike

colorism discriminatory treatment of people based on gradations of skin color

concentrated poverty said to occur when 40 percent or more of a given census area fall below the federal poverty line

content analysis method of research that systematically documents the images in various cultural artifacts

controlling image image that restricts ideas about people, particularly people of color

crime index measure of crimes that includes murder/non-negligent manslaughter, rape, robbery, aggravated assault, burglary, larceny/theft, and motor vehicle theft

critical race theory viewpoint that the media and popular culture reflect and re-create hierarchical systems of race, class, and gender in society

cultural appropriation process by which privileged groups consume and "claim" the culture of an oppressed or colonized group

cultural capital noneconomic assets—knowledge and resources—that advantaged groups get by virtue of their location in society

cultural competence ability to both recognize and understand cultural differences

cultural hegemony pervasive and excessive influence of one culture throughout society

cultural production process by which cultural images and ideas are made

cultural racism images and ideas that presume the superiority of Whites and inferiority of people of color

culture beliefs and practices that orient people to their society

culture of affirmation beliefs that provide groups with a positive identity

culture of resistance beliefs that people create explicitly to challenge controlling images in the dominant culture

death rate calculation of the number of deaths in a given population, relative to the population size, in a given period of time

deep poverty living on less than three thousand dollars a year

deindustrialization shift away from a manufacturing-based economy to a service-based economy

demographic change population change, including change in the characteristics of a given population

diaspora connection that people of color have across the globe because of the interconnectedness of their experiences

discrimination behavior that treats groups differently because of a presumed characteristic

dominant culture culture associated with the most powerful group in society

economic restructuring socioeconomic changes that are altering patterns of employment, including deindustrialization, technological change, globalization, and demographic change

environmental justice principle that all people and communities are entitled to equal protection in the environment and public health

environmental racism pattern by which racial-ethnic minorities are disproportionately exposed to environmental hazards

ethnic enclaves niches where there is a clustering of particular immigrant groups in a given occupation or industry

ethnic group identifiable group of people who share a common culture, language, regional origin, and/or religion

ethnocentrism the belief that one's group is superior to all other groups

eugenics practices that purport to improve the human race by controlling the reproduction of people deemed to be "inferior" or genetically compromised

Fair Housing Act (1968) federal law prohibiting discrimination in housing

familism pattern among Latinos of a very strong attachment to family

family household census unit that includes at least two members related by birth, marriage, or adoption

fictive kin those who are part of an extended family network, even if not biologically related

Fourteenth Amendment to the U.S. Constitution (1868) constitutional decision granting *equal protection* under the law

genocide international crime that destroys, in whole or part, a national, ethnic, racial, or religious group

genotype full set of genes found in a given organism

Gentleman's Agreement (1907) agreement between the United States and Japan that barred further entry of Japanese laborers

Gini coefficient measure of income distribution in a given group or society, ranging from zero to one

globalization increasing economic linkage between different nations

Great Migration movement of large numbers of African Americans to northern and midwestern cities beginning in the early twentieth century and lasting for almost six decades

Grutter v. Bollinger (2003) Supreme Court decision upholding the right of universities to consider race along with other factors in admissions decisions

Hart-Celler Act (1965) federal immigration law eliminating the national origins quota created by the Immigration Law of 1924 and giving priority to family reunification and occupational skill as criteria for entry to the United States

hate crime characterized by evidence of prejudice based on race, religion, sexual orientation, ethnicity, disability, gender, or gender identity

household everyone living in a residential unit

householder person who owns or rents a residential unit

human capital individual characteristics of workers, such as education, skills, prior experience, age, and marital status

hypercriminalization process by which an individual's behaviors become treated as risk, threat, or crime

hypersegregation occurs when nearly all of the residents of a given area are of the same group

hypertension condition of elevated blood pressure

hypodescent *see* one drop rule

identity person's self-conception

identity contingency something to be dealt with that derives from one's identity

identity matrix configuration of social factors that constitute one's definition of self

identity work process by which people construct and maintain positive identities

ideology constellation of beliefs that purport to justify and defend the status quo

implicit bias unconscious, negative associations held against particular groups

income money brought into a household over a given period from various sources, such as earnings

index of dissimilarity measure of the extent to which two groups are distributed across a given place

Indian Removal Act (1830) federal law mandating the removal of all Indian groups to the area identified as Indian Territory

infant mortality number of infant deaths in a given year per 1,000 births

information technology revolution process by which information technology permeates society

institutional racism seemingly sanctioned pattern of racial advantage and disadvantage

intersectional theory analyses that examine the connections between different social factors, especially class, race, gender, and sexuality

labeling theory analysis suggesting that once a person or group is identified a particular way, the label sticks

laissez-faire racism tendency for White people to minimize the effects of racism and do nothing about it

life expectancy average number of years people born in a particular year can expect to live

mass incarceration pattern by which inordinately large numbers of people of color are imprisoned

mass media channels of communication that transmit information to a wide segment of the population

matriarchy society in which women hold power

median income income level at which half the population has higher income, and half, lower

meritocracy system whereby people are hierarchically arranged solely based on their achievements

microaggressions commonplace verbal or behavioral instances that communicate insults toward people of color

minority group group with less power than a dominant group

National Crime Victimization Survey annual survey of the United States that provides information about violent nonfatal and property crimes

National Origins Act (1924) federal law that restricted the entry of new immigrants to 2 percent of the total number of people of each nationality that had been in the United States in 1890

nativism ideology that promotes the interests of people already living within a given nation

nonfamily household census unit where persons are living alone or where nonrelatives share a residential unit

nonviolent civil disobedience philosophy and practice of disrupting patterns of segregation by refusing to obey laws, customs, and norms

objectification process of treating a human being as an object or thing

occupational segregation pattern by which different groups of people are niched into certain occupations based on characteristics such as race, gender, or age

one drop rule practice wherein a certain amount of presumed "black blood" legally defined someone as Black

othermothers women who raise children other than their own

panethnicity collective identity formed when multiple ethnic groups forge a sense of shared belonging

paper sons pattern whereby many Chinese men were claimed as sons when official records had been destroyed by fire

phenotype sum total of observable physical characteristics, including those influenced by environmental factors

picture brides Asian women in marriages arranged by a broker

***Plessy v. Ferguson* (1896)** Supreme Court decision that allowed the practice of "separate but equal"

political economy linkage between power and economic systems

popular culture beliefs, ideas, images, and objects that are part of everyday life

poverty line official measure of poverty based on a 1930s calculation of the cost of a basic food budget, multiplied by three and adjusted for the cost of living

predatory lending practice of financing very high-risk loans with little review of people's ability to pay

prejudice negative attitude toward a person or group based on their presumed characteristics

race group treated as distinct in society based on presumed characteristics that have been interpreted as signifying inferiority or superiority

race-immigration nexus linkage between immigration and race, specifically how social institutions, ideology, and social practices regarding immigration reinforce racial ideas

racial division of labor organization of different tasks as based on race

racial formation process by which racial categories are created, inhabited, transformed, and/or destroyed

racial frames scripts that frame how we see ourselves and others through the lens of race

racial identity sense one has of oneself as belonging to a racial group

racial profiling practice of using race as a criterion for detaining someone on suspicion of having committed a crime

racial stratification hierarchical arrangement in society by which different racial groups have different access to economic and social resources, power, and perceived social worth

racial tax extra burden that people of color experience in living with racism

racialization process by which a group comes to be defined as a race

racism belief system that purports to justify racial inequality

redlining practice of rating different residential areas in terms of their worthiness for mortgage lending based on race

Regents of the University of California v. Bakke (1978) Supreme Court decision that colleges cannot use quotas in college admissions but can take race into account

reproductive labor work people do to maintain and reproduce the labor force

reproductive politics linkage between systems of power and intimate matters such as birth control, abortion, and pregnancy

residential segregation pattern by which different racial and ethnic groups live apart from one another

sedimentation of racial inequality structural disadvantages that have historically emerged to produce racial disadvantage

segmented assimilation process that differentiates various dimensions of integration for immigrant groups

settler colonialism process by which newcomers try to acquire land and property for the purpose of forming new communities even while overpowering indigenous (that is, native) communities

social capital (*see also* cultural capital*)* access people have to networks and relationships that further their success

social death process by which a person loses his or her humanity

spillover effect consequences of imprisonment experienced after release, making it difficult for former prisoners to succeed

split labor market theory analyzing the workforce as divided into two sectors—the *primary labor market* and the *secondary labor market*

steering practice whereby real estate agents direct people of color away from neighborhoods that are predominantly White

stereotype oversimplified set of beliefs about the members of a societal group

stereotype threat pattern whereby a group's performance is affected by the invocation of a group stereotype

structural diversity theory theory that identifies the social forces that shape families, both historically and currently

structural unemployment pattern of massive job loss caused by closing of particular industries

subprime mortgages housing loans with a higher interest rate than the prime lending rate

symbolic annihilation under- and misrepresentation of certain groups of people in the media

symbolic ethnicity allegiance to an ethnic group that is felt without having to incorporate ethnicity into one's daily behavior

systemic racism complex array of racial practices that divides social, economic, and political resources along racial lines

tracking pattern of schooling that separates students into groups according to presumed ability

transnational families families wherein members are dispersed across national borders

tri-partite society society wherein people are divided into three racial categories

unemployment rate percentage of people in a given population who are out of work based on official calculations

Uniform Crime Reports annual FBI reports of crime rates based on number of crimes reported, crimes cleared, and persons arrested

urban underclass those who are largely permanently unemployed and stuck at the absolute bottom of the economic system

Voting Rights Act (1965) federal law prohibiting discriminatory practices in voting

wealth monetary value of all one's assets minus outstanding debt, also called *net worth*

white privilege social, cultural, and economic benefits that White people accrue in a society marked by racial hierarchy

white space perception Black people have of places in which they feel marginalized when they are present

white supremacy systemized consideration of White people as superior to people of color

xenophobia fear of foreigners

References

Abrajano, Marisa, and Zoltan L. Hajnal. 2015. *White Backlash: Immigration, Race, and American Politics*. Princeton, NJ: Princeton University Press.

Acuña, Rodolfo. 2005. "Crocodile Tears: Lynching of Mexicans." *HispanicVista.com*, July 20.

Acuña, Rodolfo F. 2014. *Occupied America: A History of Chicanos*. 8th ed. Upper Saddle River, NJ: Pearson.

Adorno, T. W., E. Frenkel-Brunswik, D. J. Levinson, and R. N. Sanford. 1950. *The Authoritarian Personality*. New York: Harper and Row.

Agency for Healthcare Research and Quality. 2015. *2014 National Healthcare Quality and Disparities Report*. Rockville, MD: Agency for Healthcare Research and Quality.

Ai, Amy L., Carol Plummer, Grace Heo, Catherine M. Lemieux, Cassandra E. Simon, Patricia Taylor, and Valire C. Copeland. 2011. "Racial Identity-Related Differential Attributions of Inadequate Responses to Hurricane Katrina: A Social Identity Perspective." *Race and Social Problems* 3(1):13–24.

Ajrouch, K. J., and A. Jamal. 2007. "Assimilate to a White Identity: The Case of Arab Americans." *International Migration Review* 41(4):860–79.

Akamigbo, A. B., and F. D. Wolinsky. 2007. "New Evidence of Racial Differences in Access and Their Effects on the Use of Nursing Homes among Older Adults." *Medical Care* 45(7):672–79.

Alba, Richard D. 1996. "Italian Americans: A Century of Ethnic Change." Pp. 172–81 in *Origins and Destinies: Immigration, Race, and Ethnicity in America*, edited by Silvia Pedraza and Rubén G. Rumbaut. Belmont, CA: Wadsworth.

Alba, Richard D. 2009. *Blurring the Color Line: The New Chance for a More Integrated America*. Cambridge, MA: Harvard University Press.

Alba, Richard D. 2012. *Blurring the Color Line: The New Chance for a More Integrated America*. Cambridge, MA: Harvard University Press.

Alba, Richard, and Nancy Foner. 2015a. "Mixed Unions and Immigrant-Group Integration in North American and Western Europe." *Annals of the American Academy of Political and Social Science* 662(1):38–56.

Alba, Richard D., and Nancy Foner. 2015b. *Strangers No More: Immigration and the Challenges for Integration in North America and Western Europe*. Princeton, NJ: Princeton University Press.

Alba, Richard D., and Victor Nee. 2003. *Remaking the American Mainstream: Assimilation and Contemporary America*. Cambridge, MA: Harvard University Press.

Alexander, Michelle. 2010. *The New Jim Crow: Mass Incarceration in the Age of Colorblindness*. New York: The New Press.

Allen, Quaylan. 2013. "'They Think Minority Means Lesser Than': Black Middle-Class Sons and Fathers Resisting Microaggressions in the School." *Urban Education* 48(2):171–97.

Allport, Gordon W. 1954. *The Nature of Prejudice*. Cambridge, MA: Addison-Wesley.

Alsultany, Evelyn. 2012. *Arabs and Muslims in the Media: Race and Representation after 9/11*. New York: New York University Press.

American Immigration Council. 2015. "Giving the Facts a Fighting Chance: Addressing Common Questions on Immigration." Washington, DC: American Immigration Council. Retrieved January 7, 2017 (https://www.americanimmigrationcouncil.org/research/addressing-common-questions-immigration).

Anacker, Katrin B. 2010. "Still Paying the Race Tax? Analyzing Property Values in Homogeneous and Mixed-Race Suburbs." *Journal of Urban Affairs* 32(1):55–77.

Andersen, Margaret L. 1999. "The Fiction of Diversity without Oppression: Race, Ethnicity, Identity, and Power." Pp. 5–20 in *Critical Ethnicity: Countering the Waves of Identity Politics*, edited by Robert Tai and Mary Kenyatta. Boulder, CO: Rowman & Littlefield.

Andersen, Margaret L. 2003. "Whitewashing Race: A Critical Review." Pp. 21–34 in *Whiteout: The Continuing Significance of Race*, edited by Eduardo Bonilla-Silva and Woody Doane. New York: Routledge.

Andersen, Margaret L. 2004. "From *Brown* to *Grutter*: The Diverse Beneficiaries of *Brown v. Board of Education*." *University of Illinois Law Review* 2004(5):1073–98.

Andersen, Margaret L., and Patricia Hill Collins. 2016. *Race, Class, and Gender: An Anthology*. 9th ed. San Francisco: Cengage.

Andersen, Margaret L., and Howard F. Taylor. 2017. *Sociology: The Essentials*. 9th ed. Boston: Cengage.

Anderson, Elijah. 1999. *Code of the Street: Decency, Violence, and the Moral Life of the Inner City*. New York: W. W. Norton.

Anderson, Elijah. 2015. "The White Space." *Sociology of Race & Ethnicity* 1(1):10–21.

Anderson, Margaret. 1988. *The American Census*. New Haven, CT: Yale University Press.

Aranda, Elizabeth, and Elizabeth Vaquera. 2015. "Racism, the Immigration Enforcement Regime and the Implications for Racial Inequality in the Lives of Undocumented Young Adults." *Sociology of Race and Ethnicity* 1(1):88–104.

Aratani, Yumiko, Hsien-Hen Lu, and J. L. Aber. 2014. "Shrinking the Public Safety Net or Helping the Poor Play by the Rules? The Changes in the State-Level Policies That Affected Low-Income Families with Children in the Welfare Reform Era: 1994–2002." *American Journal of Evaluation* 35(2):189–213.

Archambault, Mark E., James A. Van Rhee, Gail S. Marion, and Sonia J. Crandall. 2008. "Utilizing Implicit Association Testing to Promote Awareness of Biases Regarding Age and Disability." *Journal of Physician Assistance Education* 19(4):20–26.

Arias, Elizabeth. 2016. "Changes in Life Expectancy by Race and Hispanic Origin in the United States, 2013–2014." NCHS Data Brief 244 (April), Figure 3 and Figure 4. Hyattsville, MD: National Center for Health Statistics. Retrieved January 19, 2017 (https://www.cdc.gov/nchs/data/databriefs/db244.pdf).

Arora, S., and T. N. Cason. 1998. "Do Community Characteristics Influence Environmental Outcomes? Evidence from the Toxic Release Inventory." *Journal of Applied Economics* 1(2):413–53.

Asakawa, Gil. 2011. "Being Stereotyped Out of Ignorance Isn't as Bad as Flat-out Racism, but. . . ." *Nikkei View: The Asian American Blog*. Retrieved May 1, 2015 (http://nikkeiview.com/blog//?s=ignorance).

Baca Zinn, Maxine. 1982. "Chicano Men and Masculinity." *Journal of Ethnic Studies* 10(2):29–44.

Baca Zinn, Maxine. 2010. "The Family as a Race Institution." Pp. 357–82 in *The Sage Handbook of Race and Ethnic Studies*, edited by Patricia Hill Collins and John Solomos. Thousand Oaks, CA: Sage Publications.

Baca Zinn, Maxine. 2015. Personal correspondence.

Baca Zinn, Maxine, and Bonnie Thornton Dill. 1996. "Theorizing Difference from Multiracial Feminism." *Feminist Studies* 22 (Summer):321–31.

Baca Zinn, Maxine, D. Stanley Eitzen, and Barbara Wells. 2015. *Diversity in Families*. 10th ed. Upper Saddle River, NJ: Pearson.

Badger, Emily. 2015. "Redlining: Still a Thing." *Washington Post*, May 28.

Barajas, Heidi L., and Jennifer L. Pierce. 2001. "The Significance of Race and Gender in School Success among Latinas and Latinos in College." *Gender & Society* 15(6):859–78.

Barak, Gregg, Paul Leighton, and Allison Cotton. 2015. *Class, Race, Gender, and Crime: The Social Realities of Justice in America*. 4th ed. Lanham, MD: Rowman and Littlefield.

Barr, Donald A. 2014. *Health Disparities in the United States: Social Class, Race, Ethnicity, and Health*. 2nd ed. Baltimore: Johns Hopkins University Press.

Basford, Tessa E., Lynn R. Offermann, and Tara S. Behrend. 2014. "Do You See What I See? Perceptions of Gender Microaggressions in the Workplace." *Psychology of Women Quarterly* 38(3):340–49.

Basset, Delfin Caronell. 2013. "Speedy Gonzales' Relationship with the Hispanic Community." *Huffington Post*, October 3. (http://www.huffingtonpost.com/2013/10/03/speedy-gonzales-hispanic_n_4039787.html.)

Baum, Dan. 2016. "Legalize It All: How to Win the War on Drugs." *Harper's Magazine*, March 27. (http://harpers.org/archive/2016/04/legalize-it-all/.)

Bean, Frank D., Susan K. Brown, and James D. Bachmeier. 2015. *Parents without Papers: The Progress and Pitfalls of Mexican American Integration*. New York: Russell Sage.

Bean, Frank D., and Jennifer Lee. 2009. "Plus Ca Change . . . ? Multiraciality and the Dynamics of Race Relations in the United States." *Journal of Social Issues* 65(1):205–19.

Bean, Frank D., Cynthia Feliciano, Jennifer Lee, and Jennifer Van Hook. 2009. "The New U.S. Immigrants: How Do They Affect Our Understanding of the African American Experience?" *The Annals of the American Academy of Political and Social Science* 621:202–20.

Behm-Morawitz, E., and D. Ta. 2014. "Cultivating Virtual Stereotypes? The Impact of Video Game Play on Racial/Ethnic Stereotypes." *The Howard Journal of Communications* 25(1):1–15.

Behnken, Brian D., ed. 2016. *Civil Rights and Beyond: African American and Latino/a Activism in the Twentieth Century United States.* Athens: University of Georgia Press.

Bell, Joyce M., and Douglas Hartmann. 2007. "Diversity in Everyday Discourse: The Cultural Ambiguities and Consequences of 'Happy Talk.' " *American Sociological Review* 72(6):895–914.

Benediktsson, Mike O. 2012. "Bridging and Bonding in the Academic Melting Pot: Cultural Resources and Network Diversity." *Sociological Forum* 27(1):46–69.

Bennett, C. 2000. "Racial Categories Used in the Census, 1790 to the Present." *Government Information Quarterly* 17:161–80.

Bennett, Lerone, Jr. 1964. *The Negro Mood.* New York: Johnson Publishing.

Berry, Brent. 2011. "Friends for Better or for Worse: Interracial Friendship in the United States as Seen through Wedding Party Photos." *Demography* 43(3):491–510.

Bertrand, Marianne, and Sendhil Mullainathan. 2004. "Are Emily and Greg More Employable Than Lakisha and Jamal? A Field Experiment on Labor Market Discrimination." *American Economic Review* 94(4):991–1013.

Bethel, E. R. 1999. *The Roots of African American Identity.* London: Macmillan.

Bethencourt, Francisco. 2014. *Racisms: From the Crusades to the Twentieth Century.* Princeton, NJ: Princeton University Press.

Billingsley, Andrew. 1968. *Black Families in White America.* Englewood Cliffs, NJ: Prentice-Hall.

Bjornstrom, E. E. S., R. L. Kaufman, R. D. Peterson, and M. D. Slater. 2010. "Race and Ethnic Representations of Lawbreakers and Victims in Crime News: A National Study of Television Coverage." *Social Problems* 57(2):269–93.

Blackside. 1987. "Fighting Back, 1957–1962." *Eyes on the Prize, film.*

Blanco, Maria. 2010. "Before Brown, There Was *Mendez*: The Lasting Impact of *Mendez v. Westminster* in the Struggle for Desegregation." *Perspectives*, March. Washington, DC: Immigration Policy Center, American Immigration Council. (http://www.immigrationpolicy.org.)

Blascovich, J., W. B. Mendes, S. B. Hunter, B. Lickel, and N. Kowai-Bell. 2001. "Perceiver Threat in Social Interactions with Stigmatized Others." *Journal of Personality and Social Psychology* 80(2):253–67.

Blau, Judith R. 2003. *Race in the Schools: Perpetuating White Dominance?* Boulder, CO: Lynne Rienner.

Block, Jason P., Richard A. Scribner, and Karen B. DeSalvo. 2004. "Fast Food, Race/Ethnicity, and Income: A Geographic Analysis." *American Journal of Preventive Medicine* 27(3):211–17.

Blow, Charles M. 2014. "Paul Ryan, Culture, and Poverty." *New York Times*, March 21.

Blumer, Herbert. 1958. "Race Prejudice as a Sense of Group Position." *Pacific Sociological Review* 1(1):3–7.

Bobo, Lawrence D. 1999. "Prejudice as Group Position: Microfoundations of a Sociological Approach to Racism and Race Relations." *Journal of Social Issues* 55(3):445–72.

Bobo, Lawrence D. 2004. "Inequalities That Endure? Racial Ideology, American Politics, and the Peculiar Role of the Social Sciences." Pp. 13–42 in *The Changing Terrain of Race and Ethnicity*, edited by Maria Krysan and Amanda E. Lewis. New York: Russell Sage Foundation.

Bobo, Lawrence D. 2006. *Prejudice in Politics: Group Position, Public Opinion, and the Wisconsin Treaty Rights Dispute.* Cambridge, MA: Harvard University Press.

Bobo, Lawrence D. 2015. "Foreword: The Racial Double Homicide of Trayvon Martin." Pp. xi–xv in *Deadly Justice: Trayvon Martin, Race, and the Criminal Justice System*, edited by Devon Johnson, Patricia Y. Warren, and Amy Farrell. New York: New York University Press.

Boguhn, Alexandrea. 2015. "White Men Will Now Host CNN and All Broadcast Sunday Morning Political Talk Shows." *Media Matters Blog.* Retrieved April 24, 2015 (https://mediamatters.org/blog/2015/04/24/white-men-will-now-host-cnn-and-all-broadcast-s/203407).

Bonham, Vence. 2015. "Race." Interview. National Human Genome Research Institute. Retrieved February 9, 2015 (http://www.genome.gov).

Bonilla-Silva, Eduardo. 2003. *Racism without Racists: Color-Blind Racism and the Persistence of Racial Inequality in the United States.* Lanham, MD: Rowman & Littlefield.

Bonilla-Silva, Eduardo. 2004. "From Bi-Racial to Tri-Racial: Towards a New System of Racial Stratification in the USA." *Ethnic and Racial Studies* 27(6):931–50.

Bonilla-Silva, Eduardo, and Karen S. Glover. 2004. "'We Are All Americans!': The Latin Americanization of Race Relations in the United States." Pp. 149–83 in *The Changing Terrain of Race and Ethnicity*, edited by Maria Krysan and Amanda E. Lewis. New York: Russell Sage.

Bouie, Jamelle. 2014. "The Most Discriminatory Law of the Land." *Slate*, June 17.

Bradley, Mindy S., and Rodney L. Engen. 2016. "Leaving Prison: A Multilevel Investigation of Racial, Ethnic, and Gender Disproportionality in Correctional Release." *Crime and Delinquency* 62(2):253–79.

Brame, Robert, Shawn D. Bushway, Ray Paternoster, and Michael G. Turner. 2014. "Demographic Patterns of Cumulative Arrest Prevalence by Ages 18 and 23." *Crime & Delinquency* 60(3):471–86.

Branch, Enobong Hannah. 2011. *Opportunity Denied: Limiting Black Women to Devalued Work.* New Brunswick, NJ: Rutgers University Press.

Branch, Taylor. 1988. *Parting the Waters: America in the King Years, 1954–1963.* New York: Simon and Schuster.

Branch, Taylor. 1998. *Pillar of Fire: America in the King Years, 1963–1965.* New York: Simon and Schuster.

Branch, Taylor. 2006. *At Canaan's Edge: America in the King Years, 1965–1968.* New York: Simon and Schuster.

Brandt, Mark J., and Christine Reyna. 2014. "To Love or Hate Thy Neighbor: The Role of Authoritarianism and Traditionalism in Explaining the Link between Fundamentalism and Racial Prejudice." *Political Psychology* 35(2):207–23.

Bridges, Khiara M. 2011. *Reproducing Race: An Ethnography of Pregnancy as a Site of Racialization.* Berkeley: University of California Press.

Briggs, Laura. 2002. *Reproducing Empire: Race, Sex, Science, and U.S. Imperialism in Puerto Rico.* Berkeley: University of California Press.

Brooks, Dwight E., and Lisa P. Hébert. 2006. "Gender, Race, and Media Representation." Pp. 297–317 in *The SAGE Handbook of Gender and Communication*, edited by Bonnie J. Dow and Julia T. Wood. Thousand Oaks, CA: Sage Publications.

Brooks, Jamie D., and Meredith Ledford King. 2008. *Geneticizing Disease: Implications for Racial Health Disparities.* Washington, DC: Center for American Progress. (http://cdn.americanprogress.org.)

Brown, Anna. 2015. "Key Takeaways on U.S. Immigration: Past, Present, and Future." Pew Research Center. (http://www.pewresearch.org/fact-tank/2015/09/28/key-takeaways-on-u-s-immigration-past-present-and-future/.)

Brown, Anna, and Eileen Patten. 2013. *Hispanics of Puerto Rican Origin in the United States, 2011.* Washington, DC: U.S. Bureau of the Census. (http://www.pewhispanic.org/2013/06/19/hispanics-of-puerto-rican-origin-in-the-united-states-2011/.)

Brown, Elsa Barkley. 1995 "Imaging Lynching: African American Women, Communities of Struggle, and Collective Memory." Pp. 100–124 in *African American Women Speak Out on Anita Hill-Clarence Thomas*, edited by Geneva Smitherman. Detroit: Wayne State University Press.

Brown, Hana, and Jennifer A. Jones. 2015. "Rethinking Panethnicity and the Race-Immigration Divide: An Ethnoracialization Model of Group Formation." *Sociology of Race and Ethnicity* 1(1):181–91.

Brown, Robert McAfee. 1984. *Unexpected News: Reading the Bible with Third World Eyes.* Louisville, KY: Westminster John Knox Press.

Brown, Susan K., and Frank D. Bean. 2006. "Assimilation Models, Old and New: Explaining a Long-Term Process." Migration Policy Institute, October 1. (http://www.migrationpolicy.org/article/assimilation-models-old-and-new-explaining-long-term-process.)

Brownstein, Ronald. 2010. "The Gray and the Brown: The Generational Mismatch." *National Journal* (July 24):14–22.

Brulle, Robert J., and David N. Pellow. 2006. "Environmental Justice: Human Health and Environmental Inequalities." *Annual Review of Public Health* 27:103–23.

Brunsma, David L. 2006a. "Public Categories, Private Identities: Exploring Regional Differences in the Biracial Experience." *Social Science Research* 35(3):555–76.

Brunsma, David L., ed. 2006b. *Mixed Messages: Multiracial Identities in the "Color-Blind" Era.* Boulder, CO: Lynne Rienner.

Bullard, Robert D. 1996. "Symposium: The Legacy of American Apartheid and Environmental Racism." *St. John's Journal of Legal Commentary* 9.

Bullard, Robert D. 2008. *Dumping in Dixie: Race, Class, and Environmental Quality.* Boulder, CO: Westview Press.

Bullard, Robert, ed. 1994. *Unequal Protection: Environmental Justice and Communities of Color.* New York: Random House.

Bunche Center for African American Studies at UCLA. 2015. "2015 Hollywood Diversity Report: Flipping the Script." (http://www.bunche center.ucla.edu/wp-content/uploads/2015/02/2015-Hollywood-Diversity-Report-2-25-15.pdf.)

Bunyasi, Tehama Lopez. 2015. "Color-Cognizance and Color-Blindness in White America: Perceptions of Whiteness and Their Potential to Predict Racial Policy Attitudes at the Dawn of the Twenty-First Century." *Sociology of Race & Ethnicity* 1(2):209–24.

Byler, Christen G. 2013. "Hispanic/Latino Fatal Occupational Injury Rates." *Monthly Labor Review* 136(2):14–23.

Byrd, W. Carson, Rachelle J. Brunn-Bevel, and Parker R. Sexton. 2014. "'We Don't All Look Alike': The Academic Performance of Black Student Populations at Elite Colleges." *Du Bois Review: Social Science Research on Race* 11(2):353–85.

Cabrera, Nolan Leon. 2014. "Exposing Whiteness in Higher Education: White Male College Students Minimizing Racism, Claiming Victimization, and Recreating White Supremacy." *Race, Ethnicity, and Education* 17(1):30–55.

California Newsreel. 2003. *Race: The Power of Illusion.* DVD. (http://www.pbs.org.)

Callanan, V. J. 2012. "Media Consumption, Perceptions of Crime Risk and Fear of Crime: Examining Race/Ethnic Differences." *Sociological Perspectives* 55(1):93–116.

Callis, Robert R., and Melissa Kresin. 2015. "Residential Vacancies and Home Ownership in the Third Quarter 2015." U.S. Bureau of the Census. (http://www.census.gov/housing/hvs/files/currenthvspress.pdf.)

Camarillo, Albert. 1979. *Chicanos in a Changing Society.* Dallas: Southern Methodist University Press.

Campbell, Michael C., Matt Vogel, and Joshua Williams. 2015. "Historical Contingencies and the Evolving Importance of Race, Violent Crime, and Region in Explaining Mass Incarceration in the United States." *Criminology* 53(2):180–203.

Cancino, Jeffrey M., Ramiro Martinez, and Jacob I. Stowell. 2009. "The Impact of Neighborhood Context on Intragroup and Intergroup Robbery: The San Antonio Experience." *Annals of the American Academy of Political and Social Science* 623:12–24.

Cannuscio, Carolyn C., Amy Hillier, Allison Karpyn, and Karen Glanz. 2014. "The Social Dynamics of Healthy Food Shopping and Store Choice in an Urban Environment." *Social Science & Medicine* 122(December):13–20.

Carbado, Devon W., and Mitu Gulati. 2013. *Acting White: Rethinking Race in Post-Racial America.* New York: Oxford University Press.

Carmichael, Stokely, and Charles V. Hamilton. 1967. *Black Power: The Politics of Liberation.* New York: Vintage Books.

Carrasquillo, Héctor A., and Virginia Sánchez-Korrol. 1996. "Migration, Community, and Culture: The United States-Puerto Rican Experience." Pp. 98–109 in *Origins and Destinies: Immigration, Race, and Ethnicity in America*, edited by Silvia Pedraza and Rubén G. Rumbaut. Belmont, CA: Wadsworth.

Carrigan, William D., and Clive Webb. 2003. "The Lynching of Persons of Mexican Origin or Descent in the United States, 1848 to 1928." *Journal of Social History* 37(2):411–38.

Carrigan, William D., and Clive Webb. 2015. "When Americans Lynched Mexicans." *New York Times*, February 20.

Carson, Clayborne. 1981. *In Struggle: SNCC and the Black Awakening of the 1960s.* Cambridge, MA: Harvard University Press.

Carson, Clayborne, David J. Garrow, Vincent Harding, and Darlene Clark Hine, eds. 1987. *Eyes on the Prize: America's Civil Rights Years, A Reader and Guide.* New York: Penguin.

Carson, E. Ann. 2016. *Prisoners in 2015.* Washington, DC: Bureau of Justice Statistics. (https://www.bjs.gov/content/pub/pdf/p15.pdf.)

Carter, Prudence L. 2007. *Keepin' It Real: School Success Beyond Black and White.* New York: Oxford University Press.

Catanzarite, Lisa. 2003. "Race-Gender Composition and Occupational Pay Degradation." *Social Problems* 50(1):14–37.

Cauce, Ana Mari. 2016. "Annual Redding Lecture." University of Delaware, April 26, Newark, DE.

Centers for Disease Control and Prevention. 2015. "Hispanic Health." *CDC Vital Signs*, May. (http://www.cdc.gov/vitalsigns/hispanic-health/.)

Centers for Disease Control and Prevention. 2013. *CDC Health Disparities and Inequality Report, United States 2013*. Atlanta: U.S. Department of Health and Human Services. (http://www.cdc.gov/mmwr/pdf/other/su6203.pdf.)

Central Intelligence Agency. 2015. *The World Factbook*. (http://www.cia.gov.)

Chae, David H., Amani Nuru-Jeter, Karen D. Lincoln, and Darlene D. Francis. 2011. "Conceptualizing Racial Disparities in Health: Advancement of a Socio-Psychobiological Approach." *Du Bois Review: Social Science Research on Race* 8(1):63–77.

Chang, Gordon H. 2010. "Eternally Foreign: Asian Americans, History, and Race." Pp. 216–33 in *Doing Race: 21 Essays for the Twenty-First Century*, edited by Paula M. Moya and Hazel Rose Markus. New York: Oxford University Press.

Chavez, Leo. 2013. *The Latino Threat: Constructing Immigrants, Citizens, and the Nation*. 2nd ed. Stanford, CA: Stanford University Press.

Chavez, Leo R. 2008. *The Latino Threat: Constructing Immigrants, Citizens, and the Nation*. Palo Alto, CA: Stanford University Press.

Chavez, Odilia. 2013. "Farm Confessional: I'm an Undocumented Farm Worker." Written and translated by Lauren Smiley. *Modern Farmer*. (http://modernfarmer.com/2013/11/farmworker-confessional/.)

Chavez-Duenas, Nayeli, Hector Y. Adames, and Kurt C. Organista. 2014. "Skin-Color Prejudice and Within-Group Racial Discrimination: Historical and Current Impact on Latino/a Populations." *Hispanic Journal of Behavioral Sciences* 36(1):3–26.

Chen, Victor Tan. 2015. *Cut Loose: Jobless and Hopeless in an Unfair Economy*. Berkeley: University of California Press.

Chesler, M. A., A. E. Lewis, and J. E. Crowfoot. 2005. *Challenging Racism in Higher Education: Promoting Justice*. Lanham, MD: Rowman & Littlefield.

Childs, Erica Chito. 2005. *Navigating Interracial Borders: Black-White Couples and Their Social World*. New Brunswick, NJ: Rutgers University Press.

Chou, Rosalind, Kristen Lee, and Simon Ho. 2015. "Love Is (Color)Blind: Asian Americans and White Institutional Space at the Elite University." *Sociology of Race & Ethnicity* 1(2):302–16.

Chow, Esther Ngan-Ling. 1996. "Family, Economy, and the State: A Legacy of Struggle for Chinese American Women." Pp. 110–24 in *Origins and Destinies: Immigration, Race, and Ethnicity in America*, edited by Silvia Pedraza and Rubén G. Rumbaut. Belmont, CA: Wadsworth.

Christian, Mark. 2000. *Multiracial Identity: An International Perspective*. New York: St. Martin's Press.

Chua, Amy. 2010. *Battle Hymn of the Tiger Mother*. New York: Penguin.

Churchill, Ward. 1993. "Crimes against Humanity." *Z Magazine* 6(March):43–47.

Cisneros, J. David. 2008. "Contaminated Communities: The Metaphor of 'Immigrant as Pollutant' on Media Representations of Immigration." *Rhetoric and Public Affairs* 11(4):569–602.

Civil Rights History Project. 2013. *Julia Matilda Burns oral history interview conducted by John Dittmer in Tchula, Mississippi*. Video. Library of Congress. (https://www.loc.gov/item/afc2010039_crhp0073/.)

Clement, Scott. 2015. "Millennials Are Just as Racist as Their Parents." *Washington Post*, June 23.

Clotfelter, Charles T. 1976. "School Desegregation, 'Tipping,' and Private School Enrollment." *Journal of Human Resources* 11(1):13–20.

Coates, Ta-Nehisi. 2015. "The Black Family in the Age of Incarceration." *Atlantic* (October):60–84.

Cobb, Jelani. 2016. "The Matter of Black Lives." *New Yorker* (March 16): 34–40.

Colby, Sandra L., and Jennifer M. Ortman. 2015. *Projections of the Size and Composition of the U.S. Population, 2014–2060*. Washington, DC: U.S. Bureau of the Census.

Coles, Roberta L., and Charles Green. 2010. *The Myth of the Missing Black Father*. New York: Columbia University Press.

Collins, Chiquita A., and David R. Williams. 1999. "Segregation and Mortality: The Deadly Effects of Racism?" *Sociological Forum* 14(3):495–523.

Collins, Patricia Hill. 1990. *Black Feminist Thought: Knowledge, Consciousness, and the Politics of Empowerment*. Boston: Unwin and Hyman.

Conner, Thaddieus W., and William A. Taggart. 2013. "Assessing the Impact of Indian Gaming on American Indian Nations: Is the House Winning?" *Social Science Quarterly* 94(4):1016–44.

Consuelo Nacional de Población. 2008. *Migration and Health: Latinos in the United States*. Berkeley: University of California Center for Health Policy Research.

Cooley, Charles Horton. 1902. *Human Nature and Social Order*. New York: Scribner's.

Cotter, Elizabeth W., Nichole R. Kelly, Karen S. Mitchell, and Suzanne E. Mazzeo. 2015. "An Investigation of Body Appreciation, Ethnic Identity, and Eating Disorder Symptoms in Black Women." *The Journal of Black Psychology* 41(1):3–25.

Craig, Maxine Leeds. 2002. *Ain't I a Beauty Queen? Black Women, Beauty, and the Politics of Race*. New York: Oxford University Press.

Crenshaw, Kimberlé. 1989. "Demarginalizing the Intersection of Race and Sexuality: A Black Feminist Critique of Antidiscrimination Doctrine, Feminist Theory, and Anti-Racist Politics." *University of Chicago Legal Forum* 140:139–67.

Crockett, Stephen A. 2015. "SAE Frat Member Apologizes for Singing Racist Song." *The Root*, March 26. (http://www.theroot.com.)

Cumminos, Peter. 1963. "Race, Marriage, and Law." *The Harvard Crimson*, December 17.

DaCosta, Kimberly. 2007. *Making Multiracials: State, Family, and Market in the Redrawing of the Color Line*. Stanford, CA: Stanford University Press.

Dalmage, Heather. 2000. *Tripping on the Color Line: Black-White Multiracial Families in a Racially Divided World*. New Brunswick, NJ: Rutgers University Press

Dalmage, Heather M., ed. 2004. *The Politics of Multiracialism: Challenging Racial Thinking*. Albany: State University of New York Press.

Daniels, Jessie. 2013. "Race and Racism in Internet Studies: A Review and Critique." *New Media & Society* 15(5):695–719.

Daniels, Kimberly, Jo Daugherty, and Jo Jones. 2014. "Current Contraceptive Status among Women Aged 15–44: United States, 2011–2013." NCHS Data Brief 173 (December), Figure 1. Hyattsville, MD: National Center for Health Statistics. Retrieved January 19, 2017 (https://www.cdc.gov/nchs/products/databriefs/db173.htm).

Darby, Derrick, and Argun Saatcioglu. 2014. "Race, Justice, and Desegregation." *Du Bois Review: Social Science Research on Race* 11(1):87–108.

Darling-Hammond, Linda. 2004. "The Color Line in American Education: Race, Resources, and Student Achievement." *Du Bois Review: Social Science Research on Race* 1(2):213–46.

Darling-Hammond, Linda. 2007. "Race, Inequality and Educational Accountability: The Irony of 'No Child Left Behind.'" *Race, Ethnicity and Education* 10(3):245–60.

Darling-Hammond, Linda. 2010. *The Flat World and Education: How America's Commitment to Equity Will Determine Our Future*. New York: Teachers College Press.

Daugherty, Brian J. 2015. "Desegregation in Public Schools." *Encyclopedia Virginia*. (http://www.encyclopediavirginia.org/Desegregation_in_Public_Schools#start_entry.)

Dave, Dhaval M., Hope Corman, and Nancy E. Reichman. 2012. "Effects of Welfare Reform on Education Acquisition of Adult Women." *Journal of Labor Research* 33(2):251–82.

Dean, Lorraine, S. V. Subramanian, David R. Williams, Katrina Armstrong, Camille Z. Charles, and Ichiro Kawachi. 2014. "The Role of Social Capital in African-American Women's Use of Mammography." *Social Science & Medicine* 104(March):148–56.

De'Armond, De'Arno, and Dandan Zhu. 2011. "Determinants of Consumer Debt: An Examination of Individual Credit Management Variables." *Journal of Finance and Accountancy* 7(1):1–17.

De Genova, Nicholas, and Ana Y. Ramos-Zayas. 2003. *Latino Crossings: Mexicans, Puerto Ricans, and the Politics of Race and Citizenship*. New York: Routledge.

de la Garza, Rodolfo O. 1992. "From Rhetoric to Reality: Latinos and the 1988 Election in Review." Pp. 171–81 in *From Rhetoric to Reality: Latino Politics in the 1988 Elections*, edited by Rodolfo O. de la Garza and Louis DeSipio. Boulder, CO: Westview Press.

Delgado, Richard. 2009. "Law of the Noose: A History of Latino Lynching." *Harvard Civil Rights-Civil Liberties Law Review* 44:297–312.

DeLuca, Stefanie, Philip M. E. Garboden, and Peter Rosenblatt. 2013. "Segregating Shelter: How Housing Policies Shape the Residential Locations of Low-Income Minority Families." *Annals of the American Academy of Political and Social Science* 647(1):268–99.

DeNavas-Walt, Carmen, and Bernadette D. Proctor. 2015. *Income and Poverty in the United States: 2014*. Washington, DC: U.S. Bureau of the Census.

DeNavas-Walt, Carmen, Bernadette D. Proctor, and Jessica C. Smith. 2010. *Income, Poverty, and Health Insurance in the United States: 2000*. Washington, DC: U.S. Bureau of the Census.

Denton, Nancy. 2001. "Housing as a Means of Asset Accumulation: A Good Strategy for the Poor?" Pp. 232–66 in *Assets for the Poor: The Benefits of Spreading Asset Ownership*, edited by Thomas M. Shapiro and Edward N. Wolff. New York: Russell Sage Foundation.

Desmond, Matthew. 2016. *Evicted: Poverty and Profit in the American City*. New York: Crown Publishers.

de Souza, B. 2007. "'Some of My Best Friends Are . . . ': Interracial Friendships, Class, and Segregation in America." *City & Community* 6(4):263–90.

Dill, Bonnie Thornton. 1988. "'Our Mothers' Grief': Racial-Ethnic Women and the Maintenance of Families." *Journal of Family History* 13(1):415–31.

Diner, Hasia. 1996. "Erin's Children in America: Three Centuries of Irish Immigration to the United States." Pp. 161–71 in *Origins and Destinies: Immigration, Race, and Ethnicity in America*, edited by Silvia Pedraza and Rubén G. Rumbaut. Belmont, CA: Wadsworth.

Dines, Gail, and Jean M. McMahon Humez, eds. 2014. *Gender, Race, and Class in the Media: A Critical Reader*. 4th ed. Thousand Oaks, CA: Sage Publications.

Dinwiddie, Gniesha Y., Darrell J. Gaskin, Kitty S. Chan, Janette Norrington, and Rachel McCleary. 2013. "Residential Segregation, Geographic Proximity and Type of Services Used: Evidence for Racial/Ethnic Disparities in Mental Health." *Social Science & Medicine* 80:67–75.

Dirks, Danielle, and Jennifer C. Mueller. 2010. "Racism and Popular Culture." Pp. 115–29 in *Handbook of the Sociology of Racial and Ethnic Relations*, edited by Hernán Vera and Joe R. Feagin. New York: Springer.

Doane, Ashley W., and Eduardo Bonilla-Silva, eds. 2003. *White Out: The Continuing Significance of Racism*. New York: Routledge.

Dorcey, Dr. L. C. 1996. Interviews by Owen Brooks and Kim Lacy Rogers, Winstonville, MI, February 27; reprinted in *Trauma and Life Stories: International Perspectives, 1999*, edited by Kim Lacy Rogers, Selma Leydesdorff, and Graham Dawson. New York: Routledge.

Dovidio, John F. 2001. "On the Nature of Contemporary Prejudice: The Third Wave." *Journal of Social Issues* 17:829–49.

Dow, Dawn M. 2015. "Negotiating 'the Welfare Queen' and 'the Strong Black Woman': African American Middle-Class Mothers' Work and Family Perspectives." *Sociological Perspectives* 58(1):36–55.

Drakulich, Kevin M. 2015. "Explicit and Hidden Racial Bias in the Framing of Social Problems." *Social Problems* 62(3):391–418.

Dreby, Joanna. 2010. *Divided by Borders: Mexican Migrants and Their Children*. Berkeley: University of California Press.

Du Bois, William E. B. 1899. *The Philadelphia Negro: A Social Study*. Philadelphia, PA: University of Pennsylvania Press.

Du Bois, W. E. B. [1903] 1996. *The Souls of Black Folk*. New York: Penguin.

Duchon, Richie. 2015. "Charleston Church Shooting Leaves Jon Stewart Jokeless." *NBC News*, June 19. Retrieved January 7, 2017 (http://www.nbcnews.com/storyline/charleston-church-shooting/charleston-church-shooting-leaves-jon-stewart-jokeless-n378236).

Duffy, Mignon. 2011. *Making Care Count: A Century of Gender, Race, and Paid Care Work*. New Brunswick, NJ: Rutgers University Press.

Dunbar, Erica Armstrong. 2017. *Never Caught: Ona Judge Staines, the President's Runaway Slave Woman*. New Haven, CT: Yale University Press.

Durkheim, Emile. [1895] 1964. *The Division of Labor in Society*. New York: Free Press.

Durso, Rachel M., and David Jacobs. 2013. "The Determinants of the Number of White Supremacist Groups: A Pooled Time-Series Analysis." *Social Problems* 60(1):128–44.

Dy, Sydney M., and Tanjala S. Purnell. 2012. "Key Concepts Relevant to Quality of Complex and Shared Decision-Making in Health Care: A Literature Review." *Social Science & Medicine* 74(4):582–87.

Eastman, Susan T., and Andrew C. Billings. 2001. "Biased Voices of Sports: Racial and Gender Stereotyping in College Basketball Announcing." *The Howard Journal of Communications* 12(4):183–201.

Eberhardt, Jennifer L. 2010. "Enduring Racial Associations: African Americans, Crime, and Animal Imagery." Pp. 439–57 in *Doing Race: 21 Essays for the Twenty-First Century*, edited by Paula M. Moya and Hazel Rose Markus. New York: Oxford University Press.

Eberhardt, Jennifer L., Phillip A. Goff, Valerie Purdie, and P. G. Davies. 2004. "Seeing Black: Race, Crime, and Visual Processing." *Journal of Personality and Social Psychology* 87(6):876–93.

Edin, Kathryn, and Maria Kefalas. 2005. *Promises I Can Keep: Why Poor Women Put Marriage before Motherhood*. Berkeley: University of California Press.

Edin, Kathryn, and Timothy J. Nelson. 2013. *Doing the Best I Can: Fatherhood in the Inner City*. Berkeley: University of California Press.

Edin, Kathryn J., and H. Luke Shaefer. 2015. *$2.00 a Day: Living on Almost Nothing in America*. Boston: Houghton Mifflin Harcourt.

Edwards, Korie, Katrina Carter-Tellison, and Cedric Herring. 2004. "For Richer, For Poorer, Whether Dark or Light: Skin Tone, Marital Status, and Spouse's Earnings." Pp. 65–91 in *Skin Deep: How Race and Complexion Matter in the "Color Blind" Era*, edited by Cedric Herring, Verna M. Keith, and Hayward Derrick Horton. Urbana: University of Illinois Press.

Elliott, Sinikka, and Elyshia Aseltine. 2013. "Raising Teenagers in Hostile Environments: How Race, Class, and Gender Matter for Mothers' Protective Carework." *Journal of Family Issues* 34(6):719–44.

Elliott, Sinikka, Rachel Powell, and Joslyn Brenton. 2015. "Being a Good Mom: Low-Income, Black Single Mothers Negotiate Intensive Mothering." *Journal of Family Issues* 36(3):351–70.

Ellis, Renee R., and Tavia Simmons. 2014. *Coresident Grandparents and Their Grandchildren: 2012*. Washington, DC: U.S. Bureau of the Census. (https://www.census.gov/content/dam/Census/library/publications/2014/demo/p20-576.pdf.)

Emerick, Nicholas A., Theodore R. Curry, Timothy W. Collins, and S. Fernando Rodriguez. 2014. "Homicide and Social Disorganization on the Border: Implications for Latino and Immigrant Populations." *Social Science Quarterly* 95(2):360–79.

Emerson, Michael O., Rachel T. Kimbro, and George Yancey. 2002. "Contact Theory Extended: The Effects of Prior Racial Contact on Current Social Ties." *Social Science Quarterly* 83 (3):745–61.

"Emilio Aguayo." N.d. Seattle Civil Rights & Labor History Project. (http://depts.washington.edu/civilr/aguayo.htm.)

Engels, Friedrich. [1884] 1972. *The Origin of the Family, Private Property, and the State*. New York: International.

Ennis, Sharon, Merarys Rios-Vargas, and Nora G. Elbert. 2011. *The Hispanic Population: 2010*. Washington, DC: U.S. Bureau of the Census. (http://www.census.gov/prod/cen2010/briefs/c2010br-04.pdf.)

Erigha, Maryann. 2015. "Race, Gender, Hollywood: Representation in Cultural Production and Digital Media's Potential for Change." *Sociology Compass* 9(1):78–89.

Erikson, Erik. 1968. *Identity, Youth, and Crisis*. New York: Norton.

Escobar, Edward J. 1993. "The Dialectics of Repression: The Los Angeles Police Department and the Chicano Movement, 1968-1971." *The Journal of American History* 79(4):1483–1514.

Espiritu, Yen Le. 1992. *Asian American Panethnicity: Bridging Institutions and Identities*. Philadelphia: Temple University Press.

Essed, Philomena. 1991. *Understanding Everyday Racism: An Interdisciplinary Theory*. Newbury Park, CA: Sage.

Evans, Bronwynne C., David W. Coon, and Michael J. Belyea. 2014. "Worry among Mexican American Caregivers of Community-Dwelling Elders." *Hispanic Journal of Behavioral Sciences* 36(3):344–65.

Ewing, Walter A., Daniel E. Martinez, and Rubén G. Rumbaut. 2015. *The Criminalization of Immigration in the United States: July 2015*. Washington, DC: American Immigration Council. (http://www.immigrationimpact.com.)

Farley, Reynolds, Howard Schuman, Suzanne Bianchi, Diane Colasanto, and Shirley Hatchett. 1978. "'Chocolate City, Vanilla Suburbs': Will the Trend toward Racially Separate Communities Continue?" *Social Science Research* 7(2):319–44.

Feagin, Joe R. 2010a. *Racist America: Current Realities and Future Reparations*. New York: Routledge.

Feagin, Joe R. 2010b. *The White Racial Frame: Centuries of Racial Framing and Counter-Framing*. New York: Routledge.

Feagin, Joe. 2013. "Race and Justice: Wrongful Convictions of African American Men." *Contemporary Sociology* 42(January):81–83.

Feagin, Joe R. 2014. *Racist America: Roots, Current Realities, and Future Reparations*. 3rd ed. Lanham, MD: Rowman & Littlefield.

Feagin, Joe R., and José A. Cobas. 2014. *Latinos Facing Racism: Discrimination, Resistance, and Endurance*. Boulder, CO: Paradigm.

Federal Bureau of Investigation. 2016a. *Crime in the United States 2015*. Washington, DC: U.S. Department of Justice. (https://ucr.fbi.gov/crime-in-the-u.s/2015/crime-in-the-u.s.-2015.)

Federal Bureau of Investigation. 2016b. *Hate Crime Statistics 2015*. Washington, DC: U.S. Department of Justice. (https://ucr.fbi.gov/hate-crime/2015/resource-pages/hate-crime-2015-_summary_final.)

Feldman, Marcus W. 2010. "The Biology of Ancestry: DNA, Genomic Variation, and Race." Pp. 136–59 in *Doing Race: 21 Essays for the Twenty-First Century*, edited by Paula M. Moya and Hazel Rose Markus. New York: Oxford University Press.

Feliciano, Cynthia, and Belinda Robnett. 2014. "How External Racial Classifications Shape Latino Dating Choices." *The DuBois Review: Social Science Research on Race* 11(2):295–328.

Feliciano, Cynthia, Belinda Robnett, and Golnaz Komaie. 2009. "Gendered Racial Exclusion among White Internet Daters." *Social Science Research* 38(1):39–54.

Feng, Z., M. L. Fennell, D. A. Tyler, M. Clark, and V. Mor. 2011. "The Care Span: Growth of Racial and Ethnic Minorities in U.S. Nursing Homes Driven by Demographics and Possible Disparities in Options." *Health Affairs* 30(7):1358–65.

Ferber, Abby. 1998. *White Man Falling: Race, Gender, and White Supremacy*. Lanham, MD: Rowman & Littlefield.

Ferguson, Ann Arnett. 2000. *Bad Boys: Public Schools in the Making of Black Masculinity*. Ann Arbor: University of Michigan Press.

Ferriss, Susan, and Ricardo Sandoval. 1997. *Fight in the Fields: Cesar Chavez and the Farmworkers' Union*. Boston: Houghton Mifflin.

Fins, Deborah. 2016. *Death Row U.S.A. Summer 2016*. Baltimore: NAACP Legal Defense and Education Fund, Inc.

Flagg, Barbara J. 1997. "'Was Blind but Now I See': White Race Consciousness and the Requirement of Discriminatory Intent." Pp. 629–31 in *Critical White Studies: Looking Behind the Mirror*, edited by Richard Delgado and Jean Stefancic. Philadelphia: Temple University Press.

Fleegler, Eric W., and Neil L. Schechter. 2015. "Pain and Prejudice." *Journal of the American Medical Association Pediatrics* 116(November 15):991–93.

Fletcher, Mark J., Stefan G. Kertesz, Michael A. Kohn, and Ralph Gonzales. 2008. "Trends in Opioid Prescribing by Race/Ethnicity for Patients Seeking Care in U.S. Emergency Departments." *Journal of the American Medical Association* 2009(1):70–78.

Flippen, Chenoa. 2004. "Unequal Returns to Housing Investments? A Study of Real Housing Appreciation among Black, White, and Hispanic Households." *Social Forces* 82(4):1523–51.

Fogel, Robert William, and Stanley L. Engermann. 1974. *Time on the Cross: The Economics of American Negro Slavery*. New York: W. W. Norton.

Foley, Neil. 2005. "Over the Rainbow: *Hernandez v. Texas, Brown v. Board of Education*, and *Black v. Brown*." *UCLA Chicano-Latina Law Review* 25(Spring):139–52.

Foner, Eric. 1988. *Reconstruction: America's Unfinished Revolution, 1863–1877*. New York: Harper and Row.

Foner, Nancy. 2005. *In a New Land: A Comparative View of Immigration*. New York: New York University Press.

Ford, Kristie A., and Josephine Orlandella. 2015. "The 'Not-So-Final Remark': The Journey to Becoming White Allies." *Sociology of Race & Ethnicity* 1(2):287–301.

Ford, Tanisha C. 2013. "SNCC Women, Denim and the Politics of Dress." *Journal of Southern History* 79(3):625–58.

Forman, Tyrone A. 2004. "Color-Blind Racism and Racial Indifference: The Role of Racial Apathy in Facilitating Enduring Inequalities." Pp. 43–66 in *The Changing Terrain of Race and Ethnicity*, edited by Maria Krysan and Amanda E. Lewis. New York: Russell Sage Foundation.

Forman, Tyrone A., Carla Goar, and Amanda E. Lewis. 2004. "Neither Black nor White? An Empirical Test of the Latinization Thesis." *Race and Society* 5(1):65–84.

Forman, Tyrone A., and Amanda E. Lewis. 2006. "Racial Apathy and Hurricane Katrina: The Social Anatomy of Prejudice in the Post-Civil Rights Era." *Du Bois Review: Social Science Research on Race* 3(1):175–202.

Fraga, Luis Ricardo. 2012. *Latinos in the New Millennium: An Almanac of Opinion, Behavior, and Policy Preferences*. New York: Cambridge University Press.

Fraga, Luis Ricardo, John J. Garcia, Rodney E. Hero, Michael Jones-Correa, Valerie Martinez-Ebers, and Gary Segura, eds. 2010. *Latino Lives in*

America: Making It Home. Philadelphia: Temple University Press.

Frankenberg, Erica. 2013. "The Role of Residential Segregation in Contemporary School Segregation." *Education and Urban Society* 45(5):548–70.

Franklin, Benjamin. [1751] 1961. "Observations Concerning the Increase of Mankind, Peopling of Countries, etc." In *Papers of Benjamin*, Vol. 4, July 1, 1750–June 30, 1753, edited by Leonard W. Labaree. New Haven, CT: Yale University Press.

Franssen, Vicky, Kristof Dhont, and Alain Van Hiel. 2013. "Age-Related Differences in Ethnic Prejudice: Evidence of the Mediating Effect of Right-Wing Attitudes." *Journal of Community & Applied Social Psychology* 23(3):252–57.

Fredrickson, George M. 2002. *Racism: A Short History*. Princeton, NJ: Princeton University Press.

Free, Marvin D., and Mitch Ruesink. 2012. *Race and Justice: Wrongful Convictions of African American Men*. Boulder, CO: Lynne Rienner.

Frey, William H. 2015. *Diversity Explosion: How New Racial Demographics Are Remaking America*. Washington, DC: The Brookings Institute.

Fryberg, Stephanie A., and Alisha Watts. 2010. "We're Honoring You, Dude: Myths, Mascots, and American Indians." Pp. 458–80 in *Doing Race: 21 Essays for the Twenty-First Century*, edited by Paula M. Moya and Hazel Rose Markus. New York: Oxford University Press.

Funderburg, Lisa. 2013. "The Changing Face of America." *National Geographic* 224(4):80–91.

Furstenberg, Frank F. 2014. "Fifty Years of Family Change: From Consensus to Complexity." *Annals of the American Academy of Political and Social Science* 654(1):12–30.

Gabbidon, Shaun L., and Helen Taylor Greene. 2016. *Race and Crime*. 4th ed. Thousand Oaks, CA: Sage Publications.

Gabrielson, Ryan, Ryann Grochowski Jones, and Eric Sagara. 2014. "Deadly Force in Black and White: A ProPublica Analysis of Killings by Police Shows Outsize Risk for Young Black Males." (htttp://www.propublica.org.)

Gaddis, S. Michael. 2015. "Discrimination in the Credential Society: An Audit Study of Race and College Selectivity in the Labor Market." *Social Forces* 93(4):1451–79.

Galaviz, Sal. N.d. "The Promised Land." Bracero History Archive, Item #3227. Retrieved November 17, 2015 (http://braceroarchive.org/items/show/3227).

Gallagher, Charles A. 2003. "Color-Blind Privilege: The Social and Political Functions of Erasing the Color Line in America." *Race, Gender & Class* 10:22–37.

Gallagher, Charles A. 2004. "Racial Redistricting: Expanding the Boundaries of Whiteness." Pp. 59–76 in *The Politics of Multiracialism: Challenging Racial Thinking*, edited by Heather M. Dalmage. Albany: State University of New York Press.

Gallagher, Mike, and Cameron McWhirter. 1998. "Chiquita Secrets Revealed." *Cincinnati Enquirer*, May 3.

Gallup Editors. 2014. "Gallup Review: Black and White Differences in Views on Race." Princeton, NJ: The Gallup Organization. Retrieved December 30, 2016 (http://www.gallup.com/poll/180107/gallup-review-black-white-differences-views-race.aspx).

Gamson, William A., David Croteau, William Hoynes, and Theodore Sasson. 1992. "Media Images and the Social Construction of Reality." *Annual Review of Sociology* 18:373–93.

Gans, Herbert J. 1979. "Symbolic Ethnicity: The Future of Ethnic Groups and Cultures in America." *Ethnic and Racial Studies* 2(1):1–20.

Gans, Herbert J. 1992. "Second-Generation Decline: Scenarios for the Economic and Ethnic Futures of the Post-1965 American Immigrants." *Ethnic and Racial Studies* 15(2):173–92.

Gans, Herbert J. 2009. "First Generation Decline: Downward Mobility among Refugees and Immigrants." *Ethnic and Racial Studies* 32(9):1658–70.

Gans, Herbert J. 2011. "The Moynihan Report and Its Aftermaths." *Du Bois Review: Social Science Research on Race* 8(2):315–27.

Gans, Herbert J. 2014. "Studying the Bottom of American Society." *Du Bois Review: Social Science Research on Race* 11(2):195–204.

Garcia, Lorena. 2012. *Respect Yourself, Protect Yourself: Latina Girls and Sexual Identity*. New York: New York University Press.

Gasteyer, Stephen P., Jennifer Lai, Brittany Tucker, Jennifer Carrera, and Julius Moss. 2016. "Basics Inequality: Race and Access to Complete

Plumbing Facilities in the United States." *Du Bois Review: Social Science Research on Race* 13(2):305–26.

Gates, Gary J. 2012. "Same-Sex Couples in Census 2010: Race and Ethnicity." The Williams Institute, University of California–Los Angeles. (http://williamsinstitute.law.ucla.edu/wp-content/uploads/Gates-CouplesRaceEthnicity-April-2012.pdf.)

General Social Survey. 2015. Chicago: National Opinion Research Center at the University of Chicago. (http://www.gss.norc.org.)

General Social Survey. 2016. *GSS Data Explorer.* Chicago: National Opinion Research Center at the University of Chicago. (http://www.gss.norc.org.)

Genovese, Eugene. 1972. *Roll, Jordan, Roll: The World the Slaves Made.* New York: Pantheon.

Georgevich, Mary. 2007. "Theme Party Provokes Outrage." *The Santa Clara*, February 15. Retrieved December 30, 2016 (http://thesantaclara.org/theme-party-provokes-outrage/#.WIO94vkrKM8).

Gerbner, George. 1972. "Violence in Television Drama: Trends and Symbolic Functions." Pp. 28–187 in *Television and Social Behavior, Vol. 1*, edited by G. A. Comstock and E. Rubenstein. Washington, DC: U.S. Government Printing Office.

Gerstel, Naomi. 2011. "Rethinking Families and Community: The Color, Class, and Centrality of Extended Kin Ties." *Sociological Forum* 26(1):1–20.

Gibson, Campbell, and Kay Jung. 2006. *Historical Census Statistics on the Foreign-Born Population of the United States, 1850–2000.* Washington, DC: U.S. Census Bureau.

Giddings, Paula J. 2007. *In Search of Sisterhood: Delta Sigma Theta and the Challenge of the Black Sorority Movement.* New York: William Morrow.

Giddings, Paula J. 2009. *Ida: A Sword among Lions: Ida B. Wells and the Campaign against Lynching.* New York: Harper.

Gilliam, Franklin D., Jr., and Shanto Iyengar. 2000. "Prime Suspects: The Influence of Local Television News on the Viewing Public." *American Journal of Political Science* 44(3):560–73.

Gilliam, Franklin D., Jr., S, Iyengar, A. Simon, and O. Wright. 1996. "Crime in Black and White: The Violent, Scary World of Local News." *Harvard International Journal of Press/Politics* 1:6–21.

Gimlin, Debra L. 2002. *Body Work: Beauty and Self-Image in American Culture.* New York: Routledge.

Glaubke, Christina R., Patti Miller, McCrae A. Parker, and Eileen Espejo. 2001. *Fair Play: Violence, Gender, and Race in Video Games.* Oakland, CA: Children Now.

Glenn, Evelyn Nakano. 1986. *Issei, Nisei, War Bride: Three Generations of Japanese American Women in Domestic Service.* Philadelphia: Temple University Press.

Glenn, Evelyn Nakano. 1992. "From Servitude to Service Work: Historical Continuities in the Racial Division of Paid Reproductive Labor." *Signs* 18(1):1–43.

Glenn, Evelyn Nakano. 2002. *Unequal Freedom: How Race and Gender Shaped American Citizenship and Labor.* Cambridge, MA: Harvard University Press.

Glenn, Evelyn N. 2008. "Yearning for Lightness: Transnational Circuits in the Marketing and Consumption of Skin Lighteners." *Gender & Society* 22(3):281–302.

Glenn, Evelyn Nakano. 2015. "Settler Colonialism as Structure: A Framework for Comparative Studies of U.S. Race and Gender Formation." *Sociology of Race & Ethnicity* 1(1): 52–72.

Glenn, Evelyn Nakano, and Rhacel Salazar Parreñas. 1996. "The Other Issei: Japanese Immigrant Women in the Pre-World War II Period." Pp. 125–40 in *Origins and Destinies: Immigration, Race, and Ethnicity in America*, edited by Silvia Pedraza and Rubén G. Rumbaut. Belmont, CA: Wadsworth.

Glick, Jennifer E., and Seung Y. Han. 2015. "Socioeconomic Stratification from Within: Changes within American Indian Cohorts in the United States: 1990-2010." *Population Research and Policy Review* 34(1):77–112.

Goetz, Edward G. 2015. "From Breaking Down Barriers to Breaking Up Communities: The Expanding Spatial Strategies of Fair Housing Advocacy." *Urban Affairs Review* 51(6): 820–42.

Goffman, Erving. 1963. *Stigma: Notes on the Management of Spoiled Identity.* Englewood Cliffs, NJ: Prentice-Hall.

Goings, Kenneth W. 1994. *Mammy and Uncle Mose: Black Collectibles and American Stereotyping.* Bloomington: Indiana University Press.

Golash-Boza, Tanya. 2016. "A Critical and Comprehensive Theory of Race and Racism." *Sociology of Race & Ethnicity* 2 (2):129–41.

Golash-Boza, Tanya, and William Darity Jr. 2008. "Latino Racial Choices: The Effects of Skin Colour and Discrimination on Latinos' and Latinas' Racial Self-Identifications." *Ethnic and Racial Studies* 31(5):899–934.

Gold, Steven J., and Bruce Phillips.1996. "Mobility and Continuity among Eastern European Jews." Pp. 182–94 in *Origins and Destinies: Immigration, Race, and Ethnicity in America*, edited by Silvia Pedraza and Rubén G. Rumbaut. Belmont, CA: Wadsworth.

Gonzales, Angela A., Thomas A. Lyson, and K. W. Mauer. 2007. "What Does a Casino Mean to a Tribe? Assessing the Impact of Casino Development on Indian Reservations in Arizona and New Mexico." *Social Science Journal* 44(3):405–19.

Gordon, Kathryn H., Yessenia Castro, Lilya Sitnikov, and Jill Holm-Denoma. 2010. "Cultural Body Shape Ideals and Eating Disorder Symptoms among White, Latina, and Black College Women." *Cultural Diversity & Ethnic Minority Psychology* 16(2):135–43.

Gordon, Linda. 1994. *Pitied but Not Entitled: Single Mothers and the History of Welfare*. New York: The Free Press.

Gordon, Linda, and F. Batlan. 2011. "The Legal History of the Aid to Dependent Children Program." (http://www.socialwelfarehistory .com/programs/aid-to-dependent-children-the-legal-history/.)

Gordon, Milton M. 1964. *Assimilation in American Life*. New York: Oxford University Press.

Goyal, M. K., N. Kuggermann, S. D. Cleary, S. J. Teach, and J. M. Chamberlain. 2015. "Racial Disparities in Pain Management of Children with Appendicitis in Emergency Departments." *Journal of the American Medical Association Pediatrics* 169(11):996–1002.

Graves, Joseph L. 2001. *The Emperor's New Clothes: Biological Theories of Race at the New Millennium*. New Brunswick, NJ: Rutgers University Press.

Graves, Joseph L. 2004. *The Race Myth: Why We Pretend Race Exists in America*. New York: Dutton.

Greenbaum, Susan D. 2015. *Blaming the Poor: The Long Shadow of the Moynihan Report on Cruel Images about Poverty*. New Brunswick, NJ: Rutgers University Press.

Greenberg, B. S., D. Mastro, and Jeffrey Brand. 2002. "Minorities and the Mass Media: Television into the 21st Century." Pp. 333–52 in *Media Effects: Advances in Theory and Research*, 2nd ed., edited by Jennings Bryant and Dolf Zillmann. Hillsdale, NJ: Lawrence Erlbaum Associates.

Greenwald, Anthony G., Debbie E. McGhee, and Jordan L. L. Schwartz. 1998. "Measuring Individual Differences in Implicit Cognition: The Implicit Association Test." *Journal of Personality and Social Psychology* 74(6):1464–480.

Grieco, Elizabeth, Yesenia D. Acosta, G. Patricia de la Cruz, Christine Gambino, Thomas Gryn, Luke J. Larsen, Edward N. Trevelyan, and Nathan P. Walters. 2012. *The Foreign-Born Population in the United States: 2010*. Washington, DC: U.S. Bureau of the Census. http://www.census.gov.

Grigoryeva, Angelina, and Martin Ruef. 2015. "The Historical Demography of Racial Segregation." *American Sociological Review* 80(4):814–42.

Grimsley, Edwin. 2012. "What Wrongful Convictions Teach Us about Racial Inequality." New York: The Innocence Project. (http://www .innocenceproject.org.)

Gruenewald, J., S. M. Chermak, and J. M. Pizarro. 2013. "Covering Victims in the News: What Makes Minority Homicides Newsworthy?" *Justice Quarterly* 30(5):755–83.

Grzanka, Patrick R. 2014. "Media as Sites/Sights of Justice." Pp. 131–37 in *Intersectionality: A Foundations and Frontiers Reader*, edited by Patrick R. Grzanka. Boulder, CO: Westview Press.

Gurin, Patricia, E. L. Dey, and Sylvia Hurtado. 2002. "Diversity and Higher Education: Theory and Impact on Educational Outcomes." *Harvard Educational Review* 72(3):330–66.

Gutiérrez, Elena R. 2008. *Fertile Matters: The Politics of Mexican-Origin Women's Reproduction*. Austin: University of Texas Press.

Gutiérrez, Elena R. 2010. "Latina/o Sex Policy." Pp. 90–102 in *Latina/o Sexualities: Probing Powers, Passions, Practices, and Politics*, edited by Marysol Asencio. New Brunswick, NJ: Rutgers University Press.

Gutiérrez y Muhs, Gabriella, Yolanda Flores Niemann, Carmen G. González, and

Angela P. Harris. 2012. *Presumed Incompetent: The Intersections of Race and Class for Women in Academia.* Boulder: University Press of Colorado.

Gutman, Herbert. 1976. *The Black Family in Slavery and Freedom.* New York: Vintage.

Guyll, Max, Stephanie Madon, Loreto Prieto, and Kyle C. Scherr. 2010. "The Potential Roles of Self-Fulfilling Prophecies, Stigma Consciousness, and Stereotype Threat in Linking Latino-a Ethnicity and Educational Outcomes." *Journal of Social Issues* 66(1):113–30.

Hall, Ronald. 1995. "The Bleaching Syndrome: African Americans' Response to Cultural Domination vis-à-vis Skin Color." *Journal of Black Studies* 26(2):172–84.

Hall, Stuart. 1997. "Introduction." Pp. 1–2 in *Representation: Cultural Representations and Signifying Practices,* edited by Stuart Hall. London: Sage Publications.

Hamilton, Brady E., Joyce A. Martin, Michelle J. K. Osterman, Sally C. Cutrin, and T. J. Mathews. 2015. *Births: Final Data for 2014.* National Vital Statistics Report, volume 64, number 12. Hyattsville, MD: National Center for Health Statistics.

Hanson, Sandra L., and Emily Gilbert. 2012. "Family, Gender and Science Experiences: The Perspective of Young Asian Americans." *Race, Gender & Class* 19(3–4):326–47.

Harlan, Sharon L., David N. Pellow, and J. Timmons Roberts. 2015. "Climate Justice and Inequality." Pp. 127–63 in *Climate Change and Society: Sociological Perspectives,* edited by Riley E. Dunlap and Robert J. Brulle. New York: Oxford University Press.

Harmon, T. R. 2004. "Race for Your Life: An Analysis of the Role of Race in Erroneous Capital Convictions." *Criminal Justice Review* 29(1):76–96.

Harper, Shaun R. 2012. *Black Male Student Success in Higher Education: A Report from the National Black Male College Achievement Study.* Philadelphia: University of Pennsylvania, Center for the Study of Race and Equity in Education.

Harris, Angel. 2011. *Kids Don't Want to Fail: Oppositional Culture and the Black-White Achievement Gap.* Cambridge, MA: Harvard University Press.

Hartnett, Caroline S., and Emilio A. Parrado. 2012. "Hispanic Familism Reconsidered." *The Sociological Quarterly* 53(4):636–53.

Havrilla, Katrina. 2010. "A Sociological Influence in Dora the Explorer." *Footnotes* 38(2):10.

Herring, Cedric. 2004. "Skin Deep: Race and Complexion in the 'Color Blind' Era." Pp. 1–21 in *Skin Deep: How Race and Complexion Matter in the "Color Blind" Era,* edited by Cedric Herring, Verna M. Keith, and Hayward Derrick Horton. Urbana: University of Illinois Press.

Herring, Cedric. 2009. "Does Diversity Pay? Race, Gender, and the Business Case for Diversity." *American Sociological Review* 74(2):208–24.

Herring, Cedric, Verna M. Keith, and Hayward Derrick Horton, eds. 2004. *Skin Deep: How Race and Complexion Matter in the "Color Blind" Era.* Urbana: University of Illinois Press.

Higginbotham, Elizabeth, and Margaret L. Andersen, eds. 2016. *Race and Ethnicity in Society: The Changing Landscape.* 4th ed. Belmont, CA: Wadsworth/Cengage.

Higher Education Research Institute. 2016. *The American Freshman: National Norms for 2015.* Los Angeles: University of California. (http://heri.ucla.edu/monographs/TheAmericanFreshman2015.pdf.)

Hill, Mark E. 2000. "Color Differences in the Socioeconomic Status of African American Men: Results of a Longitudinal Study." *Social Forces* 78(4):1437–60.

Hill, Mark E. 2002. "Skin Color and the Perception of Attractiveness among African Americans: Does Gender Make a Difference?" *Social Psychology Quarterly* 65(1):77–91.

Hine, Darlene Clark. 2004. "The *Briggs v. Elliott* Legacy: Black Culture, Consciousness, and Community Before *Brown,* 1930–1954." *University of Illinois Law Review* 2004(5): 1059–72.

Hirschman, Charles, and Douglas S. Massey. 2008. "Places and Peoples: The New American Mosaic." Pp. 1–21 in *New Faces in New Places: The Changing Geography of American Immigration,* edited by Douglas S. Massey. New York: Russell Sage Foundation.

Hobbs, Allyson. 2014. *A Chosen Exile: A History of Racial Passing in American Life.* Cambridge, MA: Harvard University Press.

Hochschild, Arlie Russell. 2016. *Strangers in Their Own Land: Anger and Mourning on the American Right.* New York: The New Press.

Hochschild, Jennifer L., and Vesla Weaver. 2007. "The Skin Color Paradox and the American Racial Order." *Social Forces* 86(2):9643–70.

Holt, Cheryl L., David L. Roth, Jin Huang, and Eddie M. Clark. 2015. "Gender Differences in the Roles of Religion and Locus of Control on Alcohol Use and Smoking among African Americans." *Journal of Studies on Alcohol and Drugs* 76(3):482–92.

Hondagneu-Sotelo, Pierrette. 2007. *Doméstica: Immigrant Workers Cleaning and Caring in the Shadows of Affluence*. Berkeley: University of California Press.

hooks, bell. 1992. *Black Looks: Race and Representation*. Boston: South End Press.

hooks, bell. 2003. *We Real Cool: Black Men and Masculinity*. New York: Routledge.

Howard, D. L, P. D. Sloane, S. Zimmerman, J. K. Eckert, J. F. Walsh, V. C. Buie, P. J. Taylor, and C. G. Koch. 2002. "Distribution of African Americans in Residential Care/Assisted Living and Nursing Homes: More Evidence of Racial Disparity?" *American Journal of Public Health* 92(August):1272–77.

Huggins, Nathan. 2007. *Harlem Renaissance*. New York: Oxford University Press.

Hughey, Matthew W. 2011. *Black Greek Letter Organizations 2.0: New Directions in the Study of African American Fraternities and Sororities*. Oxford: University Press of Mississippi.

Hughey, Matthew W. 2014. *The White Savior Film: Content, Critics, and Consumption*. Philadelphia: Temple University Press.

Hughey, Matthew W. 2015. "We've Been Framed! A Focus on Identity and Interaction for a Better Vision of Racialized Social Movements." *Sociology of Race and Ethnicity* 1(1):137–52.

Hughey, Matthew W., and Gregory S. Parks. 2011. *Black Greek-Letter Organizations, 2.0: New Directions in the Study of African American Fraternities and Sororities*. Oxford: University Press of Mississippi.

Hunter, Margaret. 2004. "Light, Bright, and Almost White: The Advantages and Disadvantages of Light Skin." Pp. 22–44 in *Skin Deep: How Race and Complexion Matter in the "Color Blind" Era*, edited by Cedric Herring, Verna M. Keith, and Hayward Derrick Horton. Urbana: University of Illinois Press.

Hunter, Margaret. 2007. "The Persistent Problem of Colorism: Skin Tone, Status, and Inequality." *Sociology Compass* 1(1):237–54.

Hurley, Ryan J., Jakob Jensen, Andrew Weaver, and Travis Dixon. 2015. "Viewer Ethnicity Matters: Black Crime in TV News and Its Impact on Decisions Regarding Public Policy." *Journal of Social Issues* 71(1):155–70.

Hyland, Shelley, Lynn Langton, and Elizabeth Davis. 2015. *Police Use of Nonfatal Force 2002–2011*. Washington, DC: Bureau of Justice Statistics. www.bjs.gov.

Imoagene, Onoso. 2012. "Being British vs. Being American: Identification among Second-Generation Adults of Nigerian Descent in the US and UK." *Ethnic and Racial Studies* 35(December):2153–73.

Innocence Project. 2016. "DNA Exonerations Nationwide." New York: The Innocence Project. (http://www.innocenceproject.org.)

Institute of Medicine. 2002. *Unequal Treatment: Confronting Racial and Ethnic Disparities in Health Care*. Washington, DC: The National Academies Press.

Institute of Medicine. 2012. *How Far Have We Come in Reducing Health Care Disparities? Progress since 2000*. Washington, DC: National Academies Press.

Irizarry, Yasmiyn. 2013. "Is Measuring Interracial Contact Enough? Racial Concentration, Racial Balance, and Perceptions of Prejudice among Black Americans." *Social Science Quarterly* 94(3):591–615.

Irving, Shelley K., and Tracy A. Loveless. 2015. *Dynamics of Economic Well-Being: Participation in Government Programs, 2009–2012, Who Gets Assistance?* Washington, DC: U.S. Bureau of the Census. (https://www.census.gov/content/dam/Census/library/publications/2015/demo/p70-141.pdf.)

Isaacs, Julia B., Isabel V. Sawhill, and Ron Haskins. 2008. *Getting Ahead or Losing Ground: Economic Mobility in America*. Washington, DC: The Brookings Institution.

Itzigsohn, Jose. 2004. "The Formation of Latino and Latina Panethnic Identities." Pp. 197–216 in *Not Just Black and White: Historical and Contemporary Perspectives on Immigration, Race, and Ethnicity in the United States*, edited by Nancy Foner and George M. Fredrickson. New York: Russell Sage.

Itzigsohn, Jose, and Carlos Dore-Cabral. 2000. "Competing Identities: Race, Ethnicity and Panethnicity among Dominicans in the United States." *Sociological Forum* 15(June):225–47.

Itzigsohn, Jose, Silvia Gorguli, and Obed Vazquez. 2005. "Immigrant Incorporation and Racial Identity: Racial Self-Identification among

Dominican Immigrants." *Ethnic and Racial Studies* 28(1):50–78.

Iyengar, Shanto. 2010. "Race in the News: Stereotypes, Political Campaigns, and Market-Based Journalism." Pp. 251–73 in *Doing Race: 21 Essays for the Twenty-First Century*, edited by Paula M. Moya and Hazel Rose Markus. New York: Oxford University Press.

Jackson, Chandra L., Frank B. Hu, Susan Redline, David R. Williams, Josiemer Mattei, and Ichiro Kawachi. 2014. "Racial/Ethnic Disparities in Short Sleep Duration by Occupation: The Contribution of Immigrant Status." *Social Science & Medicine* 118(October):71–79.

Jacobson, Cardell K., and Bryan R. Johnson. 2006. "Interracial Friendship and African American Attitudes about Interracial Marriage." *Journal of Black Studies* 36(4):570–84.

Jargowsky, Paul A. 2015a. "Architecture of Segregation: Civil Unrest, the Concentration of Poverty, and Public Policy." New Brunswick, NJ: The Century Foundation, Rutgers University. (http://apps.tcf.org/architecture-of-segregation.)

Jargowsky, Paul A. 2015b. *Concentration of Poverty in the New Millennium: Changes in Prevalence, Composition, and Location of High Poverty Neighborhoods*. New Brunswick, NJ: The Century Foundation and Rutgers Center for Urban Research.

Jeffries, Vincent, and H. E. Ransford. 1969. "Interracial Social Contact and Middle-Class White Reactions to the Watts Riot." *Social Problems* 16(3):312–24.

Joffe, Carole, and Willie J. Parker. 2012. "Race, Reproductive Politics, and Reproductive Health Care in the United States." *Contraception* 86(1):1–3.

Johnson, Lyndon. 1965. *Commencement Address*. Howard University, Washington, DC, 1965.

Jones, Jacqueline. 2013. *A Dreadful Deceit: The Myth of Race from the Colonial Era to Obama's America*. New York: Basic Books.

Jones, James H. 1993. *Bad Blood: The Tuskegee Syphilis Experiment*. New York: Free Press.

Jones, James M., John F. Dovidio, and Deborah L. Vietze. 2014. *The Psychology of Diversity: Beyond Prejudice and Racism*. Malden, MA: Wiley Blackwell.

Jones-Correa, M., and D. L. Leal. 1996. "Becoming 'Hispanic': Secondary Panethnic Identification among Latin American–Origin Populations in the United States." *Hispanic Journal of Behavioral Sciences* 18(2):214–54.

Jordan, Winthrop D. 1968. *White Over Black: American Attitudes toward the Negro 1550–1812*. Chapel Hill: University of North Carolina Press.

Joyner, Kara, and Grace Kao. 2005. "Interracial Relationships and the Transition to Adulthood." *American Sociological Review* 70(4):563–81.

Kaeble, Danielle, Lauren Glaze, Anastasios Tsoutis, and Todd Minton. 2016. *Correctional Populations in the United States, 2014*. Washington, DC: Bureau of Justice Statistics.

Kaiser Foundation. 2016. *Health Coverage by Race and Ethnicity: The Potential Impact of the Affordable Care Act*. Menlo Park, CA: Kaiser Family Foundation.

Kang, Miliann. 2010. *The Managed Hand: Race, Gender, and the Body in Beauty Service Work*. Berkeley: University of California Press.

Kao, Grace, and Kara Joyner. 2004. "Do Race and Ethnicity Matter among Friends? Activities among Interracial, Interethnic, and Intraethnic Adolescent Friends." *The Sociological Quarterly* 45(3):557–73.

Kaplan, Elaine Bell. 1996. *Not Our Kind of Girl: Unraveling the Myths of Black Teenage Motherhood*. Berkeley: University of California Press.

Kasinitz. Philip, John H. Mollenkopf, Mary C. Waters, and Jennifer Holdaway. 2008. *Inheriting the City: The Children of Immigrants Come of Age*. New York: Russell Sage Foundation.

Katz, Sheila. 2012. "TANF's 15th Anniversary and the Great Recession: Are Low-Income Mothers Celebrating Upward Economic Mobility?" *Sociology Compass* 6(8):657–70.

Katznelson, Ira. 2005. *When Affirmative Action Was White: An Untold History of Racial Inequality in Twentieth-Century America*. New York: Norton.

Katznelson, Ira. 2014. Presentation at the 109th Annual Meeting of the American Sociological Association, San Francisco, CA, August.

Kefalas, Maria J., Frank F. Furstenberg, Patrick J. Carr, and Laura Napolitano. 2011. "'Marriage Is More Than Being Together': The Meaning of Marriage for Young Adults." *Journal of Family Issues* 32(7):845–75.

Kerby, Sophia. 2012. *The Top 10 Most Startling Facts about People of Color and Criminal Justice in the United States; A Look at the Racial Disparities Inherent in Our Nation's Criminal*

Justice System. Washington, DC: Center for American Progress, www.americanprogress.org.

Kerner Commission. 1968. *Report of the National Advisory Commission on Civil Disorders*. Washington, DC: National Institute of Justice.

Keyes, Katherine M., Thomas Vo, Melanie M. Wall, Raul Caetano, Shakira F. Suglia, Silvia S. Martins, Sandro Galea, and Deborah Hasin. 2015. "Racial/Ethnic Differences in Use of Alcohol, Tobacco, and Marijuana: Is There a Cross-Over from Adolescence to Adulthood?" *Social Science & Medicine* 124(January):132–41.

Khanna, Nikki. 2011a. "Ethnicity and Race as 'Symbolic': The Use of Ethnic and Racial Symbols in Asserting a Biracial Identity." *Ethnic and Racial Studies* 34(6):1049–67.

Khanna, Nikki. 2011b. *Biracial in America: Forming and Performing Racial Identity*. Lanham, MD: Lexington Books.

Kibria, Nazli. 2003. *Becoming Asian American: Second Generation Chinese and Korean American Identities*. Baltimore: Johns Hopkins University Press.

Kibria, Nazli, Cara Bowman, and Megan O'Leary. 2014. *Race and Immigration*. Malden, MA: Polity.

Killian, Lewis M. 1968. *The Impossible Revolution? Black Power and the American Dream*. New York: Random House.

Killian, Lewis M. 1971. "Optimism and Pessimism in Sociological Analysis." *The American Sociologist* 6(4):281–86.

Kim, Ann H., and Michael J. White. 2010. "Panethnicity, Ethnic Diversity, and Residential Segregation." *American Journal of Sociology* 115(5):1558–96.

Kim, S. 2000. "Race and Home Price Appreciation in Urban Neighborhoods: Evidence from Milwaukee, Wisconsin." *The Review of Black Political Economy* 28(2):9–28.

Kim, Yushim, Heather Campbell, and Adam Eckerd. 2014. "Residential Choice Constraints and Environmental Justice." *Social Science Quarterly* 95(1):40–56.

Kimelberg, Shelley McDonough, and Chase M. Billingham. 2012. "Attitudes toward Diversity and the School Choice Process: Middle-Class Parents in a Segregated Urban Public School District." *Urban Education* 48(2):198–231.

"King's Dream Remains an Elusive Goal: Many Americans See Racial Disparities." 2013. Pew Research Center. (http://www.pewsocialtrends.org/2013/08/22/kings-dream-remains-an-elusive-goal-many-americans-see-racial-disparities/.)

Klinenberg, Eric. 2002. *Heat Wave: A Social Autopsy of Disaster in Chicago*. Chicago: University of Chicago Press.

Kneebone, Elizabeth. 2014. "The Growth and Spread of Concentrated Poverty, 2000 to 2008–2012." Brookings Institute. (http://www.brookings.edu/research/interactives/2014/concentrated-poverty#/M10420.)

Kolchin, Peter. 1993. *American Slavery, 1619–1877*. New York: Hill and Wang.

Konetzka, R. Tamara, and Rachel M. Werner. 2009. "Disparities in Long-Term Care: Building Equity into Market-Based Reforms." *Medical Care Research and Review* 66(October):491–521.

Koyen. Jeff. 2012. "The Truth about Hispanic Consumers." *AdWeek*, March 11.

Kozol, Jonathan. 2012. *Savage Inequalities: Children in America's Schools*. New York: Broadway Books.

Kramer, Michael R., Hannah L. Cooper, Carolyn Drews-Botsch, Lance A. Waller, and Carol R. Hogue. 2010. "Metropolitan Isolation Segregation and Black-White Disparities in Very Preterm Birth: A Test of Mediating Pathways and Variance Explained." *Social Science & Medicine* 71(12):2108–116.

Kramer, Rory, Ruth Burke, and Camille Z. Charles. 2015. "When Change Doesn't Matter: Racial (In)Consistency and Adolescent Well-Being." *Sociology of Race & Ethnicity* 1(2):270–86.

Kravitz-Wirtz, Nicole, Kyle Crowder, Anjum Hajat, and Victoria Sass. 2016. "The Long-Term Dynamics of Racial/Ethnic Inequality in Neighborhood Air Pollution Exposure, 1990–2009." *Du Bois Review: Social Science Research on Race* 13(2):237–60.

Krogstad, Jens Manuel, and Richard Fry. 2014. "Dept. of Ed. Projects Public Schools Will Be 'Majority-Minority' This Fall." Pew Research Center. (http://www.pewresearch.org/fact-tank/2014/08/18/u-s-public-schools-expected-to-be-majority-minority-starting-this-fall/.)

Krogstad, Jens Manuel, and Jeffrey S. Passel. 2015. "5 Facts about Illegal Immigration in the United States." Washington, DC: Pew Research Center.

Kung, H. C., D. L. Hoyert, J. Xu, and S. I. Murphy. 2008. "Deaths: Final Data for 2005." *National Vital Statistics Reports* 56(10):4–26.

Kupchik, Aaron. 2010. *Homeroom Security: School Discipline in an Age of Fear*. New York: New York University Press.

Kuppens, Toon, and Russell Spears. 2014. "You Don't Have to Be Well-Educated to Be an Aversive Racist, but It Helps." *Social Science Research* 45:211–23.

Kwate, Naa O. A., Melody S. Goodman, Jerrold Jackson, and Julen Harris. 2013. "Spatial and Racial Patterning of Real Estate Broker Listings in New York City." *The Review of Black Political Economy* 40(4):401–24.

Kwate, Naa O. A., and Han H. Meyer. 2011. "On Sticks and Stones and Broken Bones: Stereotypes and African American Health." *Du Bois Review: Social Science Research on Race* 8(1):191–98.

Lacy, Karen R. 2007. *Blue-Chip Black: Race, Class, and Status in the New Black Middle Class*. Berkeley: University of California Press.

Ladson-Billings, Gloria. 2006. "From the Achievement Gap to the Education Debt." *Educational Researcher* 36(October):3–12.

Langton, Lynn, and Matthew Durose. 2013. *Police Behavior during Traffic and Street Stops, 2011*. Washington, DC: Bureau of Justice Statistics. (http://www.bjs.gov/content/pub/pdf/pbtss11.pdf.)

Langton, Lynn, Michael Planty, and Nathan Sandholtz. 2013. *Hate Crime Victimization 2003–2011*. Washington, DC: Bureau of Justice Statistics.

Lara-Millan, Armando. 2014. "Public Emergency Room Overcrowding in the Era of Mass Imprisonment." *American Sociological Review* 79(5):866–87.

Lariscy, Joseph T., Claudia Nau, Glenn Firebaugh, and Robert A. Hummer. 2016. "Hispanic-White Differences in Lifespan Variability in the United States." *Demography* 53(1):215–39.

Lasch, Christopher. 1977. *Haven in a Heartless World: The Family Besieged*. New York: Basic Books.

LaVeist, Thomas A. 2005. "Disentangling Race and Socioeconomic Status: A Key to Understanding Health Inequalities." *Journal of Urban Health* 82(2 Suppl 3): iii26–iii34.

LaVeist, Thomas A., and Lydia A. Isaac, eds. 2012. *Race, Ethnicity and Health: A Public Health Reader*. 2nd ed. Hoboken, NJ: Jossey-Bass.

LaVeist, Thomas A., Amani Nuru-Jeter, and Kiesha E. Jones. 2003. "The Association of Doctor-Patient Race Concordance with Health Services Utilization." *Journal of Public Health Policy* 24(3–4):312–23.

LaVeist, Thomas, Keshia Pollack, Roland Thorpe, Ruth Fesahazion, and Darrell Gaskin. 2011. "Place, Not Race: Disparities Dissipate in Southwest Baltimore when Blacks and Whites Live Under Similar Conditions." *Health Affairs* 30(10):1880–87.

LaVeist, Thomas A., Roland J. Thorpe, Geraldine Pierre, GiShawn A. Mance, and David R. Williams. 2014. "The Relationships among Vigilant Coping Style, Race, and Depression." *Journal of Social Issues* 70(2):241–55.

Lawrence, Jane. 2000. "The Indian Health Service and the Sterilization of Native American Women." *American Indian Quarterly* 24(3):400–419.

Leavitt, Peter A., Rebecca Covarrubias, Yvonne A. Perez, and Stephanie A. Fryberg. 2015. "'Frozen in Time': The Impact of Native American Media Representations on Identity and Self-Understanding." *Journal of Social Issues* 71(1):39–53.

Lee, Alfred M. 1968. "Race Riots as Symptoms." *La Crítica Sociológica* 5:36–52.

Lee, Catherine. 2013. *Fictive Kinship: Family Reunification and the Meaning of Race and Nation in American Immigration*. New York: Russell Sage.

Lee, Jennifer. 2015. "From Undesirable to Marriageable: Hyper-Selectivity and the Racial Mobility of Asian Americans." *Annals of the American Academy of Political and Social Science* 662(1):79–93.

Lee, Jennifer, and Frank D. Bean. 2007. "Reinventing the Color Line: Immigration and America's New Racial/Ethnic Divide." *Social Forces* 86(2):561–86.

Lee, Jennifer, and Frank D. Bean. 2012. "A Postracial Society or a Diversity Paradox?" *Du Bois Review: Social Science Research on Race* 9(2):419–37.

Lee, Jennifer, and Min Zhou. 2004. *Asian American Youth: Culture, Identity and Ethnicity*. New York: Routledge.

Lee, Marlene A., and Mark Mather. 2008, June. "U.S. Labor Force Trends." Population Reference Bureau. (http://www.prb.org.)

Lee, S. 2004 "Marriage Dilemmas and Partner Choices and Constraints for Korean Americans in New York City." Pp. 285–98 in *Asian American Youth: Culture, Identity and*

Ethnicity, edited by Jennifer Lee and Min Zhou. New York: Routledge.

Lee, Sharon M. 1993. "Racial Classification in the U.S. Census, 1890–1900." *Ethnic and Racial Studies* 16(1):75–94.

Lemm, Kristi M. 2006. "Positive Associations among Interpersonal Contact, Motivation, and Implicit and Explicit Attitudes toward Gay Men." *Journal of Homosexuality* 51(2):79–99.

Levin, Jack, and Jim Nolan. 2016. *The Violence of Hate: Understanding Harmful Forms of Bias and Bigotry*. 4th ed. Lanham, MD: Rowman & Littlefield.

Levin, S., C. Y. Laar, and J. H. Sidanius. 2003. "The Effects of Ingroup and Outgroup Friendships on Ethnic Attitudes on College: A Longitudinal Study." *Group Processes and Intergroup Relations* 6:76–92.

Lewis, Amanda E. 2004. "'What Group?' Studying Whites and Whiteness in the Era of 'Color-Blindness.'" *Sociological Theory* 22(4):623–46.

Lewis, Amanda E., and John B. Diamond. 2015. *Despite the Best Intentions: How Racial Inequality Thrives in Good Schools*. New York: Oxford University Press.

Lewis, Amanda E., John B. Diamond, and Tyrone A. Forman. 2015. "Conundrums of Integration: Desegregation in the Context of Racialized Hierarchy." *Sociology of Race and Ethnicity* 1(1):22–36.

Lewis, David Levering. 1981. *When Harlem Was in Vogue*. New York: Knopf.

Li, Yue, Charlene Harrington, Helena Temkin-Greener, Kai You, Xueya Cai, Xi Cen, and Dana B. Mukamel. 2015. "Deficiencies in Care at Nursing Homes and Racial-Ethnic Disparities across Homes Fell, 2006–11." *Health Affairs* 34(7):1139–46.

Lichter, Daniel T., Domenico Parisi, and Michael C. Taquino. 2015. "Toward a New Macro-Segregation? Decomposing Segregation Within and Between Metropolitan Cities and Suburbs." *American Sociological Review* 80(4):843–73.

Lichter, Daniel T., Zhenchao Qian, and Dmitry Tumin. 2015. "Whom Do Immigrants Marry? Emerging Patterns of Intermarriage and Integration in the United States." *Annals of the American Academy of Political and Social Science* 662(1):57–78.

Liebler, Carolyn A. 2010. "Homelands and Indigenous Identities in a Multiracial Era." *Social Science Research* 39(4):596–609.

Liebler, Carolyn A., and Meghan Zacher. 2013. "American Indians without Tribes in the Twenty-First Century." *Ethnic and Racial Studies* 36(11):1910–34.

Lien, Pei-te, M. M. Conway, and Janelle Wong. 2003. "The Contours and Sources of Ethnic Identity Choices among Asian Americans." *Social Science Quarterly* 84(2): 461–81.

Lincoln, Abraham. [1858] 1907. "Joint Debate with Stephen A. Douglas." Reprinted in *The Outlook* 85:262.

Liosa, Alvaro Vargas. 2013. "Addressing and Discrediting 7 Major Myths about Immigration." *Forbes*, May 29. (http://www.forbes.com/sites/realspin/2013/05/29/addressing-and-discrediting-7-major-myths-about-immigration/.)

Lipsitz, George. 2011. *How Racism Takes Place*. Philadelphia: Temple University Press.

Lofquist, Daphne A. 2012. *Multigenerational Households: 2009–2011*. Washington, DC: U.S. Bureau of the Census.

Lofquist, Daphne, Terry Lugaila, Martin O'Connell, and Sarah Feltz. 2010. "Households and Families: 2010." U. S. Bureau of the Census. (https://www.census.gov/prod/cen2010/briefs/c2010br-14.pdf.)

Logan, John, and Brian J. Stults. 2011. "The Persistence of Segregation in the Metropolis: New Findings from the 2010 Census." US2010. (http://www.s4.brown.edu/us2010.)

Longazel, Jamie. 2013. "Subordinating Myth: Latino/a Immigration, Crime and Exclusion." *Sociology Compass* 7(2):87–96.

Lopez, Marc Hugo, Jens Manuel Krogstad, Eileen Patten, and Ana Gonzalez-Barrera. 2014. "Latinos' Views on Selected 2014 Ballot Measure Issues." in *Latino Voters and the 2014 Midterm Elections*. Pew Research Organization. (http://www.pewhispanic.org/2014/10/16/chapter-2-latinos-views-on-selected-2014-ballot-measure-issues/.)

Louie, Steve, and Glenn Omatsu. 2001. *Asian Americans: The Movement and the Moment*. Los Angeles: UCLA Asian American Studies Center Press.

Majors, Richard, and Janet Mancini Billson. 1993. *Cool Pose: The Dilemmas of Black Manhood in America*. New York: Touchstone.

Markides, K. S., and K. Eschbach. 2011. "Hispanic Paradox in Adult Mortality in the United States." Pp. 227–40 in *International Handbook of Adult Mortality*, edited by R. G. Rogers and E. M. Crimmins. Dordrecht, The Netherlands: Springer.

Marks, Carole. 1989. *Farewell, We're Good and Gone: The Great Black Migration*. Bloomington: Indiana University Press.

Marks, Carole C. 1990. Lecture Notes, "The Civil Rights Movement." University of Delaware.

Marks, Carole C. 1999. *The Power of Pride: Stylemakers and Rulebreakers of the Harlem Renaissance*. New York: Crown.

Markus, Hazel Rose, and Alana Conner. 2013. *Clash! 8 Cultural Conflicts That Made Us Who We Are*. New York: Hudson Street Press.

Markus, Hazel Rose, and Paula M. Moya. 2010. "Doing Race: An Introduction." Pp. 1–102 in *21 Essays for the Twenty-First Century*, edited by Paula M. Moya and Hazel Rose Markus. New York: Oxford University Press.

Markus, Hazel Rose, and Paula M. Moya, eds. 2010. *Doing Race: 21 Essays for the Twenty-First Century*. New York: Oxford University Press.

Martin, A. C. 2008. "Television Media as a Potential Negative Factor in the Racial Identity Development of African American Youth." *Academic Psychiatry* 32(4):338–42.

Martinez, Ramiro, Jr. 2014. *Latino Homicide: Immigration, Violence, and Community*. 2nd ed. New York: Routledge.

Martinez, Ramiro, Jr., and Abel Valenzuela Jr., eds. 2006. *Immigration and Crime: Race, Ethnicity, and Violence*. New York: New York University Press.

Massey, Douglas S. 2008. "Foreword." Pp. xi–xiii in *Latinas/os in the United States: Changing the Face of America*, edited by Havidan Rodríguez, Rogelio Sáenz, and Cecilia Menjívar. New York: Springer.

Massey, Douglas S. 2005. "Five Myths about Immigration: Common Misconceptions about U.S. Border Enforcement Policy." *Immigration Policy in Focus* 4(August):1–11.

Massey, Douglas S., and Nancy Denton. 1998. *American Apartheid: Segregation and the Making of the Underclass*. Cambridge, MA: Harvard University Press.

Massey, Douglas S., and Magaly R. Sánchez. 2010. *Brokered Boundaries: Creating Immigrant Identities in Anti-Immigrant Times*. New York: Russell Sage Foundation.

Massey, Douglas S., and Jonathan Tannen. 2015. "A Research Note on Trends in Black Hypersegregation." *Demography* 52(3):1025–34.

Mastro, Dana. 2015. "Why the Media's Role in Issues of Race and Ethnicity Should Be in the Spotlight." *Journal of Social Issues* 71(1):1–16.

Masuoka, N. 2006. "Together They Become One: Examining the Predictors of Panethnic Group Consciousness among Asian Americans and Latinos." *Social Science Quarterly* 87(5):993–1011.

Matsuda, Lawrence Y. 2005. "A Professor, Not a Porter." *Community and Difference: Teaching, Pluralism, and Social Justice* 261:51–75.

Mattingly, Marybeth, and Charles Varner. 2015. "Poverty." *Pathways, Special Issue: State of the States: The Poverty and Inequality Report*. Palo Alto, CA: The Stanford Center on Poverty and Inequality.

Mayorga-Gallo, Sarah. 2014. *Behind the White Picket Fence: Power and Privilege in a Multiethnic Neighborhood*. Chapel Hill: University of North Carolina Press.

Mazzocco, Philip J., Timothy C. Brock, Gregory J. Brock, Kristina R. Olson, and Mahzarin R. Banaji. 2006. "The Cost of Being Black: White Americans' Perceptions and the Question of Reparations." *Du Bois Review: Social Science Research on Race* 3(2):261–97.

McAdam, Doug. 1990. *Freedom Summer*. New York: Oxford University Press.

McAdam, Doug. 1999. *Political Process and the Development of Black Insurgency, 1930–1970*. 2nd ed. Chicago: University of Chicago Press.

McCabe, Janice. 2009. "Racial and Gender Microaggressions on a Predominantly-White Campus: Experiences of Black, Latina/o and White Undergraduates." *Race, Gender & Class* 16(1–2):133–51.

McCarthy, Justin. 2015. "More Americans Say Crime Is Rising in the U.S." Princeton, NJ: The Gallup Organization.

McDonough, Patricia. 2009. "TV Viewing among Kids at an Eight Year High." *Newswire*, October 26. Retrieved April 30, 2015 (http://www.nielsen.com).

McGill, Rebecca K., Niobe Way, and Diane Hughes. 2012. "Intra- and Interracial Best Friendships during Middle School: Links to Social and Emotional Well-Being." *Journal of Research on Adolescence* 22(4):722–38.

McIntosh, Peggy. 1988. "White Privilege and Male Privilege: A Personal Account of Coming to See Correspondences through Work in Women's

Studies." Working Paper 189. Wellesley, MA: Wellesley Centers for Women.

McKay, James, and Helen Johnson. 2008. "Pornographic Eroticism and Sexual Grotesquerie in Representations of African American Sportswomen." *Social Identities* 14(4):491–504.

McKernan, Signe-Mary, Caroline Ratcliffe, C. Eugene Steuerle, Emma Kalish, and Caleb Quakenbush. 2015. *Nine Charts about Wealth Inequality in America.* The Urban Institute. http://datatools. urban.org/Features/wealth-inequality-charts/.

Mead, George Herbert. 1934. *Mind, Self, and Society.* Chicago: University of Chicago Press.

Meier, August, and Elliott Rudwick. 1970. *From Plantation to Ghetto.* Rev. ed. New York: Hill and Wang.

Mendez, Dara D., Vijaya K. Hogan, and Jennifer F. Culhane. 2014. "Institutional Racism, Neighborhood Factors, Stress, and Preterm Birth." *Ethnicity & Health* 19(5):479–99.

Merton, Robert K. 1938. "Social Structure and Anomie." *American Sociological Review* 3:672–82.

Merton, Robert K. 1949. "Discrimination and the American Creed." Pp. 99–126 in *Discrimination and the National Welfare,* edited by Robert W. MacIver. New York: Harper and Brothers.

Middlebrook, Diane Wood. 1998. *Suits Me: The Double Life of Billy Tipton.* New York: Houghton-Mifflin.

Migration Policy Institute. 2014. "Inflow of New Legal Residents by Country of Birth, 1990–2013." *MPI Data Hub: Facts, Stats, and Maps.* Washington, DC: Migration Policy Institute.

Mills, C. Wright. 1959. *The Sociological Imagination.* New York: Oxford University Press.

Mirandé, Alfredo. 1997. *Hombres y Machos: Masculinity and Latino Culture.* Boulder, CO: Westview Press.

Mohai, Paul, and Robin Saha. 2007. "Racial Inequality in the Distribution of Hazardous Waste: A National-Level Reassessment." *Social Problems* 54(3):343–70.

Mohai, Paul, and Robin Saha. 2006. "Reassessing Racial and Socioeconomic Disparities in Environmental Justice Research." *Demography* 43(2):383–99.

Mohanty, Sarita A. 2006. *Unequal Access: Immigrants and U.S. Health Care.* Washington, DC: American Immigration Council.

(http://www.immigrationpolicy.org/just-facts/ immigrants-and-us-health-care-system.)

Morgan, Marcyliena, and Dawn-Elissa Fischer. 2010. "Hiphop and Race: Blackness, Language, and Creativity." Pp. 509–27 in *Doing Race: 21 Essays for the Twenty-First Century,* edited by Paula M. Moya and Hazel Rose Markus. New York: Oxford University Press.

Morning, Ann. 2011. *The Nature of Race: How Scientists Think and Teach about Human Difference.* Berkeley: University of California Press.

Morris, Edward W. 2005. "'Tuck in That Shirt!' Race, Class, Gender, and Discipline in an Urban School." *Sociological Perspectives* 48(1):25–48.

Morris, Edward W., and Brea L. Perry. 2016. "The Punishment Gap: School Suspension and Racial Disparities in Achievement." *Social Problems* 63(1):68–86.

Mouw, Ted, and Barbara Entwisle. 2006. "Residential Segregation and Interracial Friendship in Schools." *American Journal of Sociology* 112(2):394–441.

Moye, J. Todd. 2005. *Let the People Decide: Black Freedom and White Resistance Movements in Sunflower County, Mississippi, 1945–1986.* Chapel Hill: University of North Carolina Press.

Moynihan, Daniel Patrick. 1965. *The Negro Family: The Case for National Action.* Washington, DC: U.S. Department of Labor, Office of Policy Planning and Research.

Mueller, Jennifer C., Danielle Dirks, and Leslie Houts Picca. 2007. "Unmasking Racism: Costuming and Engagement of the Racial Order." *Qualitative Sociology* 30:315–55.

Murray, Pauli. 1997. *States' Laws on Race and Color.* Athens: University of Georgia Press.

Myrdal, Gunnar. 1944. *An American Dilemma: The Negro Problem and American Democracy.* New York: Harper Brothers.

Nakano, Dana Y. 2013. "An Interlocking Panethnicity: The Negotiation of Multiple Identities among Asian American Social Movement Leaders." *Sociological Perspectives* 56(4):569–95.

Nam, Yunju, Nora Wikoff, and Michael Sherraden. 2015. "Racial and Ethnic Differences in Parenting Stress: Evidence from a Statewide Sample of New Mothers." *Journal of Child and Family Studies* 24(2):278–88.

National Center for Education Statistics. 2013. *Number and Percentage of 9th- to 12th-Graders Who Dropped Out of Public School or Jurisdiction: 2009–2010.* Table 219.50.

Washington, DC: National Center for Education Statistics. (http://www.nces.ed.gov.)

National Center for Education Statistics. 2014. *Digest of Educational Statistics 2014*. Washington, DC: U.S. Department of Education. (https://nces.ed.gov/PUBSeARCH/pubsinfo.asp?pubid=2016006.)

National Center for Education Statistics. 2015a. *National Assessment of Adult Literacy*. Washington, DC: Institute of Education Sciences. (https://nces.ed.gov/naal/lit_history.asp.)

National Center for Education Statistics. 2015b. *Percentage of Persons 18 to 24 Years Old and Age 25 and Over, by Educational Attainment, Race/Ethnicity, and Selected Subgroups: 2008 and 2013*. Table 104.40. Washington, DC: National Center for Education Statistics. (https://nces.ed.gov/programs/digest/d14/tables/dt14_104.40.asp.)

National Center for Health Statistics. 2015. *Health, United States, 2014: With Special Feature on Adults Aged 55–64*. Hyattsville, MD: U.S. Department of Health and Human Services. (http://www.cdc.gov/nchs/data/hus/hus14.pdf.)

National Institute of Italian Statistics. 2015. (http://www.en.istat.it.)

National Opinion Research Poll. 2015. "Law Enforcement and Violence: The Divide between Black and White Americans." Chicago: AP-NORC Center for Public Affairs Research. Retrieved January 23, 2017 (http://www.apnorc.org/projects/Pages/HTML%20Reports/law-enforcement-and-violence-the-divide-between-black-and-white-americans0803-9759.aspx).

Negrón-Muntaner, Frances. 2015. *The Latino Media Gap*. New York: Columbia University, Center for the Study of Ethnicity and Race.

Nelson, Stanley. 2015. *The Black Panthers: Vanguard of the Revolution*. Film, Public Broadcasting System.

Newburger, Eric, and Thomas Gryn. 2009. *The Foreign-Born Labor Force in the United States: 2007*. Washington, DC: U.S. Bureau of the Census. (https://www.census.gov/prod/2009pubs/acs-10.pdf.)

Newman, Katherine S., and Rebekah Peeples Messengill. 2006. "The Texture of Hardship: Qualitative Sociology of Poverty, 1995-2005." *American Review of Sociology* 32:423–46.

Nielsen Company. 2011. "Social Media and TV—Who's Talking, When and What About." *Newswire*. Retrieved April 30, 2015 (http://www.nielsen.com).

Nielsen Company. 2014. "The Total Audience Report," December 3. Retrieved April 30, 2015 (http://www.nielsen.com).

Nielsen Company. 2015. "How Diverse Are Video Gamers—and the Characters They Play?" *Newswire*. Retrieved April 30, 2015 (http://www.nielsen.com).

Noguera, Pedro A. 2008. *The Trouble with Black Boys . . . and Other Reflections on Race, Equity, and the Future of Public Education*. San Francisco: Jossey-Bass.

Noguera, Pedro, and Aida Hurtado. 2011. *Invisible No More: Understanding the Disenfranchisement of Latino Men and Boys*. New York: Routledge.

Norman, Jim. 2016. "U.S. Worries about Race Relations Reach a New High." The Gallup Poll, April 11. Princeton, NJ: Gallup Organization.

Norris, Tina, Paula L. Vines, and Elizabeth M. Hoeffel. 2012. *The American Indian and Alaska Native Population: 2010*. Washington, DC: U.S. Bureau of the Census. (http://www.census.gov/prod/cen2010/briefs/c2010br-10.pdf.)

Nunley, John M., Adam Pugh, Nicholas Romero, and R. Alan Seals. 2015. "Racial Discrimination in the Labor Market for Recent College Graduates: Evidence from a Field Experiment." *The B.E. Journal of Economic Analysis & Policy* 15(3):1093–1125.

Oakes, Jeannie. 2005. *Keeping Track: How Schools Structure Inequality*. New Haven, CT: Yale University Press.

Oboler, Suzanne. 1995. *Ethnic Labels, Latino Lives: Identity and the Politics of (Re)Presentation in the United States*. Minneapolis: University of Minnesota Press.

Ocampo, Anthony C. 2014. "Are Second-Generation Filipinos 'Becoming' Asian American or Latino? Historical Colonialism, Culture and Panethnicity." *Ethnic and Racial Studies* 37(3):425–45.

Office of Immigration Statistics. 2013. *2013 Yearbook of Immigration Statistics*. Washington, DC: U.S. Department of Homeland Security.

Okamoto, Dina. 2014. *Redefining Race: Asian American Panethnicity and Shifting Ethnic Boundaries*. New York: Russell Sage.

Okamoto, Dina, and G. C. Mora. 2014. "Panethnicity." *Annual Review of Sociology* 40:219–39.

Olivas, Michael A. 2010. "My Grandfather's Stories and Immigration Law." Pp. 223–28 in *The Latino Condition*, 2nd ed., edited by Richard Delgado and Jean Stefanic. New York: New York University Press.

Oliver, Mary Beth, Keunyeong Kim, Jennifer Hoewe, Mun-Young Chung, Erin Ash, Julia K. Woolley, and Drew D. Shade. 2015. "Media-Induced Elevation as a Means of Enhancing Feelings of Intergroup Connectedness." *Journal of Social Issues* 71(1):106–22.

Oliver, Melvin L., and Thomas Shapiro. 1995. *Black Wealth/White Wealth: A New Perspective on Racial Inequality*. New York: Routledge.

Oliver, Melvin, and Thomas M. Shapiro. 2006. *Black Wealth/White Wealth: A New Perspective on Racial Inequality*. 2nd ed. New York: Routledge.

Omatsu, Glenn. 2016. "The 'Four Prisons' and the Movements of Liberation: Asian American Activism from the 1960s to the 1990s." Pp. 60–100 in *Contemporary Asian America*, 3rd ed., edited by Min Zhou and Anthony C. Ocampo. New York: New York University Press.

Omi, Michael, and Howard Winant. 1986. *Racial Formation in the United States: From the 1960s to the 1980s*. New York: Routledge.

Omi, Michael, and Howard Winant. 2015. *Racial Formation in the United States: From the 1960s to the 1980s*. Rev. ed. New York: Routledge.

Orfield, Gary. 2001. *Schools More Separate: Consequences of a Decade of Resegregation*. Cambridge, MA: Civil Rights Project, Harvard University.

Orfield, Gary. 2013. "Housing Segregation Produces Unequal Schools: Causes and Solutions." Pp. 40–60 in *Closing the Opportunity Gap: What America Must Do to Give Every Child an Even Chance*, edited by Prudence L. Carter and Kevin G. Welner. New York: Oxford University Press.

Orfield, Gary, and Erica Frankenberg. 2014. *Brown at 60: Great Progress, A Long Retreat, and an Uncertain Future*. Los Angeles: Civil Rights Project/Proyecto Derechos Civiles, University of California–Los Angeles.

Orta, Irem M. 2013. "The Impact of Cross-Group Romantic Relationships on Intergroup Prejudice." *Social Behavior and Personality* 41(1):1–6.

Ortega, Suzanne T., and Jessie L. Myles. 1987. "Race and Gender Effects on Fear of Crime: An Interactive Model with Age." *Criminology* 25(1):133–52.

Ortiz, Vilma, and Edward Telles. 2008. *Generations of Exclusion: Mexican Americans, Assimilation, and Race*. New York: Russell Sage.

Ortman, Jennifer, M., and Christine E. Guarneri. 2016. *United States Population Projections: 2000 to 2050*. Washington, DC: U.S. Bureau of the Census. (https://www.census.gov/population/projections/files/analytical-document09.pdf.)

Ousey, Graham C., and Charis E. Kubrin. 2014. "Immigration and the Changing Nature of Homicide in US Cities, 1980–2010." *Journal of Quantitative Criminology* 30(3):453–83.

Page, Scott E. 2007. *The Difference: How the Power of Diversity Creates Better Groups, Firms, Schools, and Societies*. Princeton, NJ: Princeton University Press.

Page-Gould, Elizabeth. 2004. *Research on Cross-Race Relationships: An Annotated Bibliography*. (http://greatergood.berkeley.edu/article/item/cross-race_relationships_an_annotated_bibliography.)

Page-Gould, Elizabeth, Rodolfo Mendoza-Denton, and Linda R. Tropp. 2008. "With a Little Help from My Cross-Group Friend: Reducing Anxiety in Intergroup Contexts through Cross-Group Friendship." *Journal of Personality and Social Psychology* 95(5):1080–94.

Pager, Devah. 2007. *Marked: Race, Crime, and Finding Work in an Era of Mass Incarceration*. Chicago: University of Chicago Press.

Pager, Devah, and David S. Pedulla. 2015. "Race, Self-Selection, and the Job Search Process." *American Journal of Sociology* 120(4):1005–54.

Painter, Nell Irvin. 2010. *The History of White People*. New York: Oxford University Press.

Pamuk, E. R., R. Fuchs, and W. Lutz. 2011. "Comparing Relative Effects of Education and Economic Resources on Infant Mortality in Developing Countries." *Population and Development Review* 37(4):637–64.

Pattillo, Mary. 2005. "Black Middle-Class Neighborhoods." *Annual Review of Sociology* 31:305–29.

Pattillo, Mary. 2007. *Black on the Block: The Politics of Race and Class in the City*. Chicago: University of Chicago Press.

Pattillo, Mary. 2013. "Housing: Commodity Versus Right." *Annual Review of Sociology* 39:509–31.

Pattillo, Mary. 2015. "Everyday Politics of School Choice in the Black Community." *Du Bois Review: Social Science Research on Race* 12(1):41–71.

Payne-Sturges, Devon, and Gilbert C. Gee. 2006. "National Environmental Health Measures for Minority and Low-Income Populations: Tracking

Social Disparities in Environmental Health." *Environmental Research* 102:154–71.

Pedraza, Silvia. 1996. "Origins and Destinies: Immigration, Race, and Ethnicity in American History." Pp. 1–20 in *Origins and Destinies: Immigration, Race, and Ethnicity in America*, edited by Silvia Pedraza and Rubén G. Rumbaut. Belmont, CA: Wadsworth.

Pellow, David N. 2007. *Resisting Global Toxics: Transnational Movements for Environmental Justice*. Cambridge, MA: MIT Press.

Pellow, David N. 2016. "Toward a Critical Environmental Justice Studies; Black Lives Matter as an Environmental Justice Challenge." *Du Bois Review: Social Science Research on Race* 13(2):221–36.

Pellow, David N., and Hollie Nyseth Brehm. 2013. "An Environmental Sociology for the Twenty-First Century." *Annual Review of Sociology* 39(July):229–50.

Pellow, David N., and Robert J. Brulle. 2007. "Poisoning the Planet: The Struggle for Environmental Justice." *Contexts* 6(1):37–41.

Penner, Andrew, and Aliya Saperstein. 2008. "How Social Status Shapes Race." *Proceedings of the National Academy of Sciences of the United States of America* 105(December 16): 19628–30.

Penner, Andrew, and Aliya Saperstein. 2013. "Engendering Racial Perceptions: An Intersectional Analysis of How Social Status Shapes Race." *Gender & Society* 27(3):319–44.

Perea, Juan F. 2004. "Buscando America: Why Integration and Equal Protection Fail to Protect Latinos." *Harvard Law Review* 117(5):1420–69.

Pettigrew, Thomas F. 2009. "Post-Racism?" *The Du Bois Review: Social Science Research on Race* 6(2):279–92.

Pettigrew, Thomas F., Linda R. Tropp, Ulrich Wagner, and Oliver Christ. 2011. "Recent Advances in Intergroup Contact Theory." *International Journal of Intercultural Relations* 35(3):271–80.

Pew Research Center. 2008. *Americans Say They Like Diverse Communities; Election, Census Trends Suggest Otherwise*. Washington, DC: Pew Research Center. (http://www.pewsocialtrends.org/2008/12/02/americans-say-they-like-diverse-communities-election-census-trends-suggest-otherwise/.)

Pew Research Center. 2009. "Public Backs Affirmative Action, but Not Minority Preferences." Washington, DC: Pew Research Organization.

(http://www.pewresearch.org/2009/06/02/public-backs-affirmative-action-but-not-minority-preferences/.)

Pew Research Center. 2012a. *2012 Asian American Survey*. Washington, DC: Pew Research Center.

Pew Research Center. 2012b. *2012 National Survey of Latinos*. Washington, DC: Pew Research Center.

Pew Research Center. 2015a. "Broad Public Support for Legal Status for Undocumented Immigrants." Washington, DC: Pew Research Center. (http://www.people-press.org/2015/06/04/broad-public-support-for-legal-status-for-undocumented-immigrants/.)

Pew Research Center. 2015b. "Less Support for Death Penalty, Especially among Democrats." Washington, DC: Pew Research Organization. (http://www.people-press.org/2015/04/16/less-support-for-death-penalty-especially-among-democrats/.)

Pew Research Center. 2015c. "Modern Immigration Wave Brings 59 Million to U.S., Driving Population Growth and Change Through 2065: Views of Immigration's Impact on U.S. Society Mixed." Washington, DC: Pew Research Organization. (http://www.pewhispanic.org/2015/09/28/modern-immigration-wave-brings-59-million-to-u-s-driving-population-growth-and-change-through-2065/.)

Pew Research Center. 2015d. "On Immigration Policy, Wider Partisan Divide Over Border Fence Than Path to Legal Status." Washington, DC: Pew Research Center. (http://www.people-press.org/2015/10/08/on-immigration-policy-wider-partisan-divide-over-border-fence-than-path-to-legal-status/.)

Pew Research Center. 2015e. "Persons without Health Insurance, by Age, Race, and Ethnicity, 2013." *Statistical Portrait of Hispanics in the United States, 1980–2013*. Washington, DC: Pew Research Center. (http://www.pewhispanic.org/2016/04/19/statistical-portrait-of-hispanics-in-the-united-states/ph_2015-03_statistical-portrait-of-hispanics-in-the-united-states-2013_current-35/.)

Pew Research Center. 2016. "On Immigration Policy, Partisan Differences, but Also Some Common Ground." Washington, DC: Pew Research Center. (http://www.people-press.org/2016/08/25/on-immigration-policy-partisan-differences-but-also-some-common-ground/.)

Pew Research Social and Demographic Trends. 2013. "King's Dream Remains an Elusive Goal: Many Americans See Racial Disparities," August 22. http://www.pewsocialtrends.org/2013/08/22/kings-dream-remains-an-elusive-goal-many-americans-see-racial-disparities/.

Phelps, Michelle S., and Devah Pager. 2016. "Inequality and Punishment: A Turning Point for Mass Incarceration?" *Annals of the American Academy of Political and Social Science* 663:185–203.

Philbrick, Nathaniel. 2006. *Mayflower: A Tale of Community, Courage, and War.* New York: Viking.

Phillip, Abby. 2014. "Emoji's Race Problem May Finally Be Going Away." *Washington Post*, November 4.

Philip, R. 2007. "Street Style Gives Venus Her Deadly Cutting Edge." *Daily Telegraph*, July 3.

Picca, Leslie, and Joe Feagin. 2007. *Two-Faced Racism: Whites in the Backstage and Frontstage.* New York: Routledge.

Picho, Katherine, Ariel Rodriguez, and Lauren Finnie. 2013. "Exploring the Moderating Role of Context on the Mathematics Performance of Females under Stereotype Threat: A Meta-Analysis." *Journal of Social Psychology* 153(3):299–333.

Pierce, C., J. Carew, D. Peirce-Gonzalez, and D. Willis, 1978. "An Experiment in Racism: TV Commercials." Pp. 62–88 in *Television and Education*, edited by C. Pierce. Beverly Hills, CA: Sage.

Pitcher, Ben. 2014. *Consuming Race.* New York: Routledge.

Planty, Michael, and Christopher Krebs. 2013. *Female Victims of Sexual Violence, 1994–2010.* Washington, DC: Bureau of Justice Statistics. (https://www.bjs.gov/content/pub/pdf/fvsv9410.pdf.)

Portes, Alejandro, Patricia Fernández-Kelly, and William Haller. 2005. "Segmented Assimilation on the Ground: The New Second Generation in Early Adulthood." *Ethnic and Racial Studies* 28(6):1000–40.

Portes, Alejandro, and Dag MacLeod. 1996. "What Shall I Call Myself? Hispanic Identity Formation in the Second Generation." *Ethnic and Racial Studies* 19(3):523–47.

Portes, Alejandro, and Rubén G. Rumbaut, eds. 2014. *Immigrant America: A Portrait.* 4th ed. Berkeley: University of California Press.

Portes, Alejandro, and Min Zhou. 1993. "The New Second Generation: Segmented Assimilation and Its Variants." *Annals of the American Academy of Political and Social Science* 530(1):74–96.

Potok, Mark. 2016. "Anti-Muslim Hate Crimes Surged Last Year, Fueled by Hateful Campaign." Montgomery, AL: Southern Poverty Law Center. (https://www.splcenter.org/hatewatch/2016/11/14/anti-muslim-hate-crimes-surged-last-year-fueled-hateful-campaign.)

Poveda, Tony G. 2009. "The Death Penalty in the Post-Furman Era: A Review of the Issues and the Debate." *Sociology Compass* 3(4): 559–74.

Powers, Rebecca S., Michelle M. Livermore, and Belinda C. Davis. 2013. "The Complex Lives of Disconnected Welfare Leavers: Examining Employment Barriers, Social Support and Informal Employment." *Journal of Poverty* 17(4):394–413.

Proctor, Bernadette D., Jessica L. Semega, and Melissa A. Kollar. 2016a. *Income and Poverty in the United States: 2015.* Table A-1: Households by Total Money Income, Race, and Hispanic Origin of Householder: 1967–2015. Washington, DC: U.S. Bureau of the Census. (Also available at https://www.census.gov/content/dam/Census/library/publications/2016/demo/p60-256.pdf.)

Proctor, Bernadette D., Jessica L. Semega, and Melissa A. Kollar. 2016b. *Income and Poverty in the United States: 2015.* Table B-2: Poverty Status of People by Age, Race, and Hispanic Origin: 1959–2015. Washington, DC: U.S. Bureau of the Census. (Also available at https://www.census.gov/content/dam/Census/library/publications/2016/demo/p60-256.pdf.)

Punyanunt-Carter, Narissra M. 2008. "The Perceived Realism of African American Portrayals: Effects of Racial and Ethnic Stereotyping." Pp. 325–41 in *Media Effects: Advances in Theory and Research*, 3rd ed., edited by J. Bryant and M. B. Oliver. Hillsdale: NJ: Lawrence Erlbaum Associates.

Pyke, Karen. 2014. "Immigrant Families and the Shifting Color Line in the United States." Pp. 194–213 in *The Wiley Blackwell Companion to the Sociology of Families*, edited by Judith Treas, Jacqueline Scott, and Martin Richards. Hoboken, NJ: Wiley Blackwell.

Qian, Zhenchao, and Daniel T. Lichter. 2011. "Changing Patterns of Interracial Marriage in a Multiracial Society." *Journal of Marriage and the Family* 73(5):1065–84.

Quadagno, Jill. 1996. *The Color of Welfare: How Racism Undermined the War on Poverty.* New York: Oxford University Press.

Quillian, Lincoln, and Mary E. Campbell. 2003. "Beyond Black and White: The Present and Future of Multiracial Friendship Segregation." *American Sociological Review* 68(4):540–66.

Quillian, Lincoln, and Rozlyn Redd. 2009. "The Friendship Networks of Multiracial Adolescents." *Social Science Research* 38(2):279–95.

Ramasubramanian, Srividya. 2015. "Using Celebrity News Stories to Effectively Reduce Racial/Ethnic Prejudice." *Journal of Social Issues* 71(1):123–38.

Reardon, Sean F., and Ann Owens. 2014. "60 Years After *Brown*: Trends and Consequences of School Segregation." *Annual Review of Sociology* 40(July):199–218.

Reece, Robert L., and Heather A. O'Connell. 2016. "How the Legacy of Slavery and Racial Composition Shape Public School Enrollment in the American South." *Sociology of Race & Ethnicity* 2 (1):42–57.

Reverby, Susan M. 2009. *Explaining Tuskegee: The Infamous Syphilis Study and Its Legacy*. Chapel Hill: University of North Carolina Press.

Rich, Adrienne. 1976. *Of Woman Born: Motherhood as Experience and Institution*. New York: W. W. Norton.

Rich, Meghan A. 2008. *Diversity Block by Block: Homeowners' Perceptions of Race, Class, and Neighborhood Change in an Integrated Urban Neighborhood*. PhD Dissertation, University of Delaware. Retrieved from ProQuest, AAI3291731.

Rich, Meghan A. 2009. "'It Depends on How You Define Integrated': Neighborhood Boundaries and Racial Integration in a Baltimore Neighborhood." *Sociological Forum* 24(4):828–53.

Rideout, V., E. Vandewater, and A. Wartella. 2003. *Zero to Six: Electronic Media in the Lives of Infants, Toddlers and Preschoolers*. Menlo Park, CA: Kaiser Family Foundation.

Ridolfo, Heather, Valerie Chepp, and Melissa A. Milkie. 2013. "Race and Girls' Self-Evaluations: How Mothering Matters." *Sex Roles* 68(7–8):496–509.

Riffkin, Rebecca. 2015. "Higher Support for Gender Affirmative Action Than Race." *The Gallup Poll*, August 26. Princeton, NJ: The Gallup Organization.

Rios, Victor M. 2011. *Punished: Policing the Lives of Black and Latino Boys*. New York: New York University Press.

Rios, Victor M. 2015. "Police, Punished, Dehumanized: The Reality for Young Men of Color Living in America." Pp. 59–80 in *Deadly Injustice: Trayvon Martin, Race, and the Criminal Justice System*, edited by Devon Johnson, Patricia Y. Warren, and Amy Farrell. New York: New York University Press.

Rivadeneyra, R., L. M. Ward, and M. Gordon. 2005. *Distorted Reflections: Media Use and Latino Adolescents' Conceptions of Self*. Unpublished manuscript. Normal: Illinois State University.

Rivera, Christopher. 2014. "The Brown Threat: Post-9/11 Conflations of Latina/os and Middle Eastern Muslims in the U.S. American Imagination." *Latino Studies* 12(1):44–65.

Roberts, Dorothy. 1997a. *Killing the Black Body: Race, Reproduction, and the Meaning of Liberty*. New York: Vintage.

Roberts, Dorothy. 1997b. "Spiritual and Menial Housework." *Yale Journal of Law and Feminism* 9(51):51–80.

Roberts, Dorothy. 2012. *Fatal Invention: How Science, Politics and Big Business Re-create Race in the Twenty-First Century*. New York: The New Press.

Roberts, J. Timmons, and Bradley C. Parks. 2007. *A Climate of Injustice: Global Inequality, North-South Politics, and Climate Policy*. Cambridge, MA: MIT Press.

Robinson, JoAnn. 1987. *The Montgomery Bus Boycott and the Women Who Started It*. Knoxville: University of Tennessee Press.

Rochelle, Ann. 1997. *No More Kin: Exploring Race, Class, and Gender in Family Networks*. Thousand Oaks, CA: Sage.

Rockquemore, Kerry Ann. 2002. "Negotiating the Color Line: The Gendered Process of Racial Identity Construction among Black/White Biracial Women." *Gender & Society* 16(4):485–503.

Rockquemore, Kerry A., David L. Brunsma, and Daniel J. Delgado. 2009. "Racing to Theory or Retheorizing Race? Understanding the Struggle to Build a Multiracial Identity Theory." *Journal of Social Issues* 65(1):13–34.

Rodriguez, Christina. 2014. "Comments: Symposium on Race." Presented at the annual meeting of the American Sociological Association, August (16–19), San Francisco, CA.

Rodríguez, Clara E. 2000. *Changing Race: Latinos, the Census, and the History of Ethnicity in the United States*. New York: New York University Press.

Rodríguez, Havidán, Rogelio Sáenz, and Cecilia Menjívar, eds. 2008. *Latinas/os in the United States: Changing the Face of America*. New York: Springer.

Rodríguez-Garcia, Dan. 2015. "Intermarriage and Integration Revisited: International Experiences and Cross-Disciplinary Approaches." *Annals of the American Academy of Political and Social Science* 662(1):8–36.

Roediger, David R. 2002. *Colored White: Transcending the Racial Past.* Berkeley: University of California Press.

Romero, Mary. 2002. *Maid in the U.S.A.* New York: Routledge.

Romero, Mary. 2012. *The Maid's Daughter: Living Inside and Outside the American Dream.* New York: New York University Press.

Romo, Ricardo. 1996. "Mexican Americans: Their Civic and Political Incorporation." Pp. 84–97 in *Origins and Destinies: Immigration, Race, and Ethnicity in America,* edited by Silvia Pedraza and Rubén G. Rumbaut. Belmont, CA: Wadsworth.

Root, Maria P. P., ed. 1992. *Racially Mixed People in America.* Thousand Oaks, CA: Sage.

Root, Maria P. P., ed. 1996. *The Multiracial Experience: Racial Borders as the New Frontier.* Thousand Oaks, CA: Sage.

Rose, Stephen J. 2014. *Social Stratification in the United States: The American Profile Poster.* New York: The New Press.

Rose, Tricia. 2013. "Public Tales Wag the Dog." *Du Bois Review: Social Science Research on Race* 10(2):447–69.

Rothstein, Richard. 2013. "Why Children from Lower Socio-Economic Class, on Average, Have Lower Academic Achievement Than Middle-Class Children." Pp. 61–76 in *Closing the Opportunity Gap: What America Must Do to Give Every Child an Even Chance,* edited by Prudence L. Carter and Kevin G. Welner. New York: Oxford University Press.

Royster, Deirdre. 2003. *Race and the Invisible Hand: How White Networks Exclude Black Men from Working-Class Jobs.* Berkeley: University of California Press.

Rude, Jesse. 2010. "Best Friends Forever? Race and the Stability of Adolescent Friendships." *Social Forces* 89(2):585–607.

Rugh, Jacob S., Len Albright, and Douglas S. Massey. 2015. "Race, Space, and Cumulative Disadvantage: A Case Study of the Subprime Lending Collapse." *Social Problems* 62(2):186–218.

Rugh, Jacob S., and Douglas S. Massey. 2010. "Racial Segregation and the American Foreclosure Crisis." *American Sociological Review* 75(5):629–51.

Rugh, Jacob S., and Douglas S. Massey. 2014. "Segregation in Post–Civil Rights America." *Du Bois Review: Social Science Research on Race* 11(2):205–32.

Rumbaut, Rubén. 1996. "Origins and Destinies: Immigration, Race, and Ethnicity in American History." Pp. 1–20 in *Origins and Destinies: Immigration, Race, and Ethnicity in America,* edited by Silvia Pedraza and Rubén G. Rumbaut. Belmont, CA: Wadsworth.

Rumbaut, Rubén G. 2009a. "Pigments of Our Imagination: On the Racialization and Racial Identities of 'Hispanics' and 'Latinos.'" Pp. 15–36 in *How the U.S. Racializes Latinos: White Hegemony and Its Consequences,* edited by José A. Cobas, Jorge Duany, and Joe R. Feagin. New York: Paradigm.

Rumbaut, Rubén G. 2009b. "Undocumented Immigration and Rates of Crime and Imprisonment: Popular Myths and Empirical Realities." Pp. 119–39 in *The Role of Local Police: Striking a Balance Between Immigration Enforcement and Civil Liberties,* edited by A. Khashu. Washington, DC: Police Foundation.

Rumbaut, Rubén G., and Walter A. Ewing. 2007. *The Myth of Immigrant Criminality and the Paradox of Assimilation.* Washington, DC: American Immigration Law Foundation.

Russell, Lesley M. 2011. "Reducing Disparities in Life Expectancy: What Factors Matter?" Paper presented at the Workshop on Reducing Disparities in Life Expectancy held by the Roundtable on the Promotion of Health Equity and the Elimination of Health Disparities of the Institute of Medicine. Washington, DC: National Academy.

Ryan, William. 1971. *Blaming the Victim.* New York: Pantheon.

Saad, Lydia. 2013. "In U.S., 52% of Blacks Unhappy with Societal Treatment." Gallup. Retrieved August 31, 2013 (http://www.gallup.com/poll/163553/blacks-unhappy-societal-treatment.aspx).

Sacks, Tina K. 2013. "Race and Gender Concordance: Strategy to Reduce Healthcare Disparities or Red Herring? Evidence from a Qualitative Study." *Race and Social Problems* 5(2):88–99.

Sampson, Robert J. 2008. "Rethinking Crime and Immigration." *Contexts* 7:28–33.

Sampson, Robert J., and William Julius Wilson. 1995. "Toward a Theory of Race, Crime, and Urban Inequality." Pp. 37–56 in *Crime and*

Inequality, edited by John Hagan and Ruth D. Peterson. Stanford, CA: Stanford University Press.

Sampson, Robert J., and Alix S. Winter. 2016. "The Racial Ecology of Lead Poisoning: Toxic Inequality in Chicago Neighborhoods, 1995–2013." *Du Bois Review: Social Science Research on Race* 13(2):261–84.

Saperstein, Aliya, and Andrew Penner. 2014. "Beyond the Looking Glass: Exploring Fluidity in Racial Classification and Interviewer Classification." *Sociological Perspectives* 57(2):186–207.

Sarkasian, Natalie, and Naomi Gerstel. 2012. *Nuclear Family Values, Extended Family Lives.* New York: Routledge.

Savillo, Rob. 2015. "In Five Years Diversity on Cable News Has Hardly Improved." *Media Matters.* (http://www.mediamatters.org.)

Savillo, Rob, and Oliver Willis. 2013. "Diversity on Evening Cable News in 13 Charts." *Media Matters.* Retrieved January 21, 2017 (https://mediamatters .org/research/2013/05/13/report-diversity-on-evening-cable-news-in-13-ch/194012).

Schick, Camilla. 2016. "U.N. on Aleppo: 'Massive Crimes May Be Underway.'" *New York Times*, December 13. (http://www.nytimes.com.)

Schmader, Toni, Katharina Block, and Brian Lickel. 2015. "Social Identity Threat in Response to Stereotypic Film Portrayals: Effects on Self-Conscious Emotion and Implicit Ingroup Attitudes." *Journal of Social Issues* 71(1):54–72.

Schneider, Markus P. A. 2013. "Illustrating the Implications of How Inequality Is Measured: Decomposing Earnings Inequality by Race and Gender." *Journal of Labor Research* 34(4):476–514.

Schneiderman, Howard G. 1996. "The Protestant Establishment: Its History, Its Legacy—Its Future?" Pp. 141–51 in *Origins and Destinies: Immigration, Race, and Ethnicity in America*, edited by Silvia Pedraza and Rubén G. Rumbaut. Belmont, CA: Wadsworth.

Schulz, Amy J., Graciela B. Mentz, Natalie Sampson, Melanie Ward, Rhonda Anderson, Ricardo de Majo, Barbara A. Israel, Toby C. Lewis, and Donele Wilkins. 2016. "Race and the Distribution of Social and Physical Environmental Risk: A Case Example from the Detroit Metropolitan Area." *Du Bois Review: Social Science Research on Race* 13(2):285–304.

Schwalbe, Michael. 2014. *Rigging the Game: How Inequality Is Reproduced in Everyday Life.* New York: Oxford University Press.

Schwalbe, Michael, Sandra Godwin, Daphne Holden, Douglas Schrock, Shealy Thompson, and Michele Wolkomir. 2000. "Generic Processes in the Reproduction of Inequality: An Interactionist Analysis." *Social Forces* 79(2):419–52.

Schwartzman, Luisa F. 2007. "Does Money Whiten? Intergenerational Changes in Racial Classification in Brazil." *American Sociological Review* 72(6):940–63.

Sears, David O. 1969. "Participation in the Los Angeles Riot." *Social Problems* 17(1):3–19.

"Segregation Academies and State Action." 1973. *Yale Law Journal* 82(7):1436–61.

Sellers, Robert M., Mia A. Smith, J. N. Shelton, Stephanie A. J. Rowley, and Tabbye M. Chavous. 1998. "Multidimensional Model of Racial Identity: A Reconceptualization of African American Racial Identity." *Personality and Social Psychology Review* 2(1):18–39.

Semuels, Alana. 2015a. "The Resurrection of America's Slums." *Atlantic* (August):1–7.

Semuels, Alana. 2015b. "White Flight Never Ended." *Atlantic.* (http://www.theatlantic.com/ business/archive/2015/07/white-flight-alive-and-well/399980/.)

Sewell, Abigail A. 2015. "Disaggregating Ethnoracial Disparities in Physician Trust." *Social Science Research* 54(November):1–20.

Shaheen, Jack G. 2014. *Reel Bad Arabs: How Hollywood Vilifies a People.* Northampton, MA: Olive Branch Press.

Shedd, Carla. 2015. *Unequal City: Race, Schools, and Perceptions of Injustice.* New York: Russell Sage Foundation.

Sheehan, Connor M., Robert A. Hummer, Brenda L. Moore, Kimberly R. Huyser, and John S. Butler. 2015. "Duty, Honor, Country, Disparity: Race/ Ethnic Differences in Health and Disability among Male Veterans." *Population Research and Policy Review* 34(6):785–804.

Sherman, Bradford P. 2014. "Racial Bias and Interstate Highway Planning: A Mixed Methods Approach." *College Undergraduate Research Electronic Journal.* Philadelphia: University of Pennsylvania. (http://repository.upenn.edu/cgi/ viewcontent.cgi?article=1208&context=curej.)

Shin, Laura. 2015. "The Retirement Crisis: Why 68% of Americans Aren't Saving in an Employer-Sponsored Plan." *Forbes*, April 9. (http://www .forbes.com/sites/laurashin/2015/04/09/the-retirement-crisis-why-68-of-americans-arent-saving-in-an-employer-sponsored-plan/.)

Shuttlesworth, Mary E., and Deanne Zotter. 2011. "Disordered Eating in African American and Caucasian Women: The Role of Ethnic Identity." *Journal of Black Studies* 42(6):906–22.

Silva, Jennifer M. 2013. *Coming Up Short: Working-Class Adulthood in an Age of Uncertainty*. New York: Oxford University Press.

Skiba, Russell J., Robert S. Michael, Abra Carroll Nardo, and Reece L. Peterson. 2002. "The Color of Discipline: Sources of Racial and Gender Disproportionality in School Punishment." *Urban Review* 34(4):317–42.

Skloot, Rebecca. 2010. *The Immortal Life of Henrietta Lacks*. New York: Crown Books.

Slaughter, Anne-Marie. 2015. *Unfinished Business: Women, Men, Work, Family*. New York: Random House.

Small, Mario Luis, David L. Harding, and Michéle Lamont. 2010. "Introduction: Reconsidering Culture and Poverty." *Annals of the American Academy of Political and Social Science* 629(1):6–27.

Smith, Aaron. 2014. *African Americans and Technology Use: A Demographic Portrait*. Pew Research Center. (http://www.pewinternet.org/2014/01/06/african-americans-and-technology-use/.)

Smith, D. B., Z. Feng, M. L. Fennell, J. S. Zing, and V. Mor. 2007. "Separate and Unequal: Racial Segregation and Disparities in Quality across U.S. Nursing Homes." *Health Affairs* 36(5): 1448–58.

Smith, Jessica C., and Carla Medalia. 2015. *Health Insurance Coverage in the United States: 2014*. Washington, DC: U.S. Bureau of the Census. (https://www.census.gov/content/dam/Census/library/publications/2015/demo/p60-253.pdf.)

Smith, Kristin, and Reagan Baughman. 2007. *Low Wages Prevalent in Direct Care and Child Care Workforce*. Durham, NH: Carsey Institute.

Smith, Robert Courtney. 2008. "Latino Incorporation into the United States: Local and Transnational Perspectives." Pp. 36–53 in *Latinas/os in the United States: Changing the Face of America*, edited by Havidán Rodríguez, Rogelio Sáenz, and Cecilia Menjívar. New York: Springer.

Smith, T. W., J. M. Ruiz, and B. N. Uchino. 2000. "Vigilance, Active Coping, and Cardiovascular Reactivity in Young Men." *Health Psychology* 19(4):382–92.

Snell, Tracy. 2014. *Capital Punishment, 2013: Statistical Tables*. Washington, DC: U.S.

Department of Justice. http://www.bjs.gov/content/pub/pdf/cp13st.pdf

Snipp, C. Matthew. 1996. "The First Americans: American Indians." Pp. 390–403 in *Origins and Destinies: Immigration, Race, and Ethnicity in America*, edited by Silvia Pedraza and Rubén G. Rumbaut. Belmont, CA: Wadsworth.

Snipp, C. Matthew. 2003. "Racial Measurement in the American Census: Past Practice and Implications for the Future." *Annual Review of Sociology* 29:563–88.

Snipp, C. Matthew. 2010. "Defining Race and Ethnicity: The Constitution, the Supreme Court, and the Census." Pp. 105–22 in *Doing Race: 21 Essays for the Twenty-First Century*, edited by Paula M. Moya and Hazel Rose Markus. New York: Oxford University Press.

Snow, David A., and Leon Anderson. 1987. "Identity Work among the Homeless: The Verbal Construction and Avowal of Personal Identities." *American Journal of Sociology* 92(6):1336–71.

Social Science Data Analysis Network. N.d. "CensusScope—Demographic Maps: Multiracial Population." CensusScope. (http://www.censusscope.org/us/chart_multi.html.)

Social Science Data Analysis Network. N.d. "CensusScope—Multiracial Population Statistics." CensusScope. (http://www.censusscope.org/us/chart_multi.html.)

Social Science Data Analysis Network. N.d. "CensusScope—Segregation: Dissimilarity Indexes." CensusScope. (http://www.censusscope.org/segregation.html.)

Sohoni, Deenesh, and Tracy W. P. Sohoni. 2014. "Perceptions of Immigrant Criminality: Boundaries." *Sociological Quarterly* 55(1):49–71.

Solórzano, D., M. Ceja, and T. Yosso. 2000. "Critical Race Theory, Racial Microaggressions, and Campus Racial Climate: The Experiences of African American College Students." *The Journal of Negro Education* 69(1–2):60–73.

Sotomayor, Sonia. 2013. *My Beloved World*. New York: Knopf.

Spencer, Rainier. 2006. *Challenging Multiracial Identity*. Boulder, CO: Lynne Rienner.

Spohn, Cassia. 2015. "Race, Crime, and Punishment in the Twentieth and Twenty-First Centuries." *Crime and Justice* 44(1):49–97.

Stack, Carol. 1974. *All Our Kin: Strategies for Survival in a Black Community*. New York: Harper.

Stainback, Kevin, and Donald Tomaskovic-Devey. 2012. *Documenting Desegregation: Racial* and Gender Segregation in Private Sector Employment since the Civil Rights Act. New York: Russell Sage.

Stanley, Megan, Ife Floyd, and Misha Hill. 2016. TANF Cash Benefits Have Fallen by More Than 20 Percent in Most States and Continue to Erode. Washington, DC: Center on Budget and Policy Priorities. (http://www.cbpp.org.)

Stansfield, Richard, Scott Akins, Rubén G. Rumbaut, and Roger B. Hammer. 2013. "Assessing the Effects of Recent Immigration on Serious Property Crime in Austin, Texas." Sociological Perspectives 56(4):647–72.

Stearns, Elizabeth, Claudia Buchmann, and Kara Bonneau. 2009. "Interracial Friendships in the Transition to College: Do Birds of a Feather Flock Together Once They Leave the Nest?" Sociology of Education 82(2):173–95.

Steck, Laura, D. M. Heckert, and D. A. Heckert. 2003. "The Salience of Racial Identity among African-American and White Students." Race & Society 6(1):57–73.

Steele, Claude M. 2010. Whistling Vivaldi and Other Clues to How Stereotypes Affect Us. New York: Norton.

Steele, Claude M., and Joshua Aronson. 1995. "Stereotype Threat and the Intellectual Test Performance of African Americans." Journal of Personality and Social Psychology 69(5):797–811.

Steele, Dorothy M., and Becki Cohn-Vargas. 2013. Identity Safe Classrooms: Places to Belong and Learn. Thousand Oaks, CA: Sage.

Stegman, Erik, and Amber Ebarb. 2013. "Sequestering Opportunity for American Indians and Alaska Natives." Center for American Progress. (http://www.americanprogress.org.)

Stepanikova, Irena. 2012. "Racial-Ethnic Biases, Time Pressure, and Medical Decisions." Journal of Health and Social Behavior 53(3):329–43.

Stephens, Nicole M., Stephanie A. Fryberg, Hazel R. Markus, Camille S. Johnson, and Rebecca Covarrubias. 2012. "Unseen Disadvantage: How American Universities' Focus on Independence Undermines the Academic Performance of First-Generation College Students." Journal of Personality and Social Psychology 102(6):1178–97.

Stepler, Renee, and Anna Brown. 2016. Statistical Portrait of Hispanics in the United States, 1980–2013. Age/Gender/Marital Status/Fertility, Table 10. Pew Research Center. Retrieved January 6, 2016 (http://www.pewhispanic.org/ 2016/04/19/statistical-portrait-of-hispanics-in-the-united-states/#current-age).

Sternthal, Michelle J., Natalie Slopen, and David R. Williams. 2011. "Racial Disparities in Health." Du Bois Review: Social Science Research on Race 8(1):95–113.

Stevens-Watkins, Danelle, Brea Perry, Kathi L. Harp, and Carrie B. Oser. 2012. "Racism and Illicit Drug Use among African American Women: The Protective Effects of Ethnic Identity, Affirmation, and Behavior." Journal of Black Psychology 38(4):471–96.

Stevenson, Bryan. 2015. "Just Mercy: A Story of Redemption." Talk, University of Delaware, October 6.

Stewart, Jon. 2014. "Race/Off." The Daily Show, August 28. Retrieved January 9, 2017 (https:// www.youtube.com/watch?v=T_98ojjIZDI).

Stowell, Jacob I., Ramiro Martinez, and Jeffrey M. Cancino. 2012. "Latino Crime and Latinos in the Criminal Justice System: Trends, Policy Implications, and Future Research Initiatives." Race and Social Problems 4(1):31–40.

Stromquist, Nelly P. 2012. "The Educational Experience of Hispanic Immigrants in the United States: Integration through Marginalization." Race, Ethnicity and Education 15(2):195–221.

Subramanian, S. V., and Ichiro Kawachi. 2006. "Whose Health Is Affected by Income Inequality? A Multilevel Interaction Analysis of Contemporaneous and Lagged Effects of State Income Inequality on Individual Self-Rated Health in the United States." Health & Place 12(2):141–56.

Substance Abuse and Mental Health Services Administration. 2014. Results from the 2013 National Survey on Drug Use and Health: Summary of National Findings. NSDUH Series H-48, HHS Publication No. (SMA) 14-4863. Rockville, MD: Substance Abuse and Mental Health Services Administration.

Substance Abuse and Medical Health Services Administration. 2015. "Nonmedical Use of Prescription Pain Relievers Varies by Race and Ethnicity." CBHSQ Report, June 26. (http:// www.samhsa.gov/data/sites/default/files/report_ 1972/Spotlight-1972.pdf).

Sue, Derand Wing. 2010. Microaggressions in Everyday Life: Race, Gender, and Sexual Orientation. Hoboken, NJ: Wiley.

Sue, Derand Wing, Christina M. Capodilupo, Gina C. Torino, Jennifer M. Bucceri, Aisha M. B. Holder, Kevin L. Nadal, and Marta Esquilin.

2007. "Racial Microaggressions in Everyday Life: Implications for Clinical Practice." *American Psychologist* 62(4):271–86.

Suina, Joseph. 1994. "Personal Narrative." Pp. 16–17 in *Facing History and Facing Ourselves: Holocaust and Human Behavior*, by Margot Stern Strom. Brookline, MA: Facing History and Facing Ourselves National Foundation.

Supiano, Beckie. 2015. "Racial Disparities in Higher Education: An Overview." *The Chronicle of Higher Education*, November 10.

Sze, Julie, and Jonathan K. London. 2008. "Environmental Justice at the Crossroads." *Sociology Compass* 2(4):1331–54.

Takaki, Ronald. 1989. *Strangers from a Different Shore: A History of Asian Americans.* New York: Penguin.

Takaki, Ronald. 1993. *A Different Mirror: A History of Multicultural America.* Boston: Little, Brown.

Takeuchi, David T., Lisa Sun-Hee Park, Yonette F. Thomas, and Samantha Teixeira. 2016. "Race and Environmental Equity." *Du Bois Review: Social Science Research on Race* 13(2):215–20.

Tatum, Beverly. 1997. *Why Are All the Black Kids Sitting Together in the Cafeteria?* New York: Basic Books.

Tavares, Carlos D. 2011. "Why Can't We Be Friends: The Role of Religious Congregation-Based Social Contact for Close Interracial Adolescent Friendships." *Review of Religious Research* 52(4):439–53.

Taylor, Howard F. 2008. "Defining Race." Pp. 7–13 in *Race and Ethnicity in Society: The Changing Landscape*, edited by Elizabeth Higginbotham and Margaret L. Andersen. Belmont, CA: Wadsworth/Cengage.

Taylor, Paul, and Scott Keeter, eds. 2010. *Millennials: Confident, Connected, Open to Change.* Washington, DC: Pew Research Center.

Telles, Edward. 2009. "The Social Consequences of Skin Color in Brazil." Pp. 9–24 in *Shades of Difference: Why Skin Color Matters*, edited by Evelyn Nakano Glenn. Stanford, CA: Stanford University Press.

Thakore, Bhoomi. T. 2014. "'Must See TV: South Asian Characterizations in American Popular Media." *Sociology Compass* 8(2):149–56.

Thomas, Anita J., Jason D. Hacker, and Denada Hoxha. 2011. "Gendered Racial Identity of Black Young Women." *Sex Roles: A Journal of Research* 64(7–8):530–42.

Thompson, Maxine S., and Verna M. Keith. 2001. "The Blacker the Berry: Gender, Skin Tone, Self-Esteem, and Self-Efficacy." *Gender & Society* 15(3):336–57.

Thompson, Victor. 2007. "A New Take on an Old Idea: Do We Need Multiracial Studies?" *Du Bois Review: Social Science Research on Race* 3(2):437–47.

Thompson, Victor R., and Lawrence D. Bobo. 2011. "Thinking about Crime: Race and Lay Accounts of Lawbreaking Behavior." *Annals of the American Academy of Political and Social Science* 634:16–38.

Tienda, Marta, and Vilma Ortiz. 1986. "'Hispanicity' and the 1980 Census." *Social Science Quarterly* 67:3–20.

Tierney, Kathleen J. 2007. "From Margins to the Mainstream? Disaster Research at the Crossroads." *Annual Review of Sociology* 33:503–25.

Towbin, Mia Adessa, Shelley A. Haddock, Toni Schindler Zimmerman, Lori K. Lund, and Litsa Renee Tanner. 2004. "Images of Gender, Race, Age, and Sexual Orientation in Disney Feature-Length Animated Films." *Journal of Feminist Family Therapy* 15(4):19–44.

Travis, Jeremy, Bruce Western, and Steve Redburn, eds. 2014. *The Growth of Incarceration in the United States: Exploring Causes and Consequences.* Washington, DC: National Academies Press.

Triandis, H. C. 1989. "The Self and Social Behavior in Differing Cultural Contexts." *Psychological Review* 96(3):506–20.

Trillin, Calvin. 1986. "Black or White." *New Yorker* 62(April 14):62–78.

Tropp, Linda R. 2007. "Perceived Discrimination and Interracial Contact: Predicting Interracial Closeness among Black and White Americans." *Social Psychology Quarterly* 70(1):70–81.

Truman, Jennifer L., and Lynn Langton. 2015. *Criminal Victimization, 2014.* Washington, DC: Bureau of Justice Statistics. www.bjs.gov.

Truman, Jennifer L., and Rachel E. Morgan. 2016. *Criminal Victimization, 2015.* Washington, DC: Bureau of Justice Statistics. (https://www.bjs.gov/content/pub/pdf/cv15.pdf.)

Tukachinsky, Riva, Dana Mastro, and Moran Yarchi. 2015. "Documenting Portrayals of Race/Ethnicity on Primetime Television over a 20-Year Span and Their Association with National-Level Racial/Ethnic Attitudes." *Journal of Social Issues* 71(1):17–38.

Turner, Margery Austin, and Stephen L. Ross. 2005. "How Racial Discrimination Affects the Search for Housing." Pp. 81–100 in *The Geography of Opportunity: Race and Housing Choice in Metropolitan America*, edited by Xavier de Souza Briggs. Washington, DC: The Brookings Institution.

Turner, Patricia A. 1994. *Ceramic Uncles and Celluloid Mammies: Black Images and Their Influence on Culture*. New York: Anchor.

Tyson, Karolyn. 2011. *Integration Interrupted: Tracking, Black Students, and Acting White after Brown*. New York: Oxford University Press.

Tyson, Karolyn, William Darity Jr., and Domini R. Castellino. 2005. "It's Not 'a Black Thing': Understanding the Burden of Acting White and Other Dilemmas of High Achievement." *American Sociological Review* 70(4):582–605.

Uggen, Christopher. 2016. "Crime, Punishment, and American Inequality." *Focus* 32(Fall–Winter): 1–7.

Ulmer, Jeffery T., and Brian Johnson. 2004. "Sentencing in Context: A Multilevel Analysis." *Criminology* 42(1):137–78.

United Nations. 1948. General Assembly Resolution 260A (III) Article 2. The International Convention of the Prevention and Punishment of the Crime of Genocide on December 9, 1948. Office of the UN Special Adviser on the Prevention of Genocide.http://www.un.org/en/ga/search/view_doc.asp?symbol=A/RES/260(iii), accessed January 20, 2017

U.S. Bureau of the Census. 2011. *Profile America: Facts for Features: American Indian and Alaska Native Heritage Month: November 2011*. Washington, DC: U.S. Department of Commerce. (http://www.census.gov.)

U.S. Bureau of the Census. 2012a. *The American Indian and Alaska Native Population: 2010*. Washington, DC: U.S. Department of Commerce. (http://www.census.gov/prod/cen2010/briefs/c2010br-10.pdf.)

U.S. Bureau of the Census. 2012b. *Statistical Abstract of the United States*. Washington, DC: U.S. Department of Commerce. (http://www.census.gov/library/publications/2011/compendia/statab/131ed.html.)

U.S. Bureau of the Census. 2015a. *2014 National Population Projections: Summary Tables, Table 14*. Washington, DC: U.S. Bureau of the Census.

U.S. Bureau of the Census. 2015b. *Age and Sex of All People, Family Members, and Unrelated Individuals Iterated by Income-to-Poverty Ratio and Race, Detailed Poverty Tables*. Table POV-02. Washington, DC: U.S. Bureau of the Census. Retrieved December 30, 2016 (http://www.census.gov/data/tables/time-series/demo/income-poverty/cps-pov/pov-02.2014.html).

U.S. Bureau of the Census. 2015c. *State & County Quick Facts*. Washington, DC: U.S. Department of Commerce.

U.S. Bureau of the Census. 2016a. *America's Families and Living Arrangements: 2015*. Table C3. Living Arrangements of Children under 18 Years and Marital Status of Parents, by Age, Sex, Race, and Hispanic Origin and Selected Characteristics of the Child for All Children: 2015. Washington, DC: U.S. Bureau of the Census. (https://www.census.gov/hhes/families/data/cps2015C.html.)

U.S. Bureau of the Census. 2016b. *America's Families and Living Arrangements: 2015*. Table H. Households by Race and Hispanic Origin of Household Reference Person and Detailed Type: 2015. Washington, DC: U.S. Bureau of the Census. (https://www.census.gov/hhes/families/data/cps2015.html.)

U.S. Bureau of the Census. 2016c. *State and County Quick Facts*. (http://www.census.gov.)

U.S. Bureau of Justice Statistics. 2015. *National Crime Victimization Analysis Tool*. Washington, DC: U.S. Department of Justice. (https://www.bjs.gov/index.cfm?ty=nvat.)

U. S. Bureau of Labor Statistics. 2013. "Industry Employment and Output Projections to 2022." *Monthly Labor Review*, December. (http://www.bls.gov/opub/mlr/2013/article/industry-employment-and-output-projections-to-2022-1.htm.)

U. S. Bureau of Labor Statistics. 2015a. "Employed Foreign-Born and Native-Born Persons 16 Years and Over by Occupation and Sex, 2015 Annual Averages." Table 4. Washington, DC: U.S. Department of Labor. (https://www.bls.gov/news.release/forbrn.t04.htm.)

U.S. Bureau of Labor Statistics. 2015b. *Employment and Earnings 2014*. Washington, DC: U.S. Department of Labor. (https://www.bls.gov/opub/ee/2014/sae/sae.htm.)

U.S. Bureau of Labor Statistics. 2015c. "Employment Status of the Foreign-Born and Native-Born Populations by Selected Characteristics, 2013–2014 Annual Averages."

Table 1. Washington, DC: U.S. Department of Labor. (http://www.bls.gov/news.release/forbrn.t01.htm.)

U.S. Bureau of Labor Statistics. 2015d. "Foreign-Born Workers—Labor Force Characteristics 2014." Washington, DC: U.S. Department of Labor. (https://www.bls.gov/news.release/pdf/forbrn.pdf.)

U.S. Bureau of Labor Statistics. 2016a. *Employment and Earnings 2015*. Washington, DC: U.S. Department of Labor. (https://www.bls.gov/opub/ee/2016/home.htm.)

U.S. Bureau of Labor Statistics. 2016b. *Labor Force Characteristics of Foreign-Born Workers Summary*. (https://www.bls.gov/news.release/forbrn.nr0.htm.)

U.S. Supreme Court. 1954. *Brown v. Board of Education*, 347 US 483.

Uratsu, Marvin. 2007. "Marvin Uratsu." Interview. Telling Their Stories. Retrieved December 30, 2016 (http://www.tellingstories.org/internment/muratsu/index.html).

Valenzuela, Angela. 1999. *Subtractive Schooling: U.S.-Mexican Youth and the Politics of Caring*. Albany: State University of New York Press.

Van Ausdale, Debra, and Joe R. Feagin. 2000. *The First R: How Children Learn Race and Racism*. Lanham, MD: Rowman & Littlefield.

Van Dyke, Nella, and Griff Tester. 2014. "Dangerous Climates: Explaining Variation in the Incidence of Racist Hate Crimes on College Campuses" *Journal of Contemporary Criminal Justice* 30(3):290–309.

Van Ryn, Michelle, Diana J. Burgess, John F. Dovidio, Sean M. Phelan, Somnath Saha, Jennifer Malat, Joan M. Griffin, Steven S. Fu, and Sylvia Perry. 2011. "The Impact of Racism on Clinician Cognition, Behavior, and Clinical Decision Making." *Du Bois Review: Social Science Research on Race* 8(1):199–218.

Vaquera, Elizabeth, and Grace Kao. 2008. "Socioeconomic Origin: Do You Like Me as Much as I Like You? Friendship Reciprocity and Its Effects on School Outcomes among Adolescents." *Social Science Research* 37(1):55–72.

Vargas, Deborah R. 2010. "Representations of Latina/o Sexuality in Popular Culture." Pp. 117–36 in *Latina/o Sexualities: Probing Powers, Passions, Practices, and Policies*, edited by Marysol Asencio. New Brunswick, NJ: Rutgers University Press.

Vargas, Nicholas. 2015. "Latina/o Whitening? Which Latinas/os Self-Classify as White and Report Being Perceived as White by Other Americans?" *Du Bois Review: Social Science Research on Race* 12(1):119–36.

Vasquez, Jessica M. 2014. "Race Cognizance and Colorblindness: Effects of Latino/Non-Hispanic White Intermarriage." *Du Bois Review: Social Science Research on Race* 11(2):273–93.

Vedantum, Shankar. 2015. "Despite Improving Job Market, Blacks Still Face Tougher Prospects." National Public Radio, October 1. (http://www.npr.org.)

Venkatesh, Sudhir A. 2006. *Off the Books: The Underground Economy of the Urban Poor*. Cambridge, MA: Harvard University Press.

Vera, Hernán, and Andrew Gordon. 2003. *Screen Saviors: Hollywood Fictions of Whiteness*. Lanham, MD: Rowman & Littlefield.

Vespa, Jonathan, Jamie M. Lewis, and Rose M. Kreider. 2013. *America's Families and Living Arrangements: 2012*. Washington, DC: U.S. Bureau of the Census. (Also available at http://www.census.gov/content/dam/Census/library/publications/2013/demo/p20-570.pdf.)

Villalobos, Ana. 2014. *Motherload: Making It All Better in Insecure Times*. Berkeley: University of California Press.

Villarosa, Linda. 2002. "A Conversation with: Joseph Graves: Beyond Black and White in Biology and Medicine." *New York Times*, January 1.

Viruell-Fuentes, Edna, Jeffrey D. Morenoff, David R. Williams, and James S. House. 2013. "Contextualizing Nativity Status, Latino Social Ties, and Ethnic Enclaves: An Examination of the 'Immigrant Social Ties Hypothesis.'" *Ethnicity & Health* 18(6):586–609.

Vo, Linda Trinh. 2004. *Mobilizing an Asian American Community*. Philadelphia: Temple University Press.

Volpp, Leti. 1999. "American Mestizo: Filipinos and Antimiscegenation Laws in California." *UC Davis Law Review* 33(4):795–835. (http://scholarship.law.berkeley.edu/cgi/viewcontent.cgi?article=1809&context=facpubs.)

Wagmiller, Robert L., Jr., and Kristen S. Lee. 2014. "Are Contemporary Patterns of Black Male Joblessness Unique? Cohort Replacement, Intracohort Change, and the Diverging Structures of Black and White Men's Employment." *Social Problems* 61(2):305–27.

Wah, Lee Mun, Monty Hunter, Robert Goss, and Richard C. Bock. 1994. *The Color of Fear: A Film*. Oakland, CA: Stir-Fry Seminars & Consulting.

Walker, Renee E., Christopher R. Keane, and Jessica G. Burke. 2010. "Disparities and Access to Healthy Food in the United States: A Review of Food Deserts Literature." *Health & Place* 16(5):876–84.

Walker, Samuel, Cassia Spohn, and Miriam Delone. 2012. *The Color of Justice: Race, Ethnicity, and Crime in America*. Belmont, CA: Wadsworth.

Walls, Melissa L., and Les B. Whitbeck. 2012. "The Intergenerational Effects of Relocation Policies on Indigenous Families." *Journal of Family Issues* 33(9):1272–93.

Wang, Grace. 2010. "A Shot at Half-Exposure: Asian Americans in Reality TV Shows." *Television and New Media* 11:404–27.

Wang, Wendy. 2012. *The Rise of Intermarriage: Rates, Characteristics Vary by Race and Gender*. Pew Research Center. Retrieved January 6, 2017 (http://www.pewsocialtrends.org/2012/02/16/the-rise-of-intermarriage/).

Wang, Wendy. 2015. "Interracial Marriage: Who Is 'Marrying Out?'" Pew Research Center. Retrieved January 6, 2017 (http://www.pewresearch.org/fact-tank/2015/06/12/interracial-marriage-who-is-marrying-out/).

Ward, L. Monique. 2004. "Wading through the Stereotypes: Positive and Negative Associations Between Media Use and Black Adolescents' Conceptions of Self." *Developmental Psychology* 40:284–94.

Waters, Mary C. 2000. *Black Identities: West Indian Immigrant Dreams and American Realities*. Cambridge, MA: Harvard University Press.

Way, Niobe, Rachel Gingold, Marianna Rotenberg, and Geena Kuriakose. 2005. "Close Friendships Among Urban, Ethnic-Minority Adolescents." *New Directions for Child and Adolescent Development* 107(March):41–59.

Way, Niobe, Maria G. Hernandez, Leoandra O. Rogers, and Diane L. Hughes. 2013. "'I'm Not Going to Become No Rapper': Stereotypes as a Context of Ethnic and Racial Identity Development." *Journal of Adolescent Research* 28(4):407–30.

Weber, Lynn, and Lori Peak, eds. 2012. *Displaced: Life in the Katrina Diaspora*. Austin: University of Texas Press.

Wellman, David M. 1977. *Portraits of White Racism*. New York: Cambridge University Press.

West, Cornel. 1982. *Prophesy Deliverance: An Afro-American Revolutionary Christianity*. Philadelphia: Westminster Press.

West, Cornel. 1994. *Race Matters*. New York: Vintage.

Western, Bruce. 2007. *Punishment and Inequality in America*. New York: Russell Sage Foundation.

Western, Bruce. 2014. "Incarceration, Inequality, and Imagining Alternatives." *Annals of the American Academy of Political and Social Science* 651(1):302–306.

Western, Bruce, Anthony A. Braga, Jaclyn Davis, and Catherine Sirois. 2015. "Stress and Hardship after Prison." *American Journal of Sociology* 120(5):1512–47.

Western, Bruce, and Christopher Muller. 2013. "Mass Incarceration, Macrosociology, and the Poor." *Annals of the American Academy of Political and Social Science* 647(1):166–89.

White, Augustus, A., III, with David Chanoff. 2011. *Seeing Patients: Unconscious Bias in Health Care*. Cambridge, MA: Harvard University Press.

White, Deborah Gray. 1999. *Ar'n't I a Woman? Female Slaves in the Plantation South*. New York: W.W. Norton.

White, Kellee, and Luisa N. Borrell. 2011. "Racial/Ethnic Residential Segregation: Framing the Context of Health Risk and Health Disparities." *Health & Place* 17(2):438–48.

"Who Owns What." 2015. *Columbia Journalism Review*. (http://www.cjr.org.)

Wilkerson, Isabel. 2010. *The Warmth of Other Suns: The Epic Story of America's Great Migration*. New York: Random House.

Williams, David R., and Chiquita Collins. 1995. "US Socioeconomic and Racial Differences in Health: Patterns and Explanations." *Annual Review of Sociology* 21:349–86.

Williams, David R., and Selina A. Mohammed. 2009. "Discrimination and Racial Disparities in Health: Evidence and Needed Research." *Journal of Behavioral Medicine* 32(1):20–47.

Williams, David R., and Selina A. Mohammed. 2013. "Racism and Health II: A Needed Research Agenda for Effective Interventions." *American Behavioral Scientist* 57(8):1200–1226.

Williams, Dmitri, Nicole Martins, Mia Consalvo, and James D. Ivory. 2009. "The Virtual Census: Representations of Gender, Race, and

Age in Video Games." *New Media & Society* 11(5):815–34.

Williams, Juan. 1998. *Thurgood Marshall: American Revolutionary*. New York: Three Rivers Press.

Williams, Kim W. 2006. *Mark One or More: Civil Rights in Multiracial America*. Ann Arbor: University of Michigan Press.

Wilson, Kenneth, and Alejandro Portes. 1980. "Immigrant Enclaves: An Analysis of the Labor Market Experiences of Cubans in Miami." *American Journal of Sociology* 86(2):295–319.

Wilson, Michelle Clare, and Katrina Scior. 2014. "Attitudes towards Individuals with Disabilities as Measured by the Implicit Association Test: A Literature Review." *Research in Developmental Disabilities* 35(2):294–321.

Wilson, William Julius. 1973. *Power, Racism, and Privilege: Race Relations in Theoretical and Sociological Perspectives*. New York: Collier Macmillan.

Wilson, William Julius. 1978. *The Declining Significance of Race: Blacks and Changing American Institutions*. Chicago: University of Chicago Press.

Wilson, William Julius. 1987. *The Truly Disadvantaged: The Inner City, the Underclass, and Public Policy*. Chicago: University of Chicago Press.

Wilson, William Julius. 2009. "Toward a Framework for Understanding Forces That Contribute to or Reinforce Racial Inequality." *Race and Social Problems* 1(1):3–11.

Wilson, William Julius. 2010a. *More Than Just Race: Being Black and Poor in the Inner City*. New York: W.W. Norton.

Wilson, William Julius. 2010b. "Why Both Social Structure and Culture Matter in a Holistic Analysis of Inner-City Poverty." *Annals of the American Academy of Political and Social Science* 629(May):200–219.

Wilton, Leigh S., Diana T. Sanchez, and Julie A. Garcia. 2013. "The Stigma of Privilege: Racial Identity and Stigma Consciousness among Biracial Individuals." *Race and Social Problems* 5(1):41–56.

Wingfield, Adia Harvey. 2015. "Colorblindness Is Counterproductive." *Atlantic*, September 13.

Wingfield, Adia H., and Joe Feagin. 2012. "The Racial Dialectic: President Barack Obama and the White Racial Frame." *Qualitative Sociology* 35(2):143–62.

Winograd, Ken. 2011. "Sports Biographies of African American Football Players: The Racism of Colorblindness in Children's Literature." *Race, Ethnicity and Education* 14(3):331–49.

Wise, Tim. 2007. "Majoring in Minstrelsy: White Students, Blackface and the Failure of Mainstream Multiculturalism." *Tim Wise RSS feed*, June 22. (http://www.timwise.org/2007/06/majoring-in-minstrelsy-white-students-blackface-and-the-failure-of-mainstream-multiculturalism/.)

Wise, Tim. 2008. *White Like Me*. Brooklyn, NY: Soft Skull Press.

Wise, Tim. 2011. *White Like Me*. Brooklyn, NY: Soft Skull Press.

Wolfe, Barbara, Jessica Jakubowski, Robert Haveman, and Marissa Courey. 2012. "The Income and Health Effects of Tribal Casino Gaming on American Indians." *Demography* 49(2):499–524.

Wong, Janelle, S. Karthick Ramakrishnan, Taeku Lee, and Jane Junn. 2011. *Asian American Political Participation: Emerging Constituents and Their Political Identities*. New York: Russell Sage.

Woodcock, Anna, Paul R. Hernandez, Mica Estrada, and P. W. Schultz. 2012. "The Consequences of Chronic Stereotype Threat: Domain Disidentification and Abandonment." *Journal of Personality and Social Psychology* 103(4):635–46.

Woolf, Stephen, Robert E. Johnson, George E. Fryer, George Rist, and David Satcher. 2008. "The Health Impact of Resolving Racial Disparities: An Analysis of U.S. Mortality Data." *American Journal of Public Health* 98(September):S26–S28.

World Bank. 2015. "Gini Index." (http://data.worldbank.org/indicator/SI.POV.GINI.)

Wright, Lawrence. 1994. "One Drop of Blood." *New Yorker* 70(July 25):46–55.

Yang, Frances M., and Sue E. Levkoff. 2005. "Ageism and Minority Populations: Strengths in the Face of Challenge." *Generations* 29(3):42–48.

Yi, Joseph. 2013. "Tiger Moms and Liberal Elephants: Private, Supplemental Education among Korean-Americans." *Society* 50(2):190–95.

Zambrana, Ruth Enid. 2011. *Latinos in American Society: Families and Community in Transition*. Ithaca, NY: Cornell University Press.

Zhou, Min. 2004. "Are Asian Americans 'Becoming White?'" *Contexts* 3(Winter):29–37.

Photo Credits

Cover and xix Amanda Rose Timoney, "Untitled," College Nine, University of California, Santa Cruz, 2014. **xxi** Kathy Atkinson, University of Delaware. **1** Design by Sally Rinehart and images from iStockphoto LP / m-imagephotography, iStockphoto LP / moodboard, iStockphoto LP / DragonImages, iStockphoto LP/XiXinXing, and iStockphoto LP/Maria Teijeiro. **9** PA Images / Alamy Stock Photo. **21** Library of Congress, Farm Security Administration and Office of War Information Collection, Photograph by Dorothea Lange. **26** Clark Brennan / Alamy Stock Photo. **43** Richard Levine / Alamy Stock Photo; Newscast Online Limited / Alamy Stock Photo. **51** The Advertising Archives / Alamy Stock Photo; Food Collection / Alamy Stock Photo. **66** VicHealth, Australia. **69** iStockphoto LP / Purestock. **78** Rex Features via AP Images. **89** iStockphoto LP / Digital Vision. **95** MPVHistory / Alamy Stock Photo. **101** Dereje Belachew / Alamy Stock Photo. **109** Robert Fried / Alamy Stock Photo. **118** Sipa via AP Images. **121** The Henry Ford Benson Ford Research Center. **132** Margaret Bourke-White / Getty Images. **134** Library of Congress, Shober & Carqueville Lith Co., c1886. **145** Rose-Marie Murray / Alamy Stock Photo. **156** Jim West / Alamy Stock Photo. **161** iStockphoto LP / Angelo Cavalli. **164** Stacy Walsh Rosenstock / Alamy Stock Photo. **173** iStockphoto LP / _jure. **178** iStockphoto LP / Jack Hollingsworth. **179** Blend Images / Alamy Stock Photo. **191** age fotostock / Alamy Stock Photo. **199** Ethel Wolvovitz / Alamy Stock Photo. **201** Jim West / Alamy Stock Photo. **211** Everett Collection Historical / Alamy Stock Photo. **212** Bob Daemmrich / Alamy Stock Photo. **225** AP Photo/ LM Otero. **237** AP Photo/Gary Kazanjian. **243** Jake May/The Flint Journal-MLive.com via AP. **246** Jim West / Alamy Stock Photo. **249** ZUMA Press, Inc. / Alamy Stock Photo. **259** AP Photo/Craig Ruttle. **263** David Grossman / Alamy Stock Photo. **264** AP Photo/Spencer Weiner, Pool. **275** iStockphoto LP / Boarding1Now. **282** Everett Collection Inc / Alamy Stock Photo. **289** Bettmann / Getty Images. **292** PACIFIC PRESS / Alamy Stock Photo.

Name Index

Subject Index